On Justifying
Psychotherapy

with best wishes

Ian Owen

On Justifying Psychotherapy

◆

Essays on Phenomenology, Integration and Psychology

Ian Rory Owen Ph.D.

iUniverse, Inc.
New York Lincoln Shanghai

On Justifying Psychotherapy
Essays on Phenomenology, Integration and Psychology

iUniverse books may be ordered through booksellers or by contacting:

iUniverse
2021 Pine Lake Road, Suite 100
Lincoln, NE 68512
www.iuniverse.com
1-800-Authors (1-800-288-4677)

Because of the dynamic nature of the Internet, any Web addresses or links contained in this book may have changed since publication and may no longer be valid.

The views expressed in this work are solely those of the author and do not necessarily reflect the views of the publisher, and the publisher hereby disclaims any responsibility for them.

This book is in-part based on my experiences in practice. No individuals are intended for the cases mentioned. Steps have been taken to make anonymous the identities of people who were considered for the cases mentioned. Any resemblances between persons mentioned here and real persons are entirely coincidental.

ISBN: 978-0-595-45573-7 (pbk)
ISBN: 978-0-595-89874-9 (ebk)

Printed in the United States of America

Contents

List of Illustrations

Preface and overview

This book shows the progress gained during 17 years of theoretical research in a broad view of the origins of existentialism. All the chapters are previously published papers. They represent a return and a renewal of understanding in the project of searching for the genuine roots of existential therapy, better called existential-phenomenological therapy. However, what the theoretical research discovered was not evidence for the humanistic-existential view or the deconstructive view of the original writers. Accordingly, what was found was not supportive of the majority of currently existing views of Edmund Husserl and Martin Heidegger. And this means altering the status quo between Husserl and Heidegger with respect to the major schools of psychology such as psychoanalysis, gestalt, behaviourism or cognitivism. It suggests a radical reappraisal of the role of theory, practice and research. What was found cannot be called a new existentialism either. The best term that can be used is one that Husserl and Heidegger both agreed on: "pure psychology," a form of phenomenology devoted to the everyday psychological life of people in general, a theoretical psychology.

The 20 papers in this volume are re-prints from a number of journals from 1992 to 2006. The original aim of the research was to find the aims of the twentieth century therapists Sigmund Freud, Carl Rogers and Viktor Frankl and the philosophers Edmund Husserl, Martin Heidegger, Jean-Paul Sartre and Maurice Merleau-Ponty. Specifically, Edmund Husserl's phenomenology is not just a philosophy of conscious meaning but has contributions to the theory of mind perspective, areas within qualitative and developmental psychology, social psychology and cultural anthropology. Straight away there is a divergence between this work and the pictures of Husserl and Heidegger in the contemporary understanding of what they were discussing, that has been gained via Sartre and continental philosophy.

Phenomenology is a gateway to a number of contemporary applications in philosophy, empirical psychology and therapy. However, despite its allure there is great difficulty in grasping the intention of Edmund Husserl and his peers. It is easy to become side-tracked and mis-understand the scope and application of his method. Indeed, there have been a number of fruitful mis-readings of the original intent of Husserl to create a philosophical method for understanding consciousness in its social habitat. Thanks to Iso Kern and Eduard Marbach though, a standard has been set in Husserl studies by which to measure the accuracy of interpretations. From the perspective of Kern and Marbach, the following trends appear in understanding other schools of reading Husserl.

Phenomenology is a transcendental philosophy approach for understanding how consciousness and its objects co-occur. The peers to whom Husserl can best be compared are Immanuel Kant, Martin Heidegger and Maurice Merleau-Ponty. The earliest sketch of the full phenomenological method was set out in *The Idea of Phenomenology* (Husserl, 1973a, re-translated 1999). The lectures from the summer semester of 1907 also show that what was being analysed was embodied experience by varying simple aspects of movement in relation to what appears visually, for instance (Husserl, 1997a). Despite what Husserl himself believed, phenomenology involves a hermeneutic stance. Such a stance is used contemporarily in empirical psychology in attachment research (understanding intimate human inter-actions) and the developmental changes that children go through. Both of these stances can be called "theory of mind" as they assume that the consciousness of other people exists (a radical assumption for the science of psychology).

Another area of usage of ideas to justify a stance for practice is the closely allied areas of philosophy of therapy and psychology (in contradistinction to the philosophy of the natural science experimentation with inanimate matter). In this area, there have been a number of fruitful readings of phenomenology that are usually focused on Heidegger's version, as it applies to forms of therapy, usually Freud's psycho-analysis and the outcome is called existential therapy. There is a branch of phenomenology that is applied to understand psychological distress by psychiatrists and others, called psychopathology. For this discipline, "phenomenology" is synonymous with the subjective experience of psychological suffering. Phenomenology is also seen by various areas of sociology that believe they have triumphed over Husserl's mistakes.

The remaining areas where the term "phenomenology" is used are post-Wittgensteinian analytic and linguistic philosophy, experimental cognitive science and qualitative psychology based on Merleau-Ponty's version of phenomenology. These usages of phenomenology are more loose definitions of the term and some have little or no connection to the original concerns of Kant, Husserl and Heidegger as theoretical studies in preparation for philosophy, therapy or psychology.

There is also the loose grouping that is probably best called continental philosophy that includes the stances, post-Sartre, of deconstruction, post-modernism and post-structuralism. These invoke "phenomenology" as an embarrassing mistake that only has had worth in prompting their corrections of its mistakes. But in response, books that cannot be read are not writing at all for they communicate nothing.

So "phenomenology" is a touchstone, meaning many things to many people. It cannot be a movable feast though. It does have a specific original sense and that is revealed in the essays below, in practice and theory, for a general approach to therapy and psychopathology. Finally, the difficulty concerning how to read Husserl is compounded because Husserl's stance did not reach maturity until his work *Formal and Transcendental Logic*, first published in 1929 and translated into English in 1969. The use that pure psychology is put to in this work is to put social reality of conscious meanings in society back into proper focus. The way of doing this is to understand first and then working out how to intervene will become clearer. It is assumed that proper understanding provides the confidence to be relaxed, open, flexible and cope with the stresses of practising because such a state of mind promotes the toleration of ambiguity and lack of certainty that are abundant in practice. Most of the chapters are about theory in relation to practice not about cases themselves.

Jean-Paul Sartre (1958) and Maurice Merleau-Ponty developed phenomenology into existentialism during the 1940s and commented on psychoanalysis, gestalt psychology and behaviourism (Merleau-Ponty, 1962, 1963). In later years, English language writers, particularly those with no knowledge of Immanuel Kant's transcendental philosophy, read works like Martin Heidegger's *Being and Time* and came to the conclusion that he was writing about everyday experiences and how to live authentically in relation to death, for instance. But such humanistic understandings could not be further from what Heidegger was intending and even in 1947 Heidegger (1993) refuted the sense that Sartre (1948) had made of *Being and Time* in 1945.

From the original view of the phenomenological movement, the humanistic view is non-philosophical: What phenomenology is about is a theory-first, understanding-led approach, not running to embrace empiricism which was the problem of psychologism that phenomenology was created to prevent. Psychologism is the assumption that empiricism can answer every question and set the agenda for inquiry: As though no other inquiry was relevant or justified. Specifically, Husserl and Heidegger were thinking in a way that was far from the current understanding of existential, humanistic and continental philosophy views of what phenomenology is actually about. What research into the original writers found is that the view of everyday life and how people can be helped through therapy are different to what contemporary existential therapy presumes them to be.

What Husserl and Heidegger focused on was theory before empiricism. Their perspectives are interpretations of the everyday experience of living and meaning in social worlds. Edmund Husserl's focus was on how there is meaning in a world of self and others, a public world as in the sense of the world of a family, group of work colleagues, or the world of vegetarianism, for instance. For Husserl, intentionalities, mental processes of various sorts, exist in creating senses of specific mental objects of all kinds, within contexts of sense that form "horizons" to the worlds of sense that co-occur with each object of attention.

The original phenomenological view of the relation between consciousness, others and the world for consciousness was very finely detailed and has been widely mis-understood because of the complexity of the original texts. The problem begins with a number of overviews, and what can be gleaned of the core components of phenomenology. But attending only to the published works of Husserl and Heidegger provides a misleading picture of the whole story, because even that is an incomplete account. So by way of introduction, there are five things about the key ideas explored below.

First, ideas expressed in language (theories, beliefs and concepts) arise from a detailed attention to lived experience that is investigated by the process known as imaginative variation, a thought experiment that finds invariant qualities about objects and intentional relations with them. This is not merely an attention to the objects of attention. Part of experience is being self-aware of *how* one is aware. Husserl's view included the many ways of being aware, through different intentionalities, and from different perspectives. The starting point is the whole of what appears: "The primary attitude is focused on something objective: the noematic reflection leads to the noematic constituents, the noetic reflection leads to noetic compositions", (Husserl, 1982, §148, p 353). This means that *what appears indicates how it appears. Comparing the perspectives taken towards something reveals a great deal about how the mind works.* For instance, when people are anxious they expect the worst to happen. They expect that their worst nightmare scenario is just about to happen again or may happen for the first time. The idealisation takes place is creating theory about the relation between any consciousness, and *what* and *how* consciousness is aware. The point is formalising how lived, qualitative experience occurs through attending to those lived experiences and finding the inherent distinctions between mental processes by a preliminary qualitative analysis. All the therapies including behaviourism assert the existence of intentionalities. Phenomenology is the study of conscious phenomena and interprets intentionalities in relation to their different types and overlapping senses (Husserl, 1997b). To improve on Husserl's phenomenology is to argue for a better way of interpreting the intentionalities involved in public conscious experience.

Second, introducing phenomenology can be done by noting what ideas do. Specifically, they point to something that appears or to some relationship that is potentially capable of being conscious. This pointing is called conceptual intentionality, referentiality or linguistic signification. What concepts in phenomenology point to are meanings of all kinds and the forms of being aware of them. Some of these meanings are non-verbal at first. Some might be influenced by language, whilst some seem to arise spontaneously, only then becoming verbally expressed in speech or the internal dialogue of thought.

Third, phenomenology can be explained by noting what people do with ideas. For the most part, ideas are used to discern between what is believed and what is not. They distinguish shades and nuances of credibility. This is what Iso Kern and Eduard Marbach meant when they wrote that "it is a question of *understanding that a person represents* the world in a certain way, namely, that she mentally figures to herself ... the world ... it is a matter of understanding the *motivational connections among intentional experiences* taking their course *through time* ... and [how a person] posits them as real ('believes' in them) or abandons them as merely apparent, or unreal", (2001, p 78). These comments on belief are particularly pertinent for everyday life and its therapy. Personally, I do not believe in ghosts just yet. The day that I see one I shall start believing in them, or perhaps I shall wonder if I have been working too hard and that I should get out more instead. What people do with ideas is that they connect with communities of the users and the opposers of ideas. The function of ideas is to help people negotiate themselves within and between these communities.

Fourth, phenomenology, in both its psychological and philosophical forms, has the purpose of theory-making about lived experience as a whole. The whole is a complex one comprised of various dimensions such as history, the passage of time and it runs across social domains of various sorts. Some conceptual meanings are passed down through the centuries, relatively intact; whilst other meanings change, either in what they point to conceptually or by pointing non-verbally through emotion, sensation, anticipation or memory.

Fifth, and in agreement with Heidegger and the hermeneutic tradition prior to him, understanding is not just 'learning by looking'. What counts is 'learning how to look' for what something means. Contrary to Husserl himself, who insisted that it is possible to take away meaning and peruse it with no influence from any other source. It is agreed with Wilhelm Dilthey, Martin Heidegger and Maurice Merleau-Ponty that it is impossible to be without a perspective on meaning. Meaning is ubiquitous. The perspective taken constitutes the sense that appears. It is not possible to strip away meaning from its sensual base in mere perception, or the superimposed objective re-perceptions of memory, or the additions of anticipating what the future will bring. But whilst there is no genuine meaning to find, this does not promote deconstructionism, post-modernism and nihilism. What is promoted is a self-reflexive attention to understanding how people have meaning.

How the everyday appears according to this return to the work of Husserl and Heidegger is that the traditions of hermeneutics and transcendental philosophy have something to offer in understanding the everyday world. How therapy can help is related to how and what people choose. Free will exists and current choices are shaped by the accumulation of choices and opportunities that have been made across the personal history of the individual, in their social contexts. Choices can be interpreted to exist or not. The difficulty is how to interpret what is choose-able. And contrary to psychoanalysis, there are no permanently unconscious experiences. But that is not claiming that every topic is always consciousness.

This book is a return to Edmund Husserl's pioneering work in identifying the ways in which the intentionality of consciousness points in different ways to all that is argued to exist or not. The structure of being conscious of anything is identified as the connections between *intentionality*, *sense*, *object* and *context*. The term "intentionality" means any mental process as it can be interpreted from one's own experiences or discussed with and observed in others. Intentionality is not just about how and what, one person is aware, but concerns how people are related. It is not about reified qualities 'in' a person that are fixed.

Just to say a little more of the pictures of the original writers presented here, let me provide some details concerning the first part of the work below, defining phenomenology. One problem of therapy is justifying the provision of care. For clients, the problem is how to stop the pain in the short term. One central problem of therapy addressed is the justification of clinical reasoning for its practitioners and potential clients. Martin Heidegger's focus was on references within a world that is social, temporal and historical in a very similar way to Husserl's view. The difference was that Heidegger argued that such relational qualities are part of human being itself, prior to consciousness of any such events and processes.

The personal integration of the very many official forms, or brand names, of therapy is a key concern in the sense of justifying how to practice. What is understood as important is not only heeding justifications from empirical research that has been properly executed, but satisfying the need for interpreting everyday experience by understanding intentionality and other major distinctions. The brand of integrative therapy below is one that thrives on the differences between existing schools of thought. It takes from those schools what befits individual clients and works to unify and justify the diversity of perspectives that exist. Thus integrative therapy requires a broad view of theory and research with respect to years of clinical practice, personal insight and supervision. *Integrative therapy means tailoring treatment to meet the needs and abilities of clients.* It is not just giving them what therapists have trained in, because there is nothing else on offer.

The third part of the book covers the relationship between phenomenology and empirical psychology. Because of the previous emphasis on the justification of a theoretical perspective, there is a large gap between phenomenological theory and what practice and research should be, as opposed to what empirical natural psychology makes of the subject matter.

The papers that appear are reprinted by kind permission of the following journals and publishers. Chapter 1 first appeared in 2001 as *The Attitudes and Aims of Husserlian Pure Psychology and Transcendental Phenomenology* in the *Journal of the Society for Existential Analysis*, volume 12(2), pages 287-321. Chapter 2 was published in 1999 as *Husserl and Heidegger in Comparison to Frankl* in the *Bulletin Logotherapie en Existentiale Analyse*, 9(4), pages 10-19. The book review of Robert Sokolowski's *Introduction to Phenomenology* was published in 2000, in *History and Philosophy of Psychology*, 2(2), pages 47-48. Similarly, 2000 was the year that *Husserl's Theory of Empathy: Meaning Arrives with the Other* first appeared in *Journal of the Society for Existential Analysis*, 11(2), pages 11-31. 1999 was the year that chapter 4, *The Special Hermeneutic of Empathy* appeared in the *Journal of the Society for Existential Analysis*, 10(2), pages 21-40. Chapter 6 is a reprint of *Applying Social Constructionism to Psychotherapy* that appeared in *Counselling Psychology Quarterly*, 5(4), pages 385-402, in 1992.

Of the second part of the work, chapter 7, *Are We Before or After Integration? Discussing Guidelines for Integrative Practice via Clinical Audit* first appeared in *Counselling Psychology Review*, 11(3), pages 12-18, in 1996. Chapter 8 was printed in 2001 as *Treatments of Choice, Quality and Integration* in *Counselling Psychology Review*, 16 (4), pages 16-22. Chapter 9, from 1995, is *Power, Boundaries, and Intersubjectivity* from *The British Journal of Medical Psychology*, 68(2), pages 97-107. Chapter 10 came out in 2001 as *Ethics and Multidisciplinary Prac-*

tice in the *Journal of Mental Health*, 10(4), pages 363-365. Chapter 11, *The Per-son-Centred Approach in a Cultural Context* appeared in 1996, in the edited book by Stephen Palmer, Sheila Dainow and Pat Milner, *Counselling: The BAC Coun-selling Reader*, pages 187-194, published in London by Sage Publications. Chap-ter 12, *Exploring the Similarities and Differences Between Person-Centred and Psychodynamic Therapy*, first saw the light of day in 1999 in the *British Journal of Guidance and Counselling*, 27(2), pages 165-178. Chapter 13 first came out in 2004 as *On Existential Psychotherapy: A Hermeneutic and Meta-Representational Perspective* in *Existential Analysis*, 15(2), pages 333-354.

In the third part, chapter 14 is *On the Status of Psychological Knowledge* from the journal *Changes*, 15, pages 100-106 from 1997. 1999 saw the release of *The Future of Psychotherapy in the UK: Discussing Clinical Governance* and was printed in the *British Journal of Psychotherapy*, 16(2), pages 197-207. Chapter 16 comes from 1993 and is *On "The Private Life of the Psychotherapist" and the Psychology of Caring*, a book review printed in *Counselling Psychology Quarterly*, 6(3), pages 251-264. Chapter 19 dates from 2006 and first appeared as *Attachment and Inter-subjectivity* in *Existential Analysis*, 17(1), pages 14-38. Chapter 18 is *Reference, Temporality and the Defences*, from 1998, in *Journal of the Society for Existential Analysis*, 9, pages 84-97. Chapter 19 is *Towards an Intentional Analysis of Con-sciousness?* And was first printed in *Journal of the Society for Existential Analysis*, 13(2), pages 237-265 in the year 2002. And finally, chapter 20 is *The Empirical Evidence Base as the Re-Appearance of the Problem of Psychologism*, from 2006, printed in *Existential Analysis*, 17(2), pages 371-384.

In coming to understand what the perspectives of Husserl and Heidegger were, it became obvious that contemporary readings of the originals were widely different from what the original writers had been stating. But rather than call this work on the justification of therapy "existential," I am using the term "phenome-nological" to denote its attention to the detail of Husserl and Heidegger and other key writers. It was also found that in comparison to the original writers, the deconstructive and post-modern readings of Husserl are no accurate readings at all. Existential-phenomenology was right in its attention to meaning. Sartre believed that an existential psychoanalysis should find how each individual "has chosen his being" through analysing "concrete projects" and brings out the "*ontological meaning* of qualities" which seems to be the choice of aspects of per-sonal lifestyle as being, (Sartre, 1958, pp. 599-600). Descriptions defy thought and are meaningless leading to the overall indeterminacy of meaning yet the need to account for meaning, (Merleau-Ponty, 1962, p 365). There is no inherent meaning in life or any specific situation. It is rather a matter of how to make sense of any situation including the course of one's own life or that of others. Indeed, contemporarily there is a general scepticism, suspicion and disillusionment about grand narratives that explain every situation. The scepticism has rejected free market capitalism, religion, communism, psychoanalysis and other grand narratives as naïve and over-ambitious in being able to explain. This latter scepticism is agreeable but should not become a nihilism or a cynical sneering at attempts to identify order where there genuinely is order to behold. Such remarks are unfashionable for the sceptical view.

In this work, "therapy" refers to individual talking and action therapies. The terms "patient" and "analysand" are included in the term "client". Similarly, all variations such as doctor, counsellor, clinical psychologist, psychotherapist and analyst are included when using the word "therapist". Therapy refers to all forms of therapy including counselling. The term "psychodynamic" is used to refer to all forms of therapy that are derived from Freud such as psychoanalysis, psychoanalytic psychotherapy and psychodynamic counselling. References are placed at the end of the book. References to the works of Sigmund Freud are according to the notation of the *Standard Edition* published by Hogarth. References in the text are stated in the order of their translation into English or publication in English. The changes that have been made to the original papers are to make minor corrections to make their appearance more cohesive and to correct grammar. Words like "counsellor" and "counselling psychologist" have been replaced with the word "therapist" throughout.

PART I
Defining phenomenology

The original writings of Edmund Husserl and Martin Heidegger cannot be grasped immediately and the consequences for the theory and practice of psychotherapy merely read off. What their writings mean for therapy easily becomes a matter of argument and disagreement. Accordingly, any contention concerning what they did mean *originally* is open to criticism from a number of vested interests that have already produced differing conclusions concerning the original ideas and their consequences. Currently, there are many pictures of what phenomenology is and what it provides or fails to provide, for theory, research and practice. By way of an introduction to the most basic points, the following remarks are intended to set the scene to the first part of this work and show the progression of ideas in the remaining two parts.

Phenomenology of the original kind created theory. Theory should be about something identifiable. The particular scope of theory in therapy includes the psychosocial skills of practice and conscious, publicly-accessible meanings of all kinds. Theory provides direction for practice, research and supervision. Its ideas permit some actions and discourage others. Phenomenology as philosophy is a version of Immanuel Kant's transcendental philosophy of the conditions of possibility for something to be understood in the everyday world. Transcendental philosophy considers the conditions of possibility for necessary explanations in understanding how concepts get grounded in meaningful experience, prior to practice. Immanuel Kant, Edmund Husserl and Martin Heidegger were transcendental philosophers who searched for ideal knowledge—*a priori* ideas—prior to any empirical practice. Phenomenology theorises for philosophy, applied psychology or other forms of academia. It does not proceed by rendering meaning problematic or undecided, but through explaining how it occurs.

The biggest argument in favour of transcendental philosophy is the claim that philosophy begins with the consideration of the possibility of concepts and fields of meaning of various kinds. Heidegger coined the term "existential" in relation to his a priori *analytic* of "Da-sein" (literally, the *there-being* who is human being in its contexts). Heidegger's view was not about the intentionality of Da-sein's consciousness but about its being, in an object-related sense. The word "analytic" has a specific Kantian sense for Heidegger. For Kant, what was important is finding how thought and understandings of any kind are possible via a regressive looking back from everyday meanings and experiences. Kant concluded in making conditional statements of the sort "if … then …". The basic research question is to find how thoughts, beliefs, theories and concepts relate to their experiential objects. Kant's general conclusion was that consciousness and meaningful objects together make each other possible as a whole (1993, pp. 126-129/A 105-112, Ströker, 1987).

What Husserl and Heidegger did was to develop the detail of this same conclusion. The general assumption of transcendental philosophy, and any kind of phenomenology, is that there is a regular structure to the meanings that consciousness produces. The clearly observable phenomenon, for the most part, is that there is knowledge and understanding and not chaos. A priori concepts, like those in mathematics and logic, point to something regular (pp. 94-5/B 122-3, 114-5/B 159-160). One metaphor that Kant employed for philosophy was that of the law that demands proper procedures for believing in genuine concepts that are preparatory for action. Hence philosophy finds what truly matters and distinguishes that from wasting time with irrelevancies. Kant proved through logical argument that "pure concepts" or "categories" are a priori conditions for proper understanding (p 96-7/B 126).

The conventional wisdom about transcendental philosophy is that it set sail with Kant, ran aground with Husserl but was saved by Heidegger, where it came to discover new continents. For this writer, that account is untrue. Rather, transcendental philosophy set sail with Kant and came to full sail with Husserl, but then ran aground with Heidegger. The evidence for this claim is the worth of the topics of intentionality and intersubjectivity in Husserl. But the major problem with reading Husserl are the high-context communications of his writings that do not sufficiently explain what he was trying to communicate. This is because large amounts of his published writings were never intended for publication and were written as a means of recording his insights for personal consumption.

In order to explain the abstract terminology, it is necessary to understand how the focus on the *synthetic a priori* in Kant became the search for *universal a priori* in Husserl and produced the 16 *existential a priori* of Da-sein's being in Heidegger. Specifically, Kant concluded that there are 12 "pure concepts of the understanding" or "categories" that are "a priori employed in all judgement, and provide the basis for the formation of all other, empirical concepts", (Gardner, 1999, p 116). Namely:

Of Quantity
Unity
Plurality
Totality
Of Quality
Reality

Negation
Limitation
Of Relation
Of Inherence and Subsistence …
Of Causality and Dependence (cause and effect)
Of Community (reciprocity between agent and patient)
Of Modality
Possibility—Impossibility
Existence—Non-existence
Necessity—Contingence
Kant, 1993, p 85/A 79.

Kant believed these 12 categories are used in judging and form all other empirically-related concepts. The point for the relation between philosophy and therapy practice is that phenomenology is part of the tradition of the consideration of possibilities prior to action. Kant's aim was to show how concepts arise from experience. Yet the way in which he did this has been criticised as overly logical and constructive, in the sense that he projected a number of ideas that were pertinent to his assumptions (Gardner, 1999, p 117).

What the next section shows is how Heidegger developed Kant's ideas in his influential work *Being and Time* that became the major inspiration for Sartre, Merleau-Ponty and others. It has to be noted that it was specifically Jean-Paul Sartre who was a main thinker in taking Husserl and Heidegger's ideas and applying them to criticise Freud, although Sartre was certainly not the only writer in this genre. The upshot has been to have a heavy focus on the talking cures in therapy and to relegate cognitive behaviour therapy and other forms of practice to the sidelines. Let us consider Heidegger before Husserl in order to point out the original focus of phenomenology.

Heidegger's influence for existential therapy

Heidegger developed some aspects of Kant's stance in the following way. For Heidegger, there are 16 existentials of Da-sein in relation to other Da-sein, itself and the world. Allow me to provide a brief overview of the way that Heidegger had to correct Sartre, who had mis-understood what Heidegger meant and sent existentialism into a non-Heideggerian direction. Let us pick up the story at the key phrase that Sartre mis-understood: "*The essence of Da-sein lies in its existence*", (Heidegger, 1996, §9, p 40) although it would have probably been better to write that *the essence of Da-sein lies in its mode of existence*. What Heidegger meant by

this is that Da-sein is self-reflexively aware of its own existence and able to identify its own manner of existing. Heidegger is defining fundamental ontology as an
a priori analysis of human being concerning how claims about human nature are
possible in the first place. The point is that understanding of the human condition is possible. The desired conclusions concern pre-knowledge that is prior to
any experience and make it possible. Such a prioris would have universal necessity
and validity and be constructs common to all humanity: Probably the best way to
understand this type of reasoning is to understand the laws of logic and mathematics in relation to their real-world applications. "Existentials" are the mathematics of human being.

The outcome for Heidegger is identifying existentials that are interpretative
dispositions and necessities, that by virtue of being human, grant us common
sense share-able experiences and a common humanity. If there were no existentials, there would be no understanding and a confusion of incomprehensible
experiences that would not be capable of communication and solipsism would
ensue. The existentials of Heidegger are necessities for interpreting one's own
experience as part of the greater whole. The method of deriving them concerns
self-reflection and interpretation of the sense of what it is to exist in a world-con-
text. Such an "ontological" investigation must come first. Heidegger assumed
that there are discernible underlying ontological characteristics of what is apparent to consciousness.

The following is a brief note concerning what Heidegger concluded to provide
some flavour of his thinking. It does not represent a conclusion of the detailed
analyses of *Being and Time* nor the place of existentials in Heidegger's later work.
The existentials themselves are noted by capitals. A reading of the importance of
temporality is provided in more detail in chapter 18 below and *Psychotherapy and
Phenomenology* (Owen, 2006). In overview, what can be noted of the existentials
is that the subject-object connection is made possible by Temporality that
enables the opening up of the World-whole prior to any recognition of its object-
parts. For Heidegger, all being lies inside Da-sein's world and its temporal being
is what creates the openness of the human world. Care, Taking-care and Concern
occur within that context. Moods show the Attunement to the world and Understanding (of possibility and as interpreting) is projected onto objects and meaning
is discovered. When it comes to people or physical objects, Spaciality is encountered through De-distancing oneself towards such objects. However, the role of
others is such that people are united and there is no gap between people (except
through false thinking) to create alienation, because the Truth of the matter,
according to Heidegger, is that The They forms Being-with for all persons. Truth

can be discerned by paying attention to instances of experience. Da-sein has a limit in Death and Totality, as a different type of whole altogether. The point to bear in mind is that time is most constitutive in opening Da-sein to beings of all sorts, including that of every new moment (Heidegger, 1996, §69, p 321). On the basis of there having been a past world, and the temporal absorbency of Da-sein's being, can there be conscious attention (§69b, p 332). The whole is a priori to any of its parts, concerning the relation of human being as temporal towards any being for it (§69c, p 333). Da-sein's temporal being is temporally embedded in the world (Ibid).

Heidegger's interpretation of the existentials of Da-sein's being concern its temporal nature (§4, p 10, cf §65, p 301). When he noted that "Apriorism is the method," (note 10, p 410), what he was urging was an interpretative approach to understanding the embedded, complex whole of human being as the totality of all its facets. In 1965 at a seminar to mental health professionals, he explained it this way: that "the mode of existing—is the existential analytic of Da-sein", (Heidegger, 2001, p 121). These categories of human being are "existentialia", (p 122). "The analytic of Da-sein as existential is a kind of ontology in an entirely formal sense ... a *fundamental ontology*", (Ibid). This is an explicit warning not to read *Being and Time* as "anthropology," a worldly or empirical psychology or non-philosophical qualitative study.

What this means is that an existential psychology, or therapy for that matter, uses the basic categories or dimensions of human being to interpret, judge and structure life in various ways. When taken to the psychological sphere this means that psychological causes are necessary to interpret cause and effect, in the way that ideas like formulation have come to pass in therapy. The point of understanding how consciousness works is to relate how what appears as real for clients can be accountable, understood, for them and for therapists. Intentionalities are notional and idealised forms of representing relation. The same situation can be feared, found relaxing or interesting. The situation has different senses yet it is the same situation. Natural psychological science cannot account for this apparent variability in reality, what exists from different perspectives.

Husserl and Heidegger explored a number of key terms such as the idea that there is a world of meaning. For instance, transcendental phenomenology focuses on the idea of the world: This means it finds how there are intersubjective meanings of the same objects of attention and meanings for more than one person. This exploration takes place in a theoretical and general way. Psychology for Husserl and Heidegger means emotional, relational and concerning intentionalities about conscious lived experiences such as thoughts, feelings and beliefs. The psychological objects and processes of therapy also are lived meaningful experiences. For therapists, what is required is a means of access to changing these in an ethical way. Basic understanding is the tool with which clients can understand themselves and so provide their own interventions.

Husserl and Heidegger on pure psychology

Pure psychology is a theoretical form of identifying basic ideas that would contemporarily be called a biopsychosocial perspective: Pure psychology is a tripartite stance, demanding a future consensus about *precisely* how the biological, psychological and social dimensions of human being mutually influence each other. The *biological* refers to all that is material, physical and genetically-inherited. The *psychological* refers to the dimension of free will, choice and the intentionality of being related to what is believed to exist psychologically. Belief occurs through forms of intentionality such as perceiving, anticipating and recollecting. The *social* refers to the influence of culture, society and history as they are handed down through the medium of the family and those around us. The biopsychosocial view of the ego is that there is a dynamic inter-action between all three components. More details will be mentioned below. The common point to grasp is that intentionality is the being of consciousness for both men however it is portrayed. To spend a life is to spend it through intentionalities that present cultural objects (or inner worldly beings).

However, the commonalities between Husserl and Heidegger are not well known. On the contrary to what many people think, there is documentary evidence of how supportive Heidegger was of Husserl's foray into theoretical psychology. Because their areas of difference are well-known, it is widely believed that Heidegger never supported Husserl's focus on consciousness to any degree. However, this is not true. The original emphases of both were on a priori concerns about the being of consciousness, but to different degrees. It is true that Heidegger insisted that being should be considered. But this is not to say that Heidegger had no dealings with pure psychology.

How the two men differed is that Heidegger wanted to be more focused on ontology because the "being of everything ... is constituted in this pure subjectivity, pure subjectivity is called transcendental subjectivity", (Heidegger, 1997, p 109). Ontology is specifying the nature of what exists and what relations there are. The aim of phenomenology is attending to the whole of human experience and identifying regions within it, according to the interpreted truth of the matter, rather than being influenced by the prejudices of what academia or science currently believe to be the case.

Heidegger's statements that defined pure psychology are as follows: the "intentionality of lived experiences shows itself to be the essential structure of the pure psychic. The whole complex of lived experience ... exists at each moment as a self (an "I")", (p 111). The idealisation of experience concludes on "the pure psychic" and "lays out the essential structures of particular kinds of lived experience, their forms of interrelation and occurrence", (p 112). One task is to find the nature of intentionality such as "a perception in general, a wish in general", (p 114). The aim is that:

> Pure psychology furnishes the necessary a priori foundation for empirical psychology in relation to the pure psychic. Just as the grounding of an "exact" empirical science of nature requires a systematic disclosure of the essential forms of nature in general ... so too a scientifically "exact" psychology requires disclosure of the a priori typical forms without which it is impossible to think the I (or the we), consciousness, the objects of consciousness, and hence any psychic life at all.
> p 116.

These remarks show how Heidegger agreed with Husserl concerning what a theoretical or philosophical psychology should be. The a priori foundation in particular is understanding how intentionalities of different sorts present meanings.

To summarise the story so far, the original phenomenological psychology, here referred to as pure psychology, is a theoretical concern in the sense of a pure mathematics that comes before its applications. For instance, the purpose of mathematics is designing a bridge that will stand up and not fall down. Because ideas are formative and govern the nature and direction of any practice, theoretical psychology is necessary and prior to any empirical psychology or practice of any kind. For the originators, pure psychology was not a science. Nor was it subjectivism. Nor was it merely descriptive in making its conclusions. Pure psychology interprets what is experienced. Nor was it introspection or speculation. Pure psychology points to its evidence and makes its theory-making method clear to all, for critical appraisal from other perspectives. What this means for understanding the practice of the psychosocial skills of therapy is that, most approaches might agree that lack of compassion, lack of trust of one's own experience and an over-readiness to focus on weakness in preference to one's strengths, might contribute to distress. But it takes a qualitative analysis to find out what these experiences really are for each person. What pure psychology does is provide ideas about what consciousness and its intentionalities are that can be used. Pure psychology concerns making ideas that are put to work in larger human purposes.

Pure psychology in relation to the conventional understanding of personality

This section comments on the scope and impact of Husserl's theoretical psychology for therapy with respect to the term "personality disorder".

Firstly, in comparison to contemporary schools of theoretical or empirical psychology, there is no reason why pure psychology should be tied to any one area of the current scene. Husserl and Heidegger were both clear that pure psychology is more fundamental than any approach extent in the 1920s and that still applies today. Indeed, the wholism that pure psychology is about defies current distinctions between psychoanalysis, behaviourism, gestalt, developmental psychology, social constructionism and the quantitative practices. Pure psychology is about consciousness in its habitat of other consciousness as embedded in the reality that people live. It concerns how attention is shared and demonstrated, how people communicate, model and believe what may be true or false. For instance, what interests pure psychology is *how* the consciousness of a depressed person focuses on problems, *how* their intentional focus becomes entrained with others and *how* that person creates their depressed sense of the world, others and themselves.

It is worth putting together some of the key ideas from Husserl's definitions of pure psychology by way of making more tangible his abstract perspective. Husserl focused on *a priori* theorising. In 1927, Husserl lectured that his qualitative analysis kept questions open and prevented foreclosure in advance of the research taking its course: The following citations record the scope of research in relation to the self and its beliefs.

> The term "I" [or "ego"] designates a new direction for investigation (still in abstraction from the social sense of this word) in reference to the essence-forms of "habituality;" in other words, the "I" [or "ego"] as subject of lasting beliefs or thought-tendencies—"persuasions"—(convictions about being, value-convictions, volitional decisions, and so on), as the personal subject of habits, of trained knowing, of certain character qualities.
> 1997c, §5, pp. 166-7.

The above means there is a determination to understand the nature of the lived experience of self. What is being referred to above is a general view of what it is to be oneself. For therapists, psychological researchers and lay people, beliefs are added together across time.

The remarks in the next section show how Husserl saw the self as part of a complex whole. Bet let us make the abstract comments above, more concrete. For Husserl, the ego is a combinatory style that brings together experiences across a number of contexts of time, person and place: *The past influences the present in relation to the future.* The even more precise way of stating this most basic stance is to understand that voluntary memory and involuntary retention of the past enable the present and so does the anticipation of the future. To jump ahead with one impact for contemporary psychology and therapy, is to understand for instance, that personality disorders are not pervasive across a number of fronts. But rather *personality is pervasive across the domains of being embedded in a culture, having the influence of personal history in the present, and creating-temporally-oriented understanding within the larger contexts of language, society and history.* Personality is never disordered in the phenomenological view. It always has the same form. The ego and its consciousness integrate past influences with present and future ones. What has been learned and associated gets re-presented in the present and the future. People try and prevent possible threat and damage to themselves, even in advance of there being such danger in the present.

The problems of people with the so-called personality disorders are not about the structure of their personality but about a lack of reflection, difficulty in interpreting self and difficulty in carrying out basic self-care in the psychological sense. The means of production and the 'end-products' of the life produced, concern intentionality. People who have personality disorders do not have a problem with intellectually understanding themselves but an inability or unwillingness to self-care. The explanations for such difficulties may include overcoming the sheer weight of the habits of a lifetime. Even if accurate self-knowledge is attained, there is an unwillingness to keep the self safe and limit self-harming and impulsive behaviours. The great weight of the past decades shows that the person has been persistently unable to look after themselves. This might be because they see no value in being self-caring due to low self-esteem. Because the ego is an accumulation of senses and implicit and explicit beliefs across the lifespan, the way of helping people with personality disorders is no different to any mainstream good practice that is responsive and has clear boundaries that inform and motivate clients in their own care. Any client can be helped when they own their emotions and behaviour. What further needs to happen is giving them the tools to self-care and make changes in their lives and increase their capacity for frustration and negative emotion. To tell a person that they have something wrong with themselves is dis-empowering, pejorative and robs them of hope and the means of understanding themselves so that they can make changes. When any person rea-lises that they are not wholly their current emotions and actions, then they come to realise their capability to leave the past behind and move on as best they can.

The means of helping clients who pass the check list test for personality disor-der, or do not, is to be present, responsive through providing relationship condi-tions that enable change (Rogers, 1957, 1975) and provide clear boundaries (1942, pp. 95-108). Carl Rogers called it being in psychological "contact" which was the very first enabling condition (1957) and John Bowlby described it as making a secure therapeutic relationship to promote the exploration of shameful and frightening material (1988, p 138). Other reasons for a narrow lifestyle are lack of social contact and the creation of defences that have the purpose of fend-ing off no actual threats in current perception. The defences are aimed at staving off what has happened or might yet happen. Below, the nature of the self will be returned to with a more sustained explanation. One consequence of the Husser-lian understanding of personality is that no special techniques need to be used with people who self-harm, catastrophise their view of the present and future or who have extreme difficulty in looking after themselves and others. Let us take the case of borderline personality disorder to be more specific. Marsha Linehan's approach (1993) has been shown to be effective with people who self-harm and are emotionally dys-regulated with respect to interpreted threat. (They lack egoic constancy and object constancy concerning others and are unable to distinguish their fear of what might be happening from what is actually happening). How-ever, it has to be noted that such characteristics are existent in the general popula-tion among people who would never qualify for the title "borderline personality disorder". Accordingly, it is incorrect to draw an arbitrary line concerning who has borderline personality and who does not. What needs to happen is to widen the scope of how to help with problems of self-harm, lack of object constancy and difficulty in providing basic self-care in the population at large not just within those persons who qualify for the category "borderline".

Let us return to the original intent of Husserl's comments from 1925 that were in a similar general view:

> The title Apriority means: this psychology aims first of all at all those essential universalities and necessities, without which psy-chological being and living are simply inconceivable. Only sub-sequently does it proceed to the explanation of psychological

facts, to theory, precisely their eidetic explanation, which is *for us*
the first interest.
1977a, §4, p 33.

What the above refers to is the aim of finding necessary invariant laws of what
idealised consciousness is and does for anyone. Husserl wanted to explore and
idealise, how people are connected in their mutual influences and how meaning is
transmitted, across generations and between cultures:

> The exploration of single forms of intentional psychic processes
> which in essential necessity generally must or can present them-
> selves in the mind; in unity with this, also the exploration of the
> syntheses they are members of for a typology of their essences:
> both those that are discrete and those continuous with others,
> both the finitely closed and those continuing into open infinity.
> 1997c, §5, p 166.

The above concerns interpreting a single experience to show the forms of intentionalities involved. What is being discussed is how to compare and contrast the
givennesses of what appears, and become able to work out how different forms of
mental process are occurring, by paying attention to how meanings of different
sorts present themselves. For instance, on the one hand, when people perceive
visually what appears does so in immediacy. On the other, if a strong memory is
found, the re-playing of the memory super-imposes itself on the perception of the
here and now, sometimes to the extent that the present can become 'lost' if the
memory is sufficiently strong enough.

Intentionality is interpreted through comparisons of how objects are present
in their various ways. Something that Husserl called their "manners of givenness," for instance, as remembered, as imagined, loved or hated. The comparison
of how the same person or situation appears in these ways is the raw data to be
studied. The conclusions are of the form of stating how one person is involved
with others through socially-accessible meanings. The method is comparing the
manners of givenness of the object to work out, for instance, how memories get
superimposed on the perception of the present, with the focus being on understanding active remembering and perceiving. The aim is differentiating all forms
of being aware of all types of object-meanings. Conclusions concern how the
intentionalities differ, in what they include or exclude, in terms of sense and how
they comprise wholes of different sorts of meaning.

> ... intentionality ... consciousness ... personality as such, and objectivity as objectivity of consciousness ... this twofold centering of conscious life ... furnishes every inner psychology ... the task ... of descriptively pursuing ... Every category of possible objectivities designates an index for a methodic regularity of possible psychic life; every possible real world, a regularity of possible intersubjective life.
> 1977a, §4, p 34.

What the above means is the focus of finding the invariant aspects of how consciousness operates and makes sense. It means making concluding interpretations of how and what oneself and others experience. What the above means is that theorising how the mind works joins up the portions of evidence that are considered to make a cohesive narrative, an accessible explanation.

The quotation below concerns the stance from which everyday experience is understood. What is important is teaching others how to make sense of qualitative experience.

> ... as psychologists we do not want to be philosophers ... Each can begin only as a natural, unphilosophical human being.
> ... We want to remain in the natural attitude; we want actually to be nothing else but psychologists, directed in a natural, human manner toward the objective world as actuality, and endeavoring to investigate it insofar as it is a world of mind.
> Ibid.

What the above means in concrete terms is that pure psychology stays in contact with the real world and never loses sight of the whole as biopsychosocial. However, that which is biopsychosocial is complex and has a large number of interrelated facets. One region (biological, psychological or social) impacts with the other two, in a complex manner. In this wholistic view, the individual is united with the social in: "the pure essential theory of the mental, of the individually psychic as well as of the socially psychic, and of the productions of society, is *eo ipso* simultaneously a knowledge of the world, with regard to the mentality which factually permeates it", (p 35). What he was referring to was the wholism of consciousness in the everyday human world. The object of pure psychology is understandable in the following way ...

Since we have all formed the concept of the a priori science in mathematics … we tend understandably to regard any a priori science at all as something like a mathematics; *a priori* psychology, therefore, as a mathematics of the mind. But here we must be on our guard … The psychic province … has a multiplicity of immediate essential insights which continually grows with analysis and is never to be limited. Here, mere immediate intuition delivers already a quite endless science, an intuitive and descriptive a priori … The mediate, concluding and deducing procedure is not lacking at higher stages, and it leads to higher level a priori; but by no means is the entire science of the type of a mathematics.

pp. 36-7.

What the above makes clear is the development of understanding from Kant to Husserl. The idea of pure psychology as pure mathematics is an explanatory metaphor and should not be taken literally. The ultimate outcome of a pure psychology is the creation of practices that connect with lived experience after having interpreted it in a formal way. Let us consider what this means for therapy: The practice of psychosocial skills occurs within the medium of face-to-face meetings that are a two-way communication. The bare bones of therapy meetings are that clients require an explanation of their psychological problem and then some analysis of that with them, with the expectation (implicit or explicit) that clients are being requested to try something new, based on the new understanding made.

The role that pure psychology performs is to sort through general cases. Even if these are imagined relations between one consciousness and meaning, or between people and meaning, in order to relate justified concepts via the a priori of psychology (as rules or laws). This is for understanding psychological reality and perspectives on the empathised social world of conscious phenomena. Pure psychology creates ideal laws about actual, empirical research or purely imagined possibilities, or concerning merely possible actuality. These aprioris are already existent in experimental psychology, for therapists and laypersons, even if these ideals are only implicit in their actions and way of life. In other words, theory occupies an interpretative position to what appears as psychologically real and what is psychologically possible.

Metaphorically, pure psychology is like jurisprudence in relation to the practice of the law. There is argument about rules, principles and proper procedures, in order to aid good practice and promote consistent and justified outcomes.

Jurisprudence considers principles for the practice of the law, as seen across a wide spectrum of approaches. For therapy, the pure focus is on the receipt and provision of care. Clinical reasoning concludes in finding principles about how to supply care. For the pure psychology of therapy, there could be the study of specific systems and specific institutions of providing care, to find out what they have to offer. Some of the research questions that a pure psychology asks are "what are the conditions of possibility for ____?" "What is the relationship between one therapy and another?" "What should an approach for helping ____ be like?" What is being urged is a search for theory that is grounded in lived experience about constant aspects and possible universal relations between consciousness, other consciousness and cultural objects.

For example, what pure psychology means is that depression, for instance, is a complex whole. People who are severely depressed for a long time have a variety of problems. Their personal relationships and those around them suffer as a result of social withdrawal and low self-esteem that is part of the depressive world, its totality. When the experience of being depressed is on-going, then social skills become atrophied, so that the person becomes out of practice in making contact with others. As they socially withdraw and fixate on their losses and regrets, friends and family turn away because they do not know how to respond. Family cannot help the depressed person and receive no thanks when they try. The consequences of depression are wide-ranging and connect with the abilities of the person. It does not matter even if it is suspected that the depression is mainly biological in origin, because there have been no losses in the person's life.

This observation on the nature of depression immediately shows the strength of pure psychology as opposed to natural psychological science. Specifically, natural psychological science is overly hasty and does not sufficiently attend to the experience of being depressed, as it exists in the type of social world that is the habitat of the depressed person. What natural psychological science would want to do is measure and classify the extent of depression without first wanting to know *how* consciousness does what it does and understand what it is to be depressed. The problem of natural psychological science is its excessive focus on the naturalistic attitude that believes that only natural-material cause is worthy of attention. The naturalistic attitude rules out the complex inter-connections between all three aspects of the biopsychosocial whole. It contradicts the as-yet-unknown overall inter-action between each aspect.

The common point about phenomenology is that it is a mental analysis of qualitative experience. What this means for a qualitative analysis of consciousness is that common sense everyday experience is re-interpreted as idealised forms of how we understand. Pure psychology is an introductory clarification of psychological reality in the world. Transcendental phenomenology is a more general analysis of meaning for selves and others within the meaningful world. For Husserl, it was necessary to create a specific understanding of what consciousness achieves because it does not belong to natural scientific psychology. When taken to the sphere of therapy, what this means is that if people alter their behaviour in-line with what is unreal, then they may not be hallucinating, but they are reacting to what is not perceptually present but merely anticipated or remembered, for instance.

Some of Husserl's theoretical conclusions in brief

The purpose of this section is focusing on some of what Husserl did conclude in his abstract view, before making much more concrete and specific examples in the final sections of this introduction.

Many writers would agree that self, other and world are major terms in any therapeutic approach. What these concepts point to are any self, any other and the mutuality of sense that comprises a number of shared meanings. In brief and not in full, some theoretical conclusions are noted before providing further details on the nature of intentionality and the self. For Husserl, there was no final listing of the topics that were to be investigated or had been concluded on. A great deal could be mentioned of the fine detail of the type of answer and type of reasoning that is used to find the answers. Some of the types of answer that Husserl made are the following.

The *Fifth Cartesian Meditation* provides answers about how there is a world in consciousness (1977b, §§42-62). The basic view of self, other and world was laid out in a mature form in the *Cartesian Meditations,* which is an odd name for a non-Cartesian perspective (Owen, 2006). It seemed that Husserl was trying to make an appeal to the obvious nature of the social sharing of meaning. *Formal and Transcendental Logic* answered the question of how there is space and time in consciousness (1969, §§4, 107c). The basic method was the analysis of the types of givenness of remembering and imagining, and other types of intentionality that are subject to interpretation. The Kantian research question is 'how is consciousness structured so that objects of different kinds can appear for me, including the object of myself?'

• The major contribution of useable ideas is identifying the forms of the intentionalities, the inter-relation between self, other, object and world. The being of psychological objects is often temporally-oriented and often fearful of the repetition or occurrence of interpersonal events that are not current.

• The social world is comprised of the perspectives of others. Such a theory of the world, for instance, can be put to use in actions with families, groups, cultures and societies. The term "world" can mean a world shared by two people or by a much larger cross-section who may not actually know each other at all. Empathy is the type of intentionality that provides the second-hand perspectives of what others experience. Others have their perspective that is never experienceable as my perspective, yet others are to a degree understandable by me and vice versa. To understand another person is to be part of the social world and understand their perspective on the world. Others are selves like me and remain separate yet connected.

The terms "ego" or "self" have their referent, their experiential base in anyone who is an I who thinks, feels and experiences. Selves are persons understood generally. When people are interpreted this way, it shows that human identity extends across time in its difference and sameness. The style of a self refers to a person's whole constant character (This is not an account of short-term variation that only changes slowly across the lifespan and reactions to immediate circumstances). "Self" includes how a person understands themselves, verbally and nonverbally and includes the sense of felt-agency and free will in contact with other agents, social and physical constraints and the socio-historical world. For Husserl, the basic phenomena of the self are:

• There is a pre-reflexive, self-presence and self-identification with respect to others, past and present. Even before reflection, there is an overlapping of the manifold of experiences of self that makes them mine: One's chosen and involuntary mental and physical acts. These create the sense of self called "object constancy" because there is a duration and integration of these many senses across time and place (cf Fraiberg, 1969, Solnit, 1982, Solnit and Neubauer, 1986, Akhtar, 1994, Tyson, 1996).

• The presence of bodily sensation and perception are the immediate here and now experiences of one's own constancy of being an embodied person—waking up, walking along, sitting down, dancing. These occur in relation to the embodied presence of others. What these experiences have in common is an "originality" of self-presence.

For Husserl, the self is tied to the "null point" of looking out at the world from the same physical body. The I is the same I for whom everything appears and that unifies the manifold of everyday experience across the lifespan. The "pure I" is the Identical I, the same throughout egoic experience that is made in contra-distinction to others, for they are never mine and are always other. As regards the biopsychosocial view, then the inter-action between all three aspects is as follows: The fundamental building blocks of genetic inheritance are not amenable to change in themselves. But the biological buildings blocks are in a dynamic relation with how people can cope through new social learning. The socially learned aspects are more easily open to reflection and change than the biological ones. The psychosocial part is addressed as choose-able and meaningful. It links the individual with family, work, culture and society. The component of human being that is psychosocial is expressive, value-oriented and changes across the lifespan, due to social change as a whole. Altogether, there is a biopsychosocial whole of human existence with its biological, individual psychological and social psychological parts in constant inter-action.

The above remarks are abstract and not the usual form of statement that existentialism concerns choice, freedom and authenticity. The first outcome of pure psychology is creating clear understanding about conscious experiences and mental processes of all kinds. The following remarks are intended to focus on two concrete examples. In order to provide case examples, allow me to show more detail of the sort of experiences to which apriori theory refers. First is the idea of intentionality. And second is that of the ego or sense of self.

Understanding intentionality

The major concept of intentionality is understood by the general public and is understandable by therapists who also use it without focusing on it formally. For instance, there are two major ways in that it is used with clients. It is possible to ask clients what they are feeling. This would elicit their emotions, mood and the object that they felt-about, plus what they feel and similar responses. These are all object-related, however the initial question is phrased and however the answer about the object of attention is expressed.

But it is also possible to ask *how* a specific object of attention is conscious. For instance, is it remembered? Is it anticipated? Is it only when the person says something to themselves that is anxiety-provoking that they feel their throat tightening up? The types of answer these questions elicit indicate *how* the object was conscious rather than *what* it was that was being experienced.

Such lines of questioning are common to ordinary experience. What the concept of intentionality shows is that there are two poles to conscious experience. What the *objects of attention* are—and the *kinds of attention* in which they appear. Indeed, there are many simple and compound types of being aware. The types of intentional relation include simple types such as action, speech, seeing and emotion. There are compound types such as empathising what another is saying to themselves, what another feels, what another intends to do. The intentionalities are studied as idealised forms of relation to all kinds of objects. It is this *relation-to* that is referred to in the abstract comments by Husserl and Heidegger. Therefore, one instance of what phenomenology does is making therapists more aware, in a formal way, of what and how people are aware. Of course, the same distinctions apply to therapists as well.

The usefulness of intentionality is that it is a necessary explanation. Intentionalities cannot be seen, but their interpreted end-products are experienced as recognisable meaningful objects. Similar objects are recognisable as end-products in different sense-fields (such as audition, bodily feeling, affect or through language). There are complex inter-relations between varieties of meaningful object. Some objects are comprised of composite objects where meanings of different sorts are involved. However, intentionalities are necessary assumptions concerning experience. The meaningful world occurs because mental processes make mental stuffs. Clearly, the assumption is that the constitution of meaning employs intentionalities to make the end-products of objective-meaning. The ego and its free will are involved in directing awareness of various types, towards objects of various sorts, and so produce mood, affect and influence the choice of behaviour and relating.

The nature of self

A second exemplar of the phenomenological view is to understand the theme of contextuality and being embedded within a whole of meanings. Let us take the term "ego" which means the personality or living sense of self as direct self-experience. In short, the ego is pervasive across a number of domains, simultaneously and across time.

Eduard Marbach explains that the ego includes what it does and what it can do (2000, p 91). For the most part, it unifies itself. However empirically, there are problems in being able to attain constancy of the sense of self, for instance, in the experiences called borderline personality disorder and dissociative identity disorder. Yet the same effect happens in vacillation, procrastination and other changes between objects, either simultaneously or across time. Judging oneself is often in contra-distinction to the others with whom one relates and to social contexts, where one relates. The problem of the lack of ego constancy arises in a number of areas where learning and rationality are not transferred from one domain to another.

Consequently, the traditional difficulty in being able to account for personality reflects the pervasiveness of what personality is. There are a very large number of idiosyncratic ways of being. Any serious attempt to classify people into the 11 personality types defined by *Diagnostic and Statistical Manual IV* (American Psychiatric Association, 1994, pp. 629-673) will run into trouble as people generally have two or three features of the classificatory system. Indeed, the idea that personality can be easily classified by a number of problematic symptoms in a checklist is refuted as it could never capture the many ways in which the facets of personality actually exist.

Furthermore, the complexity that human being is can only be begun to be captured by the term "biopsychosocial". Where pure psychology shines is that it honours the complex meaningful whole of inter-relations that exist for consciousness. Specifically, what exists for one consciousness may also exist for others. An ego (an I or self) is an intersubjective style that is influenced by its biological traits but is expressed and co-created across the psychosocial expanse (of intersubjectivity, of being-with and living in-between other subjects). Any ego is a pervasive style, a character, a personality. The link between beliefs (below, "convictions") and this style is as follows:

> ... convictions are, in general, only relatively abiding and have their modes of alteration (... for example, "cancellation" or negation, undoing their acceptance), the Ego shows, in such alterations, an abiding style with a unity of identity throughout all of them: a "personal character".
> Husserl, 1977b, §32, p 67.

What the above means is that there is a continuum between active and passive processes, which when voiced in the first person for ease of understanding, is the insight that one contributes to one's own problems and makes changes in-line with what one wants to achieve. What the passage above means for therapy is that explicit beliefs are subject to choice.

In a wider view, the self influences others and is influenced in return. Some aspects of self are capable of change and some are impervious, particularly once adulthood is reached. An ego absorbs the influences of its family, neighbourhood and cultural group as well as those of its society and historical epoch. An ego has free will and personal choice to some degree. As the decades roll by, the ego reaps what it sows in terms of the accrual of the consequences of its choices. Past choices add up to create further consequences that reverberate and exact an influence on self.

The words "active" and "passive" are used to denote the phenomena of free will and the involuntary processes. The ego is active to the degree that it can choose *what* and *how* to be aware of various topics. The extent to which it is involved in its own psychological problems varies, in that a fixation on the past, a fixation on problems that have not yet happened and a fearful avoidance of things that might go wrong (were they ever to happen)—such experiences are created by intentionality that plays its part in psychological problems and their help. Yet the other side of the human character are its involuntary processes and tendencies to be influenced, that to a greater degree are outside of volition and free choice. Husserl used the term "passive" process to denote phenomena of affective meaning and those aspects of memory that arise spontaneously without the skilled and explicit action of the ego. On the one hand, the ego is active in that it walks, talks and chooses and is determined to achieve. On the other, the ego is also soothed, influenced by mood and bodily sensation—that are to a greater degree, less under personal control. There are also important connections where it is possible to be contributing to one's own mood without realising that one is contributing. However, because of the phenomena of self-awareness, it is possible to catch one's being-aware, and have direct experience of how one is aware. For instance, focusing excessively on a problem in worry produces anxiety and depression. It is possible to understand how one achieves the anxiety and depression.

The natural, naturalistic and conventional types of thinking cannot grasp these mutually inter-acting influences of intentionality. Furthermore, empirical research that only focuses on separate domains is unable to grasp the whole. For instance, for pure psychology there is no difference between intrapersonal, personal, social and the interpersonal because these words refer to regions of experience that are only separate by the artifice of thought and are incapable of existing alone. If one were only to have a 'wholly personal' experience (without any intrapersonal, social and interpersonal aspects), it would be a most unusual experience because no one else would be able to understand it. Indeed, the distinction between internal and external was a major false distinction argued against by Husserl in April 1907 (Husserl, 1999). However, other traditional distinctions in interpreting human experience such as symptoms, contexts, emotion, biological traits, interpersonal style and the character of a self, refer to simultaneously existent and temporally accruing styles of experience.

After the above, it should be clear that any empirical psychology and the views of Jacques Derrida are anti-transcendental. Empirical psychology does not consider the conditions for guiding ideas. Here Derrida's scepticism and arguments against Husserl are taken as missing the point. Derrida occupies a nihilistic hermeneutic position that can be described as scepticism that attacks all other positions apart from its own (Rickman, 2004). From the position of phenomenology, certain areas of philosophy and therapy-discourse are untenable for different reasons. Linguistic philosophy is overly rational and excessively focused on semantics. Deconstruction is not aware of its own position. Similarly, any therapy approach that is hermetically-sealed to reason is suspect. The humanistic or humanistic-existential readings of *Being and Time* are far from what Heidegger was urging. Heidegger was supportive of an empirical psychology or therapy practice because he was firmly of the opinion that Kantian "Apriorism is the method", (Heidegger, 1996, note 10, p 410). For Heidegger also, theorising is the proper method and his conclusions of the 16 existentials that therapy could be about, mean noting the contours, dimensions or most basic qualities of what it is to be human.

Close

The papers of the first part of this book are introductory. *The Attitudes and Aims of Husserlian Pure Psychology and Transcendental Phenomenology* makes the distinction between pure psychology and transcendental phenomenology clear. Although it does have to be noted that there are more research attitudes in Husserl than just the two defined in the paper (Owen, 2006, p 99). *Husserl and Heidegger in Comparison to Frankl* was written for a Viktor Frankl journal and makes little comment on Frankl's excellent contributions to therapy. The purpose of the paper was rather to define the fine detail of what Husserl and Heidegger's methods of analysis are. The paper *Introduction to Phenomenology* is reprinted as Sokolowski's *Introduction to Phenomenology*. It is a book review that makes short conclusions on what the import of phenomenology is concerning the relation between self, other and world. *Husserl's Theory of Empathy: Meaning Arrives with the Other* introduces what Husserl claimed in the *Fifth Cartesian Meditation*, which is in strong contradiction to what most philosophers believe the text actually means. *The Special Hermeneutic of Empathy* introduces Heidegger's phenomenology with respect to understanding others. *Applying Social Constructionism to Psychotherapy* is included and completes the first part, although it is not about phenomenology. It is included because it shows the idea of communalisation in Husserl that is known in contemporarily as social constructionism.

The progression across part two concerns fundamental assessments of what are the core aspects of any psychological problem in relation to any proposed course of treatment. Part three is an encounter between pure psychology and natural psychological science that accuses the latter of being responsible for creating and promoting false distinctions between aspects of the meaningful whole. Therefore, from the position of psychology as science, it is difficult to rejoin the pieces. From the perspective of an interpretative pure psychology, there is primarily a whole and it is an artifice to break up the pieces.

Regarding pure psychology, Husserl and Heidegger came to the same experiences from different perspectives. For Heidegger, apriorism means the theoretical consideration of the invariant nature of the being of beings and their inter-relations. The tradition of analysis that phenomenology continues began with Immanuel Kant who called it "transcendental philosophy," meaning the consideration of the conditions for an experience or meaning of any sort. What Heidegger wrote was "we shall call the characteristics of being of Da-sein *existentials*. They are to be sharply delimited from the determinations of being of those beings unlike Da-sein which we call *categories*", (1996, §9, p 42). What he meant by "existential" was a parallel to the "categories" of understanding in Kant. Heidegger employed a similar device in creating his existential analytic of Da-sein in its contexts. Heidegger interpreted the being of Da-sein from its ordinary experiences as having ontological characteristics. Husserl did something similar, but focused on the detail of active intentionality and passive non-intentional mental processes that can be interpreted from the many manners in which an object is given, in a specific sort of intentional awareness of it. Existentials are necessary aspects of Da-sein's understanding of itself and its world that make possible the common sense understandings. The 16 existentials were interpreted from everyday experience. Without them experience would be meaningless. Existentiality is an inherent interpretive disposition of all human beings. It means understanding and interpreting in such a manner to show how Da-sein lives in its shared temporal world. If there were no existentials, there would be solipsism. The major focus for Husserl was to find the aprioris of how conscious mental acts and processes make meanings of all kinds. What this means for therapy is that theory is about how therapists believe and interpret how themselves and others make meaning.

Phenomenology as theory-making could be applied in academic areas and the resulting ideas could be put to use practically. What is not being attempted is the creation of a new brand name of therapy. What it is hoped to achieve is the wider appreciation of how a qualitative analysis of human experience can help the understanding what it is to be human. Any consideration of interventions in therapy will arise out of a proper understanding. What pure psychology provides is the consideration of how more basic enabling conditions of possibility permit or inhibit higher functions. The general mode of interpretation is to recognise that enabling conditions of possibility are biopsychosocial and permit achievements, processes and functioning of various sorts. When this comes to psychological problems it means creating a generalised view of problems and how they can be helped. Such conclusions are the following: People prioritise according to their values for short-and long-term achievement, where short- and long-term aims may conflict. Priorities can always be re-considered and made more coherent as good priorities may also entail negative consequences. Time-scales need to be realistic for the achievement of the values in question. There can be negative mood consequences because of tensions between competing good values. Higher values become achievable through the prior attainment of lower ones. For instance, artistic achievement is possible through having sufficient paint, time, sleep, food and previous experience at painting. When people feel discomfort with their current choices in life, they should change them if they can. If they choose not to make such changes, then they should not complain. When thinking about the attainment of values, then the guiding questions are "is this a good use of my time?" or "our time together?" Psychotherapy is helping people make good quality conscious choices after having considered the relevant evidence.

Because of the need to provide clinical reasoning, it is decided to press ahead with a sketch of how to theorise about observable events, conscious emotions and create psychological explanations. It is inescapable that the therapy process is about meaning change and empathised qualities of inter-action. Evidence and re-interpretation exist for all manner of beliefs and positions—some helpful and some unhelpful. What clients and therapists share are ways of assessing the evidence. However, the test of any theory is that *good understanding leads to effective action*. Indeed, effective actions can be interpreted to show how they were made. Similarly in the negative, ineffective action shows poor understanding.

1

The attitudes and aims of Husserlian pure psychology and transcendental phenomenology

For those who wish to critique or develop Husserl's phenomenology, apply it to psychotherapy or justify forms of psychological research, it is necessary to have an accurate grasp of the original practice. But amongst the many expository works on Husserl's phenomenology, there is little comment on his two types of practice and how these differ with respect to the natural attitude, the base from which they both arise. Definitive elements of Husserl's phenomenology occur with respect to the relationship between the attitudes that punctuate his methods for experiential analysis. These aims and attitudes are defined below in the following order: First, the natural attitude of ordinary lay person's involvement in the world, second, the full transcendental attitude of transcendental phenomenological research, and third, the psychological attitude of the pure psychologist. This paper argues for a specific reading of some basic concepts in the practice of Husserlian psychological and transcendental phenomenology. Phenomenology is understood as a qualitative research method for clarifying experience and producing fundamental definitions for an academic discipline. Husserl's pure psychology is an analysis of the psychodynamics of consciousness and finds the cognitive-affective processes that must be occurring in the production of meaning of any psychological sort. Accordingly, psychotherapy is understood alongside the human sciences; not the natural sciences of inanimate being. For instance, the psychodynamic constitution of the object-senses, self and other, are suggested as being the result of social activity throughout the lifespan. Some comments concerning the consequences of Husserl's position are made.

Rather than let Husserl's phenomenology lie unused, this paper seeks to define it, comment on the ability to achieve it and provide a brief overview of how it can work for therapy. An exposition ensues that provides a definition of the aims and attitudes of the two types of phenomenology, mentioned during the period 1913 to 1929. The main point to bear in mind is understanding how consciousness makes all forms of meaning: The appreciation of the work of consciousness and its non-conscious processes is the starting point for any human science or philosophy. The reading of Husserl here is one that takes him as providing a method for philosophical, scientific and conceptual grounding in lived experience.

Husserl's stance is intricate and not every detail of it can be appreciated or appraised in one paper[1]. However, some central emphases are provided below with respect to the "parallel" attitudes for research created by the "psychological" and "transcendental" reductions. Once the reductions and the research attitudes are clear, the aims of pure psychology, a pre-science to ground the human sciences and transcendental phenomenology, become clear. It becomes apparent that Husserl's stance is close to both psychoanalysis and cognitive therapy but with many differences also.

For therapists who feel that dedication to the phenomena is worthwhile, rather than scepticism or an empty adherence to unfounded traditions, it becomes important to grasp the reductions and the different "paths" for analysis (Kern, 1977, Bernet, Kern and Marbach, 1993, pp. 65-75, Sokolowski, 2000, pp. 52-6). This paper aims to be true to the "psychological path" to reduction, as portrayed in the draft for the *Encyclopaedia Britannica*, the previous drafts of that paper (Husserl, 1997b, 1997c, 1997d) and the *Cartesian Meditations* (1977b, §16). This paper clarifies Husserl's two research attitudes for understanding the constitution of the sense of the natural communal world. Once the demarcations between the "natural," "transcendental" and "psychological" attitudes become clear, it is possible to practice what Husserl urged, by making connections with other leading overviews. Both psychological and transcendental reflections concern the relation between consciousness and the pregiven world of social meaning.

When the three major attitudes are made clear, the differences in stance become fully apparent. The two reductions away from the natural attitude reveal consciousness in its meaning-making role. The two research attitudes proposed for the study of consciousness alter the natural attitude in significant ways. The first reduction, called the "psychological," or "phenomenological-psychological reduction," enables the variation of psychological essences to find genuine psychological concepts (1997c, §3). Pure psychology is a step toward the transcendental reduction and the further variation of transcendental essences to find the conditions of meaning and the concepts of philosophy that will steer the academic disciplines (1977b, §16, §57, 1997c, §4).

The objects of the two types of phenomenology, although similar, are not the same because of the different attitudes and aims of the psychological and the transcendental approaches. Each form of practice attends to different aspects that appear 'for' or 'within' consciousness, in relation to the intersubjective presence of others and their consciousness. The "object" is any object of attention or awareness. Of course, in human relations, the empathised sense of another person includes changes in the meaning of the other. For instance, the same person is loved and briefly hated, found sexy and irritating. When we focus on a person, our experiences of them become accumulated to produce an overall sense.

One common strand in phenomenological analysis is the explication of the unities of sense and meaning that arise in the natural attitude. Three related remarks concern the emphasis that what appears is constituted reality. Firstly, the *"intentional object of a presentation is the same as its actual object, and on occasion as its external object, and that it is absurd to distinguish between them"*, (1970a, Fifth Investigation, Appendix, p 595). Secondly, "there is no distinction between appearance and being ... only the one nature, the one that appears in the appearance of things" for consciousness, is what concerns phenomenology (1981a, p 179). A third comment that has the same sense is: "If transcendental subjectivity is the universe of all possible sense, then an outside is precisely—nonsense", (1977b, §41, p 84). These are expressions of the same understanding of consciousness and its relation to others and the world. The aim is that when treating conscious appearance, as its particular type, there is no consideration of its sense other than its sense for consciousness. What the reduction means in practice is that when one reduces and reflects on the sense of an object of conscious attention, phenomenologists recognise that a participant believes x about an object. Momentarily, the participant experiences a specific sense of it. But the momentary experiences accumulate into a number of personal and social senses. Object-senses are at once private and public. This stance is expressed in Husserl's terminology as the proper relation between the immanence and transcendence of consciousness, its ability to be both inward and outward[2].

What follows is a brief overview of the interpretative problems in reading Husserl. The details would take up a great deal of space. After the overview, it is then possible to turn to the two research attitudes and then the aims.

Preamble: Interpretative problems

The main problem in reading Husserl is to read 'through the words' in order to find the constancy that lies between the lines of actual phrasings. However, when Directors of the *Husserl Archives* do not fully agree on definitions of the terms "reduction[3]," "attitude" and "noema[4]," it gives cause for concern. These terms are co-extensive and are linked because an act of *reduction* produces the research *attitude of epoché* through which one becomes aware of a reduced object, a *noema*, the literal result of conscious and non-conscious *noeses*, the processes of consciousness. The situation is further confused because, generally, the English language literature considers the transcendental reduction and not the psychological one[5].

Edmund Husserl, the main protagonist in the phenomenological movement, thought nothing of changing his mind in the light of new evidence and his ongoing research into how consciousness functions. Such an aim is admirable but in the context of his voluminous and high-context writings, it promotes difficulty in understanding what he concluded on and how he practised his research. Not surprisingly, the literature on Husserlian phenomenology has not arrived at consensus on many of the main points. After a search of the literature, there appear to be no English language papers defining the three major attitudes of Husserlian phenomenology. Although there are a small number of papers and books on the practice of the original phenomenology, none of these provide full details of all aspects of it (Smith, 1977, Marbach, 1993, Fink, 1981). Without such consensus, particularly concerning the research attitudes, the original phenomenology cannot be practised.

It is the whole understanding of natural waking life that Husserl claimed to be able to alter, with his psychological and transcendental reductions, and practise the two forms of phenomenology. He made three hypotheses. Firstly, the processes of consciousness make meaning that exists as the outcome of work. Secondly, the direction of analysis is to compare the end products of the meanings that have been made, to work out the parts that created the whole. Thirdly, it is assumed that knowledge and understanding exist for consciousness and have been made by "absolute" consciousness. Therefore, the initial premise for pure psychology and transcendental phenomenology is that there should be a phenomenology of consciousness.

The "eidetic reduction" is a theorising practice that takes instances and moves through general essences towards universal essences of intentionalities. Again, there are conflations of the sense of generalisation, the shared purpose of the eidetic and transcendental reductions. In writing about eidetic phenomenology, Husserl stated: "Its ascertainments concern not realities but essences; its truths state what is valid for such essences, i.e., for everything falling under such essences as such in unconditioned necessity and universality", (Husserl, 1980, §8, p 41).

This is the sense of pure theoretical research—as opposed to applied, empirical research.

What follows are conclusions gained from textual research. The textual evidence has been weighed up and conclusions are presented below. The general method has been to keep the psychological attitude and the transcendental one, firmly separate, as Husserl stated they should be. This enables clarity to be found concerning the parallel approaches of psychological and transcendental phenomenology. The major theses that express the central purposes of Husserl's philosophy are provided in the numbered statements below NA1 to 3, TP1 to 3 and PP1 to 4.

NA1. The "worldly," natural and naturalistic attitudes are insufficient grounds for any academic discipline.

NA2. Natural philosophy, that permits the influences of the natural attitude, is ungrounded, relativistic and contains circularities and contradictions.

NA3. Natural science has been very successful in considering inanimate being. Natural science is appropriate and useful because of its ground of mathematical a priori essences, for instance trigonometry, statistics, matrices, algebra, etc. But natural science is theoretically and empirically relativistic. It lacks a self-reflexive awareness of the limits of its applicability and cannot be its own ground.

Husserl accepted the model relation of mathematics that exists within the natural sciences. Mathematics is part of the ideal theory-base that guides empirical practice and creates effective ends. Therefore, other academic disciplines should distinguish their ideal-eidetic regions of pure theory that will guide their form of practice and achieve their ends (1970a, Prolegomena, §§16, 41-2, 46, 48, 51). Ideal-essences are ontological and accurately map their region of being. The success of the natural sciences shows the success of mathematics in being able to guide the sciences of facts towards their region of being, inanimate matter. Mathematics is a good map for modelling that region of being. Hence, humanity reaps the rewards of chemistry, biology and physics. Let us now consider the grand project of transcendental phenomenology, the study of meaning for consciousness in the world.

The stance of transcendental phenomenology can be understood with respect to the attitudes of the natural world:

TP1. The initial premise is that consciousness constitutes meaning in the understood-world, the total horizon of meaning. Accordingly, transcendental phenomenology does not allow itself to fall foul of the presupposition of ignoring the whole. Each object makes sense within the whole of all object-meanings, the world. Therefore, there must be a non-worldly transcendental phenomenology of absolute consciousness to ground knowledge and understanding "absolutely," in this specific sense.

TP2. The gaze of a transcendental phenomenology is allegedly not worldly, but of a mere on-looker, or disinterested spectator, on the idealised processes of the constitution of object-meanings.

TP3. Transcendental phenomenology is a first philosophy of knowing and its own manner of knowing. It is the ultimate ground for philosophy and hence, any academic discipline including the practical technologies, natural sciences and human sciences. It uses reflection, description, imaginative variation and idealisation, to find the constant aspects of the region of relations to its objects. It understands from a perspective that is, allegedly, wholly separate from the world.

There is also pure psychology to consider. Pure psychology is preparatory for a biopsychosocial approach to psychological meaning. Phenomenological therapy is akin to this stance:

PP1. In order to establish a preliminary exploration of human knowing, there should be a pure psychology that will be effective in grounding any human science.

PP2. Pure psychology is a theoretical psychology of everyday psychological living. It understands and monitors its own progress towards its aims. It realises that it should find the inherent nature and ideal dimensions of its object: worldly consciousness, its objects and processes.

PP3. Pure psychology is self-reflexive.

PP4. Pure psychology uses reflection, description, imaginative variation and idealisation to find the constant aspects of the region of relations to its objects, as understood within the everyday world.

Let us make these points clearer. What this means for therapy is that theory and clinical reasoning guide the practical means of relating with clients, that achieve the desired end-point of effective practice (§16). Accordingly, phenomenological therapy theorises for practice, research, supervision and the on-going quality assurance of the work. It could create theory to describe the phenomena at play for clients who get better through psychological help. Its main concern would be the accuracy and consistency of theories as they describe the change process, for instance.

Starting point: The problem of the natural attitude and naturalism

The term "naturalism" covers the major philosophical, epistemological, ontological, hermeneutic and methodological problems to be overcome by Husserl's work. The "natural attitude" is the base from which natural philosophy stems. The natural attitude has neither adequate connection to natural science nor any academic worth. Natural science may have had much success in certain areas, such as chemistry and physics, but its area of competence is limited to dealing with inanimate being. For instance, when the assumptions of natural science are carried over into the domain of psychology, there arise the wholly unsuitable natural psychological approaches, the sworn enemy of pure psychology. The charges against natural psychology, from the phenomenological perspective, are legion. They include the reification of consciousness, mistaking parts for wholes and not understanding the consciousness-material body relation. Natural psychology will not take advice from philosophy. It refuses to heed its mistakes and begin to understand the nature of human identity or being, as a distributed identity across many instances and contexts. The relations of the natural attitude may be conceptualised by the following characterisation, a sketch gained from published works.

Firstly, there is nothing wrong with the natural attitude in a moral sense. It is the manner of living and ordinary involvement in life. However, for Husserl the natural attitude is grossly insufficient as a basis from which to start science or philosophy or, for instance, to gain consensus in an academic discipline such as therapy[6]. The problem with the natural attitude is that it is unreflective and uncritical in that it is absorbed in culture and society, and unthinkingly accepts whatever circulates there in an ad hoc manner (1999, p 61). For Husserl, the natural attitude has no idea how consciousness works and no interest in determining how it does so (Ibid). The state of the natural attitude is alluded to in the first three sentences of the main text of *Ideas I*:

> Natural cognition begins with experience and remains *within* experience. In the theoretical attitude which we call the *"natural"* *<theoretical attitude>* the collective horizon of possible investigations is therefore designated with one *word*: It is the *world*. Accordingly, the sciences of this original attitude are, in their entirety, sciences of the world; and, as long as it is the exclusively dominant <theoretical attitude,> the concepts "true being," "actual being," that is, real being and—since everything real joins together to make up the unity of the world—"being in the world" coincide.
> 1982, §1, p 5.

What the quotation means is that the natural attitude is insufficient to judge between hearsay and what is really more dependable. Such a state of affairs cannot be accepted by an academic discipline. It is hoped that phenomenology, as an experiential clarification producing rationality, will decide how ideas arise from unclarified experience (§47, p 106). Although the natural attitude is an inadequate ground, and unclear to those who are ruled by it. It is nevertheless understood as a wondrous accomplishment[7]. The individual may well accept the object-senses of the local culture. Phenomenology urges an investigation into the general psychodynamic processes of all individuals. The comparison of object-senses of specific types is claimed to show general links between the individual and the social milieu.

The perspective is a certain type of idealism[8]. Husserl contended that natural science, based on the natural attitude, has a number of tendencies that conflate natural attitude mistakes and deficits in clarity (1999, p 63). The resulting inability of natural science to correct or recognise its own stance, connects with the tendency to claim that natural science is the only source of knowledge. In the worst excesses of natural science, when empiricism becomes worshipped in Scientism, there can be a lack of contact with the object of a science altogether, or the jumping between different objects of adjacent sciences, or jumping between entirely different types of evidence and manners of argument. Furthermore, natural science rejects philosophy that could help it correct itself (1969, p 3). Natural science entails empirical relativism, in that its results are relative to the particular sample and methodology used. For instance in natural science, empirical results are only acceptable until the next replication of a hypothesis-testing experiment. So, concerning natural science's positivity:

The *unphilosophical character of this positivity* consists precisely in this: The sciences, because they do not understand their own productions as those of a productive intentionality ... are unable to clarify the genuine being-sense of either their provinces or the concepts that comprehend their provinces; thus they are unable to say ... what belongs to the existent of which they speak or what sense-horizons that the existent presupposes—horizons of which they do not speak, but are nevertheless co-determinant of its sense.
p 13.

The quotation above shows that phenomenology is destined to explore implications and references of meaning: Be that in science or any other area. Such meanings might not be immediately present but are referred to by prior learnings, habits and the first-ever acquisitions, the primal institutions, *Urstiftungen*, of their sense (1977b, §50, p 111, 1989, §29).

Intentional analysis of objects to find processes

What major texts such as *Phenomenological Psychology* or *Cartesian Meditations* do not make clear is that "intentional analysis" (or "explication," *Auslegung*) refers to the whole of what appears of the connections between the manners of givenness of objects and the constitutive acts and processes that made them (1977b, §§17-21). Following the above, the emphasis is on the centrality of consciousness as the starting point, in that object-oriented phenomenology serves the purpose of noetic phenomenology, the theorisation of the cognitive-affective process of consciousness in general. To treat Husserl's work as anything less than the exhortation to analyse conscious experience, is to misrepresent it and render it impotent. Certain realisations dawned on Husserl over a number of years beginning around 1898 and coming to fruition in *The Crisis* (1970b). For phenomenology, consciousness in connection with other consciousness and the world constitute sense and meaning, including those of science, philosophy and culture. This is because consciousness: "is the root ... the source of all else that is called being ... it does not refer to something further, from which it could or must have been derived", (Ms B IV 6, p 91b, cited in Bernet, Kern and Marbach, 1993, p 57, cf Husserl, 1977b, §44, p 98, 1982, §50, 1997d, §13, p 247). Phenomenology analyses the "origins of objectivity [*Objektivität*] in transcendental subjectivity, the origins of the relative being of objects [*Objekte*] in the absolute being of consciousness", (Husserl, 1956, p 382, cited in Bernet, Kern and Marbach, 1993, p 52). In this vein, consciousness is also referred to as "originary," "pre-reflective" and "pre-immanent," in that it is automatic and works before conscious attention can turn to its products[9] (Husserl, 1981a, p 174). These remarks are descriptive findings and not empty assertions.

As noted above, the method of analysis concerns the manners of givenness that indicate the ways in which consciousness created what appears (1982, §131, p 314, §132, p 316, 1999, pp. 67-9, Marbach, 1992, 1993, 1999). As an aim, it is replicable by those who accept the above remarks as first principles, and who are willing to meditate on what and how objects appear. Thus, Husserl is proposing that the adequate measure of meaning and existence is consciousness's relation to itself and other consciousness. Consciousness is the ground for knowledge and the study of it should not fall into prior assumptions such as realism, idealism, natural science and the natural attitude. Consequently, it is entailed in the use of the term "absolute" that knowledge is based on the consciousness of consciousness[10]. There is only one object of inquiry for transcendental phenomenology and that is finding the manners of the constitution of the shared world of meaning and being, by consciousness. The object of pure psychology is somewhat similar: The ordinary psychological life in the shared world.

The clue that enables this analysis to occur is a process of comparison of the manners in which beliefs, abstract ideas, manners of existence and meaning occur (Marbach, 1992, 1999). Phenomenology is a comparison through attending to *how objects appear*, are "given" for reflecting consciousness. Through comparison of senses, it tries to work out how they have been constituted. Husserl believed that the manners in which objects appear are key to understanding the conditions for meaning to occur (Husserl, 1977b, §51, p 112). For instance, the body of the other, and its senses for us, are important. Fundamentally, other persons have a united sense of mind and body. The point is that the living bodies of other persons are the medium through which meaning gets communicated through bodily expressiveness and speech. In this respect, the major focus for transcendental phenomenology is different to pure psychology. The particular types of object and givenness that are considered in transcendental phenomenology are the world, belief, existence, temporality, empathy, community and intellectual categories (Fink, 1981, p 44). In short, transcendental phenomenology is a pre-philosophy concerning the qualitative investigation of how consciousness generates the world-frame for understanding.

What psychological reflection does is similar to the transcendental reflection. Psychological reflection does not regard the source of meaning in the world via its constitutions, but rather compares and contrasts the acts and syntheses of consciousness through comparing and contrasting the manners of givenness of its many processes. In this way, it is possible to work out the essence of perceptual intentionality, for instance, in contrast to recollection, wishing, imagining, so on and so forth. For instance, visual perception gives objects as having a certain field of closeness and distance. The phenomenon of occlusion occurs whereby one object that is behind another, is not understood as the object behind, 'growing out of,' the one in front. They are understood as two separate objects with distance between them. Visual perception contains a centrality and periphery of the field, where what appears suggests the presence of its sides and back, that are not perceptually given, but are intimated by consciousness, "co-implied" by what is present.

In comparison, hearing is less directional and has some similar properties. Sounds appear in a directional manner and one sound can co-occur with another in ways that are understandable as two auditory objects or only one. For instance, a car horn and someone knocking at the door are heard as two different sounds. But a flute and a piano can be heard as playing the same song. The types of givenness that Husserl considered in pure psychology include physical bodiliness, psychological categories, empathy and community. Also, included are the psychological experiences of love and hate, the understanding of the givenness of visual art and other images, the givenness of speech and thinking to oneself.

Generally, what is being proposed is an analysis of the cognitive-affective processes of consciousness's production of the ordinary sense of the world and meaning in it. It was intended that the productions of consciousness would be investigated to find out how such senses have accrued, personally, collectively, societally and historically. The connection that is reflected-on takes the object of belief, in the manner of givenness of how it appears, and relates it back to those types of cognition and affect that must have produced it. Dependable understanding arises as the summation and comparison of many specific beliefs and appearances (Husserl, 1982, §139, p 335).

Husserl's analysis moves from specific appearances to find essences, *ideal generalities* that are the major guiding concepts of an academic discipline. It aims to find universal essences and the necessary conditions for understanding meaning, the modalities of knowing and believing, about the manners of givenness of regions of being. It claims to be able to achieve such contemplation through prolonged eidetic variation: experiments of thought concerning how guiding concepts fit together (1980, §8, p 45, 1982, §§70-75). It is claimed that specific knowledge and understanding concern generality, the ideal and universal, as well as what is empirically the case. Once some refined data is produced about the consciousness-world inter-relation, it is checked further through the variation of essences which is a specific procedure for clarifying concepts and understanding, before further philosophical analysis or argument.

Some brief remarks are required on the commonality of seeing and varying essences in the two types of phenomenology. For instance, Derrida has thoroughly misunderstood Husserl's theory of signs and essence (Moran, 2000). Firstly, essences are theorisations and generalisations about the full variety of experience: non-verbal, perceptual, sensual and bodily kinds. They are conceptualisations that will be trusted to guide the sciences and philosophy, because they have been freed from the corrupting influence of the natural attitude. However, phenomenology entails a lack of certainty concerning essences (Husserl, 1969, §84, §105, §107c) and a lack of certainty concerning evidence (1977b, §9, p 23, §63, p 151).

The method of eidetic variation primarily concerns varying the essences of the active ego, passive consciousness and the world of others, in order to find their nature and 'structure' (1977a, §9, §10, 1977b, §25, 1980, §16, p 75). The purpose of eidetic variation in transcendental phenomenology focuses on the eidetic variants gained from the consideration of what exists (1982, §49, §53, p 124, fn 79, §54, 1997d, §11, pp. 240-1). The aim is to explore the consciousness-world relation. Examples from literature, history and many other sources can be included as raw data (1982, §§70-5).

Psychological eidetic variation aims to find the invariant structures of consciousness within the social world. The purpose is to check the inherent constraints by running through "all" imaginable variants to find the conditions for the possibility of there being the meanings and experiences of ego, other, we, egoic act and automatic synthesis. These senses are investigated as they occur in actual cultural worlds, for the purpose of theorising their natures and relations. The aim is to derive the forms of the constitution of the psychological senses (1997c, §4, p 165).

The next topics addressed are the two research attitudes of phenomenology. The transcendental attitude has been heavily criticised by a number of writers. However, it is claimed that transcendental phenomenology has saving graces of its own. Whatever its faults, the fundamental insight driving transcendental phenomenology concerns attending to the manners in which objects are given to consciousness.

Comparison of the attitudes of the parallel forms of phenomenology
Introduction: The nature of transcendental phenomenology

What follows is an overview of the ground to be covered with respect to the establishment of the practice of transcendental phenomenology, through the procedure of transcendental reduction, to attain the transcendental attitude: the suspension yet maintenance of the natural attitude. Despite much ill founded criticism of Husserl's stance, this section contends that whatever the problem involved in trying to remove the influence of current knowledge, whilst seeing the evidence of the workings of intersubjective consciousness in oneself, Husserl's intentions need to be carefully attended to before any criticism of his position. This section provides a flavour of Husserl's radical proposal to establish what would contemporarily be categorised in psychology as a "cognitive-affective analysis of social constructs," a "constructivism of meaning," or a "qualitative grounded analysis of guiding concepts" for an academic discipline.

Transcendental reduction to the transcendental attitude

The transcendental reduction is a manoeuvre that produces the transcendental attitude. Through the transcendentally reduced and reflected-on consciousness, absolute consciousness is considered as an invariant. Absolute consciousness is revealed through transcendental reflection[11]. The transcendental reduction is an alleged accomplishment of will, in turning to understand one's own experience of others and the ordinary world.

The basic definitions of the transcendental reduction and epoché have many entailments. What the transcendental reduction means is spread across the text of *Ideas I,* for instance, in a manner that might first appear to be incoherent. However, the basic principle defined above is quite coherent. The attitude is to try and prevent intersubjective bias and prior understanding from affecting the results of the new radical form of investigation, of consciousness in relation to the world and others. Transcendental reduction combined with reflection is a ...

> ... *specifically peculiar mode of consciousness* ... [which relates to the original positing—fn 23] ... and, likewise in a specifically peculiar manner, changes its value.
> ... this peculiar epoché, *a certain* ... [refraining from belief—fn 24] ... is converted into the "*parenthesized judgement*" [or belief].
> 1982, §31, pp. 59-60 & fn 23 & 24.

The above remarks concern the alleged ability to de-contextualise awareness of the meaning of what appears, and the manner of belief concerning its existence, by an act of the will that can consider the same, 'unaffected,' in an attitude of non-participant observation. The same assertion is much clearer in the *Cartesian Meditations*:

> ... the world experienced in this reflectively grasped life goes on being for me (in a certain manner) "experienced" as before, and with just the content it has at any particular time ... the only difference is that I ... no longer keep in effect (no longer accept) the natural believing in existence involved in experiencing the world—though that believing too is still there and grasped by my noticing regard ...
>
> ... this "inhibiting" or "putting out of play" of all positions taken toward the already-given Objective world ... *purely as* meant in them: the universe of phenomena ... The epoché can also be said to be the radical and universal method by which I apprehend myself purely ... in and by which the entire Objective world exists for me and is precisely as it is for me.
> 1977b, §8, pp. 19-20, pp. 20-21.

It is possible to dismiss Husserl's claim to be able to achieve the above, as Merleau-Ponty did[12]. But let us stay focused on the implications of the transcendental reduction a little longer.

To appraise Husserl's claim with due care and attention means that the only sure way to criticise phenomenology or develop it, is to practice it and find out to what degree it is achievable. Thus, if the whole procedure were capable of being practised, the transcendental reduction would serve to take away the sense of the natural attitude, the totality of its understanding and contents, from contaminating the new transcendental attitude. The transcendental attitude claims that it keeps the natural attitude as an object for study, in theorising the relation of consciousness to the human world, its habitat (1982, §50, §63, 1997c, §9, p 172, 1997d, §9, p 235). It is claimed to be possible to observe any object and the whole in a neutral manner. The ultimate aim is to observe the whole, natural sense of the world in which specific events, objects and relationships occur. The observing part of consciousness, the "transcendental on-looker," is allegedly able to regard the relation of constituting consciousness to the totality of its constitutions, the world and all in it, including inter-actions with the source of meaning, the absolute consciousness of self and others. Husserl described the transcendental attitude and its purpose of working out how absolute consciousness makes meaning, as follows:

> Strictly speaking, we have not lost anything but rather have gained the whole of absolute being which, rightly understood, contains within itself, "constitutes" within itself, all worldly transcendencies.
>
> … for our new inquiries we do not "participate in these positings" [beliefs]. Instead of living *in* them, instead of effecting *them*, we effect acts of *reflection* directed to them; and we seize upon them themselves as the *absolute* being which they are. 1982, §50, pp. 113-4.

The quotation describes the belief in the ability to investigate the consciousness-world relation in a 'non-worldly' context of fresh and open understanding. The claim is that the transcendental attitude is allegedly undisturbed by the contamination of spurious ideas from the natural realm.

One way of construing the manoeuvre of the transcendental reduction is to regard it as taking up a refusal to believe in what others believe, yet in such a way that the refusal does not significantly alter the way in which the research attitude of interpretation of lived experience is carried out. If it is possible to perform a transcendental reduction and attend to one's own experience, and find universal invariant aspects of the intentionalities that others can agree, then transcendental phenomenology is viable. If the setting aside of the natural attitude is only partly attainable, then there are degrees of attainability that would support a reduction of a type that may make us conscious of what we assume, but cannot guarantee that one view is more influence-free than any other. So the objection of Merleau-Ponty is sustained. The transcendental reduction as Husserl conceived it is not achievable[13].

Also, there is variance in what appears. Husserl refused hermeneutics and insisted that transcendental phenomenology released the on-looker from the world and escaped the hermeneutic circle. Despite the experiential variance that appears, Husserl refused to acknowledge that hermeneutics had a role to play in the clarification of qualitative experience. This is a major problem that pertains to sensual, conscious experience, perceptual objectivity and the higher forms of intellectual objectivity in speech and language.

The section above put forward the attitude of transcendental phenomenology. The next section defines the research attitude of "pure eidetic psychology" or "phenomenological psychology," also called "psychological phenomenology".

This section focuses on the second type of phenomenology, the qualitative clarification of psychological experiences. This theoretical psychology has the purpose of co-ordinating the human sciences, a wide area of study.

Psychological reduction to the psychological attitude

The psychological reduction aims to preclude some worldly, cultural and societal judgements, plus the ontological and hermeneutic preferences associated with the natural psychological approaches. Natural and ungrounded psychological approaches are kept at bay for the fundamentalist new beginning of human science (1997d, §4, p 219). Pure psychologists reflect on their own consciousness, the consciousness of others and the nature of intersubjectivity as these senses appear for others in common sense everyday "personal," "personalistic," "motivational" and "practical" experience (1989, §49e, p 192, p 199). The psychological research attitude is theorising that operates within the orbit of everyday matters such as shaking hands and saying "hello". As such, it is parallel to a 'group analysis' or an analysis of meaning that seeks to work out the psychological processes involved in creating specific meanings and distinctions.

From 1908, Husserl realised that there was a major difference between pure psychology and his ultimate project of transcendental phenomenology (1975, p 59). Unlike philosophers, psychologists do not consider matters of reason, truth, existence, belief, meaning and ideas as they pertain to philosophy. Pure psychology primarily considers the senses "I," "other," and "us," "the concretely grasped "I" and "we" of ordinary conversation", (1997c, §9, pp. 171-2). Finding the nature of constitutive psychological processes is the outcome in relation to their meaning-objects in the world, culture and society (1997b, p 94, 1997c, §5). As such, consciousness is researched as just one region amongst many others that are contextualised in the natural attitude (Fink, 1970, p 118). The region of consciousness fits in with those influences and motivations from others and from the material sphere of physical causations. The range of objects that can be studied includes any object, cultural practice or value. Objects of attention are imbued with the intersubjective meaning that they have for the larger group. Husserl called this the addition of the cultural sense to the cultural object (Husserl, 1977a, §16).

The stance of pure psychology is different to that of transcendental on-lookers. Pure psychologists remain in the world, understood as it is usually believed to exist (1977b, §14, p 32, 1997c, §9, p 172). Although they investigate the essences of the region of consciousness in an eidetic manner, they do so whilst tied to the vestiges of the natural attitude. Some definitive comments on the "psychological reduction" are that it is the forerunner for the "*transcendental reduc-tion*", (Ibid). In the *Amsterdam Lectures*, the "phenomenological-psychological reduction" enables a focus on the intentionality of the psychologically-under-stood mind to take place, a focus on consciousness, contextualised in the world. Psychological grounding occurs in the manner that:

> ... the psychologist has as his object of study mental subjectivity as something real in the pregiven, constantly and naturally accepted world. As eidetic [psychological] phenomenologist, however, he explores the logos of the mental. His thematic ground is then a conceivable world as such, likewise still thought of as simply existing and pregiven.
> 1997d, §13, p 246.

What the above implies is that psychological guiding concepts should arise from clarifying the inter-relations inherent in conscious experience, to find eidetic gen-eralities and universal concepts for all psychologists who wish to start afresh and find a consensus for future work (cf Fink, 1970, p 92, p 115, p 127, 1972, p 34). Pure psychology begins with what appears and generalizes it, in the practice of eidetic variation (Husserl, 1997d, §8, p 230).

Accordingly, pure psychology has a connection to the natural world and is self-aware about how it theorises within the overall belief in it. On the one hand, the psychological attitude is not concerned with 'real facts'. But on the other, what appears to the psychological attitude may not be contextualised within the standard understanding of the natural spacio-temporal reality (§3, p 220). Pure psychology is a quasi-positive, quasi-natural-attitude based 'pre-science'. It explores what is commonly understood as the "mind" in the "pregiven world", (§12, pp. 241-2). Consciousness is understood as an ontological unity with the human body despite the different types of givenness of consciousness and the lived body to consciousness (Ströker, 1993, p 131). This is why the understand-ings derived from this form of research are tied to natural spacio-temporality, the general sense of cultural space and time-passing, the assumptions and beliefs of ordinary culture (Husserl, 1997d, §12, p 242).

Husserl asked human scientists to focus on motivation, the meaningful associ-ations and reasons why people do things (1989, §56f, p 241). Accordingly, the way to understand people is through understanding their motivations (p 242, cf 1982, §47, p 107, fn 5). For pure psychology, a "person's faculty is not consti-tuted merely as a product of association ... I come to know his formation and growth according to the style of experience properly his own", (1989, §57, p 261, fn 1). Furthermore, in meeting people and inter-acting with them, it is of the utmost importance to bear in mind that pure psychology ...

> ... is a phenomenology of man, his personality, his personal properties and his (human) flow of consciousness; furthermore, a phenomenology of the social mind, of social formations, cultural products, etc. Everything transcendent, in as much as it becomes given in consciousness, is an object for phenomenological investigation not only with respect to the *consciousness of it* ... as what is given and accepted in the modes of givenness.
> 1982, §76, p 172.

The above quotation shows that pure psychology focuses on meanings for specific others and for groups of others. It has the aim of generalising about everyday experiences of the cultural and societal world, in order to create adequate guidelines for a forthcoming empirical human science that will understand the unusual nature of consciousness in the living body and social life (1977a, §4, p 35). The same theme is reiterated in later texts where it is clear that consciousness includes an analysis of communal life, for the influence of sociality is part of "inner experience", (1997c, §3, p 164).

In *Cartesian Meditations,* it is noted that pure psychology works with "dumb ... psychological experience ... [which] must be made to utter its own sense with no adulteration", (Husserl, 1977b, §16, pp. 38-9). This is an aim to be true to the manner of all that appears—within the context of an on-going comparison to all the manners of what appears. What this means is three things: (1) Phenomenology rejects the natural understandings of realism and idealism. (2) There should be no assumptions concerning natural categories of part and whole relations, carried over from the natural understanding. And (3), it is permissable, for instance, to investigate understandings about conceptualisations and experiences of the mind's immanence and transcendence, and understandings of parts and wholes.

Husserl's research assistant, Eugen Fink stated that the pure psychology of consciousness includes "unconscious," out of awareness and pre-reflexive processes that can be explored in relation to constituting syntheses and what are termed "horizons" of sense (Fink, 1972, p 23). As a result, what are psychologically reflected-on are aspects of one's own and other persons' participation in the world. It is permissable to focus on the objective meanings, the personal or communal meaning of cultural objects, codes of cultural meaning and what must be the case for persons in general. A primary interest is in cataloguing the inter-relations and modifications that consciousness makes on its own processes and "material", (1977a, §37, pp. 145-7).

Finally, the last major point to bear in mind concerning the psychological research attitude is that pure psychologists are self-reflexive in accounting for their own relation to the acts, syntheses and objects of their participants. They do this by making clear their own relation to the same objects. The whole of pure psychology, noted above, is portrayed in the next quotation. The pure psychologist needs to distinguish between:

> 1) the description of the personal surrounding world, namely of the persons or personal communities in question, purely as it is theirs intentionally, according to their belief; 2) on the other hand, the attitude taken by the one who is exploring this personality, his attitude toward the true existence of all these objects of the surrounding world ...—he is necessarily a member with them of a personal total mankind ...
> §45, p 174.

What the above means is that: (1) participants in psychological research are asked to describe their beliefs about the meanings of their psychological objects in their surrounding worlds. Their descriptions should be attended to in the manner in which the participants experience and describe them. (2) Pure psychologists are required to 'keep separate' their own experiences and meanings. The researchers should describe their beliefs towards the same cultural objects as their participants. The researchers should make clear their own understandings to themselves and delineate them from the beliefs and meanings of their participants. It can be concluded that pure psychology is a self-reflexive, qualitative approach in which the understandings of the researcher are held apart from the understandings of the participants.

The next section of the paper concerns the general aims of the parallel forms of phenomenology that can now be better understood in the light of the above.

Comparison of the aims of the parallel forms of phenomenology
Aims of transcendental phenomenology

Husserl believed that transcendental phenomenology will analyse the "clues" or "indexes" of the manners of givenness of what exists and has sense, in the everyday world (1970b, §50, p 172, App IX, pp. 394-5, 1977b, §§17-20, 1982, §§130-2, 149-50). But there are great difficulties that lie ahead for this discipline.

This is because experience and verbally-represented knowledge of the experiential world occur all at once. Prior to reflection, on what and how objects appear and are immediately understood, there is "a knowing of them which involves no conceptual thinking", (1982, §27, p 52). The immediacy of what is understood effects and limits the psychological and transcendental research of what appears.

The motivation for the action of the transcendental reduction, as the exercise of free will, is the belief that it is unacceptable to decide on matters of truth and existence in advance of carefully being aware of the enabling conditions for what appears. The aim is that the intersubjective categories and concepts of natural science, culture and history ought to be prevented from influencing the theoretical explorations that lie ahead. Transcendental phenomenology wishes to prevent natural and empirical relativism, and theoretically remove techniques that are insufficient in relation to their objects. Culture and science are seen as arbitrary formations, with respect to the rigour and proper focus that transcendental phenomenology will have. Husserl assumed that there is a fundamental basis of conscious processes through which there are constitutions of social, cultural, scientific and historical meanings. In order to practise transcendental phenomenology, the influence of these assumptions needs to be kept at bay, in order to focus on the manner of their making.

The main aim of transcendental phenomenology is to derive generalised understandings of the invariant structure of consciousness and the world, from one's own and others' experience of it. Husserl believed that what consciousness achieves is fundamentally, *One World* for individuals and for surrounding lifeworlds of shared consciousness (1980, Supplement I, §1, 1982, §87, p 212, §151, 1989, §51, p 208). What this means is that we share one empathically-understood world. It is constituted through the senses of self and other (1977b, §50). The understanding of perceptual objects forms a basis for higher, abstract understandings and communal behaviours and beliefs. The *purpose of transcendental phenomenology is to focus on the necessary conditions of the nature and structure of consciousness that provide the shared world*[14] (§41, p 83, 1982, §49, §54, 1997c, §8, p 171, 1997d, §11, pp. 240-1).

In transcendental phenomenology, all manner of phenomena could be observed. It could use empathic understanding to work out how a group of scientists or politicians make a decision (1969, p 9). It is permissable to study how a person concludes on their identity or how a philosophical school arrives at arguments that are deemed convincing and acceptable. Furthermore, transcendental phenomenology was claimed to be the only possible ground for all philosophy and science (1981a, p 185). In short, transcendental phenomenology is a grand project for epistemology. It focuses on social meanings and shows how they have been made. Transcendental phenomenology is allegedly an epistemologically superior method, that is ontologically neutral and has overcome the hermeneutic circle and the contaminations of contextualisation within the natural attitude (1997c, §8, p 171, 1997d, §13, p 247).

Aims of pure psychology

Two important aims of pure psychology are as follows. One major aim is to find the universal invariants of consciousness and the relations between persons. Secondly, pure psychology attempts to find the *logos* of the soul, the type of reason that governs consciousness, the "logic" of psyche itself, its inherent structure of formative, often non-conscious processes (1977a, §37, p 144, 1997d, §13, p 246). Because pure psychology is not wholly removed from the natural attitude, consciousness is conceptualised in an unsuitable manner by lay persons and natural scientific psychologists as the "mind," a strange *thing*. It appears as part of the extensiveness of "external … worldly experience" that has the effect of distancing consciousness from all those who could become directly aware of their own consciousness themselves (Ibid). For instance, in *Cartesian Meditations*, there is a clear statement that my "animate organism," the sense of one's own living body or "*Leib*" in the original German, and "my psyche" are constitutions of a psychophysical unity of sense (§44, p 97). Overall, pure psychology aims to find the invariant aspects of the region of psychologically-appearing consciousness in the world. Such an approach is a theoretical grounding of psychology that tries to attain consensus about conceptual and methodological issues. It is opposed to an all-too-hasty empirical psychology that just begins without a sufficient prior understanding of the nature of its object. The theorising of guiding invariants is also described as an attempt to find the universal "eidos psyche" in the eidetic horizon of its worldly habitat (1977a, §10, pp. 68-9, 1977b, §35, p 73). This could be described as a qualitative cognitive-affective anthropology or social psychology.

However, the criticisms of Husserl's phenomenology by Heidegger have been most influential. The paper should make some mention of Heidegger's thinking of human being and its context in *Being and Time*.

A brief aside to Heidegger

Heidegger refuted Husserl because he believed that regarding mere subjectivity and consciousness, the *intuitus*, is insufficient as a beginning for an academic discipline such as psychology, philosophy or therapy. His main research question arose from the necessity of understanding being, the nature and the manners of existence of Da-sein who understands itself, as well as the non-Da-sein manners of being. The main research question is discussed as "thinking being" and "thinking the ground of thought": There is a necessity to understand the manners of existence of all that exists and how it exists, in order to differentiate the manners of being and the ways in which the being who understands exists (1996, §1). Heidegger insisted that this question must not be ignored any longer. Thus, it is a mistake to begin with understanding consciousness. For Heidegger, we must first understand Da-sein and its habitat of the with-world, the ensemble of an interactive life together through history. Through a phenomenological ontology, academics should come to understand the being of Da-sein because its form of being transcends and envelops all that exists, in its attempts at understanding. A transcendental investigation must find the possibilities or conditions for philosophy or science because knowing and understanding are part of the being of Da-sein (§4, p 10). Da-sein lives in a world and within that world all innerworldly beings are found in juxtaposition with the activities of Da-sein. The world is the overall context for all events. It is not possible to get outside of it. Therefore, there is the necessity for a limited reduction of beliefs, a smashing of icons, in order to free the spirit of genuine inquiry (§6, pp. 18-20). The bad inheritance of inaccurate understanding cannot be entirely removed and it does need to be understood with respect to what and how all being appears.

But Heidegger's answer in *Being and Time* is obscure because he mixed his metaphors and jumps between forms of written expression that try to answer the same question. The images that he used and alluded to are jumbled and ultimately secondary to the focus on the major research question and the attempts at providing an answer. Heidegger's answer was the starting point of the connection between the inwardness and the outwardness of Da-sein's being. Da-sein has a form of being that is inward insomuch that it can reach out and enclose. Da-sein transcends and brings back the sense of being. Da-sein has a form of being that is temporal and its temporality is neither inward not outward but rather both of these aspects in connection with its pre-reflexive ability to pre-understand being including that which it has not met before. Accordingly, there are five major aspects to the answer that Heidegger provided. All of these images are of its humanity.

First aspect: Da-sein's being transcends and encloses all being: "Being and its structure transcend every being and every possible existent determination of a being. *Being is the transcendens pure and simple*", (§7c, pp. 33-4). Its temporality is open to what is outside and it brings into itself and finds its being in connection with what is outside of itself also. Heidegger agreed with Kant and Husserl in this respect. This on-going reaching out to connect with other Da-sein and other forms of being is part of its being. All that exists does so for Da-sein. All being is coexistent with the being of Da-sein. Da-sein is identical with existence. The "meaning of being to be found" is Da-sein (§2, p 5). Its being is the ground of thinking and understanding.

Second aspect: Da-sein is light that is open to the world. The "*lumen naturale* in human being", (§28, p 125). It has *Ek-sistenz* and with metaphors of light, sustaining and illuminating, its being shines its light on portions of the world. To be in this way is to be ""illuminated" means that it is cleared", (Ibid). There are also metaphors of standing within a shared world and images of clearing that may refer to light or other images of a space for understanding. But the images used do not become brought together: Da-sein can be "authentic: bringing about standing-within the there ... The difference bound to transcendence ... The overcoming of the horizon as such", (§8, p 35). Illuminated means: "*Aletheia* openness—clearing, light, shining ... Da-sein exists, and it alone. Thus existence is standing out and perduring the openness of the there: Ek-sistence", (§28, p 125). The image of the circle in Da-sein's being is one that must be entered in the right way, but thoughts of circularity are not those that Heidegger would like to use but rather "standing within the clearing of presence, where neither the clearing as such nor presence as such becomes thematic for representational thinking", (§32, p 144). The "thrown project" of Da-sein uses the idea of "thrown" in a manner that is also linked to "standing-in", (§44b, p 205). Furthermore, Da-sein holds open its world through which all being is transcended and understood. This occurs through language, in speech and thought (§34, pp. 151-2). The "circle" as an image for understanding the pre-reflexive basis for conscious understanding, the objectifying attention of ordinary attention, is insufficient, Heidegger declared. Care has multiple facets, raptures or ecstasies (§63, pp. 290-2). The temporal aspect of humanity has been misunderstood and ignored for centuries. It is correct to understand human being in its own terms as a central arranging principle (§66, pp. 304-6).

Third aspect: Da-sein always already understands: "The interpretation of something as something is essentially grounded in fore-having, fore-sight, and fore-conception. Interpretation is never a presuppositionless grasping of something previously given ... what is initially "there" is nothing else than the self-evident, undisputed prejudice of the interpreter", (§28, p 141). Its form of being as being in the world is a form of being that is prior to and constitutive of conscious, surface, experience. This is why it is important to deduce the nature of the pre-reflexive. For instance, theory and thinking are derivative with respect to the deeper nature of Da-sein's being. "When we determine something objectively present by merely looking at it, this has the character of care just as much as a "political action," or resting and having a good time. "Theory" and "praxis" are possibilities of being for a being whose being must be defined as care", (§41, p 180).

Proper understanding should not make the interpretative mistake of *Vorhandenheit* when it comes to understanding non-*vorhanden* beings though. It would be a mistake to interpret the existentials of Da-sein's being according to mere *vorhanden* things that are objects or inanimate stuff. Whereas that which is genuinely constitutive of Da-sein's being is *Zuhanden*, it is connection to other persons that is most fundamental and the temporal nature of repetition, the moment and the anticipation of the future that must be won from prior ignorance (§§ 5, 68).

Fourth aspect: Da-sein is thrown into the world, as well as holding it open and always already understanding it. Da-sein is contextual, through and through, it stands within the with-world as a finite, culture-bound existence. Proper understanding arises through "clearing away coverings and obscurities, by breaking up the disguises with which Da-sein cuts itself off from itself", (§26, p 121).

Fifth aspect: Da-sein can be in harmony with its nature, its existentials, or not. If it is in harmony with its temporal being that is finite and so leads to death, then it will have thrown off the bad inheritance from philosophy and science through the ages that have ignored the question of being. Da-sein is contextual in that it is temporal and historical, individually and collectively. The answers that are given use a number of images to provide the contrary aspects of Da-sein's being. Temporality is described and deduced according to ecstasy, ecstatic, rapture and raptness (§68d, §69b, §69c) and historiography (§76, p 362). These terms repeat the 'stretching out' and 'holding within' imagery of Da-sein's transcendence, pure and simple, yet temporality is connected to others, the great importance of history's evolution and the possibilities of the future. But Da-sein's being is mortal. There is no escape from its finite, individual capacity to exist (§§65, 66, 68c). This part of Da-sein's being has also been misunderstood for centuries (§§80, 81). Life leads to death and so death is another dimension to the being of Da-sein.

For these reasons, according to Heidegger, the cultural history of therapy is important and the ground for thinking its being (cf Cushman, 1995, Richards, 1996).

Connections to future work

The above completes the clarifications of the paper. There are at least four directions in which a Husserl-inspired phenomenology can go. Firstly, it would be worthwhile to assess the Husserlian method and critique it, to comment on what could be achievable for creating genuine phenomenological methods and practices in the human sciences and any applied psychology such as therapy. There is Heidegger's opposition to be considered. That is the question of whether it is really true that Heidegger has superseded Husserl. It has not been considered how to find and use the existentials, the most central assertions about the being of humanity that can be employed within the human sciences.

Secondly, it would be worthwhile to provide an overview of the Husserlian challenges to natural cognitive science. Again, it is possible to distinguish the approaches that are closest to Husserl's and to state how there are other pseudo-phenomenological approaches that miss the point. But there are no approaches that follow Husserl's lead to the letter—whilst there are others that claim the word "phenomenological" yet fall far short of the concerns of Husserl[15] or Heidegger.

Thirdly, it would be possible to go even further into the precise details of what is required, to reflect on real instances and use such raw data to find the theoretical ideals of everyday psychological life, which is what Husserl exhorted his readers to do. It is the case that there are, at least, three fundamental phenomena of phenomenology. If these are not adequately understood, then the whole project becomes abstruse and misses its mark. But after the long presentation above, there is little space in which to do justice to, (1), the centrality of the primacy of empathy, (2), the way in which the identity of an object appears across a manifold of slightly different, varying appearances of it, and (3), there is the matter of the "seeing of a category," a linguistically-expressed understanding concerning the variance and appearance of the object. But, let us turn to therapy, invigorated and freed by the above.

Phenomenology as the analysis of human existence, in an open-ended manner, of life in general and the therapeutic situation, means there is a need to distinguish between false and genuine problems; and then distinguish between false and genuine solutions. Accordingly, one illustration of Husserl's method, its findings and applicability, is to look at what is called "psychopathology" and assess the senses of the objects, self and other, and to say something informative about the genuine problems and difficulties that face the practice of therapy. The paper closes with some notes on this subject in-line with the need to understand the motivations in psychological distress and its therapy. Despite what Husserl wrote about the need for caution with respect motivation in the social sphere, it is the case that most therapists assume that what they do is facilitative of change (1977a, §§3e, 23, 1989, §56f). Accordingly, let us try and be clear about what we think is causative of the problems of clients and how we might help them bring about changes.

The centrality of the senses of other and self

Therapy generally believes that consciousness is at work in making attachment bonds, thoughts, feelings and the valuings of esteem given to self and others. But this general agreement needs to be made more precise. Two leading questions arise. Firstly, "how do we justify our interventions?" One answer might be "making sure they fit with the specific psychodynamic and social motivations of a client". A second question is: "How do we know what clients' psychodynamics, personal and social motivations are?" A second answer might be "by looking at the whole set of ways in which people suffer psychologically, emotionally and socially".

Phenomenology assumes that there are three major types of causation accruing between consciousness and its material base, the physical, material body. Firstly, there is the material substrate where the physical effects of adrenaline, neurotransmitters and other physical and material causes alter mood and behaviour (Plomin et al, 1997). These are non-conscious physical motivations, tendencies and capabilities, due to the physical and genetic side of our nature. Secondly, there are many non-conscious, out of awareness processes, the 'unconscious'. These non-conscious processes are socially-influenced and contribute to mood, relationships and behaviour. Non-conscious processes are still 'causative' in the way in which retained experience, habits of all kinds, automatic influences and anticipations shape our experience. These processes are not wholly controlled by the ego but occur quickly and automatically, sometimes before conscious attention can attend to their workings. Finally, there are all those experiences concerning personal striving and willing, namely the ego and how it is influenced socially, culturally and societally.

Insomuch that therapists are psychologically influential and recognise that there are different types of causation, it becomes possible to connect with the nature of clients' specific motivations and work with specific clients, whilst recognising that their motivations change alongside their own set of preferences and possibilities for themselves. There are the following important intentional experiences that are concurrent and perhaps peripheral to conscious attention. Each one can be considered as a reference to an object of attention or to a presence:

• The sense of the therapeutic relationship, the co-empathy or co-attachment, between self and other.

• The work of anxiety and defence in trying to prepare the self to be vigilant and perform, but without the 'cost' of excessive anxiety that 'masochistically' attacks the sense of self or other, rendering the self less constant, less securely attaching and, generally, less able.

• Motivations to act, feel and think, according to the overall sense of specific relations to self, others or situations.

• The relation to specific "cultural objects," a general Husserlian term for any shared or public object of a culture (1977b, §16).

• Specific inter-relations between the above.

The clients' motivation to work in therapy and overcome their own pain, defences, anxieties and so forth, require a valuing of a future, end-point more than the current state of pain, or any future pain involved in having therapy. Therefore immediately, the value that clients' accord themselves plays a role in judging whether they want to work through in therapy, or whether they would prefer to stay the same and not try to change.

There are a large number of social, automatic and anticipated influences that are currently acting on relationships, feelings and behaviour. The factors to be considered include repression and taboo, the full range of various types of defence and the accompanying qualities of anxiety. These factors connect with how people interpret the meanings of their lives, in a highly complex manner. A phenomenological approach considers the whole in order to determine the constituting processes that comprise it. What are of interest are the theoretical parameters that underpin the practical means that achieve the desired ends. Therefore, what is required is some initial estimate of what the full set of object senses are. The reason for this is that the part bears a relation to the whole. The whole set of possible objects, self and other, need to be considered. Specific types of egoic and empathic constitution make each part of the whole. Once an analysis of the whole is achieved then specific, actual senses of self and other can be known adequately with respect to the whole. Phenomenological therapy primarily concerns the work of fundamental theorising.

The basic problem of practising therapy is that there is an infinite amount of motivational and causative possibilities in the lifestyle of clients. It is not possible to design a syllabus that can account for the whole range and combination of psychological influences and problematics. Therefore, a judicious selection has to be made. For phenomenology, it is contested that intersubjectivity is fundamental: Self is always in relation to the other and vice versa. Accordingly, the reflected-on senses of self and other become the embarkation point for theorising. What needs to be considered is the whole of everyday life that is tacit and the basis for knowledge and understanding. In outline for further research and corroboration, there is a need to make clear two major assumptions.

The first assumption on which this research is based is that consciousness is constitutive of the senses of other and self, that are literally *made* by our 'social mind'. Another way of stating this working assumption is to call it a 'cognitive-affective' assumption: It is assumed that human consciousness is active in doing work of a specific kind in creating the empathic senses that we have of other persons, and those which are about self, and are ego-constitutive or ego-genetic. For it is included in this first assumption that the mind is active in creating the senses of self that co-occur in inter-actions with other persons.

The second major assumption on which phenomenological research is based are views of self and other in psychological distress that are taken as being accurate descriptions of the key features of human suffering. In all these examples of long-term severe distress, anxiety and defences are found. These are assumed to be the products or results of specific cognitive-affective processes of unhappy consciousness. It is a further line of research to investigate the end-point that unhappy consciousness is trying to achieve in increasing its sense of anxiety, or in trying to blot out or pre-empt the experiencing of further painful material.

In the two assumptions above, it is the case that it is possible to compare and contrast the major forms of suffering, obtained from theorising *DSM IV*, for instance, to note the inherent patterns, and alteration of themes across the spectrum of human experience mentioned there (American Psychiatric Association, 1994). The 'structure' of unhappy consciousness could be investigated by thinking about the *inconstancy* of the objects, self and other, and the types of *insecure* 'co-attachment' or 'co-empathy' between them. The aim would be to find repeating themes concerning the presence of various continua and variations within the definitive aspects of psychopathology. The grand aim of a reformed therapy requires thorough theoretical guidelines that can be won by consciousness analysing itself. Pure psychology is an 'eidetic,' conceptual investigation of the generalities, structures and conditions of what and how objects appear. It is operative within an alteration of the natural attitude.

Both types of Husserl's phenomenology consider the manners of appearance as *Leitfaden*, guiding clues to the manner of the constitution of their sense of existence and meaning. For phenomenology to exist, it has to be the case that a reduction of some sort can be achieved, for it is the definitive mark of its practice. In the above, it is assumed that the only way of answering questions concerning Husserl's work is to replicate his practice, for instance, to clarify the whole of the experiences of suffering. There is a priority to understand the whole before trying to understand a part, such as a specific person. It would be possible to use an understanding of the senses of self and other, gained through thought and super-vision. Interventions could be based on such an understanding.

Notes

1. In order to facilitate the reading of the paper, detailed appraisals of the English language literature are placed in endnotes to avoid losing the flow of points in the main text. Attention is on providing details to support the interpretation made. It should be noted that there are a number of common elements between the two major types of phenomenology, but these do not form a focus for concerted attention. These common elements include the reflection on evidence and the method of eidetic variation (Husserl, 1982, §§70-5). Husserl was cognisant of the three different ways of contextualising the understanding of consciousness—(1) as natural and natural-scientific, (2) as pure psychological, and (3), as transcendental. "Consciousness therefore makes its appearance here in different modes of apprehension and different contexts ... as absolute consciousness and secondly, in the correlate, as psychological consciousness which occurs in the natural world", (§76, p 172). Natural refers to the common sense understanding of people as taken for granted by everyone. Naturalistic means the natural scientific focus on material being and material cause that cannot be otherwise than it is. Transcendental means the consideration of the possibilities of their condition. The general view is that the many types of intentionality and passive process do the work of creating meaning.

2. Husserl and Heidegger agreed that consciousness and being are both immanent and transcendent. Human temporal nature embraces what appears and understands it pre-reflexively, before conscious attention can turn to it.

3. Accurate commentaries are provided by van Breda (1977) who emphasises the Cartesian and Kantian themes in the transcendental reduction. Kern (1977) and Küng (1975) do likewise, either pointing out the change of focus or providing details, but not weighing up the details of the changes in sense of the reductions. The characterisation given by Ricoeur (1978) is somewhat like that of Merleau-Ponty. Ricoeur only believes that short-lasting reductions are capable of being effected. De Boer's 1978 work is informative but not concerning the noema.

4. Atwell (1969) clarifies the differences between ideal objects and moments of the whole of signification, with remarks that are in-line with *The Idea of Phenomenology*. Sokolowski (2000), Bernet (1979, p 125), Holmes (1975) and Larabee (1986) contribute readings that lend themselves to the interpretation of the noema as membership of a set of variants about a core, constant identity. These are insightful and paint a picture of the noema as a polythetic concept, as a basis

for an eidetic a priori science with colleagues. Worthwhile interpretative help comes from some early writers such as Salmon (1929) who provided details of the basic aims of Husserl's work. Fink's papers from 1934 and 1939 are helpful. There is an area of debate concerning whether a noema is an ideal concept of higher intentionality or whether it is the givenness of imagination, recollection or an exemplary occurrence of any object or synthesis of consciousness. The most authoritative comments on the noema are those by Marbach (1992). To a degree, there is agreement with Bernet who views the noema as an object of belief (Bernet, Kern and Marbach, 1993, p 50, p 176). Ströker (1993, pp. 95-111) focuses on the identity and difference of noema as constancy. Ströker (1987, pp. 57-60) claims that only the transcendental approach entails the noema and that it has no connection to the natural attitude. As the natural attitude is connected to the psychological one, it then becomes unclear according to her work, if the noema, an object or referent for reduced consciousness, can appear for psychological research. However, Bernet, (Bernet, Kern and Marbach, 1993, pp. 95-101) uses the term in a general sense. Ströker is one writer to point out the presence of many instances of a noema that contribute towards the recognition of the experience of constancy in what appears of the same thing, idea or person (1993, p 100, Sokolowski, 2000, p 19, cf Husserl, 1977a, §9c, p 58, 1977b, §18, p 41, 1999, pp. 68-9). Marbach (1992) provides clear details that the direction of analysis goes back from the manners of givenness, as "clues" or "indexes," to compare and contrast the intentionalities that have created them (1977b, §18, p 42, §21). Atwell (1969) and Holmes (1975) are insightful and agree on a picture of the core noema as the appraisal of definitive features of an object. No papers state the major difference between the psychological and transcendental approaches (Fink, 1981, p 44). Scanlon is one English language writer who comes close to shining some light on pure psychology (1972).

5. The confusion among the interpreters reflects Husserl's frequent changes in wording and meaning over a 50-year period. For instance, a variety of comments during the years 1927 to 1928, could easily be taken as stating that the sense of existence of the world had actually been extinguished in the "phenomenological" reduction (1997c, §3, p 163, 1997d, §6, p 222). So without further attention to the clarifications by Husserl, it could seem as though the introductory "psychological-phenomenological" reduction was also a full rejection of the natural attitude when it is not. What appears to a sustained attention is that the "phenomenological-psychological" reduction is an introductory manoeuvre (1997b, p 98, 1997c, §9, p 172). There is some confusion in terminology and

stance because Husserl also mentioned a "phenomenological reduction" and a "phenomenological-psychological reduction".

6. Both Husserl and Heidegger claimed to distance themselves from the natural attitude and its assumptions about the relation of its meaning, or sense, versus its many sensual appearances and manners of being, referred to as the "ontological difference", (Heidegger, 1996, §20, p 88 fn, cf Husserl, 1999, p 68, Sokolowski, 2000, p 50). In the natural attitude, there is the projection of initial understanding that may not fit the nature of what appears and is, arguably, not a suitable approach for knowing it.

7. Eventually, the natural attitude is understood as an accomplishment of consciousness in mediated contact with other consciousness (Husserl, 1970b, §§52-4, 71, 1977b, §§41-50).

8. Bernet, Kern and Marbach call Husserl's position *"epistemological* idealism", (1993, p 57). Husserl aimed to treat consciousness as consciousness and not as neurons, inanimate matter or computational problems in a computer or other inappropriate and misleading understandings. Husserl took a perspective that opposed all traditional dualities in philosophy (Husserl, 1997c, §16).

9. There is a confusion of terms. The absolute constitutive consciousness is called "transcendent," "time-constituting" and "pre-reflexive". Transcendental consciousness is considered to be "absolute", (Husserl, 1982, §49, p 110, 1997c, §9, pp. 173-4). This usage of "transcendental" is the Kantian epistemological sense concerning the conditions, possibilities and necessities for constituting the conditions for knowledge and experience: "conditions of the "possibility of experience" are the first," most primordial conditions to be ascertained (Husserl, 1997a, §40, p 119, cf Kant, 1993, p 43/B 25). Consciousness is "transcendent" in a different sense, in that it constitutes the meaning of all parts of the world, of other persons and things. There is a third sense in which "transcendent" can be used and that is in a temporal sense because the senses of objects first learned in the past *transcend*, go across time and come into the present or future (Husserl, 1977b, §38, p 80, §50, p 111, 1989, §29, p 120, p 124, §60c, p 281, Supplement II, p 324).

10. The term "absolute" refers to the "absolute" consciousness that constitutes meaning in a complex manner. "Absolute" as portrayed in *Ideas I* is deceptive and does not mean what it might first appear to mean. Primarily, the correlations that are reflected on are connections between acts or syntheses and objects: *"empirical*

unities ... of intentional "constitution" ... merely "relative"" to the processes that make meaning (1982, §54, p 128). Secondarily, absolute consciousness is "absolute" because Husserl deemed it to be absolutely constitutive in the sense that it is the fundamental means of recognizing and verifying that which appears as evident, to the senses or the intellect (Sokolowski, 2000, p 92).

11. Transcendental reflection is the alleged ability to reflect on how oneself creates senses in co-operation with other persons (Husserl, 1977b, §§41-50).

12. In discussing Husserl, Merleau-Ponty criticized him from what can only be a position of 'replicated' experiential understanding: "All the misunderstandings with his interpreters ... have arisen from the fact that in order to see the world and grasp it as paradoxical, we must break with our familiar acceptance of it and ... from the fact that from this break we can learn nothing but the unmotivated upsurge of the world. The most important lesson which the reduction teaches us is the impossibility of a complete reduction", (Merleau-Ponty, 1962, p xiv).

13. Heidegger's "de-construction" and "destructuring" of the bad inheritance from history is close to Husserl's transcendental reduction. This is because Husserl advocated a reduction of traditional philosophy and history (Husserl, 1982, §18, p 34). He required phenomenologists to leave behind "all hitherto prevailing habits of thinking", (p xix). There should be a prevention of reification (§22, p 41) plus the removal of the tendencies of natural science (§32, p 61).

14. Heidegger disagreed. He thought that consciousness was insufficient in order to understand human being. For him, human being is situated, contextual and finite in a number of ways. Therefore, consciousness is not the essence of human being but one aspect of its being. The reality that appears for human being does not require a major focus on conscious awareness. Consciousness is not the only condition for the truth of being or the reality of what is real (Heidegger, 1996, §43a, p 190, §69b, p 328). For Heidegger, consciousness and the intersubjective lifeworld of shared experience are superficialities based on the condition of the temporal-historical being-with of the being of Da-sein and the worldhood of the world (§§17, 18). The latter is the condition or ground for the meaning of being. For Husserl, being can only be being-for-consciousness. Consciousness does work of specific sorts in understanding the meaning of being. Phenomenology should determine how consciousness does this. For Husserl, there are the many types of egoic intentional, and non-egoic non-intentional, relations to the object of consciousness (1999, pp. 68-9).

15. The case of contemporary cognitive science and psychology are particularly good examples of the lack of cohesiveness, the jumping between types of evidence and concordant manners of justification, for action in the creation of acceptable knowledge claims. In mainstream psychology, there is a panoply of methods that favour materialistic neurology, neuroscience, artificial intelligence and the use statistics and experimentation. There is permitted a consideration of psychiatric states plus evidence from artificial intelligence, sociology and anthropology. Contemporary psychology focuses on the material substrate of consciousness, rather than meanings-for-consciousness. For Husserl, psychology made in the image of naturalism, becomes an arbitrary pseudo-science. For instance, natural psychological science's "objectivity" is a higher type of construct on the basis of conscious and unconscious experience. According to Husserl, natural science and natural scientific psychology are ungrounded and cannot be their own grounds.

2

Husserl and Heidegger in comparison to Frankl

This paper initially focuses on defining phenomenological research according to Husserl and Heidegger. It then makes connections between phenomenology and Frankl's stance. It ends with making some points with respect to the general state of therapy theory, practice and research concerning effectiveness and received-quality.

Phenomenology is a fundamental qualitative analysis of meaning that goes before any further research or empirical work. Its instigator was Husserl, a philosopher of mind and science. The implication of Husserl's work is that academics should know how the mind works in constituting meaning of all sorts. If academics cannot do this, then they cannot assert any claim with certainty. Husserl proposed a revolutionary method that was aimed at co-ordinating the work of academic disciplines. He proposed that academics should investigate the workings of minds in general by an analysis of awareness. The method assumes that meanings are the products of cognitive and affective processes. The total set of meanings of a specific type indicates the forms of the processes that made them. His method is defined below.

Husserl influenced his student Heidegger in proposing a similar perspective that had a broader focus on the ways in which people live and meanings occur. Frankl also analyzed his life experiences and proposed a number of principles for structuring therapy made from his analysis. His approach focused on the difference between satisfying and purposive living—and that which is a denial or forgetting of potential. Because Husserl and Heidegger were sketching out a new approach, what they wrote was more general and does not compare to the insights that Frankl received. However, there is common ground between all three views and room for further development and understanding psychodynamics in order to develop new, more satisfying ways of living.

This paper has three main parts. It provides brief overviews of Husserl and Heidegger's qualitative research of consciousness and the manner of human living. These details are kept brief and are not closely argued with respect to the texts in which the methods are presented. The point of the paper is making assertions about how to practise phenomenology. It relates these remarks to the practice of therapy. Towards the end of the paper, some specific remarks are made about Frankl's work and the state of research. The first two sections that follow concern short overviews of the stances of Husserl and Heidegger. The sections after that discuss the implications of the practice of phenomenology.

Overview of Husserl's phenomenology

Husserl's contribution to psychology can be described as fundamentalist. His work can be paraphrased as being a specific request. Husserl pointed out that knowledge arises from experience. For him, consciousness constitutes meaning. He urged academics of any sort to find axioms and guiding concepts with a degree of certainty. He proposed that academics must turn to their experience and reflect on what appears to themselves, about the functioning of consciousness in relation to any shared meaning, any object. The aim is to understand how the object appears. The term "object" is an ontologically neutral one, not denoting any reification of human being or process of consciousness.

Husserl's general stance was organising a discipline by finding the guiding concepts that would co-ordinate the actions of its practitioners. This aim is based on his early work as a philosopher of mathematics. For him, a guiding relation in the philosophy is the recognition that there is something cohesive about the cardinal numbers and the way that the concepts "one" and "two" point to all instances of ones and twos, for instance (Bernet, Kern and Marbach, 1993, De Boer, 1978, Ströker, 1993). The type of referentiality of the ways in which these concepts point to all instances of actual "ones" and "twos" is of a universal type. Husserl wanted to find such universal essences about consciousness.

His discipline of "pure psychology" is the study of consciousness in the everyday world. It was hoped that this theorising would be sufficient to ground the human sciences and be a first introduction for philosophers who were concerned with how human beings know. Pure psychology would be followed by Husserl's transcendental phenomenology, a second more general scrutiny of consciousness. Husserl thought that transcendental phenomenology was the ultimate and absolute perspective from which it would be possible to organise philosophy, psychology and the sciences.

Now that the overview is in place, let us go into some more detail of how to practise phenomenology starting with Husserl's approach. There are only a small number of papers within the whole of the English language literature on phenomenology that actually carry out some phenomenological analysis and none of these go as far as working through "eidetic variation" to a conclusion (Marbach, 1992, 1993, 1999, Owen, 1994, Smith, 1977, Spader, 1995).

Husserl's method of reflection and seeing essences

Without any preamble, this section defines the full procedure of how to practise Husserlian phenomenology.

1. Remember or imagine having an experience of an object of a specific kind. A specific inanimate object, an experience, belief or meaning of any sort indicates the egoic acts and automatic syntheses of consciousness that constituted it. In pure psychology, the object is understood in a psychological research attitude: It is a remembered or imagined example that occurs in the consensually real world of a specific culture. The researchers acknowledge that their attitude towards the object of the participants is not the same as the attitude of the participants towards their object. What is remembered or imagined is the whole of the connection between consciousness and the constituted sense of the object.

2. The specific type of the manner of givenness or appearance of the object indicates how it appears that way. Researchers must attend experientially to the whole experience of the object. The connection between the qualities of the object in relation to other ways of imagining, thinking, feeling and perceiving it need to be described as they appear—in the context of how they appear. Generally, there are inter-relations between the object, in relation to past appearances of it and the whole set of processes that made it. The many appearances of it may even indicate the first ever encounter with the object. This analysis of current awareness does not preclude future references and horizons that might also be pertinent. The point here is to compare and contrast the specific correlation between the manner of givenness of the object—and be able to compare and contrast the types of constitutive acts and syntheses.

3. Once a sufficient amount of data has been generated and a set of contributing intentionalities have been identified, further imaginative variation takes place. This is achieved through imagining arbitrary examples of the object and different types of relation to it. Eidetic variations are thought experiments where the 'raw data' of appearances are modified with respect to related or potentially similar

objects. The point of such imaginative changes is to create new permutations in order to check and decide on the invariant features of the object and relations to it. Eidetic variation stops when such constant features of the relation and the object are found. In this revolutionary way, attention is given to what appears.

Generally, there are inter-relations between the egos who 'receive' the finished constitutions of constituting automatic cognitive processes and there are relations between what appears and how the object has been constituted throughout the lifespan. The analysis is comparative in two ways. Firstly, it compares and contrasts manners of giving acts, syntheses and given objects and interprets the parts and whole of what appears. Secondly, it compares and contrasts imagined versions of the same, to find their being. The process is successful once an invariant universal essence is decided.

The above three steps are an account of how to practise Husserlian phenomenology in the psychological stance. The aim is to take experience of which we are only implicitly aware and cease on-going experiencing—and begin to "see" or reflect on it generally. Thereby making explicit the link between what has been made and the manner in which it was made. This is an inherently comparative process that occurs with respect to the totality of acts, syntheses and objects of adjacent sorts. The major focus for Husserl was to concentrate on the cognitive processes of consciousness, as a matter of priority, in order to achieve "noetic phenomenology" of intentionality or "noetics", (Husserl, 1982, §85, p 207, §144, p 344, §147, p 353, Marbach, 1992). Phenomenology makes definitions that communicate something understandable to other persons so that they might agree or disagree (Husserl, 1982, §66, p 152). The aim is to establish a community of concept-users who progress together along the same path (Owen and Morris, 1999). The classic focus of phenomenology is to work from one's own experience of any object. It is a qualitative pre-scientific focus on how the mind works, as derived by the clarification of experience. It is hoped to produce agreement about theory that is used empirically in the actual world, in solving problems and furthering human aims.

Accordingly, there is no need to invent psychodynamic processes or ideas about the unconscious. The meaningful products of consciousness indicate the processes that made them. In conclusion and without the detailed workings, it is the case that the types of suffering, say in *DSM IV*, share a small number of problematic processes. There appear to be four major types of processes involved in unhappy consciousness. In providing the conclusions, it is possible to relate back all the manners of the givenness of self and other to find the following.

In relation to empathising the other, making a sense of others, the following possibilities occur:

a) Cannot create a sense of the other, cannot attach to others.

b) Cannot create a constant sense of the other.

c) Creates an inaccurate sense of the other.

d) Creates a sense of the other in relation to a needy insecure self.

e) Creates a benign and secure sense of the other in relation to a secure self.

In regard to self only:

a) Cannot create a cohesive constant self.

b) Cannot create a sufficient sense of self.

c) Displaces anxiety on to others or things, places.

d) Creates an inaccurate sense of self.

e) Self can create a benign and constant sense of self in relation to a benign, constant and secure other.

In short, the above points are the overall aims of Husserl's exploration of consciousness. A further section below briefly compares and contrasts Husserl's approach to Heidegger's.

Overview of Heidegger's phenomenology

In brief, Heidegger's phenomenological work before 1930 focused on similar themes to Husserl's but with a number of important additions (Grieder, 1988). Firstly, Heidegger's stance was hermeneutic. He saw knowledge and conscious meaning as arising out of human being's ability to have an overall contextualised experience, its human world. For Heidegger, any person, experience or event has its meaning through the immediate ability to understand something, because humans project their world as a frame for understanding, around what appears.

The main point about Heidegger's work was relating ontology to hermeneutics. In particular, immediate understanding, is a fundamental characteristic of human beings. He connected phenomenology with the German hermeneutic tradition that began in the eighteenth century and has followed through into Gadamer and other writers. For Heidegger, phenomenology was about finding references by which any person, experience or event makes sense. There are two types of such analyses that I have called the "pure" and "applied" styles (Owen, 2000a).

The "applied" style of analysis is clearly understood by reference to the examples of using a hammer and the car indicator in *Being and Time* (Heidegger, 1996, §33, p 147). The key principle is that anything can be meaningful for human beings. Anything is understandable as a sign. Immediate understanding of any person or object occurs because of its referentiality to the whole set of experiences that a person is.

There is a second type of analysis that is called "pure" because it is more concerned with philosophical texts and concepts. The aim of the pure type of analysis is to check current meanings in etymology or philology. The aim is to take a current concept and compare and contrast its usage and lived meaning, to ancient meanings of the same concept or practice. The idea is to check the current understanding of the concept to see if it is an accurate one with respect to human purposes.

A couple of key quotations from *Being and Time* are as follows. In the applied analysis, the experience of picking up a hammer and using it for a specific task is one particular way of encountering the world of tools for human purposes:

> For example, the thing at hand we call a hammer has to do with hammering, the hammering has to do with fastening something, fastening something has to do with protection against bad weather ... Which relevance things at hand have is prefigured in terms of the total relevance. The total relevance that, for example, constitutes the things at hand in a workshop in their handiness is "earlier" than any single useful thing ...
> §18, p 78.

This type of analysis of the lived references between things and persons is "semiotic". It is a pragmatic analysis of how things exist in relation to the manner in which human beings exist.

As regards hermeneutics, the "circle," the inter-relation between the part and the whole, is an inter-relation of mutuality. This is not an inexorable problem but just the way things are when they are understood.

> What is decisive is not to get out of the circle, but to get in it in the right way. This circle of understanding is not a circle in which any random kind of knowledge operates … [The] first, constant, and last task is not to let fore-having, fore-sight, and fore-conception be given to it by chance ideas and popular conceptions, but to guarantee the scientific theme by developing these in terms of the things themselves.
>
> §32, p 143.

This mention of the "things themselves" is an ironic remark as it means developing a tried and tested experiential understanding of any research topic. Like Husserl, Heidegger was against bad understanding. A good interpretation or good concept is one that really explains the phenomena.

Heidegger's applied method

Heidegger's hermeneutic method was less technical than Husserl's. Heidegger's aim was to refine descriptions of essences of the manners of human being. This occurs in two ways, pure and applied. However, any description of what appears is not about consciousness but concerns the attitude and relation to the being of the research object in the human world. For Heidegger, this relation of insertion in a world is fundamental and he called it the mode of being-in-the-world. The following is an account of only the applied type of analysis.

In disclosing the essences of human being in fundamental ontology, interpretation occurs via the totality of involvements in the world. For example, the experiences of using hammers and car indicators are examples of the way in which experiences, persons and codes of meaning are inter-related. Consequently, a revealing or disclosing form of writing or speech should make present what exists between people (§7b, p 28). For Heidegger, phenomenology should communicate by indicating the object with its context and mode of existence. When this is attempted, what is disclosed is human immersion in a universe, the totality of references in a human world where each innerworldly-being is capable of being projected-on and so viewed differently. Beings and the manner of understanding and interpreting are shown best in the effects produced by signs: Any experience or thing can be a sign that points to referents and other contexts. Such sets of codes and contexts concerning signs could include intersubjective praxis and the influence of history, other people or the sedimentation of meaning in culture and science. The totality of the set of references extends contemporarily—and into the future and past. It is the case that things make sense through the cumulative effect of temporality, the cultural world and history.

When it comes to understanding other people, the focus is to begin at a level of interpreting specific experiences of empathy by understanding the totality of empathic experience in the world. Any spoken phrases or gestures make sense according to the totality of significations, as in the hammer and car indicator examples. But for understanding others, the research attitude uses solicitude (*Fürsorge*) and encounters the other as the other encounters us.

Heidegger's claim was that non-phenomenological approaches to understanding other persons are incorrect. For instance, at a non-phenomenological level of understanding, empathy is often assumed to be actual, emotional knowledge of the other's mind. Knowing the minds of others is assumed to be an easy capability. Traditional "natural" scientific psychology assumes that its base material, the empathic knowledge of others, is a fact of the sort that can be explored and measured. Phenomenology disagrees. Heidegger showed that the other is always pre-reflexively understood. The being of the other is "co-constituted" [*mitkonstituiert*] via its immanent-transcendent existentiality of being, an opening or clearing for innerworldly being (§24, p 105). He believed that the other is passively apprehended without any egoic, active intervening processes of introjection, interpretation of the other and the assumption that the other is 'like me'.

Also, in meeting with other people, empathic mistakes and assumptions show us our own inaccurate understandings of people in general and in our specific encounters with specific others. If we acknowledge our mistakes and learn from them, it helps us get around the world more easily. Thus the type of experiential learning about the pre-reflexive experience of being-with others, aided by therapy or not, is consistent with a Heideggerian approach.

Brief discussion of the two approaches

Before moving onto to Frankl and making various comments about therapy, it is necessary to say a little about the material covered so far.

Husserl's main emphasis was to focus on the egoic acts of consciousness and the automatic processes over which the ego has no conscious control. He took experience which is not ordinarily reflected on and "objectified" it. This does not mean that he reified it, but rather understood it as it appears in its own manner.

Heidegger's applied method focuses on action, living and doing in a wholistic manner. *Being and Time* focuses on the automatic pre-reflexive way in which appearances occur, because for him, meaning is literally "constituted" by temporal existence. This temporal manner of living is also connected with historical and social influences.

As far as this aspect of phenomenology goes, then there is only a subtle difference between Husserl and Heidegger. Both men agreed on the fundamentality of the frame of the human world, cultural influences, in constituting meaning through temporality, social life and history.

However, if Heidegger's approach is preferred over Husserl's, it can be seen that there are a number of idealistic aspects to Husserl's philosophical stance. In 1913 Husserl believed in the possibility of a reduction to experiential truth without the contamination of language, history, habits of thinking and ontology (1982, p xix, §18, pp. 33-4, §31, p 59, §87, p 212). His method involved relating instances of what appears to imagined possibility, in order to find its universal and invariant aspects. For Heidegger, this hermeneutic naïvety was unacceptable. Heidegger believed in the possibility of partial reductions that strip away some false conceptualisations and beliefs. This could be achieved in a number of ways: Through mistakes that upset our expectations, revealing the truer nature of what exists (1996, §16). Through anxiety stripping away our sense of being at home in a community, thus revealing us as fundamentally alone in the world and facing death (§40, §53). It is also necessary to attempt to strip away the obscuring, bad inheritance of historical beliefs about human nature, for instance, of false ideas about human temporality and the understanding of history (§§1, 5, 6, 66, 76).

What a phenomenological hermeneutic exploration can do is clarify and refine understanding, and compare it with the direct experience of what appears. *The ultimate test of whether we know something or someone is if our understanding fits the experiences.* Such proven understanding is hermeneutically capable of showing more of any phenomena that appears, rather than it's opposite: Concepts that do not fit experience, that continue to obstruct and mystify, prevent accurate understanding. What phenomenology is against is the production of "maps" that do not represent the "territory", (Husserl, 1970a, Sixth Investigation, §20, pp. 727-8).

Heidegger was explicit about his principle of how any instance has an immediate and on-going meaning with respect to meanings of its type, and that past and future connections play a role. Thus the major difference between the approaches to meaning of the two men is as follows. For Husserl, the mind has intentional references to what exists and has meaning. The reflective exploration of the mind involves comparisons of what appears with respect to the interplay of acts, syntheses, things, the ego, horizons of understanding and with respect to retained senses of meaning, that were once conscious but are now only tacitly quasi-present. For Husserl, what appears bears a relation to the whole of past actual and imagined experience. Theory concerns universal essences about intentional relations that are found by scrutinising a full set of imaginable possibilities. Universal essences apply to all instances of the same intentionality-object relationship. But for Heidegger, references and comparisons are made with respect to the part and its connection to the whole. Heidegger's "applied" research attitude acknowledges that we are caught up in the world in many different ways. We must compare and contrast these ways in order to know ourselves and other persons, for instance.

Husserl's pure psychology is relativistic and analysed belief in the consensually real world but it is not explicitly hermeneutic. Husserl believed in the necessary starting point of faithful description. His research attitude was one of the mental investigation of imagined possibilities, alongside the contemplation of empirical, fictional or other personal experiences.

To round up this section, it can be seen that overall, phenomenology is against inaccurate understanding. Understandings are wrong when they are insufficient or inadequate in relation to lived experience. The practical outcome is that insufficient methods of approach to practical problems must be abandoned. The charge against non-phenomenological approaches is that they maintain a lack of thought and adopt inaccurate conventions passed down and accepted without question. What phenomenology concerns itself with is learning from experience in a revelatory manner. It is revolutionary and debates fundamental concerns so that communal progress can be made. Following Heidegger, all understanding is part of human being and involves finding the sufficient means of contextualising what appears. The aim is to experience lived meaning and be able to conceptualise it in a manner that is proven by prolonged experience. Consequently, theorising is closely related to practice and research (Heidegger, 1996, §69b, pp. 327-8). Theorising involves any kind of interpretation about a client or oneself. It requires projecting the therapy world around the client and their signs. As such, formulation, assessment, intervention and review involve interpretation.

With these remarks in place, it is now possible to progress to make various connections with Frankl's approach to therapy and finally comment on empirical research.

Comparisons with Frankl's approach to meaning in life

There are number of overlaps between phenomenology and Frankl's logotherapy. Both agree that meaning, in a broad sense, is central to human existence and therapy. Viktor Frankl's approach to therapy concerns itself with a number of ways of finding, exploring and changing the lived-meaning and the sense of purpose of life (Frankl, 1964, 1967, 1973). It has its own theory of the source of meaning and its own ideas about the facilitation and change of meaning. Within logotherapy, it may also be possible to encourage, challenge, reframe and set interventions that directly alter or instil a purposive striving in life. Logotherapy has its classical themes of finding a purpose in life and moving away from ignoring one's own capabilities, limitations and potential. From a phenomenological perspective a major question is—how is meaning or understanding itself sufficiently understood? This section discusses the subject of meaning as a lived reference within a human world.

An initial insight can be gained through looking at the ubiquity of hermeneutics in therapy. Hermeneutics is a topic that is largely ignored in the natural scientific psychology of therapy. Phenomenology is opposed to natural psychological science covering over the phenomena of meaning in life. For phenomenology, meaning occurs at three inter-related levels. The most fundamental level is the pre-reflexive one: the immediate engagement and contact with self, others and world. Once reflection begins, the pre-reflective engagement and its forms of apprehension ceases. Reflection may not be a neurotic stagnation. In reflection, the ego is active in turning attention to what appears to gain an awareness of what occurs and what is meaning-producing. But the reflective level is an intermediate one as there are influences from the larger social world, which percolate through the ego and into the pre-reflexive. Insomuch that the ego gains habits and automatic abilities through repetition and learning in the larger social world.

Thus, there are three levels of understanding. (1) The pre-reflexive realm contains social and egoic influences. It is the immediacy of what is understood without conscious thought, that just appears the way it does within the surrounding understanding of the frame of the cultural world. (2) There are reflected-on meanings that appear wholly for one person with respect to the social world. These too may be fixed or unstable, ambivalent or fragmented, or topics that are not yet explored. (3) There are the meanings of language, culture and the social world, conventional, fairly-fixed intersubjective meanings. These three levels are inter-related with constitution passing between them. If this understanding is accurate, then interventions can be understood as effecting meaning according to these three levels.

If we take hermeneutics seriously, then there are many different styles of hermeneutics in life, and on both sides of the therapeutic relationship. The depressed or pessimistic person sees a milk bottle that is half full and complains that it is half empty. The optimist sees the same bottle and is happy because there is still some left. But seriously, the client's problems arise through self-interpretation in a style or genre of hermeneutic processes. The neurotic problem is interpreted into existence through comparison to a selection of instances from the world. Meaning and purpose are references to something, some past, present or future situation. On the one hand, there is the client who has their own frame of reference, which at the beginning is the ground to be explored and understood. On the other hand, there are therapists who are also focused on this ground, but inevitably understand it in their own way and show their understanding to the client in a response of some sort.

Phenomenology understands human beings as having a realm of private experience into which societal, historical and cultural experiences flow. But we never experience the experiences of others as they experience them. This is the problem of empathy or the problem of other minds. The phenomenological way of understanding therapy is to bear in mind that we never experience clients' experiences. Rather, empathy about clients is a mediated experience that occurs with respect to our total experience of meeting other people. People understand themselves and each other through empathic and hermeneutic processes. If we come to agree with clients and become able to understand their view of themselves, others and the world, then this is a verbal agreement or one that is based on an understanding of body language. We never have the same experiences as others, although we have the possibility of coming to agree on the same descriptions. Consequently, the scope of therapy focuses on their view of the problem, their nature and capabilities, interests and motivations. Our comments can be heard if we can place them within their worlds and we speak within their frame of reference. Through a number of meetings, it is possible to establish the sense of the shared world of mutual experience in the consulting room. Understanding the ubiquity of hermeneutics implies that selves can understand others, but selves never experience their feelings as they feel them.

Accordingly, the shared space between phenomenology and logotherapy concerns finding a purpose in life with others. For phenomenology, meaning occurs through interchange with others in which meaning circulates between people. Human aims are not just personal ones and are not simply towards unending and exhausting striving in life. Meaning occurs intersubjectively through exchange in culture and society. Any person can earn their self-esteem through an exchange with others where they do some meaningful task in which they contribute to the shared good of others and thereby feel good about themselves. Such a lack of the attainment of meaning occurs in some forms of neurosis. For instance, part of the difference between feeling good or bad about oneself may include a fixation of attention on a small number of items that become a focus for excessive concern, as in the case of depression.

Phenomenology in relation to therapy has openness to experience with respect to ethics and values. Openness to self encourages accurate insight. Openness to the other encourages accurate empathy. In insufficient attention and understanding, there lie those experiences where a person is not open to, but distanced from their own experience, their own lived-meanings. The direction of the cure is towards a greater self-acceptance, happiness, relaxation and dependable senses of self and others as worthwhile and trustworthy. To be constant and secure is not to be boring but having a sense of providing a sustained, loving attention towards others and feeling that oneself is worthwhile, cohesive and not needy or caught up in excessive passions.

As regards ethics, values and the quality of our attention to the other, then a Heideggerian perspective would deny the possibility of a theory-free or value-free stance. In section 26 of *Being and Time,* Heidegger sketched out what is close to a Foucaultian analysis of relationships. Overall, values and ethics are to be explored. Our understanding must fit with human nature and not go against it. If we start with temporality, then a good deal of human meaning and value in the west is laid out according to linear time. The neurotic person feels they must have done something by the time they were 21, 30, 40 or 50, etc. Winter is a time for family parties and summer is a time for holidays. In these instances, time is wrongly used to measure of self-worth. A certain specific age or season acts as a sign for achievements that must have occurred. If they do not, there is a sense of failure and hopelessness where the person berates themselves according to the adoption of the standards of others.

There is also the topic of the introjection of values from others to consider. For instance, the problem of "individualism" is ruining lives. When "individualism" is introjected, it alienates and goes against community. The introjection of meanings and values that promote an excessive, overly-individualistic, self-contained understanding of people are such that self-punitive, non-communal, materialistic, narcissistic and aggressive behaviours become the norm. For phenomenology, there is a tension between the adoption of introjects, target ideals, that are too high—versus the skills, abilities and inherited tendencies that are sufficient to be capable of meeting the target ideals. If the neurotic person has unhelpful, unrealistic introjects, that they cannot achieve, there is trouble. Either the target ideals must be lowered to meet the actual abilities, skills and aptitudes of the person. Or the social skills and abilities are too low and need to be raised to meet the ideals. Either way there is a tension.

Overall, a simple life that is in-tune with human community and certain core values is more healthy and achievable. For instance, such values are having a sense of self-worth that is achieved through altruistic acts, loving and playful contact with others—no matter how small they are. Being a good enough parent, a good enough partner, doing as well as one can and being honest are achievable values. The overly individualistic aims are achievable only with great difficulty because they create conflict and competition.

One connected topic between phenomenology and logotherapy is the effect of belief in meanings that have been constituted (Owen, 1992a, p 396). The medical terminology notes the presence of "placebo" and "nocebo" effects. The placebo effect is one where a useless sugar coated pill has the same anaesthetic effect as diamorphine. It has this effect because the patient believes they are being given a painkiller. The nocebo effect is seen in cases of voodoo death where a curse is issued and the afflicted person dies within three days. In this case the fear produced by the curse is sufficient for the afflicted to give up life altogether. We see similar nocebo effects in diagnoses of cancer and the iatrogenic effects of judgemental therapists. Following Husserl and Heidegger, it is the attitude of approach that constitutes the overall meaning of the problem.

There have been attempts to analyse how meaning occurs. One paper by Rice and Sapeira has gone far in the direction of finding how good meanings are connected to bad ones. They note that the nature of neurosis concerns the poor interpretation of evidence, for instance, in the cases called transference, projection, poor empathy and lack of insight (Rice and Sapeira, 1984, p 32). They also note that there are positive and negative intentions and meanings that surround the problematic behaviours or feelings. But if therapists 'follow' the bad for long enough, it leads to the 'good' and the discovery of the good can change the bad (pp. 33-43). The point being that there are connections between the good and the bad (cf Carl Jung's concept of the shadow, Melanie Klein's theory of object development). Accordingly, therapy has the task of having clients realise "the good in the bad". It is a project of discovery and healing. When people realise their strengths in adversity, it is a reminder that they themselves are not all bad, for instance.

Closing by way of therapy research

For phenomenology and logotherapy, meaning is a central topic. This is not just cognitive and linguistic forms of meaning but the direct and immediate felt-sense of any experience. If we take seriously the principle that an instance of any occurrence or category occurs with respect to its totality, and that the part makes sense in connection with the whole. Then much doubt is thrown upon the standards of randomised control trials, hypothesis-testing and hypothetical-deductive means of obtaining psychological knowledge. One case is research dominated by the medical model. It uses the drug metaphor that has been severely criticised by its own practitioners (Owen, 1999, Stiles and Shapiro, 1989).

The current developments towards the empirical validation of all forms of health care are laudable exercises in some ways. Such a trend puts quantitative research to the forefront and gives it permission to be the judge of what is effective and good value for money. But for phenomenology, this form of research is not acceptable. Quantitative research shows what is statistically the average for client groups who have a pure presentation of single sets of symptoms. It requires a large sample size to work effectively. Generally, it is non-hermeneutic and reifies the lived effects of the intersubjective processes it should be try to understand. Ordinary qualitative research focuses on meaning and may not always account for the hermeneutic stance and interests of the researchers. For Heidegger, the current understanding gets refined in repeated attempts to meet the other, the 'object' of research.

But there are other allied concerns. The twin projects of "clinical reasoning" and "clinical governance" are meant to be following the propelling force of quantitative research. Clinical reasoning is the trend to have agreed forms of interventions for specific situations whereby the best form of clinical practice might occur for users of the health services. This might seem very sensible at first sight. But the difficulties are getting any agreement in a maverick field such as therapy. The problem is one of a lack of standardisation and almost a refusal to look at the quantitative findings in detail.

Clinical governance is a good idea. This is making the Chief Executives of Health Service Trusts legally responsible for the quality of the services provided by their hospitals and clinics. Of course, Chief Executives devolve the responsibility to clinical governance specialists and managers in quality audit. However, the point is that quality audit will be carried out by quantitative research that alters meaning and may not understand the mechanisms by which change occurs and care is provided and received. Many projects have measures of behavioural change that do not fit the manner in which meaning-change occurs through therapy.

In closing, allow me to clear up a popular misconception about phenomenology. Phenomenology is not just about relating consciousness to others, things and the world. It is against the natural attitude, an unreflective way of being that assumes far too much. It is against the natural sciences that think that quantification, based on a materialistic way of thinking about the world, is sufficient. Consequently, a phenomenologically-oriented therapy is not primarily against empirical science, cognitive-behaviour therapy nor psychoanalysis, nor is it automatically for humanistic therapy. What it is against, in its critique of the natural and naturalistic approaches, is inaccurate understanding. Inaccurate understanding occurs when an interpretation stands outside of a sphere of interpretations that do not tally with a consensus of understandable interpretations (Rickman, 1998). Inaccurate understandings beget methods, manners of thinking and relating that do not meet human abilities. Inaccurate understandings cover over a phenomenon so it cannot be understood. A phenomenological approach to therapy is about beginning with adequate descriptions of client and therapist experiences on the shared path of recovery. The quality and effectiveness of therapy is governed by clients' wishes and abilities. Only with their active participation might therapy move towards the maximum amount of recovery possible for each client in their home context. Phenomenology demands that we speak about what we know and that we attend to each object in a sufficient manner.

3

Sokolowski's Introduction to Phenomenology

In some ways this latest offering on Husserlian phenomenology is extremely helpful and achieves what no other English language publication has so far. Namely, it successfully encapsulates the central points of Husserl's massive output. It puts forward strong arguments for Husserl's stance within one introductory undergraduate text in an easily accessible way. Yet, there is a major inadequacy with the text, for there is not one quotation provided, nor any reference to Husserl's texts, published or unpublished. In assessing this work, I shall mention its strong points first, and then remedy its weaknesses by supplying details of those texts that provide supporting evidence.

In overview, I claim that an *Introduction to Phenomenology* is the most authoritative and concise portrayal of Husserl's stance in the English language to date (Sokolowski, 2000). It is a major contribution that stands alongside the work of Kern, Marbach, Ströker and Bernet who are Directors of the *Husserl Archives*. It is suitable for undergraduate courses in philosophy of mind, cognitive science, psychology and the social sciences. Along the way, Sokolowski also scores by emphasising that it was Husserl who overturned the traditional immanent-transcendent and idealist-realist dichotomies with his understanding of intentionality. This was a major achievement for Husserl in *The Idea of Phenomenology* (1999). Accordingly, it is also the case that for something to be *in consciousness* is not at all like something being *in a box* because there is no exterior to consciousness. Derrida is also put in his place for making Husserl into a straw man who can then be easily found at fault. Links are made to post-modernism and the schools of Husserl interpretation in America.

Husserl's work is important because it is an attempt at a qualitative grounding of major concepts to achieve consensus in science or an academic discipline, before beginning any quantitative investigation. It is claimed that such grounding is required in order to create productive co-operation. Sokolowski's book is useful for providing details of the three major phenomena on which phenomenology is based. Husserl was a seminal thinker but his writings are abstruse. The following remarks should bring extra clarity to understanding Sokolowski's book and specific works by Husserl.

The first of these phenomena could be called "the primacy of empathy" because Husserl's philosophical position begins with the two-way empathic relation between two or more persons. Such a basic understanding allows for multiple perspectives on the same cultural object, any perceptual or intellectual object or practice that belongs to a culture. "The primacy of empathy" is a phrase to describe Husserl's starting point for his theorising of how consciousness produces meaning: A theorising that begins with the acknowledgement that different persons have their own perceptual perspective on, say, a visually-perceived cultural object. From such a basis, each person gains a specific understanding of that object, whilst knowing or possibly knowing, that other persons have different perceptual and meaningful perspectives about 'the same' object. From this, it follows that more complex objects, and contexts for understanding, also comply with the empathic ability to acknowledge others' perspectives as well as one's own (Sokolowski, 2000, p 32, Husserl, 1980, Supplement I, §1, 1982, §151, 1977b, §§43, 49). The following quotation from a lecture by Husserl in 1931, concerns the inter-connectedness of all human consciousness. The conditions for knowing anything for Husserl involved the connection between the collective and the individual: "communalized transcendental life ... constitutes the world as an objective world, as a world that is identical for everyone", (1997e, p 498).

Accordingly, the premises of Husserl's most basic stance may be expressed in the following way. Concerning the relation of any two persons who are considering the same visual object, the first premise is that one person understands that the other sees the same object. The second premise is that one person understands the object in relation to many others who have also understood it, for instance, in different cultures or at different times in history. Therefore, the world as it appears for any one consciousness is a single appearance of the world, with respect to the totality of other persons' views of the world. Additions of sense occur to any one person's understanding of the same object. Also, it is the case that any one person's view of the same object is inadequate with respect to the potential sum total of all views. Another way of expressing Husserl's most fundamental view is to write that *what exists for one consciousness is the world for that consciousness plus the world seen by others*. Husserl's philosophy is based on theorising from such a perspective.

The second major phenomenon on which Husserl focused, and which is given a clear account by Sokolowski, is the relation between a definitive experiential understanding and the very many specific instances and contexts from which the definitive central understanding arises. Heidegger referred to the same phenomenon as the "ontological difference", (1982, §4 and other works). Husserl described it in the terminology of the relation of the core noematic senses to the full noematic senses. The same phenomenon occurred for Husserl in the relation of a universal essence to a range of eidetic instances (Sokolowski, 2000, p 19). Husserl's original formulation from 1925 is as follows, "the multiplicity must be an object of consciousness as multiplicity, as plurality … Otherwise we do not win the … identical, as the *hen epi pollon*," literally, the "one over many," meaning that there would be a failure to achieve the recognition of identity, despite many variations in appearance (Husserl, 1977a, §9c, p 58). Consciousness is able to identify new instances as belonging to a set of prior instances. When consciousness cannot recognise new instances, there is the experience of confusion.

The third major phenomenon on which Sokolowski shines a good deal of light, is the seeing of categories, which is related to the second phenomenon above. Categorial intuition is the bestowal of linguistic meaning by consciousness, which is understood as an intentional achievement of spoken or thought meanings (1982, §§124-7). In particular, seeing a category is the achievement of meaning expressed in syntax and language that is based on the experiential sense that a reflected-on understanding has (Sokolowski, 2000, pp. 89-90, Husserl, 1977a, §16, 1982, §94).

So, I find that Sokolowski's book has a great deal to recommend it because it puts right many mis-understandings that plague Husserl studies. On the downside, it is aberrant as a scholarly text because no links are made to supporting textual evidence.

4

Husserl's theory of empathy: Meaning arrives with the other

This paper points to an omission in the psychology that underpins practice and research. The omission is the lack of attention to the importance of the topic of the way in which we understand how we experience other people, how we empathise. This paper demonstrates this omission and briefly recaps Husserl's theory of empathy. This paper does not provide an overview of the whole story of phenomenology nor can it fully state Husserl's position or analyse other interpretations of what he meant. However, the paper has the aim of indicating the gap in understanding that is evident in "ignoring the other" in the majority of quantitative natural science approaches. The interpretation of the *Fifth Meditation* is in-line with the work of the Directors of the *Husserl Archives* that appears in English translation. This paper amplifies and explains comments by Kern (1993a) and Ströker (1993).

There is almost a complete absence of consideration of how we come to be able to understand other persons in psychology, the behavioural and human sciences. For instance, the PsycLIT Silver Platter database of five compact discs covering the period 1887 to 1995 contained only approximately 20 entries on the subjects of Husserl, empathy, the problem of other minds and associated terms[1]. This paper introduces the implications of the lack of attention to empathy. This is because there is a major problem in understanding other people. We may often think we understand others but we never have direct access to their thoughts and feelings. Consequently, self gives the feelings and senses that we have about others to them, in a manner that is not immediately evident. It is the purpose of this paper to lay out some of the basic principles of Husserl's approach to understanding the other. Husserl spent approximately 30 years in proposing a pure psychology, a theoretical venture to ground and make cohesive applied work in the general sphere of psychology.

Historically, Husserl's work has gained greater acceptance in philosophy. There the problem of other minds, or the problem of empathy, had been the topic of prolonged debate in eighteenth and nineteenth century German philosophy particularly[2] (Stein, 1989). But in contemporary psychology, the absence of consideration of the other is lamentable because psychological knowledge needs to be grounded via a consensual understanding of how one human being experiences another. The lived experience of other people occurs before any rating and statistical analysis. Accordingly, if it is agreed that the object of psychology is the lived experience of people, it follows that some consideration of *how* we achieve the senses of other persons is required in order to relate psychological claims of any kind, and for any purpose, to the object of attention. This paper claims that it is necessary to have an explicit theory regarding how one human being understands and experiences others. Although these experiences that are clarified by science, occur within the totality of socio-cultural life in which we ordinarily live, it is not enough to ignore the mental processes through which we empathise other persons.

Husserl's approach

One of the clearest examples of the problem of empathy is provided in the collection of research papers written in 1912 now called *Phenomenology and the Foundations of the Sciences*[3] (Husserl, 1980, §44, pp. 94-98). However, it was not until 1929, the year of writing the *Cartesian Meditations*, that Husserl arrived at what can be considered as something of an answer to the paradox of the apparent acquaintance with the mind of the other and its absence in not being directly given to us[4] (1975). Husserl's phenomenology of social experience was intended to establish a scientific community with a new method of philosophical grounding that would lead scientists, academics and practitioners, out of their state of philosophical lack of awareness. This state of epistemological and ontological non-awareness is called the "natural attitude" by phenomenology. The natural psychological sciences would be one place where such a lack of reflection could be overcome, so that theories and practices may be justified within an explicit consensus and understanding that includes understanding one's own position within the whole set of possibilities.

Husserl called the cognitive-affective process that constitutes the senses of others "empathic presentation[5]". Empathic presentation is the technical term for the generation of empathic senses of other persons. This process has the features of creating the vicarious experience of the apparently immediate understanding of the inner motives and emotions of another person or persons. Paradoxically, these experiences are not experienced as part of one's own consciousness, but are felt as real or imagined, for instance, within one's own consciousness but belonging to others. For Husserl, what the self experiences is never the actual experiences, feelings and motives of another consciousness. He did not believe in mind reading. What is experienced is understood as the constitution of the sense of the other in self. The precise psychodynamics of this constitution is the puzzle that Husserl claimed to have solved.

The Husserlian understanding of empathy starts with a model of consciousness that rejects the natural attitude assumptions that reify consciousness. It is claimed that non-phenomenological approaches project the distorting, natural attitude understanding (1981a, p 192). It is alleged that an empathic part of consciousness constitutes the ordinary awareness of our feelings for, and understandings of, others. In the *Cartesian Meditations*, a transcendental reduction produces an allegedly neutral attitude with respect to being-senses. This attitude is for the purpose of bracketing assumptions about oneself, others, culture, empirical psychology and human nature (1977b, §44, p 96). Husserl claimed it is possible to see the essences of our experiences of others and finally decide on the conditions for the possibility of such experience. This is the heart of the concern for Husserl.

Husserl's approach was critical insomuch that he is claiming that psychology should be focused on consciousness, one's own and that of others. Natural psychological science focuses on behaviour, biological processes, the brain, chemical and electrical processes in the brain and then claims to have found something about consciousness. For Husserl, the human sciences must focus on their specific object[6] of consciousness and other people.

Such a focus on empathy is central to initiate a philosophical reflection on "purified," immanent experiences, by excluding what could be doubted and what is specifically part of the surface, constituted feelings we have for others. One's own experiences can be reflected on in a depersonalised and dissociated manner. The reduction allegedly produces a sphere of pure ownness that belongs wholly to oneself (§44, p 96, §48, p 106). After the reduction[7], the observing part of reduced consciousness is regarded as an anonymous non-participating observer. The inter-relation of self, other and world, with cultural objects in it is described in the following manner:

> In changeable harmonious multiplicities of experience I experience others as actually existing and, on the one hand, as world Objects—not as mere physical things belonging to Nature, though indeed as such things in respect of one side of them ... I experience them at the same time as *subjects for this world*, as

experiencing it (this same world that I experience) and, in so doing, experiencing me too, even as I experience the world and others in it....

... I *experience* the world (including others) ... as other than mine alone [*mir fremde*], as an *intersubjective* world, actually there for everyone, accessible in respect of its Objects to everyone. And yet each has his experiences, his appearances and appearance-unities, his world-phenomenon ...
§43, p 91.

What the above means is that the following selection of phenomena is taken into account. Husserl believed that the following five points are most basic in our understanding of ourselves in relation to others and they to us:

1. In empathy there is the understanding that there is a transposability of perspective. If two people are looking at the same vase, the one understands that the other has a different perspective on it. In empathy, one person understands that two or more people each have "appresentations," additions of senses, one to the other. It is also the case that the other may well understand that others have a different perspective concerning the same vase. When self empathises other, self realises they are persons who are like self in a fundamental manner.

2. Consequently, it is assumed that persons participate in one world, co-constituting its meanings and objectivities. Empathy would be better called "co-empathy".

3. Mutuality and reciprocity exist with respect to the appresentations of co-empathy, because empathy is a two-way communion, a connection between people.

4. Consequently, there is a single world of shared appresentations of the local cultural-world senses to objects, at a fundamental level. This position does not deny ethnocentricity and racism, but is a claim that even hatred and discrimination are communicable through our fundamental transpersonal humanity.

5. Through the mutual addition and transposability of senses is constituted the natural attitude. At the natural attitude level, the ordinary ontic level of understanding, each individual person has their own individual perspective and an illusion of privacy and separation from each other and the world. This last point could be called a 'false sense of alienation'. It is false because people are enjoined in an all-embracing mutuality and inter-mixing that occurs through their com-

mon psychophysical Nature. Human beings are complex inter-relations of consciousness, intersubjective actuality in consciousness, history and physical nature[8] (De Boer, 1978, p 458).

The transcendental reduction requires setting aside the usual senses of the presumed received wisdom about others and human nature: "But in the case of *our* abstraction the sense "Objective," which belongs to everything worldly—as constituted intersubjectively, as experienceable by everyone, and so forth—*vanishes completely*," (Husserl, 1977b, §44, p 96). There is an alleged rejection of language (§44, p 95, §48, p 106) in order to attend to pre-intersubjective non-verbal senses, like in meditation, with the aim of comparing that to fully public meanings as in the usual case. Attention turns to the psychophysical Nature only of what appears of oneself, as an example of human beings in general and their social contexts. What remained, for Husserl, is the direct seeing of the essences of automatic and non-egoic syntheses by which consciousness creates meaning and spans time (§51, pp. 112-3). Also it appears that the empathic senses that were constituted for the first time in infancy remain as accessible sources of their ongoing future additions to the perceived bodies of others (§44, p 93).

Husserl's philosophical process started with our everyday experiences of empathy, as in the five points noted above (§43, p 91). By means of the transcendental reduction, it is alleged that an absolute sphere of immanent seeing is produced, in which it is possible to see essences of the constitution of the sense of others, self and the intersubjective constitution of forms of meaning. The psychophysical Nature of one's living body itself is revealed only after the transcendental reduction as …

> … a kind of "world" still, a Nature reduced to what is included in our ownness and, as having its place in this Nature thanks to the bodily organism, the psychophysical Ego, with "body and soul" and personal Ego—utterly unique members of this reduced "world".
> §44, p 98.

What the above means is that pre-intersubjective human Nature is still a world of sorts, evident by attention to our own living bodiliness and that of others in spacial connection with us, and the way in which meanings are apparent to all.

There are three processes of constitution at the heart of the creation of the sense of the other. First, there is a primal institution of the first-ever empathic sense of another person. This happens during infancy. Primal institution is the first-ever successful learning of an object's meaning. Within such a process there

is a first-ever pairing of categories of associated senses and a first-ever appresentation of the cultural sense onto the cultural object. For instance, primal institution
occurs in an example where a child visually perceives inanimate things and learns
to understand them over a period of time.

> ... objects given beforehand ... the already-given everyday world
> ... in which we understand their sense and its horizons forth-
> with, points back to a *"primal instituting,"* in which an object
> with a similar sense became constituted for the first time ... for
> the first time the final [use-] sense of scissors [occurs]; and from
> now on he sees scissors at the first glance *as* scissors.
> §50, p 111.

So it is claimed that a primal institution of the first sense of any object, or the first
sense of another human being, involves the creation of basic categories of the
experience of objects. These first senses are up-dated with new ones across time.

Husserl concluded that the primal institution of an object's sense occurs
through two other allied involuntary processes. The first and future attainments
of any objects' senses require these two processes. For there to be an understanding that the adult carers of the infant are human, the infant has to be able to constitute the sense of itself and the sense of the other. This occurs through "pairing"
and is a general process of the constitution of senses, not just those concerning
the constitution of the senses "self" and "others" (§ 44, p 98). Generally, pairing
is a cognitive-affective process of the constitution of basic categories of meaning
and the on-going attainment and refinement of such experience.

The term "pairing" was a general finding from Husserl's analysis of experience. It applies to the creation of many categories of sameness and difference in
experience. The specific categories "self" and "other" have a pivotal role in the
creation and maintenance of categories of higher intellectual understanding.

> Pairing is a *primal form of that passive synthesis* which we designate
> as *"association"* ... In a *pairing association* the characteristic fea-
> ture is that, in the most primitive case, two data are given intu-
> itionally, and with prominence, in the unity of a consciousness
> and that ... as data appearing with mutual distinctness, they
> *found phenomenologically a unity of similarity* and thus are always
> constituted precisely as a pair.
> §51, p 112.

Husserl started from the position that we are linked to others through empathic syntheses that literally constitute the presence of the other, in a complex manner, within ourselves. From the evidence of his direct experiencing he argued that what exists in ourselves is a vicarious experience whereby the mind of the other, which is never present to us, quasi-appears as though it is present. Part of this process incurs repeated appresentations from self to others and then the retention of the sense of the other into self. However, the third simultaneous synthesis is appresentation, the addition of senses when the perceptual object appears within lived experience. What enables this to take place is the recognition of fundamental similarity between self and others, which are based on the recognition that both self and other, are a psychosomatic unity of meaning and felt-sense. This adding occurs in a similar manner to that in which we experience external objects in three dimensions, instead of just two: When we look at a cup, although we do not see its oblique sides or its rear, such views are appresented to the front view that we do see.

Furthermore, pairing occurs for consciousness. The cognitive-affective processes of each person's mind are assumed to function in a similar manner. It is mutual and reciprocal in joining people together (§55, p 122). The initial and continued recognition of similarity that occurs, between two or more human beings, is a form of the seeing the category: "we are human and both have a unified mind-and-living-body". What is seen as the bodies of others are given the sense of lived bodies and living consciousness, over there. This process happens for all persons. Others employ the same processes. The three processes of synthesis are claimed to be the most fundamental processes for empathy and intersubjectivity to exist as they do. It is because of the primal institution of sense, the pairing and on-going appresentation and retention of experience that any recognition occurs. What accrues is the universal co-constitution of the senses of self and other within humanity. In 1929 Husserl was confident that the common human bodily form was at the root of creating publicly accessible meaning and the shared sense of others as understandable.

> It is clear from the very beginning that only a similarity connecting, within my primordial sphere, that body over there with my body can serve as the motivational basis for the *"analogizing" apprehension* of that body as another animate organism.
> §50, p 111.

Husserl's studies tried to lay aside natural-attitude cultural assumptions. His thought experiments led him to believe that this process involved the mutual and simultaneous appresentation of empathic meaning constituted through one's past. Consequently, others are felt to be living persons, "like me", but "over there", (§54, pp. 118-9). He concluded that because of human beings' apperception of themselves as a unity of consciousness, their living bodiliness and their physical bodiliness, they understand the physical bodies of others by immediately adding to them the sense of one's own unity. After such an addition, the other is felt to be other because they are physically over there and not "me here". This continuing transfer and accrual of meaning constitutes the sense of self, other and intersubjective connection. The other is a target for projections of passive, non-conscious processes, whereby self experiences become given to the other (§53, p 117). As a consequence in the natural attitude, a constituted experience comprised of the previous processes, the other is felt to have the being-sense of an existent person. The other is empathised as having their perspective There where they are. Their bodiliness indicates that they are another self and reciprocity and mutuality apply.

> ... as we find on closer examination, I apperceive him as having spatial modes of appearance like those I should have if I should go over there and be where he is. Furthermore the Other is appresentatively apperceived as the "Ego" of a primordial world, and of a monad, wherein his animate organism is originally constituted and experienced in the mode of the absolute Here, precisely as the functional center for his governing. In this appresentation, therefore, the body in the mode *There*, which presents itself in *my* monadic sphere and is apperceived as another's live body (the animate organism of the alter ego)—that body indicates "the same" body in the mode *Here*, as the body experienced by the other ego in *his* monadic sphere. Moreover it indicates the "same" body concretely, with all the constitutive intentionality pertaining to this mode of givenness in the other's experience.
> Ibid.

The presence of the physical bodies of people act as unities that maintain the public phenomenon of meaning that is retained by each individual. Each meeting with another is part of an overall learning experience, through which the individual gets to learn about the shared cultural world in all its details and complexity. Therefore, we are mutual targets and the bearers of meaning for each other, of the temporal accumulation of empathic objectivity and other kinds of higher intellectual sense. Thus, in a further twist, the realisation that we all have the same unified psychosomatic existence, becomes the basis for the establishment of other forms of objectivity and meaning.

> It is quite comprehensible that, *as a further consequence*, an "empathizing" of definite contents belonging to the "*higher psychic sphere*" arises. Such contents too are indicated somatically and in the conduct of the organism toward the outside world—for example: as the outward conduct of someone who is angry or cheerful, which I easily understand from my own conduct under similar circumstances. Higher psychic occurrences, diverse as they are and familiar as they have become, have furthermore their style of synthetic interconnexions and take their course in forms of their own, which I can understand associatively on the basis of my empirical familiarity with the style of my own life, as exemplifying roughly differentiated typical forms. In this sphere, moreover, every successful understanding of what occurs in others has the effect of opening up new associations and new possibilities of understanding; and conversely, since every pairing association is reciprocal, every such understanding uncovers my own psychic life in its similarity and difference and, by bringing new features into prominence, makes it fruitful for new associations.
> §54, p 120.

The above refers to how specific contents of the everyday world arise through conditions of possibility that constitute codes of conduct and communication in culture and society. Husserl is claiming to have shown that through his analysis of the living body, it indicates how the social body also operates. The importance of empathy for phenomenology, and the sciences to be founded on it, is that empathy is mediated through our understanding of the signs, sounds, movements and gestures of the bodies of others. That which we experienced as infants, acts as a template for on-going social learning throughout the lifespan. Therefore, habit and automatic processes build up immediate expectations and abilities of recognition[9].

The bodily presence of others throughout life acts as a sign for the retained, accumulating associations and references of the sense of otherness, that accrue in each consciousness in constituting a collective sense of memories and meanings. We do not immediately transfer our sense to others, but they invoke in us the sense of our own retained or imagined having been where they are, which also adds to prior pairing and appresentation (p 118).

Thus the totality of the actual social world is constituted and retained by egos and consciousness. From the immanent processes of each individual arise the beginnings of meaning and forms of intersubjectivity that are mediated communally (p 119). The cultural senses, the public meanings of a group, are based on the continual holding of a shared sense of human being:

> The first thing constituted in the form of community, and the *foundation for all other intersubjectively common things*, is the *commonness of Nature*, along with that of the *Other's organism* and *his psychophysical Ego*, as paired with my own psychophysical Ego. §55, p 120.

It is through the primal institution, the pairing of self and other, and the continued connection between self and other that cultural senses may pass in transmission from one person to another. It is also the case that thing-constitution, the constitution of a cultural sense to a cultural inanimate object, is not more fundamental than the empathic constitution of the senses "animal" or "human", (§61, p 145).

Consequently, when Husserl asked 'what are the primordial, conditioning experiences for objectivity to exist?' His answer was that our link with the other is the first and most fundamental objectivity. Accordingly, there is no solipsism but an intersubjective creation of common objectivities and meanings. Empathy, the vicarious feelings and responses in self, is part of an intersubjective co-constitution of the shared experience of the same objects in one, fundamental cultural world. This overall process has come to be known as transcendental intersubjectivity—the exploration of the conditions of possibility of the intersubjective constitution of meaning with others in the world. Through his exceedingly complex and condensed presentation, Husserl claimed that his analysis demonstrated the necessary conditions of intersubjective nature that are necessary for the establishment, and any possible agreement about, any objective meaning. A theme which was present at least as early as 1912 (1980, §1, pp. 1-2). The consciousness of other persons is a mediated presence, indicated through their speech, movement, bodiliness and gestures.

The absence of the other

The strongest implication that arises from an understanding of Husserl's approach in the *Fifth Cartesian Meditation* is that the perspective presented there spans the categories that currently exist in the behavioural sciences between social learning theory, psychoanalysis and developmental theories. Husserl asked 'precisely how does it happen that we are both apparently in contact with the feelings of others and yet never so?' Following Descartes, Husserl stated not I think therefore I am, but 'because of primal institution, pairing and appresentation I am in a shared cultural world'. Husserl answered that even though we never have the contents of their minds directly given to us, as we have the lived contents of our minds given to us, it is still the case that we can understand others. From time to time such an understanding may be accurate. For Husserl, it is the case that the inter-action between absolute consciousness, the other and the cultural content co-constitutes the world-sense that surrounds experience[10].

Phenomenology, as pre-science and pre-philosophy, rules out logical argumentation alone as being an overly assumptive model for the justification of knowledge. It also abandons the assumption that knowledge is somehow separate from mere experience, or distant from the presence of others. On the contrary, through primal institution and pairing in early life, intersubjective, intellectual and other forms of knowledge are based on appresented senses. Such learning may be accurate or inaccurate, according to one's perspective. Husserl's theory of empathy formulates how the social construction of meaning occurs.

Phenomenology is an attempt to set aside assumptions in the hope of finding the common invariant aspects of how meaning is made in the world. What remains after such an attempt is that the pure flux of conscious awareness has an intersubjective sense given through appresentation and retention of earlier perceptions and experiences, through learning (1977b, §44, p 94, §48, p 105). Also, the recognition of the sense of self co-exists with the recognition of otherness in pairing. Husserl argued that intersubjective syntheses are the most basic condition for the co-constitution of an objective shared world, because the constitution of the world is a shared process of accumulating evidence to which people contribute and are shaped by what they create. This sharing occurs in pervasive, simultaneous syntheses of empathy that are the mutual transfer and addition of a primordial sense of otherness to others. On the basis of empathy occurs the co-constitution of objects having social meanings, whereby culture and history accrue through time. In short, our experiences of the world, and everything in it, are grounded on empathy, according to Husserl (Bernet, Kern and Marbach, 1993, pp. 7, 165).

But in the *Fifth Cartesian Meditation,* Husserl recorded some conclusions rather than providing his workings. Also, the type of theory is one that is directly comparable to a psychodynamic image of consciousness. His theory included the connections of the appresentation (projection) and retention (introjection) to habituation and social learning. Indeed, there are a number of similarities between Husserl and Freud. Both claimed to have been able to find the definitive characteristics of the acts and syntheses of consciousness. Freud worked on the processes of transference, projection, defence and so forth. Both were engaged in the qualitative clarification of experience.

Of course, there are many more complex, higher combinations of empathic syntheses and acts of the ego based on them. For instance, our inner creation and participation in the inner lives of others may or may not be validated by them. Self can empathise with another's empathising. Being a citizen in society is related to empathy, expectation and habituation, which are complex syntheses, as are changes in the types of relationships that people have throughout the lifespan[11]. It is also the case that Husserl's theory of empathy is a theory of how we come to have culture and cultural senses that are accessible to all, or at least potentially open.

Husserl felt that the type of argument that he provided in the *Fifth Meditation* was the answer to understanding the manner in which consciousness and meaning are both public and private, immanent and transcendent. Like a moebius strip, the apparent transcendence of public meaning also holds for the individual—and what is individual is often understandable publicly[12]. Husserl and Heidegger also expressed this perspective in terms of the world. For Husserl, the cultural world or cultural context is that which is immanent and projected out in understanding any specific cultural object. It is also that which surrounds experience as an ultimate context, one that constrains that which can be understood within the context (Trân, 1986, p 35). In the *Fifth Meditation,* Husserl's answer is that the transcendence of the cultural world becomes retained in the immanence and transcendence of consciousness, through the lifelong learning of meaning that is based on the fundamental role of understanding the feelings and motives of others' bodies. If it were not for our ability to make feelings "for" others and attribute others with a consciousness "like ours," then there would not be any understanding as human beings have it. Like Descartes, Husserl implied that this is an evident truth. It is not because I think that I am. We understand and exist in a meaningful world as we do because of primal institution, pairing and appresentation that are continually up-dated with new appresentations from others.

The obscured emphasis of the original perspective

The impact of pure psychology has been small during the twentieth century. The approach of grounding psychology has many thought-provoking points to offer contemporary workers. The manner of arguing and consideration of evidence contains the features of psychodynamic cognitive-affective processes. Husserl argued that there are automatic tacit processes in the occurrence of our senses of other persons. Such a first-ever learning happens first of all as an infant and is extended throughout the lifespan. Ultimately, the senses we have of other persons are regarded as social learning that becomes more refined throughout the lifespan. Husserl's theorising includes the perspective that the meaning of the behaviour of others is an achievement of habits of cognitive-affective processes. The contemporary implications of this perspective are that it may be possible to connect disparate perspectives in cognitive science, developmental psychology and the history and philosophy of psychology in order to progress with a fuller understanding of the persons whom the researcher meets and the theoretician idealises.

The feelings we have about other people may not always be the focus of conscious attention. Yet in conversations and close proximity to other people, more often than not, they appear to be in a mood of some sort. They may look deep in thought or vacant, happy or distressed. So much is often obvious. But we may not know how we know this. This paper has set aside the relevant answers made by Mead and Freud as regards the sense of other people for the purpose of concentrating on Husserl's approach. The omission of the manner of creating the sense of the other is a most pertinent one, considering that we are not alone in the world.

Two other pertinent implications arise. Firstly, there has been much mention of the self and theorizing about the ego in relation to the unconscious. But if there is to be a justifiable theory of psychology, might it not be best to start with what is given in our experience of other people? According to phenomenology, in order to build theories that can guide practice, it is better to start with direct experience, rather than to start with conceptual assumptions. Secondly, if there is no agreed theory of how we experience the other, in the culture in which we participate, there is room for error because knowledge and argumentation concerning how to treat others is built on assumption. Such knowledge is not justified and argued from consensually-agreed experience. Accordingly, the paper turned to the major significance of empathy and intersubjectivity, with the aim of showing how apparent phenomena have a hidden constitution.

Practical conclusion: One example

This final section makes some comments about the contemporary situation of justifying theories and claims to psychological knowledge by empirical research. A particular area of therapy research is chosen to illustrate the differences between a grounded pure psychological approach—and the standard natural scientific approach. The history of therapy research has been dominated by natural psychological science. Currently, there is a move towards adopting empirical methods to base theoretical practice and inform therapeutic decision-making within sessions. However, within such a turn, where is the consideration of the other as a basis for such theorising and justification? Empirical justification is an attempt at making important decisions for the future of the profession, but without a clear view of how we understand others and culture, without having an agreed understanding of the overall context for how we make such justifications. It is precisely the role of phenomenology to understand the context for thinking and reasoning, as it is a fundamental analysis of meaning, as indicated above.

The major difference between the clarification of experience and the empirical forms of psychology, including some of the qualitative approaches, is the nature of the phenomena for phenomenology. This is also the case for therapy and areas like personality theory where the phenomena are not measurable. What is not measurable, what is not observable by raters, cannot be subject to statistics and cannot be considered by natural scientific psychology. The discrepancy between phenomenology, therapy and personality theory, on the one hand; and natural psychological science, on the other, can be made more evident in the following example.

Natural psychological science, whether discourse analysis or an experimental approach, only begins with observable events, whether on audiotape, videotape or through direct observation. For the natural psychological scientist, there must be something observable in the behaviour, actions and words of the participants.

For phenomenology, therapy and personality theory, the basis of evidence is the sense of self and the sense of the other, in self, or between self and other. But such senses are not available to the type of observation and measurement that natural psychological science uses. For natural psychological science, the sense of self, ego, and the empathised sense of the other, our feeling that we know the other, is not genuine data and cannot be a part of its science.

But on the contrary, the genuine data for phenomenology, therapy and personality theory is that which is immanent, of oneself, and potentially not at all apparent to anyone else unless they are having similarly describable experiences.

This leads to a tangle of problems of different varieties. There are theoretical and practical problems in how to consider the most basic types of evidence. Phenomenology, therapy and personality theory prefer feeling, insight and empathy for their data. There are research problems, because the prima facie types of evidence are not agreed and neither is any means of concluding from them. This means that the creation and use of psychological science has no place of consensus within its broad field of differing approaches. Such a lack of consensus renders the drive to conclude on empathic evidence problematic (Roth and Fonagy, 1986, Bohart, O'Hara and Leitner, 1998, Elliott, 1998).

But, since the beginnings of evidence-based practice, theorising and clinical audit are formative in therapy practice, it would be prudent to have a consensually-agreed model of how to understand and practice. It would be preferable to have psychological theories that are based on what is given rather than unjustified conceptual assumptions and ontological prejudice. It would be ethical to demonstrate to clients, if necessary, and to other professions, how we justify our understanding of clients and ground our responses, generally.

Husserl's philosophy of psychology was focused on finding the processes of the mind by analysing what appears. For him, if we cannot account for how we understand the other, we cannot justify a theory concerning human behaviour or create justifications for how to act in sessions. According to Husserl's phenomenology, there are significant sins of omission from psychology because the fundamental processes through which we experience other people are tacit. Husserl worked on this particular point from 1905 until his death in 1938 (Husserl, 1973b, 1973c, 1973d). In Husserl's terminology, empathy is a "passive synthesis," an involuntary automatic and rapid cognitive-affective process of consciousness based on the recognition of a fundamental similarity functioning without the conscious action of the ego.

In conclusion, there are many problems and paradoxical questions that could be asked about Husserl's phenomenology and how it is relevant in informing the debate about what can be counted as evidence in psychology, the behavioural and human sciences. There is still much work to be done in applying Husserl's pure philosophy and psychology in these worlds.

Notes

1. I have not found any coherent theory of how we experience other people in PsycLIT, The Philosophers Index, Sociological Abstracts and the Psychological Bulletin. The small number of entries on the sense of other persons on the PsycLIT database includes contributions by Drüe, (1963), Fluckiger and Sullivan, (1965), Hunsdahl, (1967), Carr, (1973) and Jennings, (1986). Sokolowski's work, although authoritative and a simple to read overview of Husserl, has surprisingly little to say about the importance of empathy as world-constituting and meaning-constituting (2000).

2. The first writers on empathy include Paul Stern (1898) and Theodore Lipps (1893, 1903a, 1903b, 1907). A notable contribution was from Max Scheler of which the second revised edition was translated as *The Nature of Sympathy* (1954).

3. This original work deals with the role of the body in relation to philosophy, psychology and ontology (Husserl, 1980, Supplement I, §1, pp. 94-8). However, the particular research text included there is only a conclusion. The detailed working behind that conclusion is omitted. In 1913 in "*Ideas I,*" we find comments that précis the work that had been done on empathy so far (1982, §151, p 363). In 1915 in *Ideas II*, we find another approach to empathy, but the problem of understanding the whole now becomes diluted because the comments made in this collection of papers are diffuse (1989, §51, p 208).

4. The text that became the *Meditations* was first presented as two lectures at the Sorbonne in 1929 (Husserl, 1975). The translation of the *Fifth Cartesian Meditation*, (1977b, §§42-62) is currently the most mature English translation.

5. To understand Husserl's work on empathy and intersubjectivity, it is necessary to know about his analysis of the acts and syntheses of consciousness. Husserl's understanding of the acts of consciousness begins with his distinction that perception in the five senses is the most basic form of presentation: One where perceptual objects are regarded as current and actually existing. But there are other types of givenness. Husserl's analyses of memory, imagination and the semiosis of visual art revealed that their essence concerns the presentation of prior perceptions. He argued that these acts re-present, "presentiate," an object that is either not currently present, or may not potentially have ever existed. See Eduard Marbach (1993). Presentations are a group of processes within consciousness that re-present an absence. In recollection (active long-term memory) we remember

what is not currently present but which was once so. In imagination we create something that is not currently present, may never have been or may never be. In empathy we create the sense of the other's feelings, thoughts, motivations and intentions, although we never experience the contents of their minds and bodily sensation. Another form of presentation is called "appresentation" the addition of meanings and senses to what appears. Appresentation is a central theme in phenomenology that is barely acknowledged except by Gurwitsch (1974). Husserl's clearest presentation of appresentation is in *Phenomenological Psychology* (1977a, §16).

6. The term "object" is an opaque one in Husserl. It is a general term and claimed to be ontologically and ethically neutral. When it is applied to other people, it does not reify or objectify them. Rather, what it means is a general term for the recognisable pattern, meaning or perceptual sense that appears. Also, some objects are discreet items such as a book, or the silhouette of a book. Others are abstract: "society," "compassion". However, it is a basic ability of consciousness, that out of temporal and actual multiplicity, unities of sense occur (Husserl, 1991, Note 39, p 294).

The original German text of the *Fifth Meditation* also needs to be carefully considered in relation to the question of precisely what Husserl was describing and analysing. Some lines in the German original can be translated as follows (Husserl, 1950, §42, page 122, lines 23-28): "We ought to work for insight into the explicit and implicit intentionality, in which the other ego announces and proves itself on the basis of our transcendental ego, in the same way, in which processes create themselves in myself and the sense of the other proves itself under the headings of the other in unequivocal experiences as being in its way a self", (cf 1977b, §42, p 90). The same basic thought is expressed later, when Husserl returned to the same theme, (§44, page 127, lines 12-21): "We state in this context one important phenomenon. In the abstraction *remains for us a uniform correlated level of the phenomenon world*, of the transcendental correlates of the continually unequivocal progressing world experience. Despite our abstraction we can continually progress in the experiencing reflection", (cf 1977b, §44, p 96). The passages refer to the pre-intersubjective lived experience of selves that are the object of comparison.

7. Husserl alleged that the transcendental reduction enables phenomenologists to stand outside of themselves and the world, in order to see both clearly and the complex intentional relations between them through time. Husserl believed he could contemplate the natural attitude experiences of empathy, which are now

understood as accumulations through time, and possible sources for understanding the essences of empathic intentionality and the intersubjective constitution of objectivity (Bernet, Kern and Marbach, 1993, p 75). His concern was to understand the character of empathy and intersubjectivity by seeing and varying all possible aspects.

8. The term "animate organism" tries to reflect this concern. It is a translation of "*Leib*," living body. "Bodily organism" is a translation of "*körperlichen Leib*".

9. In this sense Husserl's conclusions on empathy agree with a general concept of psychodynamic transference. Transference for Husserl is inaccurate mis-empathy. It has an intersubjective component that is responsible for the mixture of self-fulfilling prophecy and evoking such behaviour in others, in confirming the prophecy.

10. Heidegger had a different view of empathy and took more of a contextual route to understanding how we constitute empathic feelings. To explain his perspective would take up a good deal of space. But briefly, because of human temporality and the overall context of the world, and through our nature of being pre-reflexively in contact with each other, we experience ourselves as already with others (Heidegger, 1996, §§13, 69). There are a few sparse details of his approach to the other in the summer lectures of 1927 (Heidegger, 1982, §20a, p 278).

11. A phenomenological understanding of empathy can be acquired by reading section 151 of *Ideas I* where, once more, Husserl provided an overview of his conclusions. The incomplete PhD thesis of Edith Stein, a supervisee of Husserl, and later his research assistant, laid out a Husserlian position in 1916 that psychological knowledge is based on empathy (Stein, 1989, §4, p 19). Stein went on to develop her own approach in her habilitation thesis of 1919 on psychological causality (published with Husserl's full approval, Stein, 1922). In all these remarks, it is important to bear in mind that for phenomenology, consciousness is both immanent and transcendent. If it were only immanent it would never be able to have access to the public cultural world nor have any awareness of inanimate objects (Husserl, 1999). There is little on empathy in the *Paris Lectures* where Husserl propounded an earlier stance. *Cartesian Meditations* is perhaps one of the most definitive Husserlian texts but it is very condensed and contains many interpretative ambiguities that can only be overcome through attending to the clarifications made by the Directors of the *Husserl Archives* (Bernet, Kern and

Marbach, 1993, p 159, Ströker, 1993, pp. 130-1). Unfortunately, Husserl confused his method in *Cartesian Meditations*, something that he only later realised. For instance, after seemingly indicating that the transcendental reduction focuses only on an ego (1977b, §44, p 96, p 98, §47, p 104, §58, p 134 and §61, p 146); he explained himself that the reduction reveals the presence of the sense of self, otherness and world (§44, p 93, §44, p 94, p 98, §45, p 100 and §51, p 112). Despite this, it is possible to recreate a Husserlian position that corrects this confusion.

12. A moebius strip is a three-dimensional strip of paper with a number of twists in it. When a strip of paper is twisted once, the resultant surface has only one side.

5

The special hermeneutic of empathy

This paper takes some introductory steps in the direction of sketching the major theme of empathy in Husserl and Heidegger's phenomenologies. A great deal could be written about these subjects. The paper briefly recaps Husserl's position and uses it as an entrée for a presentation of Heidegger's answer in *Being and Time*. The title of this paper is taken from Heidegger's call for a "special hermeneutic" of empathy which will offset the illusions of separation between human minds and "will have to show how the various possibilities of being of Da-sein themselves mislead and obstruct being-with-one-another and its self-knowledge, so that a genuine "understanding" is suppressed and Da-sein takes refuge in surrogates", (Heidegger, 1996, §26, p 117). What this means is grounding of the empirical practice and theory of therapy and the human sciences, in an understanding of empathy that is close to the phenomena as they appear after a reduction of previous ontological beliefs and conceptualisations. Other relevant writers are omitted to make a focus specifically on Heidegger's phenomenology and ascertain what such an approach to empathy would be like.

If we believe that therapists' relations to clients are the most important practical aspect then it should follow that our theorising should reflect this central attention. Setting aside ethics as one place where this attention is defined in global guidelines and turning to the theories that define practice. Then it is claimed that there is an insufficient attention concerning how to behave and think towards the public. A couple of theories mention empathy in passing but do not have any account of it that functions cohesively as a basis for their actions with respect to others. The phenomenological philosophies of Husserl and Heidegger supply an empathic basis for making such a sufficient attention in therapy, psychological research and the human sciences. From the establishment of a theory concerning how we understand others, have experiences of them and relate toward them, it is possible to connect with an understanding of ethics and progress to other aspects of the complex ways of making decisions about how to intervene and meet with them.

In order to organise the flow of argument in the paper, four sections have been devised in order to take the reader through the steps that led Heidegger to formulate his answer to the problem of empathy, also called the problem of other minds. The problem concerns how we constitute feelings about other people. In everyday life, we do have feelings about others. We find that, generally, other people are understandable. More often than not, we find that we can fairly accurately understand when another is sad or happy. But simultaneously with such experiences, on the one hand, we never have access to the minds of others. If we do not believe in telepathy, then there must be some means of being able to understand how others feel and have potentially accurate experiences about them. On the other hand, we never feel the other's pain nor have the experience of the colour blue as the other actually experiences it.

Therefore, philosophical, ethical and practical problems arise if theories and beliefs about ourselves in connection with others are incorrect. If we do not know with agreed justifications about how to act in the therapy situation, then it could be argued that we should not be acting in it at all. The value of finding a solution to the problem of empathy is beginning to create an agreed basic context of analyses in the human sciences and the allied professions. Therapy is particularly an area where a grounded and agreed application of basic psychological knowledge would help.

Empathy and the problem of other minds

Phenomenology grounds conceptualisation and justification in philosophy and the sciences. It is a pre-science or a pre-philosophy. Phenomenology concerns itself with fundamentals in the crossover from lived experience to knowledge claims in speech and language (Bernet, Kern and Marbach, 1993, Heidegger, 1996, §33, pp. 146-150, §69b, pp. 327-333).

The practical point of discussing empathy is that conclusions about the views of client, therapist or researcher, are closely related to the initial view of practice and research findings (Husserl, 1981a, p 192, Heidegger, 1996, §69b, pp. 327-8). Kant, Husserl and Heidegger would agree that initial understanding occurs in perceptions and empathies of others. If there is to be a conceptual consensus that brings part of the field of practitioners together, there should be discussion of justifications concerning *how* we understand other people and *how* we address ourselves to their understanding of their personal world.

Empathy arrives in the English language to translate the German word *Ein-füblung* which itself was derived from the Greek *empathiea* that means to feel into the consciousness of another person, animal or understand a work of art[1]. At the natural level, empathy is assumed to be an emotional or intellectual knowledge of the other. A second assumption is that knowing the minds of others is an easy capability of the sort that can be explored and measured by the natural science approach. This is not the case for phenomenology. The problem with many therapies is that they implicitly or explicitly assume telepathy or confuse perception with empathy. The mystery is that we never have direct experience of the mind, thoughts, feelings or motivations of others. Yet we often feel that we do. So how does the empathic sense of the other become accessible to ourselves?

Husserl's early statement of the problematic

The primary research question that Husserl's phenomenology focused on was the theorising of empathy that is considered as being constitutive of a shared human world of culture and meaning. Husserl's early work on the problem of empathy, as evidenced by his writings of 1912, was that he had been able to decide that there are major differences for the three standpoints of the (1) natural attitude, (2) the reflective attitude of phenomenology, and (3), the pre-reflective[2] experience on which both the natural attitude and reflective attitude are based. For natural psychological science and non-phenomenological approaches, our feelings about other people are there as facts and are nothing to be concerned about. After a reduction, reflection on the way in which consciousness must constitute our senses of other people begins. In 1912 Husserl believed that the other's living body is empathised as the carrier of sensations and acts. It is their animated body that carries the meaning of the other for oneself as a person in a surrounding world. The other "pure Ego has its *surrounding world*, has its *Here* and *Now* in relation to which its physicalness is oriented … its animate organism, in a way similar to that in which *my* Here and Now is related to *my* animate organism", (Husserl, 1980, Supplement I, §1, p 94).

However, what is most important to bear in mind is that the "Objectivity of one's own psyche presupposes mutual understanding", (p 98). This phrase means that even before reflection or awareness of any kind begins, there is an immediate mutual and pre-reflective understanding of the other for, or within, oneself. This presence occurs before becoming aware of any specific experience about others and one's relation to them. Shared meanings are "intersubjectively graspable … through the only possible medium of mutual understanding, through animate organicity," born of the lived body of oneself and the other (§2, p 101). The meaning of the other in self-presence, before any specific attention is turned to any aspect of another, actual person, is relevant to Heidegger's solution to the problem of other minds. Husserl's position is that "psychic reality is founded in the organismal matter," the living bodily material (§4, p 104). This means that bodiliness is the medium of showing interest in the shared world.

Seventeen years later, Husserl still held that we never have direct access to the consciousness of others, but the way we constitute this sense arises within infancy (1977b, *The Fifth Cartesian Meditation*). Husserl argued that a first constitution of the sense of another occurs when the infant adds their unified sense of themselves to another human being for the first time (§50, p 111). Meanings occur through a "primal institution" of their sense. Primal institution is the first-ever achievement of the sense of another person as a human being with an immanent life-stream of consciousness "like me". In all later life, variegated senses of specific others occur by still being able to experience the primal institution of the infant's sense of the first other. Therefore, in adult life we empathise other persons to be human beings like ourselves due to social learning. This fundamental sense of otherness is claimed to arise involuntarily within each person's consciousness and enables cultural and intellectual meaning to occur.

Husserl claimed in the *Fifth Meditation* to demonstrate how we constitute the everyday sense we have of others by deriving it from within our own consciousness. He analysed the way in which involuntary processes of consciousness constitute the sense that specific others are live human beings. The method denies that straightforward argument is sufficient for a fundamental grounding of concepts. Husserl claimed a method that requires philosophers and scientists to return to consciousness and begin theorising the intentionality in relation to objects that appears to oneself. Husserl believed that phenomenologists should see and describe the invariant aspects of the conditions of possibility for consciousness and its objects. Husserl's concern was to make qualitative-philosophical reflections on our experience with others, concerning some of its definitive qualities and instances. Readers may like to try this for themselves[3].

Heidegger's position on empathy within a meaningful world

Existential and phenomenologically-oriented therapists use their understanding of Heidegger's early work to shine some light on how to justify an approach to practising and thinking in a fundamental manner. The way of reading *Being and Time* below is that the work is seen as journeying, exploring and deepening the themes that Heidegger investigated as the text progresses. *Being and Time* covers all manner of topics and several readings of it could be justified by careful argumentation. The one preferred here takes into account a small number of its sections as central. Division One provides direction and purpose, but it is Division Two where the main philosophical focus takes place.

The specific sections that found the basis for the particular conclusion about Heidegger's view of the constitution of the innerworldly meaning of being are those sections concerning the world (Heidegger, 1996, §13) and the constitution of inner worldly beings in a human world or cultural context[4] (§69). The semiotic examples of signs, references and the examples of the place of the total set of signs (§17, §18) are very telling. But it is specifically section 69 that is argued to be the most important section in *Being and Time* for understanding the contextualising the frame of the world in how it supplies references of meaning in a prereflexive manner. In terms of making sense of the commitment to a special hermeneutic of empathy, what is clear is that it involves de-construction or destruction, a reduction in a limited sense, before a new construction.

The examples that Heidegger provided in *Being and Time* are revealing. The examples of the analysis of the being of signs as indicative of the relation between Da-sein and its world, such as the car indicator, show that these signs make sense within the overall context for road users. With this remark, Heidegger stated a key principle that *specific objects make sense within the context of a tacit understanding of the whole*. This understanding is predicated on the nature of Da-sein and the being of the sign together (§17, §18). For instance, the experience of choosing a hammer is discussed as a totality of the use of the felt-sense of a specific hammer in comparison to experiences of using other hammers. Such an automatic, pre-reflexive subliminal presence reveals the difference between the full set of experiences of the usefulness of a hammer vis a vis past experiences of hammers and other tools[5] (§15, pp. 64-5, §33, p 144-5, pp. 147-8, §69b, p 330).

Similarly to Husserl's philosophical and historical reductions, Heidegger also wished to remove incorrect understanding, yet acknowledged its formative power through the metaphor of the hermeneutic circle: A device that Heidegger used to introduce the formative place of prior and future temporal understanding in shaping what is interpreted-as in the present. For instance, "just as praxis has its own specific kind of sight ("theory"), theoretical investigation is not without its own praxis", (§69b, pp. 327-8): A statement that has many implications for therapeutic knowledge claims and daily living. The hermeneutic circle is also a context for the various understandings of human being[6].

Heidegger's phenomenology believes that Da-sein inevitably projects its faulty assumptions onto experience. Including those understandings and experiences that happen pre-reflexively, before higher thought has been able to verbalise what has been understood without words. In section 69 particularly, Heidegger laid out his ideas concerning how innerworldly being lies inside Da-sein's world (p 334). Either side of this remark he seemed to equate Da-sein with its world (pp. 333, 335). Da-sein has learned about its world that "arises from a retention that awaits; on the basis of such retention, or as such a "basis," Da-sein exists in a world", (p 326). However, the point about focusing on the constitution of the world, and the constituting effect of the sense of a world, is that the sections on other Da-sein are much more easily understood (§§25-27). Most of the impact about understanding other people, in relation to the question concerning how we understand others as having minds and feelings of their own (§26), is only understandable on the basis of realising the important role of the world. In section 26, there are several criticisms of Husserl's position on empathy. However, the world is pre-reflexive 'in' and 'for' Da-sein (pp. 111-2). Heidegger preferred an implicit reduction away from theorising to describe the pre-reflexive experience of sociality, which is the contrary to the natural attitude and natural science assumption of separation between human beings.

Heidegger's answer concerning empathy

How might we understand empathy when we have no access to the other's consciousness? Heidegger started from what appears and described how we find each other, in this particular case Da-sein's "being-with". Heidegger provided an answer to the problem of other minds when he commented that the assumed split between human being and its form of existence in a human world, the "subject-object split," is erroneous. The transcendence of Da-sein's being is such that it is able to have direct access to the being of other persons and the world (1982, §20a, p 275, 1996, §7c, p 33). At a surface level of the mind, and at the more fundamental level of the being of Da-sein, the immanence of "personal" experience is not separated from transcendent others or objects of the world. Thinking that there is a gap to be crossed is false.

For Heidegger, the experience commonly called "empathy" can be best described as meeting the other as one who is "encountered from the *world*", (§26, p 112). What this indicates is that ontologically human nature is such that: "Being-with existentially determines Da-sein even when an other is not factically present and received", (p 113). The aspect of Da-sein's being called "being-with-others" is a major ontological characteristic of human being (p 115). It occurs alongside our continued orientation in time and the associated attitudes for understanding: ""Empathy" does not first constitute being-with, but is first possible on its basis, and motivated by the prevailing modes of being-with in their inevitably", (p 117). Thus, Heidegger's position is that human being has such a nature that its being-with constitutes what we experience as empathic feelings about others (§§25, 26).

Heidegger refuted any claim concerning the nature of empathy that involved accounts of crossing a bridge between people, from self to the other. Following Heidegger, there is no separation between the inside and outside of an individual. Such a description is flawed. Consequently, we can see that Heidegger believed that the other is apprehended without any other intervening processes of introjection, interpretation of the other and the assumption that the other is "like me". The problem of the seeming opacity of other minds is a problem due to the variable ability to interpret the actions of others and begin understanding from the wrong starting place. This is exemplified in the mistaken, natural attitude tendency to see people as "individuals" who are capable of being understood in complete separation from their being, temporality, history and social context.

Another version of an ontological mistake is the detached attitude of those human scientists who claim to be objective and minimise their emotional contact with those whom they seek to understand. But how could they work without a pre-reflexive basis for understanding and contact? Another way of stating this is to write that conscious intersubjective experience of others is part of the full extent of human experience. Da-sein's being is being-with in relation to others. It has the potential to provide immediate experience of others, although there are times when this sense changes or fails. Empathy and psychological insight into self and other can occur or fail. However, the surface, everyday phenomena of empathy need to be carefully investigated in an involved self-aware manner, not a detached one. The basis for such a thorough contextualisation of any part of the totality of empathic life is the context of Da-sein's being as a totality (pp. 116-8).

There are several influential factors that Heidegger omitted from his description in section 26. Four sets of themes need to be acknowledged as the full context for the analysis, yet they did not form a precise presentation[7]. These are the themes of power and self-responsibility; the individual and the collective; authentic and inauthentic views of Da-sein; and the associated analysis of Da-sein's being-with as fallen, thrown and so forth. Heidegger did not pursue the way in which the dominating forms of relating, "leaping in," and their unsociability made a motivation for "empathy" and co-operation as possible occurrences. Da-sein's being empathic can only exist by being based on a more fundamental ontological nature of being-with. Although he did indicate that these other factors are involved. A continuum of power-relations lie between leaping in and leaping ahead, that act as motivations for surface effects.

Therapy examples: Counteracting the absence of the phenomenon of empathy

The problems that arise from insufficient understandings of the nature of empathy are seen in a variety of areas within therapy and the human sciences. No focus on the other at a pre-reflexive level means ignoring those who are the attention of therapy and the human sciences. This analysis could draw on many sources, but this paper only mentions three cases of psychodynamic and humanistic practice and quantitative empirical research.

Firstly, there are inconsistencies concerning the understanding of the other within the psychodynamic approach. Freud used the word *Einfühlung* in his writings to express the necessity of gaining good conscious rapport with clients at the beginning of therapy (Shaughnessy, 1995, Freud, 1913c). Shaughnessy claims that in Freud, empathy is an attempt of therapists to understand, in an emotional manner, the conscious feelings, thoughts and motivations of clients. This may involve therapists comparing their own empathic experience of clients with their own experience of themselves. The problem is that hypothesised unconscious to unconscious communication is the main area of focus for psychodynamic therapists: "everyone possesses in his own unconscious an instrument with which he can interpret the utterances of the unconscious of other people", (Freud, 1913i, p 320). On the one hand, there is conscious experience of the other, on the other hand, an alleged communication of an entirely different sort between the two persons? The question is how do the two understandings fit together?

One example of unconscious communication is in a paper by Beres and Arlow (1974). A paper quoted as a prime example of the verity of unconscious communication. It is supposed that unconscious communication might be causative or motivational for conscious communication of the constituted form of empathically being-aware of the emotional state of the other. Neither Freud nor Beres and Arlow specify how the emotional state of one person crosses over or becomes understood by the other. These writers describe conscious events allegedly concerning how their conscious thoughts and feelings become touched by the free associations of clients. So it is hypothesised that analysts are able to make sense of clients.

But the question concerning what form of communication passes between human beings is confused. Is empathy a feeling that moves from one person into the conscious mind of the other? Is empathy an ability to be open to one's own "unconscious" processes as they connect with the preconscious and then the conscious aspects of one's own consciousness? If it is the latter, then the nature of the unconscious communication is still not described but merely alleged to have occurred. Overall, it is not clear how psychodynamic therapists claim to have an experience of another's consciousness or to have converted unconscious aspects of their own unconscious into conscious experience.

Another case worthy of attention are the writings of Rogers who vacillates on the nature of empathy. At one point, there is a definition of empathy as the "as if" understanding of others. Empathy concerns having a conscious understanding of others but without having direct access to their feelings and motivations. The quality of this understanding is sensing "the client's private world ... but without ever losing the 'as if' quality" that oneself and the other are separate individuals (1957, p 99). But the sense of empathy is not, and can never be, the first-hand perception of the attitudes of the client (Ibid). Elsewhere, Rogers confused empathy with telepathy when he wrote that empathy is "entering the private perceptual world of the other and becoming thoroughly at home in it", (Rogers, 1975, p 4, see also Rogers, 1951, p 29). He could only have meant this figuratively, it could not be literally true. Later Rogers moved to another position on empathy:

> ... I am perhaps in a slightly altered state of consciousness, indwelling in the client's world, completely in tune with that world. My nonconscious intellect takes over. I [nonconsciously] know much more than my conscious mind is aware of. I do not form my responses consciously, they simply arise in me, from my nonconscious sensing of the world of the other.
> Rogers, 1986a, p 206.

The above is perhaps a better description of what occurs in having pre-reflexive experiences of other people and the description is made without hypotheses concerning unconscious processes, although it uses the term "nonconscious" to describe the type of becoming aware.

Thirdly, the absence of conceptualisations of empathy are noticeable in psychology, the empirical discipline that seeks to justify what are acceptable guidelines for practice. It is not clear in this case about the precise way in which feelings get across any notional gap between human beings where ostensibly, at a conscious level, it would appear that we each have separate minds and bodies. As there appears to be no empirical investigation about the transmission of empathy between human beings, then it is a wonder how the human sciences to exist. To repeat Husserl and Heidegger's view: If the human sciences cannot account for the specific processes by which we receive or create the senses of others throughout the lifespan, they have not begun in earnest.

The experience of empathy seems to be completely denied in "objective" and "scientific," psychology[8]. For instance, psychologists and psychiatrists who are influenced by natural science are taught to carry out interviews in a scientific and objective manner and lay aside their subjective feelings when gathering data in research projects. But, how are they to achieve their aims without acknowledging the experience of empathy? Insight and empathy barely feature in empirical psychology, yet surely they come before the use of statistics or a qualitative approach (Owen, 1997). Is it not the case that psychologists would agree that empathy and insight are two fundamental practical qualities that form the ground, or pre-reflexive experience, of understanding others before rating their actions? Surely, the empathic experiences come before the use of statistics or qualitative research? If raters cannot use insight and empathy and only employ "objectivity" to make their scores, then the process of attending to the participants in scientific research is not fully defined. However, if raters use insight into themselves, and empathy towards the other, then they are not being 'objective' in the required scientific manner.

Therefore, for the statistically-based approaches, it is something of a mystery as to how the alleged objectivity arises in psychological research. For an ontologically-grounded Heideggerian approach there is no mystery in these terms. It is part of the interpretation of the being of Da-sein to be-with others[9].

The centrality of empathy for therapy

In considering the points above, what can the reader take away for use in understanding how to practice? Firstly, the starting point for Husserl is that consciousness occurs within a surrounding context of intersubjectivity and other consciousness. The reciprocal actions of intersubjectivity are closely related to the constitution of the sense of empathy: the sense that we have of other persons in that we find others, more often than not, understandable.

Secondly, those experiences that are called "transference" and "counter-transference" are understandable as learned relationship habits, behaviours and anticipations that have been accrued over the years. Childhood events may lead to dispositions and attachment patterns that can be overcome through therapy. Adult trauma can also lead to adult, problematic attachment, anticipations and self-defeating behaviours.

Other psychological theories imply that people have a full merger with the other as in the Rogers (1975) example above and its ontological critique. Yet other theories operate from a position that what therapists consciously, or even unconsciously, think and feel about the shared relationship is far more important than what clients experience. Overall, therapy is in conceptual disarray and locked into beliefs without any consensually agreed justification. Possibly, the way to take therapy closer to the actuality of experience is to take it away from accepted notions of the self-contained, rational self, and consider the other as other within the context of empathy in society. Perhaps, these basic concepts are fundamental for ethical developments and effective practice.

There could be many ways in which therapy could be criticised and bettered. Such grounding by a philosophical approach would be to prepare for future empirical research of a new kind. The profession is an amalgam of approximately 400 recorded, formalised styles of making a professional relationship with persons in distress, who have problems with daily living and in their relationships to self and others (Karasu, 1986). Each one supplies its own set of meanings and assumptions about human being and the concomitant choices for action in the world. Each suggests and justifies specific ways of relating to others, thus inhibiting other types of relationship. In some cases, the degree of unhelpfulness, in allegedly helpful therapeutic relationships, can reach pathological proportions. Therapy could look at its own procedures for working, researching and agreeing theory by which to act, rather than building obscuring mythologies that are based on unagreed theory and evidence that has never been personally experienced. The multiple practices and professional discourses of therapy mainly refer to relationships that are claimed to provide a healing experience by facilitating insight, empathy and independence, reducing lacks of self-knowledge, inaccurate evidence-gathering and dependence on harmful or constricting ways of life. Therapy is not one discourse but a set of competing discourses that claim to be helpful. Could it be that therapy is confused and in need of some help from persons outside of its closed doors? If there are insufficient justifications and clear agreed knowledge for the practice of therapy, why should unproven, unagreed beliefs be practised with clients?

Traditional western philosophy prefers the armchair approach to the clarification of concepts and justifications before any empirical approach (Gorovitz et al, 1963). Phenomenology, in either the Husserlian or Heideggerian forms, should also take the armchair about what appears before empirical work of any sort. The phenomenological aim is to describe our relations to others and find out how, or whether, it is possible to ground a concept of empathy for further theorising of the relation between self and other in everyday and therapeutic experience. Phenomenology works to focus on fundamental concerns about the theorising of empathy and otherness in therapy. The problem is that the many theories, practices and means of justification that comprise this area have no shared agreement on the nature of empathy. Some theories do not mention the client, the other. Some explicitly want to manipulate the other into what is previously assumed to be psychological health. Most of these professionals claim they know others better than they know themselves. This occurs because the theories have a dogmatic belief in the suitability of their theory.

Drawing the pieces together, we have a direction towards a special hermeneutic of empathy that occurs experientially in meetings with others: Becoming aware of how self and other are empathic in a broad sense, with each other and other persons. What is brought to the situation are often the natural attitude assumptions of the factual being and interpretation of others: For instance, empirical assumptions, *DSM IV* classifications and stereotypes. But the various schools and specific professions have created images of humanity in traditional and institutionalised forms. What others have written comprises a closed world of signs about what exists about the being of others, the actual interpretation of clinical signs by one human being "over" another.

To invoke the form of Heideggerian analysis mentioned above, it would mean that a specific experience with a specific other person makes sense within the context of one's whole life experience. It follows that therapy concerns being able to make fine distinctions at an experiential level about intersubjective situations. Work and life experience contribute to experiential learning through the checking and refinement of empathic experiences throughout the lifespan. However, there is a type of intellectual ontological analysis with the special hermeneutic of empathy that would constitute an ontological critique of empathy in therapy and the human sciences.

Phenomenological therapy is structured by considering fundamental theoretical, ethical and practical considerations in the light of the above comments. An agreed conclusion would substantiate the claim that a concept of empathy can serve as a grounding, first principle for practice. In this light, one problem is the lack of a sustained consideration of empathy in practice, theory and research. The sphere of relationships is a major focus in consideration of the other: Through careful consideration of the theorising of the other, more accurate thinking and therapeutic behaviours could be identified. To validate the theoretical position laid out above, what is required is further precision about the ideals of the original arguments and an evaluation of them with respect to evidence and an appreciation of the variability of the objects self or other, within an understanding of the overall constancy of them.

In conclusion, the lived understanding of human being that is always already present, pre-reflexively, that comes before statistics and the qualitative approach, is considered as being of the utmost importance for therapists, theoreticians and researchers. A Heideggerian analysis produces an emphasis on the assumptions of conventional knowledge, which is currently absent. Its emphasis is on making a sure knowledge of self and others, that could be based on correct and incorrect insight and empathy, alongside an ontology of everyday life that might enable recognition of the possibilities of differing hermeneutic preferences that contribute to error and misunderstanding in relationships. Those communications, which turn out to be truly insightful and empathic, require further analysis to find out how they can be identified and how they occur. The topic of empathy is central to therapy. Practice and ethics should be set according to this emphasis.

Notes

1. The etymology of the word "empathy" comes from the Greek *empathos*, comprised of *en*, inside, and *pathos*, feeling, passion, pain or emotion.

2. Since at least 1905, Husserl was aware that consciousness constitutes what we are aware of before the intellectual ability to name or describe it. The understanding of any object occurs "before the animating apprehension can commence … in the moment in which the apprehension begins, a part of the datum of sensation has already elapsed and is preserved only in the retention" of what has just elapsed, of what we have just become aware (Husserl, 1991, Appendix V, p 115).

3. Personally, when I have tried this I have come to realise that my consciousness was automatically constituting empathic senses within a surrounding sense of intersubjectivity, of people in general. Consequently, as regards the problem of empathy, it may be that social experience is pre-reflective and that the sense of individuality arises temporarily, out of a more general social sense as background to our objective awareness. The recognition of specific senses of other persons and specific features and qualities of them occurs temporarily out of a vaguer context (Scheler, 1954, Stein, 1989). This may occur because of an ability to understand ourselves as a bodily on-going experience, a part of a larger shared, pre-reflective life.

4. Kant, Husserl and Heidegger agreed that the ultimate constitutive aspect of Da-sein is its temporality—"if the being of Da-sein is completely grounded in temporality, temporality must make possible being-in-the-world and thus the transcendence of Da-sein, which in its turn supports the being together with innerworldly beings that takes care, whether theoretical or practical", (Heidegger, 1996, §69b, p 333). According to both Husserl and Heidegger, the true horizon for personal and philosophical understanding is claimed to be the nature of temporality and the human world. It is suggested that through temporality occurs the connection of consciousness with the world and others. One focus might be on the full spectrum of experiences that are called insight and empathy and their relation to culture, society and the world, in the horizon of temporality. Writers who guide the interpretation of this paper emphasise the role of Husserl in understanding *Being and Time* (Haar, 1993, Kisiel, 1993, von Herrmann, 1996). *Being and Time* is an attempt at clarifying and developing Husserl's earlier phenomenology, as defined in *Logical Investigations, Ideas I, On the Phenomenology of the Consciousness of Internal Time, Ideas II* and other works (Husserl, 1970a,

1981a, 1982, 1989, 1991). Heidegger's starting position follows on from Husserl's early works from 1900 to 1925 and cannot be sufficiently understood without a grounding in them (Husserl, 1973a, 1973b, 1973c, 1973d, 1977a, 1977b). Heidegger's process of destruction and reclamation is similar to the transcendental reduction (Bernet, 1994a) and is termed the de-construction or reprise, *wiederholen* by Heidegger (1982, §5, 1996, §6), or the "destructive retrieve" (Kocklemans, 1977). What they have in common is an attempt to break through to the experiential basis that concepts point to, before speech and assumptions.

5. This is the "applied" version of two major approaches in *Being and Time*. A second type of more formal ontological analysis comments on the way that conceptualisations of human being have differed from age to age and culture to culture. When applied to therapy, such an analysis of specific forms of it would be to compare and contrast the way that human nature is understood: in cognitive-behavioural work as opposed to the person-centred approach, for instance. The applied type of analysis is defined in the examples of hammering and car indicators and could be applied to the qualitative-experiential knowledge of specific clients and therapists. The second type of intellectual "pure" analysis is more apt for analysing texts and ideas. Therefore, there are two ways of focusing on the being of empathy. Its sufficient mode of interpretation is to bear in mind what theory and prior experience bring to praxis. This means attending to (1) the thematization of empathy in awareness and the position of empathy in the total world of the human experience of others. (2) The de-construction and ontological analysis of theoretical accounts of the being of empathy through the ages.

6. The image of a circle in understanding is a helpful one to orientate readers in grasping what Heidegger was trying to show. But it should not be taken as being a sufficient image, for Heidegger abandoned it as an approximation: "in the structure of understanding in general, that what is faulted with the inappropriate expression "circle" belongs to the essence and the distinctiveness of understanding itself", (§63, p 290). The image of circularity is a surface understanding that is properly understood as a temporal inter-relation. During the first Division, the circle in pre-reflexive understanding lies between the interpretative ontological schemata that Da-sein already has, and what appears is already understood as something already recognisable, by courtesy of what has gone before and what we expect will occur (Gadamer, 1976, Maddox, 1983, Phillips, 1996). The hermeneutic circle describes the tension that exists between what appears to the senses and the way these appearances are immediately interpreted in indicating the nature of what appears. The image of the hermeneutic circle would have been

well-known to readers as the topic of hermeneutics was over a hundred years old at the time of publication of *Being and Time* and had been well developed by Dilthey and called the *second aporia*:

> The whole must be understood in terms of its individual parts, individual parts in terms of the whole. To understand the whole of a work we must refer to its author and to related literature. Such a comparative procedure allows one to understand every individual work, indeed, every individual sentence, more profoundly than we did before. So understanding the whole and of the individual parts are interdependent.
> Dilthey, 1976, p 262.

It is the role of hermeneutics to venture answers to the problems of ontology and epistemology and apply such answers in the human sciences, for instance. Hermeneutics as a science, will attempt to investigate the second aporia and seek to determine how valid understanding can be separated from invalid. "So the first, important, epistemological problem which confronts us in the human studies is the analysis of understanding", (Ibid). Husserl knew full well the dangers of ontological projection and he wanted his phenomenology to prevent this (1981a, p 192, Thurnher, 1995).

7. Heidegger obscured a clear analysis by bringing to the text many themes which render his analysis complex through an imprecise presentation. Also, it is not possible to give a detailed analysis of the discussion of these themes that would detract from a focus on the being of empathy. A detailed derivation of this position would take many thousands of words and is not possible within the confines of this current paper. It has to be pointed out that this interpretation of Heidegger emphasises the phenomenological aspects in *Being and Time*.

8. Literature searches of the natural scientific approach to psychology have produced a small number of research papers on the "constancy of the object," to use a psychoanalytic phrase (Blatt, 1995, Blatt and Blass, 1990, 1996, Blatt and Shichman, 1983, Kernberg, 1977, Stern, 1985). There is a small amount of research in the crossover between cognitive science and the constitution of the senses of self and the other in psychoanalytic child development. There is empirical work on the visual recognition of the other, but not on the precise details of relation between the senses of self and other. Constancy of the object refers to

recognition of the same object despite its many different senses and could refer to a person, situation or meaning of any sort.

9. Heidegger's statements about the ontological nature of Da-sein are not causative hypotheses. Rather they are statements about the nature of the manner of existence of Da-sein. They do not suggest specific reasons why things occur but try to describe without prejudice how Da-sein lives or how things are. Human behaviour is over-determined. One specific action is neither caused nor motivated by one specific factor. Nor does one specific action have one specific meaning. On the contrary, specific actions have multiple causes, motivations and meanings, both for the actor and spectators who observe the action.

6

Applying social constructionism to psychotherapy

Social constructionism is the view that many of the abstract quantities, our relations according to these, and the relationships of everyday life, are human-made processes in contexts. We have been born into these or we can gain access to them by our credentials in society. Social constructionism has so far investigated personhood, gender roles, sexuality, cross-cultural aspects of healing and mental health and different types of socially appropriate roles and emotional displays. Fields of science, study and debate are seen as historical processes occurring in human contexts of supporters and dissenters, who gather round in a complex changing pattern. Explanations are not regarded as indisputable facts or truths, but only as more or less adequate approximations: parts of discourses between schools of thought. Abstract quantities, the attribution of qualities to people and events between people—are regarded not as fixed things but as descriptions or explanations that are created, maintained and passed on through speech, writing and between people in the present moment.

The social constructionist view

Social constructionism is a reminder that all values, ideologies and social institutions are made by human beings (Gergen, 1985, Harré, 1988, p 13). At first glance this may not seem profound or far reaching, but it takes some time to allow the full implications of this view to become appreciated.

An example from astronomy illustrates some key points. At one time, it was taken to be a fact that the Earth was the centre of the universe and that the other planets revolved around it in circular orbits. In 1663 Galileo thought differently and posited that the Sun was the centre of the universe and that the Earth and other planets revolved around the Sun. To the orthodox establishment Galileo's view appeared to be a heresy and he was put in prison. It took many years for it to be accepted that the Sun is the centre.

Social constructionism is the claim and viewpoint that the content of our consciousness, and the mode of relating we have to others is taught by our culture and society. It includes the viewpoint that real and abstract metaphysical quantities we take for granted are learned from others around us. Social constructionism has an important message for therapists and this paper fills in some relevant background before discussing its implications for theory, training, research and practice. Any theory about universal human nature is placed in question.

The institutions under study by social constructionism include the family, marriage, male-female relations, psychological "illness," and hence assumptions about health. Psychological healing can be seen as combining mind and body, emotions and cognitions. The therapies come under the heading of healing as they seek to alleviate discomfort and promote understanding of the human situation as a curative act.

Roots of social constructionism

Social constructionism is a development of an earlier branch of sociology, instigated by Marx and Mannheim, called the sociology of knowledge (Abercrombie, Hill and Turner, 1988, p 237, Stark, 1958). This earlier discipline is based on Marx's premise that *ideology* is linked to *base*: that it is no accident that what people think is directly related to the economic base of the mode of production in which they are involved within society. Marx once wrote that "social existence determines consciousness" and this phrase was the basis of social constructionism (Marx, 1972, p 4, Berger and Luckmann, 1966, p 17). Marx argued that a belief system is largely determined by the economic base and mode of production of the believers. This is the basis of the concept that there is a relation between ideology and social structure within society. Marx's economic and political analysis was based on the relation between beliefs and identifiable recurring patterns of social behaviour.

The roots of this mode of thought can be found in German philosophy in the writings of Brentano, Husserl and Heidegger (Heidegger, 1962). Existential philosophy and the radical inquiry of phenomenology were the first views that chose to set aside what was currently known about a subject in order to look again, more closely, without the excess baggage of previous assumptions and results (Cohn, 1984).

How social constructionism sees

The social constructionist view is like that of phenomenology as it involves questioning, searching, clarifying, checking and constantly re-evaluating opinions in the light of new data. It is a view that states that theories map reality but that the descriptions contained in theory are *not* that reality, but are, rather, explanations of phenomena. Understandings are socially created by a group of believers. In doing this, social constructionism challenges the bases of conventional knowledge by making an inquiry into what is usually taken for granted.

Theories, explanations and discourses exist in time and place. A "supporters club" that is in contact with other supporters clubs decides a theory's lifespan. The careers of the supporters are often at stake. A consequence is that supporters of a popular theory are on safe ground. Supporters of minority theories are more at risk of their movement dying out. To pass one's own understanding to others is to swell the ranks of one's own position by currying favour with others.

Parallel paths to social constructionism are relativism and its precursors, phenomenology, existentialism and phenomenological sociology. Berger and Luckmann's book *The Social Construction of Reality*, first published in 1966, subtitled *A Treatise on the Sociology of Knowledge*, was a leading work in phenomenological sociology. Their work applies to ideologies and metaphysics of all kinds. They apply social constructionist method and illustrate the social construction of everyday life. They pay particular attention to what is taken as being ordinary experience. Involved in the view is an extended concept of mind as social relating that mediates the flow of circuits of speech, and echoes through many groups of speaker-listeners. This is spread across individuals, and makes psychology social. Harré takes concepts and "mind" itself as the products of speech, writing and other symbolic exchanges that take place according to local norms. In short, all beliefs are created by past conversations, in action with present conversations, that help to draw the past anew. Bakhurst outlines the Russian cultural-historical school of Vygotsky, Leontiev, Luria, Voloshinov, Bakhtin, and Ilyenkov. Bakhurst describes a philosophy of mind that considers the capacity to think as the ability to live in a meaningful world (Bakhurst, 1990, Wertsch, 1985).

Relativism suggests that there are parallel universes of experience for people of different ideologies that give rise to separate realities, sets of truths, knowings and personal experiences. For instance, people who believe in ghosts may have experienced them in their senses. For them, ghosts are believed to exist and have been felt, seen or heard. Those who do not believe in ghosts are probably much less likely to experience them in their reality. Such is the power of belief.

Some social constructionist views

The assumptions that social constructionist inquiry has for its subject include norms and appropriate—versus and abnormal inappropriate behaviour, thought and emotion—by considering who is acting on whom and in what context, for whose gain and loss.

For instance, the self is a misnomer according to social constructionism because it implies individuals who are out of context, not as people who are in a world with others (Harré, 1988, p 128). It is a mistake to create a separate self just because we have a separate body and that we can each say "I". What we talk about comes from our inter-actions with others. In a similar vein, the existential therapist Cohn stressed the importance of individual person's determination by social contexts and the inter-action with others. The individual self is considered as an abstraction (Cohn, 1985, p 217). In another paper, Cohn quoted the psychoanalyst Foulkes who once wrote that "the old juxtaposition of an inside and outside world, constitution and environment, individual and society, phantasy and reality, body and mind and so on, are untenable", (Foulkes, 1948, p 10, cited in Cohn, 1990, p 1). People are not individuals in the sense that they are alone and isolated. In this view, individuals are points in a flux, or single places of resonance within a field of forces that pull and push the participants in different directions. People are like ants in an ant colony or like the legs of a millipede that move in step with each other. Furthermore, we cannot be individuals in the narrow sense of being distant and separate from others. We continually breathe-in the influences of others and breathe out messages of how to be that are then breathed-in by others. In this sense, it is impossible to strive to be an individual because one can never be one: people can only swim with or against the tide of others. People are multifaceted and may behave, think and feel quite differently in different contexts.

Thought, according to Harré, is located on a continuum between public and private displays (Harré, 1984, p 129). Cognitions are displayed in talking and writing. A person can choose to try and hide an emotion from the view of others, or not communicate a thought, but still the thought or emotion exists at some level. Harré's view follows Vygotsky in that individual "minds" are abilities created by making private speech from that which was once public (Vygotsky, 1978). Knowledge and belief systems are consequently regarded as collective, consensual and discursive.

The display of emotion is also located somewhere along a private-public continuum. Emotions are played out as though on a stage (Harré, 1988, p 13). People are regarded by social constructionists as being consciously aware of the choices they are making about the type of emotional display they say or feel they have no power controlling. People are seen to be consistent in the type of appropriate behaviour that is open to them, according to their role and status, and hence they have choice of the stereotypical displays open to them (Holland and Skinner, 1987). In this view, emotions are well-known observable, regular and subjectively-felt ways of relating to others. They are displays of behaviour according to the social rules and ethics of the clan or tribe to which a person belongs.

The emotions and cognitions that go with the behaviours form a part of a power-play between participants in a drama. Emotions are socially-made conventions of appropriate behaviour that are easily recognisable to members of that social set. A study of the Ifaluk people of the Western pacific shows that their emotional responses are different to those in the West. One example is when the researcher Catherine Lutz is with a woman and a little girl. The girl approaches Lutz, does a little dance, makes a silly face and waits. Lutz interprets this action as the girl being cute and she smiles at her. The woman reprimands Lutz saying "Don't smile at her—she'll think you're not justifiably angry", (Lutz, 1987, p 290).

Similarly, displays of psychopathology might be made in order to put duress on others to re-balance power, or move in transition to a socially different place (Littlewood and Lipsedge, 1987, p 295). Littlewood and Lipsedge conclude their cross-cultural study of psychopathology by pointing out that the system of suffering and healing involves three stages: dislocation, exaggeration or inversion and restitution. People who suffer are first seen as non-dominant individuals within their social context. They react in a predetermined way by taking one of the psychopathology behaviours, after a period of powerlessness. The psychopathology breaks the standard social rules of society, either by the person grossly exaggerating certain aspects of their role or society's core values (for instance, when men become over-manly or women excessively feminine). Or by the person inverting their normal role (a man becoming womanly or a woman manly). The final act in the drama is the intervention of the healer who restores the person to a new role in the old social context, or perhaps helps the person transfer to a new social context altogether. Cross-culturally, healing supplies restitution and recombination with others. This subject is touched on again below.

Social constructionism views relationships between people according to stereotypes of social institutions of idealised relating that actual participants either conform to, or differ from. It questions the assumed values and morality of the day. Problems in relating are seen as being due to the lack of fit of any one person to the idealised roles that are open to them in society.

A theory of the relativity of knowledge is required to offset the bias of any one particular view that occurs and to place an emphasis on the differences in the large number of life-worlds that are in existence. Reality is laid down by many generations of humanity (Onians, 1951). Teams of people are required to innovate a theory. Adherents are required to further the cause and new converts for it to expand. Theories in themselves are held to be indeterminately true or false. What is of interest is what is done with the theories.

Truth and reality are linked and confused sometimes and it is worthwhile considering their relation before going further. Usually, the first meaning of the word "truth" that comes to mind is one of an Absolute Truth, something that is a verifiable fact that will hold forever, which is not open to reinterpretation or dispute. This version of Truth is one of dogmatism. In the social constructionist perspective this version appears akin to the beliefs of a "Flat Earth Society". It shows the rejection of new data and the refusal to make new interpretations about phenomena. The social system of a Flat Earth Society cannot and will not take on board any criticism of its doctrine and is a closed system.

Truth is according to who is making a claim to whom and where the action occurs in time and place. "Truth" often turns out to be a way of supporting oneself and discrediting alternative theorists' views about the nature of what might be. The history of the discourses of science is one of clashes of opposing groups for status, opportunities and power. "Facts" about human behaviour cannot exist in the absolutist sense because everything is open to dispute and differing interpretations. Psychology and the human sciences are *not* made of facts and this also includes social constructionism itself. Studies are opinion-making and the production of more theories, concepts and explanations. While some are trying to build up theory and establish themselves as market leaders in training and therapeutic practice, social constructionism pulls down theory and questions the collaborators' motives.

Kuhn (1970) wrote that science is not a series of discoveries or methodologies but a series of socially—constructed paradigms about sets of phenomena. Immature sciences, according to Kuhn, use a large number of paradigms (models or theories). The scientific work done in such cases is not cumulative as the different factions do not pull together. The results of one researcher or working group only have a small effect on the scientific community as a whole. When a single paradigm is finally accepted by a majority, then the total work becomes cumulative. Scientific communication is not understandable to those who do not share the same paradigm, because such communication is stated only in the language of that paradigm. Scientific revolutions involve changes in what becomes admissible as procedure and evidence: who admits the new material, finances it, publishes it, supports it—and who rejects the old paradigms. After a scientific revolution, old findings, experiments and instruments are found to be naive and are discontinued.

But a paradigm cannot be falsified because science cannot define the real. For instance, physicists no longer make claims of reality but seek to give the best explanation that they can. A quest for reality is outmoded modern science and belongs to the nineteenth century. Physicists realize that their methods of analysis can never explain all phenomena, so certain groups of phenomena are chosen and a model is built for those cases. A large amount of data that is inconsistent with a paradigm increases the dissatisfaction with that paradigm. When a new paradigm is offered that gives a more adequate explanation of a large number of phenomena, this qualifies it and the old paradigm is rejected. The opinion of Kuhn is born in mind and discussed below.

However, error exists in making any judgements, and, rather than there being different truths that refer to different realities about the world, that different people believe to differing degrees. An alternative view is to suspend all belief in Truth and consider the possibility that there are different errors to which people subscribe and pay allegiance. In the case of therapy, the possibility of doubt and error could be admitted and taken into account when acting on rationalisations about clients. These need to state when and how to relate to clients and how to keep an open mind about them.

The link between knowledge and personal experience is also interesting as it shines some light on the experiential basis of phenomenology. What becomes personal experience for therapists includes the personal assessments of training, life experience, past experience with other clients, and the experience of personal therapy. Phenomenologists believe that all we can know is based on the five senses through which we perceive the world and communicate with others. Knowledge, including every day understanding, is a series of specific judgements, conclusions and generalisations about what we have felt, heard, seen, smelt and tasted. Everyday understanding of clients and non-psychologically trained lay folk is as much socially constructed as that of mental health professionals who have taken a specialised training (Semin and Gergen, 1990). The sense of the term "knowledge" encompasses lay peoples' understandings as well as mental health professionals. Knowledge is not allowed preference over hearsay, folklore or superstition. Knowledge and personal experience are united and subjects for a social constructionist inquiry.

One way of starting a social constructionist inquiry is to believe theories about therapy, human nature and morality are incomplete. Time is required to explore the consequences of this. Given that ideas are partial and provisional, they have an apparent clarity that promotes dismissing inquiry, in favour of the acceptance of a faith. This is an easy acceptance by immediately joining a bandwagon rather than taking the difficult path and thinking things through. Social constructionism means giving up fixed ideas in preference for a life with doubt and searching.

Some feminist writings on gender roles take a social constructionist perspective (Ardener, 1981). Feminists state that many social institutions are *man*-made and male dominated. Their critique of male-female relations is that they largely benefit men at the expense of women. Feminists argue that human qualities such as the ability to provide childcare, assertiveness, and the desire to care for others at the expense of oneself are not innate natural qualities that belong solely to one gender. Rather, male-dominated society controls the number of roles open to men and women and the extent of each role. Stereotypical men are credited with an aggressive, rational and unemotional character; whilst women are deemed to be passive, caring, intuitive and emotional. The permissions for both genders have changed and some greater freedom for women has occurred whilst men have not generally given up their more powerful position. Social constructionism sees women's subordinate status to men as being facilitated by some women who side with men and continue the cycle of oppression. Feminists reject this complementary system of oppression and collusion with the oppressors.

Harré has extended the usual social constructionist perspective to include an emphasis on what he terms "discursive practices". This is a linguistic construction of reality that considers the ways in which meanings are passed on and created in how we speak about the world and create the beliefs we adhere to and on which we act. He also mentions the collection of works on the social influences of memory and the ways in which truths are reinvented in concordance with the current state of affairs.

Social constructionist concepts

When the world is seen through social constructionist spectacles, it appears differently to mainstream psychologists and therapists. The links between people through time and place, and the flows of ideology, assumptions and descriptive metaphors are noted to link generations together.

To avoid the confusion of logical types between unique personal experiences and political selfhood, that is part of the membership in a community of others, judgement is required to distinguish relationships between people; and relationships of people to abstract quantities, things or events. The understanding of life that social constructionism provides is that it splits it into two categories that have been named "content" and "structure" (Owen, 1991). The conceptual distinction between content and structure teases apart two inter-twined yet distinct categories. The two are not the same and must be separated so that clarity may be gained in the ensuing analysis.

Content consists of two subgroups. The first is *justifications* of all kinds including rationalisations for doing things with or to others. In fact, justifications are a link between *structure* and *content* as they form part of a specific knowledge of a people, yet are ways of defining how to relate to others within, and outside, the home group. The second subgroup of content is all else that can be spoken about: namely all ideology, beliefs, "truth," "fact," opinions and all else that people say and believe themselves to do. Justifications are made separate because they are the link between content and structure.

It is important to consider how justifications are held. The importance of justifications is seen when considering what is actually done with the beliefs that are held. Many actions are taken with justifications that are self-serving for the member of the group who is subscribing to a belief. Justifications are not arbitrary as they explain to others and oneself why a course of action is suitable or "rational". Therapists relate to clients on the basis of their theoretical justifications that are open to bias, error, doubt, lack of discussion, questioning and the disregard of the criticism of others.

Content is all that is believed or known to exist. It is the total series of interpretations of observable events between people and things. Also, our relations to abstract concepts such as god, right and wrong, are a part of content. Content is subject to error and any claims to its validity in a particular situation must be held in doubt. Following on from Galileo and the analogy about the changing theories of the nature of the universe, the same principle can be applied to theories about any subject, including the practice of therapy. Because Kuhn and others show that theoretical views change though time, the procedure of a specific therapist gathering data about a specific client is also subject to error and doubt. Any judgement or diagnosis about a client's suitability for therapy, personality type, relationship to others or abstract quantities, is subject to disagreement and error in its quantification or classification.

Structure refers to face-to-face relationships between people. It is observable or recordable actions, events and interpersonal behaviours. It does not refer to a person or group's relations to abstract quantities such as the Roman Catholic Church in general, but to the relation to a specific Catholic church in particular. Structure concerns the patterns of social structure that may be found in an army platoon, a factory, a classroom, a hospital or a training school for therapists.

Social constructionism sees human being as processes of relationship in contexts. The three major types of relationship that exist are to *content, structure* and *justifications*. When we are in relation to content, we are relating to, or according to, spoken or written words. Content is the semantics of abstract quantities defined in language: such as a "good marriage," "a wife's proper role," "love" or "unbearable sadness". When we relate to structure we are with others in the living present moment and doing something with them. When we relate to justifications, we take up some position to social rules by making an appeal to some sort of reasoning, so that we may feel or think in some way about someone or something.

The relation between structure and content can be likened to watching TV: to observe content only is like listening to a TV with the picture turned off. In order to observe the power relations between people, it is often necessary to ignore what they say, to watch closely what they are doing, which is like turning the sound down to concentrate on watching the picture. Both content and structure occur at the same time.

During the twentieth century there have been massive changes in both the structure and content of Western society. Behaviour of all kinds, particularly between men and women, and in permitted sexual expression, are very different now compared to the norms of behaviour at the beginning of this century. For instance in Britain, since women over the age of 21 gained the vote in 1928, the rise of feminism and the appearance of "new" men are evidence of changes in the balance between men and women in society. New roles and opportunities are being attempted, so men and women can relate to each other in different ways. These are attempts to redefine what are appropriate and inappropriate.

Two explanatory diagrams

Equal Opportunity Programmes now exist to redress discrimination that was once the norm. During the last 30 years there has been a threefold increase in the number of divorces, when previously it was highly unlikely that a couple would split. Likewise there has been some acceptance of gay and lesbian couples as a viable and non-pathological choice. There has also been a decrease in male authoritarian power.

Changing beliefs set by self.   Changing beliefs set by others.

Beliefs slow to change. Set by self.   Beliefs slow to change. Set by others.

Figure 1-A theoretical construction to show the differences between four combinations of structure and change of content of a culture. The horizontal dimension is belief set by the cultural structure of others. The vertical dimension is change of cultural content.

The aim of the diagram is not to categorise people in fixed boxes but rather to make distinctions and judgements about what we can expect when we look at the world with social constructionist spectacles. Figure 1 is based on Douglas's cultural theory from social anthropology that explains the differences between people in their personal experiences of interpersonal relationships, interpretations, justifications and explanations (Douglas, 1978).

The horizontal dimension of the diagram above represents structure. The two areas on the left-hand side are contexts where individuals are able to be self-governing in life. The right-hand side represents contexts where individuals decide to fit in with the wishes of others or are constrained and dictated to by the actions of others.

The vertical dimension is one of rate of change through time of content. The top notes that change is taking place. The gradations up the vertical axis represent changes from a totally fixed belief system at the bottom of the diagram with increasing amounts of change, as a person or people are situated further up the vertical axis. At a mid-point between the top and bottom lines, slow change increasingly occurs, to give way to more rapid change. The top line represents a place of rapid change in ideology. The four areas or spaces produced hypothesise different contexts for living.

The top-half of the diagram symbolises social contexts in which already existing beliefs change through time. It represents contexts in which meanings are constantly being created and destroyed in a flux of moving and evolving ideologies. The tension between the left- and the right-hand sides of the diagram represents the tension between being constrained by others on the right-hand side, like children, prisoners, the unemployed, some women or junior employees in a company. The right-hand side describes the environment such as children trying to be independent, free-wheeling members of society, women who have gained choices in life, or company employees who are self-determining.

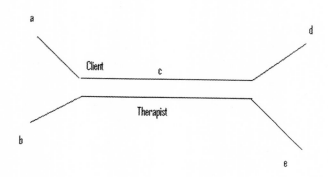

Figure 2-Five areas of social construction: Before, during and after therapy.

a- Culture-bound syndrome

b- Training of the therapist

c- Therapy meetings

d- Healed or disgruntled client

e- Enriched or guilty therapist

The five parts to the diagram above can be spelled out as follows. In figure 2 above, sections a, c and d are the most relevant for therapists. Section a is the part of the client's life leading up to starting therapy. It is the portion of time in which the person becomes "ill," to use a shorthand parlance.

Section a is called, by medical anthropologists and sociologists, a culture-bound syndrome (Hughes and Simons, 1985). This is a specific psychological and psychosomatic syndrome that exists only in a certain place at a certain time for a certain people. It leads the client to the therapist. Western culture-bound syndromes include the type A behaviour pattern (Helman, 1987), psychosomatic disorders in general (Helman, 1985), mental illness (Eisenberg, 1988), obesity (Millman, 1974, Rittenbaugh, 1982), agoraphobia (de Swaan, 1981, Littlewood and Lipsedge, 1987, p 306), anorexia nervosa (Garner and Garfinkel, 1980, Prince, 1983, Schwartz, 1986, Littlewood and Lipsedge, 1987, p 307) and exhibitionism (p 312). Psychopathology is a social event that is a social institution of suffering. These include conversion hysteria (McEvedy and Beard, 1970, Chodoff and Lyons, 1955) and suicide by overdose (Kreitman and Schreiber, 1979).

What makes culture-bound syndromes identifiable is their local nature and uniqueness in specific countries or at specific times in history. For instance, male exhibitionism is common in Hong Kong but rare in Japan. Overdose by prescription medicine does not occur in China. There is little obesity in countries with much poverty.

Cross-cultural views of other aspects of living also show up the assumptions that can blind us to hidden processes. Two examples of this are the studies of depression (Kleinmann and Good, 1986) and bereavement (Eisenbruch, 1984a, 1984b). Sexual behaviour is also culturally and societally determined. Foucault researched sexuality through the ages (Foucault, 1987, p 211). He found direct parallels between the permitted modes of thought and sexual expression in ancient Greece with contemporary behaviour in the West.

Section b on diagram 2 above refers to the prior life of the therapist. It includes his or her life-experiences of suffering and therapy that contribute to his or her current attitudes and refers to the current social context in which the therapist lives.

Section c on diagram 2 refers to the therapeutic alliance itself. It is the time in which client and therapist are together and in which the communication of meanings and the use of symbolic forms passes back and forth between the two, as they read each other for intentions and hidden agendas.

Section d is the time after therapy for the client. Two extreme possibilities arise. Either the client may feel transformed and uplifted by the relationship that has just finished. Or, the client may feel that they cannot be helped: That the therapist is "sicker" than they are. Other variations exist between these two extremes.

Section e is the after-effects of the meetings for the therapist. He or she may feel a witness to the client sorting out his or her life in a safe place, provided by their skills. This might be deeply worthwhile and enriching for the therapist. Alternatively, the therapist may feel that the client is yet another person whose pain was too great or too inaccessible for them to be helped. The therapist may feel he or she has let the client down or made a mistake when trust had been placed in him or her, beyond the ability of the therapist to deliver to such expectations.

In applying the terms "content" and "structure" to therapies of different sorts, the first action is to lay aside the content of therapy. That is to lay aside the theories, and the overt material of what client and therapist say they do, in order to scrutinise what actually takes place. The structure of a particular session or of the course of many sessions of therapy, is about the types of relating that occur between the participants. This is intimately linked to the content, of what is said in the sessions between the two parties, but the emphasis in regarding structure is on analysing, at a deeper level, the underlying struggles for power, the collusion and submission between the two.

In more general terms, it can be seen that therapy has been socially constructed right from its infancy. Freud withdrew two sets of theories because they were met with criticism. He withdrew the seduction theory that young children had been sexually abused by their elders and that this abuse was more widespread than had previously been thought (Schimek, 1987). He withdrew his theory that men could also be hysterical, because it was met with incredulity and hostility when he presented it to the Viennese Imperial Society of Physicians in 1886 (Ellenberger, 1970, p 437).

Human needs

It is difficult to draw conclusions about the universal needs of humanity on a world-wide cross-cultural scale. But what seems to come through research into cross-cultural material is that there are some distinct needs that human beings share and these are interwoven.

Onto-epistemological needs are those concerning *to know what exists*. Ontology and epistemology are inseparable because knowing about something necessarily posits the existence of that object, quality or event, that is known. People need to make sense of life and psychological theories fit the bill. The need to know what exists is also related to a human ability *to make exist what is known*. Like the chicken and the egg, it is a matter of debate as to which comes first in knowing about something that exists, or whether something first exists, which is then known. Onto-epistemology is the study of beliefs that are held about human nature and the world. Beliefs and knowings determine how people perceive and act in their world, which in turn, determine their beliefs about their world. In this way, onto-epistemological premises become self-validating (Bateson, 1972, pp. 313-4).

Part of knowing what exists is inextricably linked to explaining, describing and understanding people and the world through the great discourses, myths and narratives of the world. The word "mythopoetic" strictly means myth-making or pertaining to the creation of myths. Mythopoetic needs can be seen in the universal occurrence of having events explained and being able to explain processes to others. Mythopoetic needs indicate the hermeneutic sense of *needing to create a narrative* and *take part in the narratives of successive generations*. These narratives provide understanding that wards off anxiety, doubt and indecision at being presented with a confusion of different explanations. These narratives include the various discourses of science and philosophy, the sacred traditions of the world religions and the studies of humanity. The sense of mythopoetic encompasses the offering and accepting of explanations.

Finally, there is a need to be certain and reduce anxiety that produces the ability *to have faith* as a separate category altogether. These are boulomaeic needs because they are about being able to place trust in knowing what exists, not merely to know that something exists or not.

The word "faith" has five major senses. It includes belief, trust or confidence; yielding belief to something or someone in an act of giving faith; it is used with an imperative quality about something that is or should be believed; it is a power to produce belief; and, finally, it is the duty of fulfilling one's trust: An obligation imposed by trust placed in something or someone. Faith is about an ideology or someone's ability. It is placed by the faithful onto the object or person of trust. People imbue someone or something with a spirit of faith that comes from themselves via others, because of the need to believe in something.

It seems that faith comes to fill up some human lack or yearning. Boulomaeic needs produce healing in double-blind drug trials and religious experiences. It is intimately linked to the two previous needs in so much that a need to have faith contributes to a need to know what exists and a need to explain. Mental health professionals exhibit faith in the beliefs of human nature in a similar manner to the previous myths of Adam and Eve or the Hindu gods. Psychologists put their faith in statistics, the computer metaphor for memory, and the belief that psychology is an objective science producing a discourse of facts.

Nocebo and placebo

The Latin verb *Nocebo*, meaning, "I shall harm" is the negative effect of faith. It is the causative factor in examples of voodoo death where people have been so afraid of a curse that they have aged many years in a few days and died because of the knowledge that they have broken a taboo, or that they have been named by a powerful person as a wrongdoer (Lex, 1974). The equivalent of this happens in the West in cases of cancer or HIV infection where approximately one third of those diagnosed as having cancer give up on life and die very rapidly. If something is generally believed to be a terminal illness or life threatening, then there will be fear and anxiety on finding out one has that illness or condition.

The placebo effect has been well-studied in cancer and is routinely taken into account in drug trials. It can be measured as being 30 to 60 per cent of the healing effect of some pharmaceuticals: The effect of an inert pill given in double-blind medical trials can be as effective as the medication in 30 to 60 per cent of the people to whom it is administered. By comparison to therapy, it can be seen that no research takes place before a new therapy is launched onto the market. Some trials of the effectiveness of therapies have produced nothing but muddle and confusion (Stiles, Shapiro and Elliott, 1986). The placebo effect has been admitted to therapy research design and this has also been discussed (p 173, Parloff, London and Wolfe, 1986, p 338). Also, multivariate factor analyses of different types inherently skew the same set of input data, so producing different outputs according to the biases of the mathematical models used.

A body of research does exist however, on the view that placebo effects may be happening in therapy. Research into the characteristics of good placebo responders shows that they are generally able to inhibit critical and analytic modes of thought. They may see conceptual or other relationships between events that appear random to others. Placebo non-responders have been found to be "rigid" and "not psychologically minded", (Shapiro, 1971). Evans (1977) concludes that the placebo response is not correlated to suggestibility, but is in fact due to arousing cultural expectations and beliefs in the treatment method. Torrey lists six factors that he believes are at work in all healing on a pan global scale. He concludes a comparison of Western and indigenous Nigerian therapy that both:

> ... healers share the world view of the client and are able to put a name on what is wrong; they often have therapeutic personality characteristics; their reputation is usually sufficient to raise the client's expectations; and they utilize techniques that generate emotional arousal and give the client a sense of mastery.
> Torrey, 1986, p 186.

Perhaps a sense of order, a rightful place in one's social context or an explanation of what is wrong, what caused it, who one is and how one should behave, are all-relevant.

Power and desire

Some clients abdicate power and choice in favour of viewing themselves as weaklings in the face of an almighty therapist who should give them advice so they can get out of their predicament. In such a situation, the therapist is supposed to know what is wrong, what causes the problem, who is to blame and what to do. Sometimes the client looses power during the therapy and can only regain it on leaving and continuing without support. Power between people is a systemic or co-dependant process involving oppression by one party and collusion or acceptance of that oppression by the other. Power does not exist wholly in one party or the other. In the case where there is an open conflict between two parties, neither one is the controller. Only in the case where one submits or agrees to the imposition of the other's force or will, is there a true state of power. Of course, if the one who submits takes away their compliance, then the more powerful one's needs are exposed as being unmet and this is an act of taking back power, away from the dominator. Subservience and domination go hand in hand. If a person does not wish to be dominated then they must rebel. Also, if one party knows he or she is desired by the other, the desired person can lead the desirer at will.

It takes both parties to make the relationship in individual therapy. The power balance swings between the strong therapist, who has the upper hand, because he or she is nominally less wounded, and the client. The client shows weakness because he or she has come to the sessions to speak of their distress and confusion at life's dilemmas.

People also show their desires when they give commands or issue orders. In effect, they are saying "do as I bid". Some people are only too willing to satisfy others' desires at the expense of themselves. It is enlightening to think about who gives the orders in therapy sessions and who obeys or acquiesces, and satisfies the other's desires. The manner in which behaviour modification programmes, social skills training and medication can be imposed on clients of psychiatric services and psychology departments show the imposition of the will of the professionals onto the public in an effort to do something to them.

Implications for practice

Applying social constructionist ideas to therapy reveals an insight that it is impossible to measure the amount of truth or falsity in the claims of therapy and psychology researchers. Following on from Kuhn's analysis above, each theory is currently indeterminate in its ultimate truth or falsity. Theories are explanations that can be considered as explanatory narratives or myths that are currently held, but are open to change in a long-term perspective. In short, there are no new human phenomena just new explanations.

According to Kuhn, the large number of therapies and their explanations suggest that therapy is immature as a science. Over 360 therapies have been counted by one researcher (Omer and London, 1988, p 171). One book has 66 therapies summarised (Corsini, 1981). Each therapy has its own rationale and procedures. Furthermore, therapy schools are not co-operative but in direct competition for supporters and new members. There are a few major therapies, perhaps a dozen world-wide. Through time, the older established schools are on the decrease whilst new ones come into vogue to challenge the market leadership of the older ones. The total number of supporters of the great number of fringe therapies is comparatively small.

Psychoanalysis, behaviourism, cognitive and systemic therapies are well-established. The terms of each of these therapies are not easily translatable into the languages of the others. In fact, it could be argued that the data of any one therapy is confined to the specific situation in which it arises. A social constructionist view of therapy theories is that they are based on what is let through by the gatekeepers of each discourse. Theories can be seen as successive adequate explanations, which tie an explanatory string though a series of observable phenomena. What is admitted, as knowledge to the participants in a particular discourse, then may set off new effects downstream as the news disseminates through channels of communication.

A fault of many therapies is the lack of critique of the therapist's own actions with clients, and the beliefs and justifications that may be put forward to clients. Therapist responsibility lies in personal and collective methods of facilitating a well-reasoned mode of relating to clients and a non-psycho-toxic content of therapy. This is in opposition to those who accept their training without question. In applying the concept of structure to therapy the question is: "What is caring and ethical behaviour between oneself and a particular client?" In applying the concept of content to therapy the question arises "Is the thinking that has created the ideology, justifications and mode of relating between us both sufficiently rigorous?" Another couple of simple questions that may help in providing more ethical therapy are asking what each client wants and asking how they will know when they do not need to come for therapy any longer. Both of these latter questions will set up client-oriented solutions to therapy and make the therapy go in the direction that clients want to take.

The research journals for therapists periodically review material. There have been reports that supporters of a certain therapy find that their particular brand is best (Stiles, Shapiro and Elliott, 1986, p 167). Dissatisfaction with poorly performing theories, or ones that have a high degree of graduate drop out, will mean they eventually die out as time and market forces decide which therapies shall go forward. The most attractive explanatory models get the largest following until another model is brought onto the market that fits phenomena together in a more satisfactory manner. It would be interesting to see what a more precise analysis will show of what is ethically and philosophically correct practice, and for whom and by whom, therapy is carried out.

In Britain there seem certain class distinctions and professional rivalries between different sets of mental health professionals. In a generalisation, each training institute of the professional bodies favours a certain approach and style that sets the orthodox standards for its membership: For instance, behavioural therapy by psychiatric nurses, systemic family therapy by social workers, cognitive behavioural therapy by psychologists and individual psychoanalysis in private practice. Psychiatrists on the whole, favour medication and this can be effective in controlling or diminishing psychotic symptoms.

Error occurs in trying to gain insight and knowledge into oneself or another. People can hold themselves in question and can question and disagree with others about their motives. To act on one's untested insight, intuition, theory or experience is to act with bias. It is therapist pathology to act out one's theory to the detriment of clients. Theories can hold prejudices and presuppositions rather than focusing to the client.

When neurosis and psychosis are seen as culture-bound syndromes of a particular group within a particular society, in a particular time and place, suffering is a shared cultural and societal phenomenon throughout a country. When a person "acts out" they are acting out the conflicting forces within their society that run through them from the institutions of their family and the social structures which surround it and hold it together.

Psychoanalytic therapy is often based on telling the client the cause of what gives them pain. Behavioural therapy is about getting clients to act differently so they can begin to do what they currently cannot. The cognitive therapies are based on helping people think differently about themselves and their circumstances. Gestalt and other therapies have an emphasis on helping clients be more assertive and so relate differently to others. Alternatively, the basis of therapy could be relatively free of therapists' *content*. A content-free way of thinking, relating and describing is required for the client to appreciate fully their own psyche and be active in their social context. A therapy that is not blinded by its theory is required in an attempt to see what actually might be for client and therapist. A therapy entirely without theory would be confusion. So a combination of knowledge and care is required. Therapy can be helping clients to find what is appropriate for themselves, taking into consideration their context and moment in their personal history.

A relevant viewpoint to initiate an analysis of relationships is to concentrate on the meanings that certain phrases and movements may have. Dow proposes a theory about how meaning-laden symbols, words or events are transacted between client and therapist in all forms of healing (Dow, 1986). He suggests that healing is created in one of two forms. Either the therapist directly manipulates the client's symbols, and so creates new meaning and combinations for the client. Or, the therapist attaches his or her own symbols to the client's symbols, in order to create a healing experience. Such a view may lead to further insights into the process of therapy sessions. Moerman suggests that symbols and placebo processes play a part in medicine and his views have direct parallels for therapy (Moerman, 1972). He concludes that the construction of healing symbols is in itself a healing force. He views healing as a symbolic process that causes placebo reactions due to the power of socially created meanings. Prince (1976) on the other hand, comments that Freud and other writers have viewed physical and emotional imbalance as nature's attempts at self-healing. Prince does not dismiss interpersonal healing effects, but emphasizes placebo effects in healing.

The desired therapeutic *structure* could be such that it draws in clients because it provides them with adequate safety and they understand what it is that they are letting themselves in for. Therapy should be provided that clients want to have. Therapy could be tailored to their needs and abilities and help them be contribute and participate. Another direction that could be investigated is to help clients explore their meanings, values and context more. It could concentrate solely on clients' concerns to a much greater degree. Help may have to be given to enable them to establish a framework for this, that is safe and appropriate for them. Therapy could be more focused on the interests of the clients. It could be more open-minded in meeting and accepting others. It could reject the need of some therapists to satisfy their interests and control the sessions. Therapeutic *justifications* could also be open to explanation and agreement with clients.

Therapy could be more based on what can be seen, heard and felt. It could abandon any claim to truth in an absolute sense. When a therapist is present with a client, what happens between them is a unique meeting that can never be the same. Interpreting others through one's own system holds up the other for judgement against therapists' values. The client's independence needs to be promoted and the use of the client's trust taken ethically, as we are often supposed to know what is unknowable. When the therapist eschews the common belief that he or she is an expert or an authority, then new ground is entered.

As far as the practice of therapy is concerned, it would be valuable to build up a much finer vocabulary to talk about *justifications*, *structure* and *content* within therapy sessions. An analysis of the structures of power in therapy and an analysis of the content of symbolic processes between client and therapist is overdue. The power we have as therapists by virtue of our position, can be used in manipulating the client wittingly or unwittingly.

As a closing note, phenomenological approaches to therapy can also be of use in training and supervision. If we stop to ask ourselves what we are really doing and what we are trying to achieve, then new insights always come through. Both existential therapy and the person-centred approach eschew theory in trying to sit with a client and allow therapists to dare to be themselves.

In the social constructionist view, absolute truth is a fascist concept. In conclusion, the major problem in therapy is not the client but the therapist. There is still much more unknown about psychotherapy and human nature than there is known. The lack of absolute knowledge effects relationships with others and is an area to be explored in therapy sessions and for the profession as a whole.

PART II

The intentionality model: Towards the integration of the psychotherapies

Part I defined the methodology and stance of the interpretation of pure psychology. Clearly its scope is outside the jurisdiction of the psychological science view of therapy. Pure psychology as basic understanding is clearly within the scope of transcendental argument as concerning how consciousness and its objects make each other possible (Kant, 1993, pp. 126-9/A 105-112). Specifically, some issues need to be explained and could never be tested. This second part concerns the application of phenomenological ideas for the purpose of basic thinking towards the integration of the many brand name schools of interpreting and practising.

On integration

The term "integration" within therapy is primarily about the justification of any means of understanding and intervention, by a school or a specific therapist. It requires the creation of a formal means of clinical reasoning, in order to justify how the needs of clients are understood and best addressed by any intervention. The role of pure psychology is thinking how to amalgamate and comment on already existent styles of practice. The role of understanding in pure psychology in the first part, enables its conclusions to underpin the chapters of the second part. The term "integration" means using a reasoned selection of interventions in order to help specific clients. What is being urged below is not the establishment of a new brand name of practice but for therapists to pick up the responsibility to understand how they justify themselves and their interventions. It is hoped to mix the personal and the professional in a way that remains open to new developments in research into the effectiveness of therapy, the components of change-making processes and findings concerning the on-set and maintenance of psychological problems.

Conventional wisdom would balk at the possibility of adding together two different types of theory and practice. This is because purists believe that the brand name forms of practice are incompatible. But from the point of view of pure psychology, that understands the ubiquity and centrality of consciousness, intentionality and the intersubjective, such systems are capable of comparison and unification by thinking through their understanding and interventions. In this view, talking and relating are the backbone of the on-set of distress, the maintenance and amelioration of psychological problems. For pure psychology, brand name forms of practice are concordant because they concern talking and relating about generally understood cultural objects such as trauma, anger and depression and many more.

The integration of the therapies acknowledges that there are at least 400 recorded brand names of practice (Karasu, 1986). There are three types of approach to integration: "technical eclecticism ... theoretical integration ... [and] common factors", (Norcross and Newman, 1992, p 10). Technical eclecticism concerns the ability to select the best interventions for a specific type of problem and a specific client. Theoretical integration brings together two or more forms of theory and practice. And is a theoretically-based approach to finding the best elements of previously existent approaches. The common factors approach finds the essences of the forms of practice and might be an empirically-based means of determining what is effective. The approach in these pages is firmly a focus on understanding the nature of distress, and the way that meaning exists, prior to anything else. Thus understanding through phenomenology produces an amalgamation and comparison of theory and empirical findings thus including research to find the components of what may work. In these pages, intentionality and the complex experience of being-in-context are used to think through how to unite aspects of different forms of theory and practice. The intentionality model is practising in a way justified by a multi-disciplinary approach not allied to any one school of justification, but drawing on a number of relevant areas.

Justification without there being a consensus

Each brand name approach assumes it knows the causes of problems, how they are maintained and how to change them. Yet across the field, there is no agreement on the detail. What it means to have a lack of consensus across therapy is that there are no guidelines to go from *identifying a problem* to *knowing how to act*. Clinical reasoning includes "if ___, then ___" statements that make links between specific situations and lines of action. But if there is no agreement about basic rules across the many schools of practice, then there is no means of getting outside of particular views to find common knowledge. Nor can scientific psychology answer the pertinent questions or provide certainty. Consequently, from the perspective of looking at the whole profession, therapy schools are parochial and insufficiently justified.

Perhaps no theoretical model could ever accurately map all possibilities that are the whole of psychological life. But the profession accepts this difficulty in offering help to the public. What is suggested as helpful is more fully involving clients in their own self-care. For instance, in helping them formulate their psychological problems. Intentionality is the key for connecting with the common sense discourse of what it is to remember, imagine, anticipate or avoid. Even people with a limited education can grasp the idea of intentionality and apply the principles of self-care because intentionality refers directly to how they have their experiences.

But if there is no consensus, then there can be neither competence nor incompetence in the legal sense, and consequently, there is no safeguard to the public. And to state the same thing in the negative, legally defensible practice does not exist across the profession but only within each school. Currently, there is only competence or incompetence within a single school of practice. To get legal redress for incompetence requires some idea of what a reasonable therapist of a specific school would do in a given situation.

One reason why there maybe so many brand names types of therapy is that each lays claim to an approach or a region of human experience. From the phenomenological view, the traditional boundaries between these types of practice and the regions claimed are untenable. This is because there is no means of confining the influence of an intervention to just one dedicated area. For instance, cognitive interventions try to re-configure rationalising processes to help increase self-awareness and control, for instance. Or interventions can be used to increase the self-awareness of how a person continues to choose something harming or limiting, overcoming a way that had previously been automatic and not been adequately conscious.

Despite the proliferation of brand name approaches, there is still a need for the profession as a whole to offer a united front to the public. Legally speaking, the practice of ethics starts when clients are asked to give consent for assessment or therapy. Legally and practically, they must have understood what it is that they are consenting to: This means achieving understanding of what may help best. This is achieved through helping clients understand why assessment or an intervention is a preferable course of action. To quote from the UK Department of Health advice on consent, clients "need sufficient information before they can decide whether to give their consent". If they are "not offered as much information as they reasonably need to make their decision, and in a form they can understand, their consent may not be valid", (Department of Health, 2001a). This judgement also applies in the negative: Knowing when some proposed treatment would hurt clients or cause more pain than gain, so as to know when not to offer therapy. And even when not to offer an assessment because any type of therapy would be unhelpful and there would be nothing to be gained by assessment.

The ability to justify practice goes hand in hand with explaining the most fundamental aspects of it to clients. This returns us to the claim that the most pressing problem of therapy concerns how to justify practice at all. In overview, therapy changes understandings so that clients will change themselves or be helped in how to change themselves. This means that how clients decide to put in effort into making changes in their lives is a major topic. Therapy assumes that free will is possible. If there were no free will and no ability to change under-standing, then speaking to someone about problems would be pointless, as would attempting to alter one's behaviour in-line with one's understandings. The fact that psychological change does occur through the media of talk, action and psychological influence confirms the existence of free will.

In conclusion of this section, from the phenomenological perspective, the problems of practising therapy are the problems of how to justify a complex set of psychosocial skills when there is no overall consensus. In summary, the field of therapy has no consensus and that has a number of consequences. Empirical research as a means of justification is limited in terms of the type of answers it can provide. Empirical research cannot provide justification concerning the ideal or pure knowledge that guides practice. For instance, empirical research cannot create statistics, or design methodology, or deductive methods, or understand the basic ways of making sense of what appears. The major import of pure psychology is providing theory for integration by making alternative explanations of conscious meaningful phenomena. Such theories concern the intentionality of consciousness, understanding the nature of self and the importance of empathy as providing the perspective of the other and their intent.

Understanding intentionality in everyday experience and therapy

The "intentionality model" is a model for integrative therapy practice that links the awareness of clients to the interventions of therapists. The model is experientially-based in the sense that psychological distress is assessed in terms of the basic building blocks of how mental processes, the intentionalities, create the outcomes of emotional distress and persistently negative mood. Let us start from the beginning once more. The intentionality of consciousness refers to the many ways in which people can be conscious of the same object of attention. It is possible to be conscious through conceptual intentionality in speech and internal dialogue, for instance. It is possible to be conscious of the same item through seeing it in visual perception. It is possible to remember the same. This is the re-playing of a previous perception and realises that memory occurs in current perception. Figure 3 attempts an overview of the meaningful situation as it occurs in individual therapy.

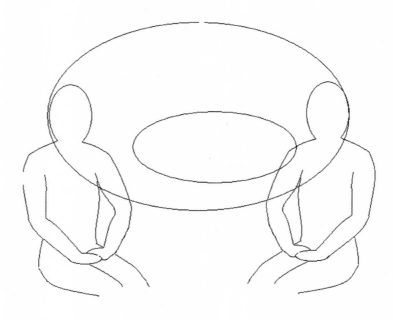

Figure 3-The shared context of the relationship and the context of the
culture at large.

Let us go to the heart of the matter: The intentionality model is an explanatory
model based on the idea that therapies are approaches to creating changes in the
lived meanings of events. It sees the nature of psychological problems as comprised of intentionalities of different sorts.

An example concerning intentionality and attachment

Worry is one building block of the combined problem of generalised anxiety disorder and insecurity of attachment, for instance. One form of worry is a problematic situation that is clearly anticipated and repeated a number of times
throughout the day. When the intentionalities are considered, there is no need
for a formulation prior to the event, although basic behavioural principles might
apply (classical conditioning and negative reinforcement). Let us take one exam-

ple to see how the ideas work. The intentionalities might be of this sort: That a catastrophic event is anticipated visually in vivid colour. For instance, a single mother anticipates the death of her only son. The accompanying emotion that goes with the visualisation is grief and confusion, prior to his death as an actuality. The psychological meaning of the process is attachment related. The mother loves her son and anticipates the worst possible scenario. If she did not care about him, then there would be no anticipatory pain. One context for making sense of this worry is attachment theory. This anticipatory and attachment-related problem causes acute anxiety and depression, and shows an insecurity of attachment from the mother to the child that may produce further insecurity of attachment or a rebellious reaction from the child.

A helpful intervention can employ the same intentionalities but works towards different ends. Firstly, the mother keeps her worries to herself and does not explain them to her family or her son. Secondly, the boy is not exposed to risk and is well-behaved and takes no risks that would lead to injury or death. After formulation with the therapist, the client can choose to redirect her visual anticipation onto a scene that is more reassuring and better represents her son's abilities to be self-caring and safe. The emotional state that goes with the new visualisation promotes a sense of well-being (instead of insecurity of attachment, anxiety and depression). The ability to intervene can also be seen clearly when the forms of intentionality that comprise the problem of insecure attachment and worry are understood. The ability to intervene requires a prior explanation of the problem and the pinpointing of the intentionalities involved. This could be achieved through discussion or written down as a formulation diagram on paper. Once the client carries out the visual anticipation of the new scenario, then there is an experiential change of sense in full. The client can then reflect back on her process of worrying in other cases, where she takes a problem and focuses on it for long periods of time, for up to 18 hours a day. Now she can apply the same overall process to herself because she fully understands the method of actively choosing what she thinks about. She can catch herself during the process of worrying and bring it to a close.

Conceptual intentionality in talking therapy

The change process in talking therapy can be clarified through paying attention to the intentionalities that are current for clients and within the inter-action with therapists. Interventions in sessions are most often in language and address the intentionalities of clients' experiences. For instance, the internal dialogue of clients may drive anticipations, memories, behaviour, emotions and the capacity to relate differently to others and self. Similarly, the relating therapies target the territory of influencing the ability to relate and use all manner of means to achieve such changes. The view of the intentionality model is that all aspects of human nature are inter-related, so any one type of intervention potentially can affect all other aspects.

Following Lester Luborsky (1994), who believes that 40 per cent of the benefit of having a talking therapy comes from the direct experience of being with the therapist, this influence can be clarified in the following way. The intentionality of empathy is the means through which people provide the sense of each other. The 40 per cent of the total of benefit claimed by Luborsky concerns the attribution of feeling and intention of the sense *given* to therapists by clients. He also found that 10 per cent of the total impact comes from specific interventions that alter the senses of the same objects of attention. What this means for talking therapy is as follows.

Talking therapy has its remit in highly complex situations, where a specific focus cannot be pinpointed, where self-help methods are rejected by clients, or for other reasons, where clients are unwilling to employ self-help. Discussion promotes spontaneous alterations in meaning that occur through the medium of conceptual intentionality. The influence of meeting with therapists sets a new context for understanding self, personal history and other significant relationships. The precise details of the intentionalities at play vary in each case. Let us take one concrete example.

A young man has stopped taking cocaine yet he is still paranoid and disillusioned with people generally. The approach taken by the therapist was to provide open-ended discussion because he had rejected the self-help method of considering the evidence that supported the belief that he was being followed by people who might kill him. What happened in sessions was that he was trusting of the therapist and talked openly about his fears and experiences. The major theme that he brought to the meetings was his view that people disappoint. For him, even good people do and say weird things and cannot be trusted. How can he protect his children in such a world?

For him, the intentionalities at play were empathy that was inaccurate, a misattribution of negative intent to people in general. He had had good reason to be generally suspicious as the whole of his childhood was spent in a violent neighbourhood where he had to fight to be a man and protect his mother. He also had been involved in criminal activities and years previously, he had believed that friends who were criminals might murder him. This negativity was not present in the therapeutic relationship and this was fedback to him. He did permit a formulation on paper of his paranoia and this brought him relief through explanation. Through discussion and greater understanding of his personal history and the chemical effects of the cocaine in producing long-lasting anxiety and paranoia, he was able to understand himself and begin to think that his thoughts and feelings about others were inaccurate and not the truth of the situation. This shows the major difference that therapy brings according to the intentionality model, that *there is a difference between a sense of an object and the overall meaning of the object itself.*

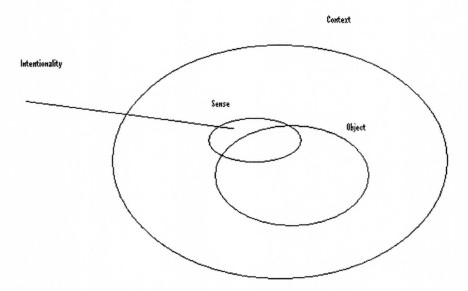

Figure 4-The inter-relation between intentionality, sense, object and context.

Let me recap the major points of the intentionality model. The intentionality model permits integration of interventions by focusing on the relation between consciousness, other consciousness and meanings of all kinds. It has theoretical entailments such as disputing the idea that there is such a thing as the "unconscious proper," that there are permanently unconscious mental objects or senses (Freud, 1940a, p 160). Once this false idea is abandoned, for instance, it permits reconciliation between the different focuses of psychodynamics and cognitive behavioural therapy, for example. The intentionality model provides sound explanation by appeal to the qualitative facts of meaning as public and understandable: between therapists and clients, and in society as a whole. Psychological problems are understandable experientially as forms of intentionalities that together comprise post-traumatic stress disorder or borderline personality disorder, for instance. Psychological interventions become recognisable as preparing for, and creating changes in meaning, by helping clients occupy new perspectives on what already exists. Specifically, changes in meaning arise through *changing the object* of attention; or *changing the intentionality* towards it; or *spending less time in attending* to it; or *changing the surrounding context* that co-appears and in which the object is understood. The psychosocial skills of therapists are helping clients' self-care and facilitating changes in meaning.

The intentionality model can make a contribution because it spots the necessary interpretations that people have to make about the human situation. All approaches justify action through stating that something 'causes' problems and that justifies interventions. It is not the content of thoughts that is important in this respect, but defining the forms of thinking and evaluating complex situations, that helps overall.

The relation between justified practice, a priori and the everyday

It is believed that the proper relation between theory and practice is that theory comes first. Theory is not the sole measure of what is real but rather determines what should be considered. This alternative is putting the pure before the applied. The pure is further refined by the applied to create a new pure: in an ongoing interplay between the pure and the applied. There is an ethical necessity to offer a number of choices including what is most effective to produce help, minimise risk and promote self-care in the short-term. The usefulness of ideas is providing a medium to explain and justify mutual tasks with clients who have no point of reference. The link between ideas and the justified practice of therapy is that interpreting a priori concepts of pure psychology (of compatibility, incompatibility and necessity of explanation) meet with the psychological reality of the common sense experience of clients. The basic need is for understanding that shows the phenomena well. Let us take one more idea from Husserl.

The qualitative fact that the senses of objects accrue across time was apparent to Husserl from 1913, both objects of attention and the intentionalities that made them, are united across time producing coalescence, recognition and identification (Husserl, 1982, §118, p 283, §131, p 313). There are many and varied senses of the same object. These are added together and reconciled. Otherwise negative consequences of various sorts ensue, such as being unable to account for the inability to *add together* oneself (coming to know and explain oneself)—in relation to knowing others and being able to understand them also.

The consequences that unfold across the following pages are that Husserl's terminology provides a vocabulary and a methodology of theory-making and interpreting the sense of self, others and forms of being-together. The intentionality model is not a new brand name in therapy, but a reminder of the scope of what therapy is and does. Specifically, therapy pinpoints some factors within highly complex meaningful situations and enables a new perspective to be taken on such experiences. The common situation can be expressed in a number of ways.

Because intentionality can explain qualitative experiences, the integrative approach of pure psychology, the "intentionality model," argues that there should not be a focus on the current styles of intervention (or the regions of human being that brand names of therapy have appropriated as their own). From the perspective of understanding consciousness as intentionality entrained with the consciousness of others, what needs to happen is providing help through understanding the function of problems and how they began and are maintained as attempted solutions. From such a base, it becomes possible to move forward, with client and therapist in a collaborative team effort. Confronting, arguing and indoctrinating clients to believe something is not part of therapy and is bad practice that should never be attempted. It is better to show clients how to make sense of themselves through using ideas such as intentionality so they can explain and link their experiences in new ways. This provides relief through explaining, for instance, how they are sensitive to specific possibilities and actualities.

The reprinted papers of the second part of this work are as follows. *Are We Before or After Integration? Discussing Guidelines for Integrative Practice via Clinical Audit* discusses the basic premise of how to integrate the therapies. *Treatments of Choice, Quality and Integration* rounds up a number of pertinent issues in relation to the need for brief therapy, accountable practice and incorporating the findings of research that show that cognitive behavioural therapy is far ahead of other forms of therapy in putting itself through the rigor of empirical testing. *Power, Boundaries, and Intersubjectivity* discusses the ethical dimension in response to the blanket claim that all therapy is oppressive in that it makes clients enter slavery. *Ethics and Multidisciplinary Practice* briefly provides some notes on the ethical dimension. It is indisputable that there is a need for legally defensible practice. But pre-empting lawsuits is not in itself being ethical. If consent cannot be gained, then there can be no treatment. If there has been no explanation, there can be no treatment. Therefore, the explanation provided must be understandable by each client in order for him or her to provide consent. If clients have no understanding of what is being offered, there should be no further action because consent cannot be obtained in this circumstance.

The Person-Centred Approach in a Cultural Context is included because the theme of congruence in person-centred therapy is one that is closest to the expressiveness of the human body in phenomenology. The three core conditions of person-centred therapy are clearly enabling conditions in a practical sense, and close to the theoretical-Kantian one. The purpose of the paper is to extend understanding of what happens in any meeting between two people. Similarly, *Exploring the Similarities and Differences Between Person-Centred and Psychodynamic Therapy* is an exercise in understanding the difference between two major forms of non-directive talking therapy, merely for the purpose of finding how they agree and differ. Finally, *On Existential Psychotherapy: A Hermeneutic and Meta-Representational Perspective* makes comments in the light of what Heidegger, Sartre and Merleau-Ponty were urging—and comparing that to contemporary advances in child development and theory of mind. When there is an acknowledgement of temporality and intersubjectivity, then there can be an attention to the social developmental perspective that can take account of social influences that occur in a sequence across time. This emphasises the role of the influence of the past and makes psychopathology more understandable through meta-representation: The ability to compare and contrast the different senses that are obtained through *taking different intentionalities* towards the same object and *changing the contexts for understanding*. Altogether, Husserl's approach has promise in being able to understand human experience and the sense of identity.

7

Are we before or after integration? Discussing guidelines for integrative practice via clinical audit

Rather than give an overview of the attempts at integration, this paper stands back from the details of theory, research and practice, to discuss the broader themes of integrative practice (Norcross, 1986, Goldfried and Newman, 1992). The beliefs expressed in this paper are partly derived from my own beginning at teaching and practising in an integrative manner. The recurring theme is a need to justify interventions according to evidence. However, the evidence cited by each author is not consensually-agreed.

Introduction

Following the work of Richard Nelson-Jones, this paper suggests that there are three major choices, responsibilities and developmental tasks for an organised integration (Nelson-Jones, 1982, 1985, 1988). These tasks address a problem that lies within the field of practice, theory and research. These tasks are (1) the acknowledgement of interpretative free play, (2) the problem of an ideal of integration that could bring together many different practices and models, and (3), the problem of agreed evidence. In answer to these tasks, three novel perspectives are suggested that are linked to clinical audit. This discussion starts by noting that integration assumes that contradictory yet mutually connected theoretical perspectives for practice are being attempted to be brought together. This paper discusses the nature of these contradictory demands and forces.

The paper begins with the consideration of three observations concerning assumptions about human nature and the range of practice in the UK. First, it is claimed that cognition occurs concurrently with emotion, behaviour, self-reflection and the presence of non-verbal processes that are difficult to describe in language. The evidence for this remark is Zajonc (1980) who disagrees that cognition is always prior to, and causative of, emotion, thought and behaviour. He found that emotion is quicker to arise and so comes before cognition and Rachman has agreed (1981). Second, there are many practitioners who describe their practice with reference to humanistic, cognitive-behavioural and psychodynamic terms. Third, the British Psychological Society book list for trainees has a series of perspectives in it and recent state of the art publications like the *Handbook of Counselling Psychology* lists eight paradigms for practice alongside a gamut of other topics to be born in mind (Woolfe and Dryden, 1996). These publications imply that a wide awareness of the possibilities is being suggested. If these observations are agreed, then are we *before* the official integration? Or *after* the unofficial integration? By an *official integration* I mean an integration of theory, practice and research that has been accepted by a professional body or by a majority of practitioners. Whereas an *unofficial integration* is one where individual practitioners, departments and training schools permit their own local integration of ideas and practices from different traditions.

Theoretical and practical evolution

During the last 20 years there has been a rising interest in the possibility of integrative practice. This has occurred alongside evolution in what had been separate fields of practice, namely the four major styles of therapy: psychodynamic, humanistic and the cognitive and behavioural approaches. Each of the four forms of practice have been developed by the criticisms and research of their own practitioners. Omer and London (1988), for instance, bring together research material on the demise of separate schools of therapy. Furthermore, Omer and London do not believe that there ever has been an overall paradigm to which practitioners had belonged (p 172) which implies that the field as a whole has always been fragmented.

Those who made the developments to which Omer and London refer, previously mixed two or more ways of working in an ad hoc manner and called this new approach "eclectic". Initially these innovators chose interventions without the background of a unifying theory. They were practising before any official integration. Consequently, this paper discusses practice in the context of the large number of theories that are available to guide integrative practice. It is also argues that the space mapped out between the four major styles of therapeutic relating is a space worth traversing according to the needs of individual clients. For instance, there are many insights to be gained from comparing and contrasting these styles of working, and indeed, this space is the area of legitimate therapy. Other purists would find integrative practice abhorrent, as they prefer to stay within the consistency of one model of practice. Also, for some it might be a matter of concern that there are multiple standards and methods of practice, some of which might be even considered unethical or unproven in their effectiveness.

Task 1: Acknowledging interpretative free play

When the large number of schools are discussed, often no mention is made of interpretation and the interpretative free play that exists due to the varying degrees of expertise of the practitioners and the varying perspectives that exist within a single school of thought (Westerman, 1993). Through the years, and across the country, conceptual drift and variation occurs as terms are gradually redefined and employed differently. Hence, within each department, therapy is enacted in a slightly different manner. Practitioners are not robots and each one interprets the ground rules, their training and clients differently.

Interpretative free play is part of the procedure of embodying and enacting theories and beliefs. It is a major area in which it is difficult, if not impossible, to ensure consistency and regularity of actual practice. This free play exists in interpreting any situation or guideline for practice and its importance is not to be under-estimated. As a consequence, it could be argued that there are as many theories and practices as there are practitioners. Another way of stating this thought is to write that not only do all practitioners have their own variation on the group theme, but also, given the variance in the characters of practitioners, it is the case that there are no distinct schools of therapy at all, but only individual practitioners each practising their own style. As a corollary, it might also be the case that schools of therapy exist to satisfy a need for agreement and mutual support in the justification of each style of working. In short, practitioners continually mix ideas that they use in justifying actions with clients. For instance, there is the case where a trainee who might have a "cognitive" personality, say, learns, person-centred therapy. Even though they have a veneer of person-centred skills and a person-centred vocabulary, are they truly a person-centred therapist when their style of relating to others is driven by intellectual reasoning?

Therefore, a local, unofficial integration of the therapies has begun; yet the national official integration has not. Unofficially, practitioners mix and match concepts in practice in a relatively ad hoc manner. This process is legitimate and concerns acquiring insight and empathy through practice, supervision and training, and building therapeutic discernment and skills throughout a career. What occurs is that each person integrates their own practice according to what they value, without a fundamental, agreed theory that takes into account all the complex variables and forces in the field. So, if there is no universally accepted paradigm for practice, and all practitioners "invent" their own form of therapy by applying their interpretations of the principles of one or more schools, then what is an acceptable way of creating a cohesive, official integrative approach that brings together practice, supervision, ethics, theory, research and other factors? The next section discusses the main problem that an official integration would tackle.

Task 2: The ideal of integration as a problem

The integrative approach may be defined as one that seeks to find out what type of therapy, by what sort of therapist, works best for a specific type of client, with a specific type of problem, who is in a specific set of life circumstances (Paul, 1967, Norcross and Goldfried, 1992). By definition, the process of official integration should search for core commonalities within each of the four major schools. This is to be achieved within an official, integrated and cohesive view of therapy as a whole. This ideal of an integrative approach aims to overcome the inadequacies of a random eclecticism and provide a cohesive and consistent theoretical model that draws on some aspects of the major schools. Integration appears to be an answer because therapy is continually evolving and reconsidering its approaches. Therefore, such integrative practice would eventually be able to join together some of these elements into a cohesive whole. But this also implies that some attitudes, ways of relating and techniques will be omitted. This will be a problem for those who wish to practice in ways that are no longer official or who wish to innovate and experiment.

In order to make a therapy that is consistent with integrative values and approaches, then there is a confusion of ideas, values and practices from which to choose. As regards the practice of integration, there are many aspects to the whole field in which therapy is situated and pulled in various directions. Some of the major dimensions include long-term and brief work; group, family, couple and individual; gender-sensitive and cross-cultural. There are a variety of specialisms for sexual problems, sexual abuse or eating disorders and the list could continue. These numerous possibilities give rise to a dismay at ever being able to conclude on an official, unified integrative theory because not all aspects are capable of integration and it would take much work to consider which therapeutic procedures are appropriate for specific therapeutic situations. Overall, it is a tall order to produce a single path through these conflicting forces—but this is the path to integration. One leading question is to ask "what evidence is there to prefer one mode of practice or a specific intervention over another in any case?"

Task 3: Are we before or after evidence?

A further problem that appears is that despite 40 years of therapy research there is little agreement or knowledge about what works (Luborsky, Singer and Luborsky, 1975, Stiles, Shapiro and Elliott, 1986). Practitioners do not share an agreed starting point and an empirical base. Currently, there are two forms of research that vie with each other to investigate therapy: The quantitative and the qualitative. But the continued development of psychology is not a choice between either the quantitative approach or the qualitative approach, but rather a tension and inter-dependence between the two. Consequently, if further integration is the correct course of action, and empirical research has not yet shown us what is effective, then it is also possible to turn to theoretical or ethical analyses of therapeutic guidelines. Because there are many interventions from the different schools of practice, then there are many possible ways of proceeding during each session. If there is no agreed evidence for practising in one manner or another, then therapy is operating *before* the establishment of agreed proof *and* the discussion of the ethical dimension that occurs within different forms of practice.

Research shows that there are claims and counter-claims. If there is no evidence that is acceptable to the majority of practitioners, then the whole project goes forward on shaky ground. Evidence is a major subject as dependable knowledge provides the basis by which informed decisions can be made. If there is no reliable knowledge, then there may be uncertainty and anxiety about how to proceed. Some way out of this deadlock is required. A possible line for research is to take a "trouble case" perspective which would focus on the nature of therapeutic relationships, processes and outcomes. This approach is introduced below.

Perspectives for an answer: Audit in the organisational context

Another way of looking at the practice of integrative therapy is to view it within its context between colleagues, referees, supervision, training and society generally. In this way, the contextual and background issues that shape the relation between theory, research and practice are taken into consideration. The responsibility that supervisors or managers of a department, for instance, have for the quality of contact with the public is a shared responsibility. If certain therapists are making interventions that are generally not accepted, or could be seen as ineffective or irresponsible, then the managers of the unit have a responsibility to intervene and advise that a different course of action to be taken. This organisational context is part of the human system and ambience of the therapy team. Clinical audit that relates the service that clients receive to the practice of the service providers, can consider the provision of care. Such is the nature of the shared responsibility of practice. If there is no unified model for the department as a whole, then people practice as they like and obey the minimum requirements of a code of ethics.

Audit as trouble-case research

Trouble-case research could help establishing where the boundary of ethical and effective practice lies. To do this, it is necessary to picture the choices for relating to clients in a manner that emphasises the choice of therapeutic relating. This form of qualitative research could use the following procedures in clinical audit, to investigate complaints in an even-handed manner, to analyse client feedback and understand client-therapist agreement and disagreement. Surely, it is the case that therapists meet with the full range of clients and presenting problems. Therefore, therapists meet the same problems of, say, coming to an impasse, or having clients who drop out without having accepted the chance to make the changes that they came to receive. One aim for integrative theory could be to follow closely the twists and turns in therapeutic relationships and so predict the ground accurately. Currently, there are cases when practitioners follow a single model of practice and clients do not improve. What has gone wrong, if anything? These cases are of interest because they show how the theoretical model used is either incorrectly identified, or the model is incorrect, or the model may have been correctly identified but applied incorrectly.

The process of going through how difficulties have arisen and how mistakes have been made, is helpful for on-going learning and preventing problems happening again. Following an initial assessment interview within integrative practice, a treatment of choice model can be chosen. If clients respond to this approach, then this could be due to many factors including placebo effects. Also, some clients may not be telling the truth in research. Even if they have felt that therapy was not helpful for them, they may not admit it. Trouble-case research starts when clients do not respond. There are several possibilities here:

1. The client-therapist mix may have been unhelpful for both parties. In this case, clients need to be referred to someone else with a different approach and therapists need to be given clients who do not exceed their abilities.

2. The initial choice of model may have been unsuitable, or the initial assessment was incorrect for the possible reason that clients did not give, or were not able to give a full picture of themselves at assessment. In either case, an ineffective model has been applied.

3. The model chosen was incorrect for clients or therapists have not been able to engage clients in it. In this case, further training, supervision and attention is required to help reduce this outcome.

4. The model that has been identified is correct, but it has been incorrectly applied for a number of possible reasons that may include the lack of expertise. The situation might be rectified by taking action, as in case 3 above.

5. The model may have been correctly applied by therapists, but they may be at fault elsewhere in the view of clients. In this case, therapists may have insufficient attention to any signs that clients were dissatisfied, if any were shown. Video work and training may help in giving the necessary evaluation and feedback.

6. The therapeutic model may have been correctly applied but it was unsuited to them and the approach will have to be changed so that clients can be engaged in a new therapeutic process whilst staying with the same therapist. Rather than referring to another worker, it may be possible to save the situation through identifying any deficits in skills and awareness. The matter could also be rectified in supervision or personal reflection.

7. There could be the possibility that clients no longer want help and do not wish to change for a variety of reasons. If this is the case, therapists can do little except ask what the reasons are for leaving and so continue to try and re-engage clients if they still wish to work on their problems.

Matters arising: Practice and training

In order to integrate therapy in an organised manner, a model is required to link personal qualities and interpersonal behaviours to a process of developing an integrative model and providing feedback via supervision. In this manner, on-going learning, supervision and personal development can be connected to the development of the department as a whole. Clear outcomes will increase the probability of knowing how to distinguish and provide the necessary care to clients and staff.

One way of getting clarity on integrative practice in its context is to imagine that we have a blank sheet of paper for the initial and on-going training of integrative therapists. One could start by drawing up a person specification and job description that could be used in finding ideal candidates. The person specification would ask for those who felt they had the pre-requisite qualities of warmth, empathy, insight and a consistent ability to talk with clients on any subject. This would specify candidates who can strike up intimate long-lasting, good quality relations with others of both genders, and all sexual orientations, cultures, ages, educational backgrounds and social classes.

The job description would define specific tasks to be carried out and state therapeutic processes as interpersonal tasks. These would include an inventory of skills for accurate conceptualisation of possible processes and outcomes, empathic qualities, self-awareness, adequate life experience, nurturance, skills for reflecting and interpreting, monitoring oneself, so on and so forth. As regards the personal qualities versus skills debate, it might be useful to bear in mind that ideal therapists would have both a mature and tolerant personality and transferable skills for the job. This raises the question about what are the preferred skills and aptitudes for integrative work. In this manner, the boundaries of the most basic role, skills and qualities that practitioners should posses could be agreed. Each practitioner can practice as they please, within the bounds of a unified frame of practice within the current professional code of conduct as ratified within their department or with their supervisor.

The question also arises about what kind of training each course could produce according to the professional organisation to which it belongs. Is it the case that every training course makes its own integrative mixture? Does a course alone have the right to specify those aspects which it feels are ethically correct and empirically effective? However, it is only reasonable that each course and practitioner has an amount of freedom to practice as they wish, as long as they abide by a code of conduct and work within a permitted theoretical framework. As regards the current models of integrative practice, one problem that needs to be avoided is rampant intuition. Instead of destructive or inaccurate intuition, accurate empathy with clients and accurate insight into oneself are central and can be grounded only by validation from them.

An aim of choices for clients and therapists

An integrative theory could be built from the consideration of the decision-making possibilities that exist within the major forms of work. In addition to the theoretical problems, there is the practical aspect of how to integrate on-going career development within a cohesive framework due to the conflicting aspects of theory, research, supervision and personal reflection. Each aspect needs be taken into account and given a specific emphasis.

The view of Nelson-Jones is that the work should be integrated and this is the approach that has been used as a model here. Another currently existing model for helping workers choose suitable interventions is multimodal therapy which is similar to the medical model of analysis for the provision of appropriate care (Lazarus, 1976, 1986). But any integrative approach could end up as multi-muddle therapy, when it is not clear which aspect should take preference at any one stage in the proceedings. In addition to this confusion, if medication is being taken, it damps down the abilities of clients to respond emotionally, gain access to their memories, and think and feel, to the full extent of their ability.

Conclusion

What have been avoided in this discussion are the specifics of integrating two or more forms of practice. This paper takes a wider view of the whole enterprise. Some examples to illustrate this confusion are the possibility of integrating two approaches. It is a point of debate whether the behavioural approach is made humanistic by the addition of the reflection of feelings and an emphasis on the empathic understanding of phobic clients. Some would agree and some not. For instance, does the cognitive approach really fit with the psychodynamic emphasis on creative silence? Some psychodynamic workers would say that nothing should replace creative silence and the process of attending to unconscious communication. Does the cognitive approach fit with the person-centred need to be congruent, value and empathise? Again, some would strongly agree and some would strongly disagree. For instance, some believe that a cognitive approach and that of Carl Rogers could not fit together because of the mutually exclusive need of cognitive therapy to challenge current thoughts, assumptions and behaviours; whereas the person-centred therapist is always bound to empathise with what clients feel, and move them away from cognition towards the rediscovery of their organismic true self. Yet others feel that specific cognitive techniques can be added to the person-centred emphasis on the therapeutic relationship to make "empathic challenges" of client's self-limiting assumptions.

One way of trying to integrate these disparate views is to consider that each meeting is new and each therapist varies their approach with specific clients across their career. Each session is a time for applying oneself, researching and theorising. Consequently, practice is a rough set of guiding principles, some of which are more relevant to one client-therapist meeting than another. Although there is a growing interest in the possibility of an integrative framework, there is yet to appear a single theory, that takes into account key aspects of the leading approaches. Given the very large number of schools, it is difficult for a single therapy to arise that considers all the possibilities for interventions, either from theory that guides practice, from ethics, or from research into effectiveness.

Therapy can perform radically different tasks for clients. It can also be seen as an ethical decision-making process about how to live and treat others. It can help make and break emotional bonds through processes of unlearning and relearning, so facilitating cognitive and behavioural change. Assumptions and truth claims concerning the differing interpretations that are made of human nature provide guidance. The initial frame of understanding that therapists or researchers have defines their consequent inter-actions. These are areas for future debate and agreement.

8

Treatments of choice, quality and integration

In light of the position paper, *Treatment Choice in Psychological Therapies and Counselling,* National Health Service (NHS) staff who practise the psychological therapies are recommended to work in specific ways with specific needs or disorders (Department of Health, 2001b). This recommendation exemplifies one aspect of the scientist-practitioner model of research, theory and practice as stated in the aim of outcome research as: "*What* treatment, by *whom*, is most effective for *this* individual, with *that* specific problem, and under *which* set of circumstances," (Paul, 1967, p 111). The apparent clarity of this aim raises a number of questions. It requires precision concerning treatment, therapist and client types, disorders and the social contexts of clients. But, setting such questions aside, because it is a requirement for staff to follow these recommendations, the aim of this paper is to explore what enables evidence-based practice. Thus, links are made to adjacent concerns of working in a general role, offering clients a treatment of choice, suggested by the evidence base, and discussing the role and nature of quality assurance. It ends by suggesting that integrative practice is a likely orientation for many who are practising more than one orientation.

Practice according to research evidence

There have been a number of Department of Health and NHS Executive publications that define guidelines for the provision of health care in the UK (Department of Health, 1995) and specific papers that define guidelines for the quality assurance of the psychological therapies and mental health work (1999a, 1999b, 1999c, Joint Home Office/Department of Health Working Group, 1999, Parry and Richardson, 1996). The consequences of these papers are manifold. Primarily, psychological therapies are meant to follow the evidence base that shows there is effective treatment for a specific disorder. Although non-quantitative types of research are permitted, they are not accorded the same influence as randomised control trial (RCT) research which is the preferred mode of inquiry:

> **Type I evidence**—at least one good systematic review, including at least one randomised controlled trial
> **II**—at least one good randomised controlled trial
> **III**—at least one well designed intervention study without randomization
> **IV**—at least one well designed observational study
> **V**—expert opinion, including the opinion of service users and carers.
> Department of Health, 1999b, p 6.

For a brand name therapy or set of techniques to be practised, there should be reference to the effectiveness of the outcome of it for a disorder. Having an evidence base makes the difference between being allowed to practice in a specific way or not. According to the above, the gold standard for research is the RCT that employs the drug metaphor for psychological therapy (Stiles and Shapiro, 1989). This standard has been criticised because it assumes that clients are inert material on to whom active ingredients are poured by identical therapeutic technicians (Stiles et al., 1995). It assumes conformity and consistency of the specific types of therapy practised, the therapist and client personalities and the interaction. It ignores the difficulties of diagnosis and assumes uniformity of treatment, homogeneity of the disorder and the client's social context (Kiesler, 1966).

Again, the scientist-practitioner model comes into view. It is assumed that workers assess accurately and formulate, possibly according to what is known about the aetiology of causation and the factors that currently maintain the problem. The model assumes that a specific treatment will meet client need in a manner that initiates and deepens the therapeutic relationship. The point is that there is a gap between the research situation and the real life flexibility, spontaneity and automatic social skills of doing the work. This is called the difference between research efficacy and actual clinical effectiveness. The Department of Health are in the process of publishing a number of national guidelines for best practice. Currently, there is one for depression (1999d). There will be further standards for practising with personality disorders, schizophrenia, anxiety and eating disorders.

But the above recommendations are not the only ones that are shaping current practice and service delivery. It is clear from the perspective of the research question "what works for whom?" that what is being encouraged are specifically proven interventions that fit specific client psychological needs and preferences. The aims for "comprehensive ... co-ordinated ... user-friendly, accessible ... safe ... effective ... evidence-based [and] cost effective" treatments of choice have a number of consequences despite the cautious remarks that indicate the lack of certainty in some important areas (Parry and Richardson, 1996, pp. 5-7). It means that there is no reason to provide a long-term treatment when a short-term one would do. There is no reason to provide individual therapy when a group approach would be more cost effective, if it were of equal overall effectiveness. There is no reason to provide psychological help alone if combined psychological help and medication is proven to be most effective, so on and so forth. What this means for the orientation of the individual worker is this:

a. If there are a number of workers who have specific orientations that have been proven to be effective, then suitable clients can be referred. This might be the case for workers who have had a single training in a brand name therapy, such as psychodynamic, person-centred or cognitive-behavioural. The brand name practitioner can have a role circumscribed by specific research, most of which supports the effectiveness of cognitive-behavioural work (see below).

b. Generic workers are potentially more cost effective than persons who have a single approach because they can take a wider range of referrals. The point of integrative work is to practice according to a reasoned rationale concerning how best to meet the needs of clients (see below). Therefore, integrative work is the case for those who have been trained in more than one brand name of therapy. It is assumed that integrative workers are as competent in specific interventions as single brand name practitioners.

c. But, if treatments of choice do not work, or are not accepted by a specific client, and practitioners believe that another approach or technique that is known to them could be helpful, then it would still be possible to use an orientation that was not the one first suggested by the evidence base.

d. The three cases above require workers making a therapeutic alliance with clients. Clients should give informed consent to their treatment and be helped to become participants in it. Accordingly, any psychological treatment needs to be delivered with flexibility according to client needs, preferences and abilities. But, it then becomes apparent that real practice is the opposite of receiving a manualised research therapy: The real situation demands that workers implement a tailored therapeutic process for specific clients.

The remarks above are notes towards the aim of providing treatments of choice for specific client problems. The next section defines the key features that a quality assurance system can provide. Such a system connects with the above and goes further towards strategic planning and delivering best practice. Two further sections explore the entailments of the points above.

Quality assurance

Clinical governance and clinical audit are quality assurance procedures that endeavour to ensure good practice and the on-going improvement of services. The principles and entailments of quality assurance are generally not well-known but can be summarised clearly. Please let the following remarks be taken in the sense of creating clarity about service provision through quality assurance. The comments are grouped according to the aims, administrative necessities and general therapeutic strategy for service delivery (Burwick, 1999).

1. Overall, the aim of quality assurance is to create genuinely effective and ethical help according to the needs of clients.

2. The ethos of quality assurance can be summed up as two maxims. Firstly, "do what you say and say what you do". And secondly, "improve what you do and prove you are improving it".

3. Quality assurance aims to standardise good practice. The major aspects of working practices are documented and standardised. This is called having a "documented quality procedure". For instance, there could be the creation of short, written guidelines for each Trust on how to manage risk, what to say about confidentiality at a first session and how to refer in the possibility of suicide or in a psychiatric emergency.

4. In administrative terms, the provision of therapy and other elements of service provision are *corrective and preventative action* that documents how something has been effective in helping clients and serving the general psychological needs of the local population.

Yet administration is also focused on effectiveness. For instance, continual professional development (CPD) should not be 'one way,' according to the needs of the practitioners who attend it. CPD of a specific sort should be evaluated according to its effectiveness in helping clients with specific disorders. There is no reason to have CPD of orientation x, when orientation x has not yet been shown to be helpful. The outcome research about orientations x, y and z determines what type of training is provided.

5. Systems like CORE's pre- and post-therapy outcome measures are a national standard for collating and comparing the results of psychological help. The regular use of such a system would be one way of ensuring therapeutic- and cost-effectiveness (CORE System Group, 1998).

6. The staff who are providing treatments of choice are required to prove they document their procedures and that the documentation is an accurate record of what actually happened with clients. Again CORE can play a role in this.

7. Procedures can be altered or suspended only by the owner of the procedure. This person may be the Quality Manager of the Trust. Procedures can be altered or suspended by a clear set of meta-rules for changing them. There could be yearly or bi-yearly reviews of the effectiveness of the quality procedures, according to clearly defined and achievable outcomes.

8. Staff need to work co-operatively to improve the quality of client care. Administrative practices and the work of the department are given as close scrutiny as practice, in order to achieve the desired aims. For instance, reception staff could have customer care training. There could be audits of the capability of staff to practice according to the documented models of practice.

9. Finally, as regards strategies for service delivery, a treatment of choice is employed for a specific disorder according to interpretation of the evidence base. Other orientations may be employed when a treatment of choice has failed to be effective or when clients have not been willing to participate in it. The quality assurance procedure assesses the degree to which clients' needs are met. There is a need for on-going monitoring of the progress of clients according to such an evidence base.

What is demonstrated is the necessity of empirical research that shows the suitability of specific brand name therapies, for specific disorders. The concomitant is that when there is no research base, there is nothing to suggest that any particular brand name could be practised. But quality assurance aside, there are still further entailments of the move to practising and managing the services according to what the evidence base suggests.

Therapeutic muddles

There are a number of problems entailed in the items b, c and d, mentioned above. The major points entailed in the above can be further clarified: The aim of quality assurance, and the principles of best practice defined by an evidence base, is that departments as a whole offer treatments of choice for specific client needs. But practitioners are either purists—or they are integrative in that they practice with interventions from more than one style, made concordant through clinical reasoning for choosing one intervention over another. Three points arise in connection with what staff should be practising, seen from the perspective of a wholistic understanding of human nature.

Firstly, interventions assume a whole, a living ensemble of relations with others, culture and society plus the workings of consciousness. No psychological help could function outside of this whole.

Secondly, each brand name practice presumes it makes some sort of change on one or more aspects of the whole. The parts are the well-known therapeutic orientations of cognitive and behavioural, interpersonal and systemic therapy, etc. Each brand name type promotes change by emphasizing a specific part of the whole way of living, thinking, relating and behaving.

Thirdly, it follows that a specific type of intervention may have multiple effects in more than one of the domains that are claimed as the domain of the brand name orientation. For instance, any specific intervention may have a cognitive effect in that it promotes thought and reflection. It may have an interpersonal effect in that it promotes change in relationships, to self and other. Such changes will alter parts of the overall human system, so that cognitive-affective processes may alter in-line with the new experiences brought about through therapy.

Therefore, it may be the case that there are *no pure orientations of theory and practice*. If what is meant by a pure, brand name therapy is an approach that only focuses on cognition, or behaviour or psychodynamics or relationships with others, then it is obvious that interventions on only these aspects of the lives of clients would fail.

A wholistic integrative approach

An integrative approach means that practitioners have a wide base for assessing and understanding what is the nature of distress and how to help. Currently, each brand name therapy claims that it intervenes on parts of the human whole. None of these therapeutic enterprises could work unless the parts were inter-connected, one to the other. Thus, styles of practice and theory overlap because there are psychodynamic, cognitive-affective processes and habits that are linked to systemic relationship patterns, past and present, which are linked to specific and general cognitions, affects and behaviours, so on and so forth. The whole is comprised of many influential factors. I am arguing for the relevance of integrative, 'wholistic' therapy over any one brand name approach that only focuses on a part of the whole. This is because only a general form of therapy, that is ready and able to focus of differing parts of the whole, is more adept at trying new therapeutic techniques, attitudes and strategies.

Generally, staff have become sufficiently skilled in the use of more than one therapeutic model. But the initial understanding of client need shapes the treatment and the type of the help that will be offered. Initial understanding also defines what is thought to be ineffective and not offered. But when there is no consensus in the field about aetiology, effectiveness and theoretical perspective, there is a need to take a wide view about what is effective. It is best practice to be flexible and offer a range of interventions according to what might be helpful to peoples' different abilities and life situations. But any type of psychological process assumes that what it does is provide psychosocial influence. It is the case that the nature of the psychosocial whole is learned. A general social learning perspective minimally assumes that therapists can influence clients for the better and change meaning in the presenting problem plus associated aspects of clients' lives. Therefore, to promote the reasoned co-existence of different therapeutic models, I list nine key elements for an integrative approach.

(1) The many personality theories that exist describe aspects of a multifactorial whole. Overall, let us assume that human development occurs according to social nurture and genetic nature (Plomin et al., 2000). Obviously, psychological help cannot alter our genetic inheritance. It can only hope to alter psychosocial elements of the whole. There is no sufficiently reliable evidence to support personality theories. Some bodies of evidence show no known aetiology for the axis I disorders. Accordingly, there is no reason to place all belief on any one model of the whole of human nature and its development. Those developmental theories are agreeable with a social learning perspective and are useful in the practical situation of providing help. This is particularly so when they describe the phenomena where clients find themselves requiring help. Through the provision of suitable relationship conditions and techniques, change and maturation may recommence.

Generally, social learning theory is also (2), at the origin, cause and development of psychological problems, and (3), there are different factors at play in the on-going perpetuation of these problems. Human nature is multifactorial in that one disorder may result from the interplay of different stressors with inherited personality characteristics, different early and adult life experience, plus the cumulative effects of personal choice and the influence of others and culture. It is not possible to be precise. Early in the occurrence of a specific disorder, it may have been difficult to achieve a defensive status quo. But through many repetitions, the same state may have become apparently automatic: it occurs spontaneously and without conscious control.

(4) Understanding the process of therapeutic change could include information from evidence-based practice, clinical reasoning and clinical governance. Currently, there is no sufficient evidence to believe in the superiority of any one explanatory model (Stiles, Shapiro and Elliott, 1986). Accordingly, if it is the case that there is little consensus concerning the justification of findings, one should not impose unproven psychological theory onto the public.

(5) The ranges of permissable interventions include those listed by empirical research (Chambless et al., 1998, Gabbard, 1995, Roth and Fonagy, 1996, Nathan and Gorman, 1988). The greatest proportion of these works support cognitive-behavioural therapy and almost entirely omit findings from other types of practice due to their inability to perform according to quantitative standards. Interventions can be chosen through discussions with informed clients and by attention to their wishes, capacities and one's own judgement concerning how clients might be empowered. The readiness and ability of clients to change, their current emotion and mood, can also guide clinical reasoning.

(6) Therapeutic stages have been identified by Rogers (1942, pp. 30-45) and Prochaska and Diclemente (1992). Specifically, clinical reasoning can focus on the needs and wishes of clients, in-step with their readiness and ability to change. Choices can be offered to clients. (7) Theoretical considerations and clinical reasoning should be concordant with the overall attempt to provide evidence-based practice, inside the "New NHS", (Parry and Richardson, 1996). There are also ethical requirements for workers to set clients at ease and enable them to participate to the best of their ability.

(8) An integrative approach is inclusive of more than one therapeutic model and aims to be culture-appropriate and gender-sensitive. Psychological work is tailored to the needs of the individual's mental state and the specifics of how they are living as part of their family and culture. (9) Regular review sessions and the monitoring of clients' mental states mean the chosen approach should be altered if interventions are not helping clients. Progress should be monitored through discussion with clients. The worker may also suggest that certain issues may need

to be looked at, so clients may approach what is difficult for them, yet when tackled, will be helpful to them.

The remarks above bring the exploration of the issues surrounding evidence-based practice to a close.

In closing

This paper analysed the aims set by the Department of Health for the provision of psychological therapy in the NHS. It defined the key features of a quality assurance system. Quality assurance ensures the delivery of good practice through audit to insure improvement to services. The overall aims are cost-effectiveness, standardisation, creating consensus where there is none and the pursuit of better services. But if a form of practice over-emphasizes a *part* of human existence rather than aiming to understand the *whole*, then it may have lesser clinical utility.

In closing, firstly, psychological help should be offered according to client need. But these needs are diverse. Those who practice a single brand name limit their flexibility and the ways that they meet client-need. Such narrow and rigid of thinking does not follow the difficulty that abounds in understanding the human condition. To work only according to one brand name is like trying to play chess by only moving the pawns. It does nothing to connect with the complexity of factors that are actually involved.

Secondly, there are other Department of Health documents that call for the modernisation of working practices and the shattering of previous boundaries between staff. Furthermore, there appears the possibility of parity of pay and conditions. However, there is a great deal of overlap between persons who provide psychological help. For instance, psychiatrists, occupational therapists, nurse therapists, counsellors, psychotherapists, clinical and counselling psychologists vie with each other to provide psychological care. Currently, each may belong to combined or separate management structures and may likely be on different pay scales. Some practitioners may have more than one manager. Potentially, some practitioners may be attending to the same client needs, but are being paid at different rates. If the NHS Executive and the Department of Health believe that there should be parity on pay and prospects for those who shoulder equal responsibility, then the future consequences of these trends are not yet clear.

9

Power, boundaries,
intersubjectivity

The first part of this paper is a brief overview of the keynote speech given by Jeffrey Masson at the Sixth Conference of the Society for Existential Analysis, London, entitled *Issues of Power in the Psychotherapeutic Relationship*, in which Masson raised various questions about the alleged inappropriate behaviour of therapists and the boundaries of the professional role that must not be overstepped. These criticisms are addressed. The overall aim is promoting a discussion of the therapeutic relationship and its founding assumptions.

Overview of Masson's address

Jeffrey Masson has gained notoriety by daring to publish letters and material critical of Sigmund Freud's theoretical and therapeutic work (Freud, 1986, Masson, 1984, 1993a). At the Sixth Conference of the Society for Existential Analysis, Masson gave a keynote speech entitled *Issues of Power in the Psychotherapeutic Relationship* (Deurzen-Smith, 1994, Masson, 1993b, 1994, Kitzinger, 1994). One major theme of his paper is a request to assess and debate some of the major claims of therapy to be effective and ethical: particularly claims that are not being noted: "It makes me nervous, when the presuppositions are not even being discussed", (p 33). The assumptions contained within the keynote speech are the subject for discussion. They need to be clearly distinguished in order to analyse them. Some of the questions that shall be addressed include: what is the true nature of interpersonal power? And, what are its boundaries as regards therapist and client roles? This will be done by attending to the actual experiences that are being referred to.

The exegesis begins by enumerating some of the major points that Masson made. (1) Abuse is alleged to always take place due to any power imbalance, and these imbalances abuse and re-abuse all. He dismisses the possibility of considering the cases in which therapy can be freeing and life-enhancing, although he freely acknowledges this within the same paper. (2) Masson assumes that the power differential in therapy is inevitable for various reasons inherent within the therapeutic situation. Consequently in his view, therapists are not only always abusive because of the alleged inherent power imbalance, but also, they are in a comparatively secure position. Masson considers clients as having no real power except to leave therapy. (3) Masson assumes that it is not possible to have a "patronising" use of power, as that would be unethical, as it does nothing to reduce the power imbalance that causes abuse in non-reciprocal relationships in general. (4) Contained within this thought is the belief that it is incorrect to reform a practice that is both unethical and so severely imbalanced that it is unable to be therapeutic. (5) With reference to the concept of the unconscious mind, Masson assumes that the unconscious can be correctly known by therapists, but such knowledge, in addition to the training and professional expertise of therapists, actually increases the power imbalance. And finally, (6) Masson claims that therapy should be equal and not have any power differential.

Perhaps one accusation that readers can agree with is that Masson points out that in comparison to clients, therapists are not so much in need (p 24). But if we agree with that observation, it does not follow that the inherent non-reciprocity of the therapeutic relationship, and its imbalances of power and knowledge, automatically abuse. I cannot understand how Masson can justify his comment. Therapists have to know how therapy may proceed, and know through receiving a training therapy, to know how it feels to be treated in a certain manner.

However, Masson claims that therapy is inevitably detrimental to clients. He feels that all individuals in positions of power and influence inflict, exploit and abuse (Masson, 1993b). He commented that exploitation is not consensual, but a form of seduction due to the imbalance of power that provides a sexual-sadistic pleasure for the more powerful (Masson, 1994, p 29). It seems to Masson, that being powerful also means that it is possible to control the less powerful persons. During his speech Masson mentioned that there are social structures of hierarchy, dominance and submission into which we are born (Masson, 1993b). Masson used this to theorise that hierarchical social structures in the family and society produce conditions that give rise to experiences of the early abuse of trust, which then make possible and probable, further abuses of trust in adult life. An example of the discrimination, exploitation and misunderstanding in therapy, to which Masson objects, is when therapists cannot accept some of the choices of clients, or do not understand the experiences to which they are referring (Masson, 1994, p 30). Also, Masson points out that clients may be denied equal rights and the automatic privileges of therapists to speak and act, which portrays the therapeutic relationship as one where only therapists are in control and permitted to express themselves.

Masson assumes that power always lies with therapists and that clients have none. But this is not the case. Clients have many ways of getting attention. Clients are able to leave therapy and could heap insults onto therapists, with or without provocation, which can be part of a power-struggle in the relationship. Also, clients can be abusive and have the power of refusing to take part in therapeutic relations and can, for instance, make therapists wonder if they will attend their next session. Furthermore, Masson accuses many who are in the "enlightenment business" of not wanting to acknowledge criticism of their claims to knowledge about human nature and their ability to help. During his address Masson never considered the case that there could be such a thing as a positive use of power, as it is implied that this would be patronising, and hence should be omitted because it is unethical. Therefore, another question raised within Masson's keynote speech can be phrased as "is it possible for a use of power to help clients?"

Jeffrey Masson has published criticisms of therapy before and during his speech he made an appeal for the abolition of the profession as a whole. This appeal seems to be inspired by a utopian ideal that in a perfect world there should be no need to enter into a non-reciprocal relationship with a therapist. Masson explained this appeal for the abolition of therapy by making an analogy to the debate on slavery before it was abolished, as a way of explaining his stance. The debate on slavery became polarised by two factions: one was for abolition and the other for reform. With this analogy Masson explained his radical request for abolition: that it is incorrect to reform something that should be abolished on ethical grounds alone (Masson, 1993b). It is clear from this statement that Masson assumes that therapists are unethical and non-therapeutic, because they are always in a 'one up' position, in which they could take advantage of clients. Yes, the inevitable power imbalance is due to the real desires and needs of clients that make therapy sought-after. But why does he conclude that therapy is always unethical and unhelpful?

Another alleged controlling aspect of psychoanalytic therapy that was criticised is the consequence of the idea of the unconscious. Masson characterised the practical outcome of the concept of the unconscious, as it is enacted in the therapeutic relationship, as "you don't know about it. I do", (Ibid). This comment also refers to the aspect of therapy given by the difference between the expertise of therapists in general and the public. A true aspect of the situation is that therapists have had training, personal therapy and practical experience and clients have not. This state of affairs has been called a "hierarchy of enlightenment" by Claire Baron (Baron, 1987, Masson, 1994, p 25). But this initial condition of therapy is another thread of Masson's challenge to the profession.

The fundamental inequities that Masson distinguished set up a hierarchy within the relationship where therapists are not only 'one up,' but also, he feels that this automatically rules out the right conditions for successful therapy to take place. We can see that therapists are in the place of an expert, and are accordingly, capable of being perceived as authorities on human nature. But many practitioners are reticent and careful in making claims. On the contrary, the general reception given to clients, usually aims to be safe, positive and accepting.

What follows below, in the main body of this paper, is a discussion of the connections between power, boundaries and intersubjectivity with the aim of initiating a discussion of the relation between these three qualities. Masson commented that there could be such a thing as an informed consent for therapy, which is a reprieve on his previous call for its abolition (p 31). As a final note, Masson brought his address to a close by asking therapists to free themselves of non-therapeutic intrusions and processes in the performance of therapy. This is also, I would imagine, an ideal aim that professionals will share. I feel sure that there is much of worth that Jeffrey Masson has to say which can only be beneficial. However, the analysis of the assumptions he is making needs to be broadened to take in extra material that is currently being omitted.

On interpersonal power

In addressing the major issue of interpersonal power, one question to ask is how can we know if power "in itself" is good or bad? Or, whether it is always present within a relationship? Further questions include those about whether "power" only exists as it is perceived, but may not exist "in itself". There are three major senses of power: having control over others, being able to act, and, having control over oneself. One way of discussing the interpersonal reality of power is to bring in one of Freud's distinctions to promote awareness of its qualities and inform debate. Freud's model of the power relation is one where the supported, overtly powerful person tries to control the supporting one. Freud's idea of secondary gain demonstrates the covert power of the controlled, weak or sick person, who makes use of the symptoms of illness to manipulate others: "ill health will be her one weapon for maintaining her position. It will procure for her the care she longs for ... it will compel him to treat her with solicitude if she recovers; otherwise a relapse will threaten", (Freud, 1905e, p 44). This quotation forms a basis for opening up discussion about the possible truth of interpersonal power below.

Concentrating on this distinction illuminates the intersubjective nature of power: the primary gain of a symptom is freedom from anxiety and conflict in the sufferer, by avoiding something (negative reinforcement). The secondary gain of a symptom is the powerlessness it provides that may influence and even manipulate the more powerful person. On the one hand, the overtly powerful have an obvious ability to control others. However, those who are assumed to be "powerless" have a covert power. Freud believed they have the strength to become even weaker and take away all support whatsoever.

Possibly there are several other ways in which we can talk about power? Power is said to be "given" in acquiescence. Power is "taken away" in conflict, disagreement and negotiating compromises. Another major question raised by the discussion of the nature of power is to wonder if there is any freedom from exploitation and repression, within therapeutic sessions or in the outside world? Generating the qualities of freedom, safety and acceptance are important because they can help clients venture into new ways of being for the first time. But the Freudian description is a one-dimensional model of the relation between overt power and covert power. If we can set this aside for a while, it may be possible to turn to our own experiences of this situation in which we can grasp what happened for us, without the clutter of conventional thought or our usual bias. The actual experiences we have of these subjects can be the source for our discussions. In addition to Freud's one-dimensional model, there are cases in human relations in which people want to be rejected, hurt others or be humiliated.

Boundary

As a way of making finer distinctions within this debate, it is necessary to introduce a concept of roles and limits, to distinguish more clearly the charges being made against therapists. It is possible to discuss the term "boundary" and analyse some of its assumptions and consequences. In fact, boundary refers to a variety of interpersonal and intra-subjective experiences, and is used as a metaphor for noting movements across any given boundary, threshold or limit. Generally, *boundary* concerns what is alleged to be the appropriate intersubjective behaviour of clients and therapists. Furthermore, a clear adherence to such roles is also assumed to enable therapy to be ethical and effective.

The concept of boundary was made explicit, and a central structuring principle for the enactment of psychoanalytic therapy, in the work of Robert Langs who has used "frame" synonymously with "boundary". The frame or boundary of the way in which therapy is enacted is a "metaphor for the implicit and explicit ground rules of psychotherapy or psychoanalysis", (Langs, 1979, p 540). Robert

Langs clearly assumes that there are specifically correct ways of setting up the therapeutic relationship and orienting it along certain lines. For him, the style of relationship that is encouraged is one where therapists are silent and supportive, but do not show themselves, and do not allow any deviation from the aim of analysing events in terms of breaches of the assumed correct boundary for therapy, and the possible intrusive effects of therapists.

It is quite feasible to extend "boundary" to refer to, for instance, the difference between public and private behaviour, as in the roles of different generations in a family: grandparent, parent and child, as well as within or outside the family, and within or outside the home. "Boundary" could also refer to transgressions or movements through, across, or on the body; within, on the surface and outside of the skin, and thus could be used to conceptualise eating and sexuality, for instance. Boundary could also be used in a temporal sense: for being early, on time, or late, and so even help describing the relation between past memories, present and future experiences. What the usages seem to have in common is that boundary refers to the theoretically assumed, as well as the actual, extent of personal power or autonomy, freedom and constraint.

With the concept of boundary comes various assumptions contained within the thought of Robert Langs. For instance, he believes that both laypersons and correctly trained therapists recognise the truth of the disruption caused by breaking the boundaries of conventional roles for client and therapist. Any behaviour of therapists that deviates from a silent, impassive listener is also an alleged causative factor, as it is assumed there is a specific set of items that are claimed to constitute the appropriate roles of client and therapist behaviour. If the boundaries or rules for the alleged correct deportment of therapy are broken by "manipulativeness, seductiveness, and infantilizing qualities," on the part of therapists, then the "breach of boundaries, and the defensive usage of such interviews … almost always negate any positive aspects for the patient", (Langs, 1989, p 188). To repeat the claim of Robert Langs in another way is to believe that there is a causal link at work. This concept clearly shows the assumption of causative forces between concepts—and the actual performance of the therapeutic role. If clients or therapists break these expectations for the correct performance of roles, then the alleged proper boundaries for therapy have been overstepped. Also, it is implied in this conceptual metaphor for understanding face-to-face relations, that boundaries can be adhered to or broken, open or closed: But to what or whom? And under what conditions?

Current debate uses boundary in several senses and refers to different expectations of appropriate behaviour. But what are the assumptions that are covered in any discussions about what is deemed appropriate behaviour? It is often assumed that some schema automatically defines the boundaries of appropriate behaviour. Therapists make clear or hidden assumptions about what is appropriate behaviour in any given context. If "boundary" is used without explicit definition, then the standards of behaviour that are being assumed can only remain as unworkable ideals for defining role performance. Also, it could be pointed out that if two key aspects of human civilisations are *totems* and *taboos* (those things which are loved and worshipped and those which are feared and avoided), then it seems that what is deemed as beyond the boundary of a defined role, the alleged appropriate behaviour in a given context, is taboo and not encouraged or generally permitted.

Intersubjectivity

Now the paper turns to a third subject for consideration that may illuminate the nature of interpersonal power in the therapeutic relationship. In addition to the concept of boundary, which enables readers to consider their own experiences that are being referred to, one concept from the existential-phenomenological approach is mentioned in brief, and its consequences are explored. This concept is similar to that which has been provided by Paul Ricoeur (Ricoeur, 1967a, p 211). It is not the intention to summarise this perspective, but some of its key attitudes are directly demonstrated (Bernet, Kern and Marbach, 1993).

It is possible to see the relation between the terms *boundary* and *intersubjectivity* that can be defined as *that which exists between subjectivities* and refers to the shared cultural norms and social practices which allow specific instances of face-to-face communication and understanding to take place. Intersubjectivity has several key facets and refers to the *co-constitution* of human affairs, where our own reaction to others is shaped and formed by our interpretation of them. And vice versa: their reaction to us is shaped by their interpretation of us. Edmund Husserl, the German phenomenological philosopher, was the originator of this perspective that takes into account our social nature, and, by an analysis of our own experience, tries to find the inherent patterns, values, choices, ethics and processes involved. Husserl noted that what is purely personal may also be shared with others. At one point, he clearly showed the importance he gave to intersubjectivity and its relation to the personal "transcendental" ego, which is not the same as the personal ego, the actual everyday self, but is a philosophically-considered self-in-general.

> Any evidence gained for worldly things, any method of verifica-
> tion, whether pre-scientific or scientific, lies primarily in me as
> transcendental ego. I may owe much, perhaps almost everything,
> to others, but even they are, first of all, others for me who receive
> from me whatever meaning or validity they may have for me.
> Husserl, 1981b, p 320.

Husserl is saying that experiential and philosophical knowledge lie both within
and between each individual. Therefore, intersubjectivity is a key concept because
it attempts to incorporate the social nature of knowledge and experience, within a
notion of the mutuality and reciprocity of face-to-face meetings on which human
events are based. So, we can see at once that people depend, in varying degrees,
on themselves and others.

As regards the full spectrum of the phenomena of meeting with others that
intersubjectivity refers to, this emphasis on the intersubjective believes that it is
impossible to *not* be affected by *any* relationship we have with another person, or
even a more abstract quantity. It is consequently argued that there can never be
neutrality in relationships and involvement with the world. This comment is pertinent to therapy when it can be seen that therapists are regarded as never acting
as an impartial mirror in which clients only see themselves and their own motivations. Therefore, intersubjectivity means that we are inevitably *in relationship
with* others, self, ideas and things. Intersubjectivity is a key concept in understanding the irreducibility of human experience to simple representations. A further consequence is that therapists who take this view see therapy as largely about
the practical consequences of intersubjective understanding. This understanding
takes place when we simultaneously see ourselves in comparison to others. Also,
we are able to see ourselves being looked at, whilst we see others looking at themselves.

Discussion

By way of bringing these thoughts together, one response to the debate initiated
by Masson is to acknowledge the power imbalances within therapy. But how can
the profession learn from this? If the debate Masson has initiated enables the profession to provide less discriminatory therapy, then precisely which situations are
we trying to avoid? There are probably therapists who are unwittingly abusive, in
so much that they desire power and intimacy, believe they are a perfect mirror of
clients, or are "invisible" to them, whilst trying to remain hidden to them but
contribute an absence to the relationship. Accepting Jeffrey Masson's claim that

there is a power gradient in favour of therapists, and to the detriment of clients, then one interpretation of the nature of the harm done by incorrect therapy is to claim that negative effects arise because therapists deny or denigrate the realities of clients. In these cases "subtle abuse" could take place when a person's reality is eroded or undermined by indoctrination, or the unwitting acceptance of another's, arguably, inaccurate interpretations of oneself, which could take away faith and trust in one's own interpretation of reality, and could lead to non-therapeutic doubt about oneself: "invalidation".

It is perhaps a truism to say that adherence to our own way of understanding the world, to our way of life, is both inevitable and constricting. Following my interpretation of Masson's theory of abuse, to counteract this tendency, practitioners need reliable personal insight, based on attention to sifting through one's own knowledge of our own part in the shared social reality. If we accept that defensive illusions of power exist to overcome anxiety at not being able to find neat answers, it follows that therapists also have defences against clients, which could be attempts to reduce their own, and clients' anxiety and guilt, which may arise in the therapeutic situation.

Also, these thoughts lead me to believe that it is easier to reject an insult, rather than the subtle abuse caused by someone you like, who has won your trust. When someone directly insults you, his or her destructive comments can be pushed aside. It is sometimes easier to recognise an abusive comment when it is obvious. But, if an apparently inoffensive comment is toxic and corrosive by its effects, then this is harder to recognise immediately for what it truly is. Again, under different circumstances, it may be justifiable to challenge clients and enable them to doubt their own strongly held assumptions of negative and limiting thoughts and behaviours, harmful illusions and myths. Therefore, doubt and an ability to vary some quality that had previously been held constant, can have either positive or negative consequences for the individual.

Returning to some thoughts on Freud's distinction of primary and secondary gain, we can see that many seem unaware of the full degree of the power struggles in everyday relating. This lack of awareness is carried over into therapy where the locus of control is most often with therapists. For example, to recap one of Masson's assumptions about the abusiveness of therapy: by definition clients are actively seeking help in reducing their own pain and confusion. But are there cases to the contrary? For example, when some clients are sufficiently perceptive and capable of making the judgement that a therapy or therapist is not suitable for them. So, some clients may be weak in comparison to therapists and have an imperfect knowledge of the therapy market and what the treatment should be like. If therapists had a greater awareness of their own contribution, they could create a remedy for the power imbalance and become effective facilitators in helping clients find their meanings and values. Therapists are in a position where clients can be re-abused, either purposefully or inadvertently. However, this same criticism could be made of many other situations in everyday life. But that is not the point that I think Masson was trying to make. I feel that what he is saying is that therapists should be particularly sophisticated in knowing how to deliver their therapeutic presence, and that should include specific skills around the areas of empathy and knowing how one may be currently being empathised.

One worst-case scenario is the combination of easily led clients, with therapists who have a lack of skills, poor judgement or even abusive intentions (Masson, 1994, p 24). In this case, if clients have poor judgement about potentially abusive therapists, or if their judgement is temporarily under par, these poor conditions could contribute towards a lack of autonomy for clients and an acceptance of inappropriate behaviour in the sessions. It is in this case that therapists can get away with abuse. Because if clients are well-informed and knowledgeable about what should occur, they already have some knowledge about what comprises good therapy. But this presupposes that clients are sufficiently clear-sighted about themselves and the correct performance of the therapist they have chosen.

Masson, during his address to the Society for Existential Analysis, commented that clients need to know who therapists are. He pointed out that clients are often concerned with the personal history, marital status and character of who they are seeing (p 24). He believes that they seem to have a need to work out if they should trust this stranger, to whom they are about to bare their souls. Indeed, clients could be working out their criteria for trusting therapists. But, just how much are clients entitled to know about therapists and the theory that informs their way of helping? Masson urged therapists to tell clients what they can and cannot expect. Thereby implying that clients could have a "bill of rights" that could be discussed with them at the first meetings (p 31). Masson also suggested that a future project for practitioners is to develop a consideration of where they personally stand on the issues of gender, class and race, and acknowledge that we come from different cultural backgrounds.

If we accept Masson's suggestion that therapists have the upper hand in power and control, even if they declare themselves to be non-directive, then how could therapy gain its full restorative and ethical effect? Could it be based on the intersubjective negotiation of power and expectations? Is it possible to create a therapeutic relationship that is safe, ethical and yet expand awareness and promote positive change? Such an experience of negotiation and agreement could enable clients to create safety and inform them about what to expect. This may even help them see themselves differently and find new meanings and empowerment in their relationships outside of therapy.

One final point to be noted is Masson's request that therapy should be egalitarian. But is it at all possible to have equality in everyday life, let alone therapy? Masson says that equality, the elimination of the power differential, is what he wants: "The goal is equality. How can therapy be made more equitable?" (p 30). If we look at our own inter-actions within our peer groups, is it possible to say that these are equal? Or without some power of attraction or repulsion, or of sometimes working towards satisfying only one person's aims? So, it may be the case that this ideal of equality is impossible. If it is impossible to have equality in relationship, it is possible to conclude that it is useless to pretend that equality could exist in therapy. If the power differential does not hurt clients, then therapy is an acceptable form of treatment.

Conclusion

One possibility for minimising the harmful effects of therapy is to move further towards "self-realisation," where clients have more knowledge of the field, can make informed choices and are more responsible for judging the quality of the relationship in which they participate. This could produce more autonomy and sound judgement all round, rather than imposing definitions of reality and meanings. The many subjects touched on in this paper require much research in the form of a hermeneutic and ethical analysis of therapy, that would be in addition to other forms of research. Perhaps one consequence of this discussion is that it could institute a more egalitarian approach that would investigate the inheritance from science and psychoanalysis, such as the beliefs and methods based on neutrality, objectivity, detachment, non-engagement, and the possibility of a one and only true knowledge of reality. But this approach asks more questions than it solves. Therapists who have had their own therapy should be able to be aware of the possible effects of themselves on clients. But the safeguard that a training therapy promises, that therapists are able to know their blindspots, has no guaranteed results.

By way of recapping, it is worth emphasising that one of the aims, of searching for assumptions and analysing them, and any consequent acceptance or rejection of them, is to ground the a priori presuppositions of theory and practice in the experiences common to practitioners of similar types of therapy. Bringing these points home to our treatment of clients, it shows us that we should become morally aware of our own position. One subject for further debate and research in this manner is to investigate the possible consequences of an egalitarian relationship in therapy, where the power differential is minimised, alongside a more complete understanding of the factors leading up to unhelpful therapy.

In considering the role of insight in therapy, an answer to Masson's criticisms is to aim for the possibility of knowledge about the awareness of one's own oppression, discrimination and exploitation, and to be aware of these subjects at large in society. To have knowledge of how violence is being done to and by oneself, is a possible beginning of being able to stop such violence continuing. If one is able to point to the chains by which we hold ourselves down, then it may be possible to remove some of them. The awareness that therapists can be abusive might produce an awareness of the probable consequences of our actions, but it cannot rule out mistakes in professional judgement and abuse. Therapy has the potential to be abusive, but it is not necessarily abusive in all cases. However, until therapeutic abuse can be rigorously defined, it is impossible to define good practice by clear boundaries, codes of conduct and complaints procedures. If we accept that there is an imbalance of power, this is not necessarily to believe that it automatically leads to abuse. Perhaps some relationships are inherently non-reciprocal, but not necessarily negative. They could be mutual and complementary, where the parties concerned could gain positively. But abuse does occur when therapists take advantage of their position of comparative strength. Power differentials and imbalances are everywhere, and therapists need to acknowledge and confront them, in order to reduce any toxic effects in practice.

10

Ethics and multidisciplinary practice

Because mental health work is stressful and complex, and the possibilities of poor decision-making may result in the death of clients or harm to the public, there is a need for creating concordance to aid ethical reasoning. National and local guidelines can help. But what may also help is to have one ethical code of conduct for all co-workers. This editorial states a case for having a single ethical code.

In multidisciplinary work, colleagues might believe they are acting in a client's best interest. But because of different agendas and budgets, colleagues may wish to act differently. It may not be possible to eradicate differences of professional opinion. Particularly when there are different notions of what is important according to the professions of psychiatry, psychiatric nursing, psychiatric social work, occupational therapy, counselling, psychotherapy, clinical and counselling psychology. Therefore, what steps can be taken to ensure the quality of care?

The radical challenges of the National Health Service Executive and the Task Force on Modernisation seek to improve care and cost-effectiveness by informing the evidence-base and altering the current status quo between the professions. Where care is delivered in multidisciplinary teams and co-working with other primary care colleagues, there is still the need for consistency of care, control and co-ordination of the services. But in order to create consensus, there is a necessity for compromise.

At first glance, the major aim of ethical practice is simple. The professionals involved should co-operate for the well-being of clients, considered in the context of the good of others and society. Firstly, clients have needs and rights yet some of them may run the risk of being sectioned under the Mental Health Act. Secondly, the complexity of biopsychosocial problems requires professionals to assess ambiguous requirements. Because many professionals are bound, by both National Health Service documentation on best practice and the orientation of their training and current practice, there is a need to promote clear, shared ethical principles that aid specific instances of ethical reasoning. There are six ethical principles to which most codes of conduct adhere.

1. Beneficence—to help clients and try to achieve the greatest good for them.

2. Non-maleficence—to avoid harming clients and try to achieve the least harm.

3. Justice—to offer the same opportunities and help and avoid prejudicial treatment and discrimination.

4. Respect for autonomy—to promote the independence of clients and allow all concerned to implement a range of choices.

5. Confidentiality—to protect clients in their right to privacy.

6. Veracity—to be truthful to clients, oneself and colleagues. And avoid having secret communications with third parties.

These principles from moral philosophy are clear but it is trying to weigh opposing tendencies that makes ethical reasoning difficult. For instance, confidentiality is one major topic that at first might appear to be straightforward. But there are competing needs to provide confidentiality for clients—'against' the inquiries of third parties. Yet there is the need to share information with colleagues. Therefore, if 'levels' of confidentiality can be offered, it will promote trust and self-disclosure and satisfy the requirement to monitor risk to oneself and others (Bond, 1993). Also, offering confidentiality to clients does not mean offering secrecy about their concerns. Secrecy between professional and client is unethical because it might detract from meeting the needs of the public and the law.

Many of the counselling, psychology and psychotherapy codes of ethical conduct have clauses that outline the ways in which different levels of confidentiality can be offered (Palmer-Barnes, 1998). The possibility of changes in the level of confidentiality should be made clear from the outset. The conditions under which confidentiality is offered need to be stated clearly. Telling clients about the terms and conditions of the help being offered is called 'contracting' or 'setting boundaries'. There need to be clear, written guidelines for staff that deal with how to act in potentially ambiguous and unknown situations.

But there are grey areas where even the psychological therapy associations have little specific guidance on how to act. The most important but least discussed situations are those where:

• Clients are suicidal or self-harming: Once a team member knows of such risk, the team as a whole should know so that they too could take action.

• Clients are a risk to minors and the public: The actions of the team should connect with legal precedents.

• Clients deteriorate although the help that is being provided may have been judged to be the most appropriate according to the research base: There is a need to maintain overall contact with clients and not alienate them from receiving a service.

• If clients are psychotic or being treated against their will under the Mental Health Act, there is a need to know how to act if persons are deemed to be out of control, in danger or sectionable.

• Occasionally, professionals might be impaired due to stress, substance abuse or are over-estimating their current ability to perform their job function (Owen, 1993): Support is required for those who are impaired.

• Professionals who are in initial training or who are switching to a new job function or re-enter training, require adequate supervision and feedback: It is unethical to require a person to achieve a new task without helping them to achieve the minimum standard of performance.

• Finally, working according to an evidence base means that it is unethical to rely on treatments that are not supported by empirical research. Yet clients need to be offered a choice and be permitted to refuse what is offered.

The provision of services has an ethical dimension that should be more explicit than the unclear assumptions of everyday ethical living. Accordingly, a single code of ethics would promote best practice and increase conformity of action in multidisciplinary working. A single code would help balance opposing forces and provide quality of care.

11

The person-centred approach in a cultural context

Person-centred therapy has led the way in producing non-directive therapy. This paper investigates ways in which the person-centred approach can be extended and bettered, so practice can take into account new areas that are not mentioned in the literature. The clarification and development of guiding ideas, and the feedback of research and practice, come to enrich practice that evolves, step by step. The major point of the person-centred approach is to set aside any notion of therapists as aloof professionals. It requests them to be natural, honest and earnest in reaching out to clients. For instance, Merry (1990) has emphasised person-centred therapy as a way of being with clients, rather than the application of technique: A statement that opposes person-centred relating to the use of skills. For others, person-centred therapy is seen as the release of innate qualities within therapists, yet it is also a set of skills that can be taught and encouraged. This opposition of skills and innate capabilities is commented on.

Carl Rogers tried to balance the need for intellectual rigour with a need to create therapy that acknowledged innate human qualities (Rogers, 1961, 1965). In particular, there is one paper in which Rogers (1990) touches on the subject of cultural relativism, and this is part of the ground that will be discussed. Below, the nature of meeting with clients is considered and it is suggested that all therapy is a cross-cultural event. The stages are as follows: It is suggested that therapists need to be aware of the full qualities of clients, and the importance of the social and physical contexts in therapy. Key ideas from social anthropology are used to focus awareness on the cultural and sub-cultural differences. These issues point to the topics of identity and how there are different assumptions of appropriate behaviour within any culture. A brief analysis of some assumptions is made. Including the assumption that the *treatment* given to clients is appropriate to them.

Relationships exist within contexts

The anthropologist Hall points out that communication has components to it apart from speech and non-verbal behaviour in the present moment (Hall, 1977). There are three aspects to communication that create the social action and reaction of a relationship. Firstly, Hall writes that the *communication code* is the explicit medium used for the transmission of information between the parties involved. Communication codes are speech, pauses in speech, proxemics (the study of space between people) and kinesics (the study of gestures). However, to understand a message, its context needs to be known.

Internal contexts are internal to senders and receivers, as their internal frames of reference. This context is comprised of beliefs, experiences, attitudes, the cultural whole and ideas of causation about misfortune and suffering. Therapists' internal contexts include their training, state of mind and beliefs about the efficacy of therapy, previous experience of clients and the range of problems worked with. Clients' internal contexts are shown in how they present their suffering to therapists, their personal explanations of their suffering and their understanding of what therapy will be. Therapy is subjectively effected by the mood that occurs between therapist and client, be it happy, confident, or anxious and preoccupied. The internal contexts that therapists have include the influence of their specific training school.

External contexts are the physical and social settings in which therapy takes place. For instance, Langs (1988) has written on the importance of creating a basic sense of safety and trustworthiness by having consistent boundaries such as set times for therapy, a set fee and ensuring confidentiality. Rowan (1988) has written on the importance of the external context, for instance, where the room says a great deal about the owner's status, education, theoretical orientation and therapeutic style. This setting may have additional symbols such as books, diplomas in frames hanging on the wall, cushions on the floor, or notes on the therapist's desk. These items intimate something about the nature of the process-taking place. Other external contexts in which therapy takes place include hospitals, universities, schools or drop-in centres. These contexts contribute to the effect where the same therapist working in different settings could be viewed differently.

Defining culture

Leach defines culture as: "That complex whole which includes knowledge, belief, art, morals, law, custom and other capabilities and habits acquired by man as a member of society", (1982, pp. 38-9). Keesing defines it as "systems of shared ideas, systems of concepts and rules and meanings that underlie and are expressed in the ways that humans live", (1981, p 68). Culture is the *common* sense, the set of implicit and explicit, conscious and tacit guidelines that people inherit as members of a particular family, religion, profession or other social group. Culture tells people how to view the world and make sense of it. It gives cohesion to a group and shows people how to behave and misbehave, and provides ways of transmitting these guidelines to the next generation, or newcomers to the group. A culture teaches its members how to live in their shared world and how to interpret that world in the same way thereby providing a sense of identity and cohesiveness. Personal identity is culturally-created and culture influences the current lived states of illness and health. As a concomitant of this, no one is without prejudices based on their own cultural beliefs about morals, values, social, religious, economic, educational, political, ethnic or sexual criteria. This is particularly true in class-bound Britain. We all have culture and an upbringing. The values and beliefs we have limit us. If we did not have values or beliefs, we would be indifferent to everything.

Culture touches every part of people's lives. The people who are known face-to-face, and who have been known, play an influential role in shaping belief. Culture is found in a shared heritage, in a certain place, in words, history, education, rituals and an established class system. It is also present in the learned behaviour and emotional expression of a group. Thus, the knowledge and ability to respond appropriately to others is gained from the group to which a person belongs. A group's categories of good and bad, their ethics, roles, power and status, all comprise their culture.

Social anthropology, the study of culture and social networks, holds many relevant insights. For instance, the group that influences an individual may be a series of individuals or a tightly knit club. To think culturally is to not emphasise individuality, but to concentrate on the group dimension. "Positive" cultural thinking is having an awareness of probable areas of difference between oneself and clients. It is also the case that cultural thinking can be used negatively in stereotyping, where a person's individuality may be lost. Culture can be studied by agglomerating individuals into groups: For instance, men and women, young and old, urban and suburban, therapists and clients. A mode of dress, daily life, diet, spiritual beliefs, myths and explanatory models, including health beliefs and ideas about human nature, distinguish different groups. After children are born, their every experience is taught and shaped by culture.

The creation and maintenance of culturally-held beliefs are the social networks of a group of people because an individual's social network is the essence of their being in a world with others. However, there is a certain tension between a group and an individual. Individuals want to belong to others. Yet to do so may involve having to suppress part of personal nature in order to conform, due to the desire to be with others. Therefore, agreement with others often gets the upperhand over personal values, as the effects of peer group pressure show.

Example of medical anthropology

Medical anthropology is the study of healing and health beliefs in different cultures. Its purpose is not only to record the health practices of people who live in desolate areas or in impoverished countries. It is useful in the development of therapy and the client-centred approach. Medical anthropology analyses the lived experiences of health and illness in the contexts of cultural meanings and beliefs throughout the world. For instance, Helman (1990) provides an introduction to the scope of medical anthropology. Littlewood and Lipsedge (1987) give an alternative theory of psychopathology from a cross-cultural viewpoint.

In the West, one of the main cultures people belong to is their work (Mars, 1994). Clear examples of job cultures that are well-known are the police, nursing and teaching. In the professions there are certain implicit and explicit right and wrong ways of behaving. Only people with certain personalities find it most natural to fit into a specific human environment such as the job culture of a specific profession. As far as regards therapy, therapists take on the beliefs and values of their training schools. The risk in becoming enculturated is that the cultural view people have blinds them to what can be seen. Such shortcomings are inevitable to a degree. But the possibility of mutual mis-understanding, between individuals from different cultures, makes a need to create cross-cultural communication in therapy.

Emic-etic divide in therapy

Problems arise when cultural beliefs and assumptions lead to a culture-clash when each party's hidden rules conflict. In cross-cultural confrontation, each party can accuse the other of being irrational. I would like to temporarily re-define rational and irrational in the following way: If something is "rational" then it is agreed. If something is "irrational" one does not agree with it.

Anthropologists have three key concepts to describe the difference between insight into oneself and empathic knowledge of other people. An *etic* viewpoint is one that construes other persons, culture and the world in such a way as to fit data on to predetermined concepts. This contrasts with the understanding that clients and cultures have of themselves, which anthropology calls an *emic* viewpoint. To get an emic understanding of another's cultural view requires stepping out from one's own internal context. The word *ethnocentric* can also be used to describe how cultures clash. An ethnocentric clash is one where the opinions of one group predominate over the opinions of other groups. Ethnocentricity is the holding of culture-bound views and believing that one's own cultural bias is the only possible truth. Examples of ethnocentrism are racism, sexism and other forms of bias. Differences between emic and etic viewpoints can also be summarised as follows:

emic/client-centred	etic/therapist-centred
I am in two minds about it...	Cognitive Dissonance
It's my nerves...	Stress
I am stupid and ugly...	Low self esteem
I just can't cope...	Inadequate personality
I'm alright really...	Denial
I don't known why I come here ...	Resistance
They make me angry...	Blamer not taking responsibility

Medical anthropology considers the concepts that healers have and their understandings of the suffering of clients as "disease". Diseases are often assumed to be abstract things or independent entities that have a recurring identity. They may be assumed to be universal in form, progress and content. The symptoms, prognosis and treatment are considered to be similar, regardless of the individual or cultural group in which they occur. Taking these notions and applying them to therapy, we can see that therapists' notions of 'disease' contrast with clients' experience of 'illness' (Eisenberg, 1977). One writer, Cassell uses 'illness' to mean "what the patient (client) feels when he goes to the doctor" (therapist) and disease is "what he has on the way home from the doctor's (therapist's) office", (Cassell, 1976, p 42). Illness can be defined as the subjective response of clients to suffering. It is made up of how clients have learned how to interpret the origin and significance of their suffering, and how they should or should not behave in relation to those around them, and remedy their suffering.

This debate demonstrates that therapy is a cultural product alongside many other aspects of social life. Therapists have actions that are stylised ways of responding and constructs that are ways of understanding and working out clients' needs according to a preconceived scheme. For example, you will never actually see a false self, critical parent or superego. These belong to therapists. With the above discussion in place, it is now possible to regard therapy in the following manner: *Because client and therapist belong to their own cultures, communication in therapy is cross-cultural*. When clients come for help they are being interpreted according to theory. Therapy concentrates on the assumptions used when clients make understandings, but perhaps therapy should look first at the assumptions within its own practice. In another paper, I have criticised the cultural assumptions that I feel are implicit in humanistic approaches (Owen, 1989). What follows next is a brief analysis of four assumptions.

Therapy is appropriate for all clients: For clients to have appropriate care means that there has been a consideration of the various styles of relating and the possibilities for help that are available. For therapists to be able to deliver an appropriate approach requires them to choose a specific way of relating. For instance, there may be cases when therapy is inappropriate because clients would find it too disturbing, or are unable to integrate the new information on themselves and their understanding of others. There may also be cases when the needs of clients are too great to be met.

Therapists do no harm: Prior to the writings of Robert Langs (1988) there had been insufficient thought about the possibility that therapy could be harmful to clients. It must not be assumed that everything that happens within the bounds of a therapy relationship is helpful and freeing for clients. It is generally the case that after the selection of suitable trainees, clients teach therapists how to be effective, accurately empathic and skilful.

Interpersonal communication is relatively problem free: Following the above, the cultural assumptions of therapy inevitably come into conflict with the assumptions of clients. In the example of clients who come once or twice for therapy and never come again, what happens during such meetings? It might be the case that clients' needs have not been met. Or, clients empathise therapists as being unable to meet their needs.

An example may make these issues more vivid. A young Pakistan-born Muslim woman is referred by her GP. She speaks in a broad Yorkshire accent. Her marriage has broken up and she wants to be with her baby. In a great rapidity of words she tells her therapist that her mother-in-law is keeping her child and that when she herself was two years old, spirits possessed her. She currently cannot sit still, cry or sleep. She fears she has had a curse put on her. Her referring medic asks whether she is manic. What do you reply? Do you break confidentiality? Do you keep on seeing her? What are the underlying factors to determine appropriate care for her? This is a complicated problem because three sets of cultural assumptions are in collision. The doctor assumes that it is acceptable to consult with a therapist about treatment. The client may have too high a degree of distress to be helped by therapy alone.

Therapists and clients should have experiences in common: Some believe that for there to be an ease of understanding between therapists and clients, it is preferable or even necessary, for each to share some aspect of cultural background such as race, gender or sexual orientation. If this assumption were taken to an extreme, there would be no therapy at all, for no two people have precisely the same background experiences as described by reference to age, gender, class, religious or political views and the like. On the contrary, it is the case that those therapists with a wide life experience can make empathic relationships with clients with whom they have little in common, and this ability is what makes effective therapy.

Implications for person-centred practice

If person-centred therapy has the aim of providing appropriate care for each client, then this care is appropriate according to the individual's personality, cultural group, educational, moral, political, sexual, family, religious and other relevant considerations. The provision of appropriate care takes into account both internal and external contexts as therapists take responsibility to prepare a total healing encounter for each client. According to this redefinition of person-centred therapy, therapists need to design a therapeutic structure in which each case takes into account the individuality and cultural context of each client. To create appropriate care, therapists need to have a good appreciation of clients' understanding. Person-centred therapists need to be culturally-sensitive in the service of clients. What is in the spirit of the person-centred approach is to regard both the cultural background and the uniqueness of clients.

If the intention of person-centred therapists is to give appropriate care, what do we have to offer clients that might not be acceptable to them? One implication concerns the naming of clients' problems, and the possible labelling of clients. Using theory to name a problem of living can either be a useful practice for therapist needs, or, it could be damning them by giving them a bad name. In using theory to guide practice, it is suggested that therapists need to vary their interpersonal style and be aware of the assumptions and justifications that they use. In order to provide appropriate care, therapists need to step outside of their view of the world, and empathise the views of clients.

When therapists from the world of caring and sharing, self-responsibility and professional status meet clients from a world of pain, inability and indecision, the consequence might be difficulties in communication and understanding. For person-centred therapists to evolve their practice while staying true to being with clients in a person-centred way, then the assumptions and justifications buried within theory and practice need to be brought out and discussed. A major implication of person-centred work is to be flexible in interpersonal style with clients. Also, therapists need to note how their opinions differ from those of their clients', due to their inevitably different cultural identities. This is a step towards creating more appropriate, more person-centred therapy in the service of particular clients. Therefore, once person-centred therapists are attending to the worldviews of clients, they are working with specific experiences and understandings of illness and felt-inability.

If all therapy is cross-cultural, then effectiveness in cross-cultural communication with clients is a major concern. A tension for person-centred therapy is that therapists are themselves while playing a role within the person-centred discipline. Perhaps we are naturally and automatically a little different with each client and that this is an uneasy resolution to being oneself and using skills in a person-centred manner.

Discussion points

1. Define therapist culture in regard to the assumptions of the four major styles of different practice—humanistic, cognitive, behavioural and psychodynamic.

2. Is it possible for therapists and clients of different cultures to work effectively with each other? If so, what needs to take place?

3. To what extent can a person of one culture understand those of another? And what limits this understanding?

4. What should therapists value and aim towards, when working with clients of different backgrounds so that the therapeutic encounters may be more person-centred, rather than concentrating on therapist assumptions?

12

Exploring the similarities and differences between person-centred and psychodynamic therapy

This paper compares person-centred therapy to the psychodynamic approach defined by Hans Strupp and Jeffrey Binder. Strupp and Binder's broad-based time limited therapy is chosen because it is a precise manual of how to practice that has been assembled from 30 years of research and experience. The paper shows that person-centred practice and theory are psychodynamic in a general sense because they refer to unconscious processes. Furthermore, it is proposed that person-centred practice could be enriched by reconsidering its differences and similarities with psychodynamic therapy, thereby establishing greater clarity about each form of practice and further defining the boundary between these similar forms of relationship and feeling-oriented work.

The perspective taken

Two influential ways of working are the psychodynamic set of practices, as represented by Strupp and Binder (1984) and the person-centred style that has been clarified by more recent writers in the UK, USA and Canada (Farber et al., 1996, Mearns, 1994, 1996, 1997, Mearns and Thorne, 1988, Rennie, 1998, Thorne, 1992). This paper compares and contrasts these approaches so that person-centred practitioners may have a wider understanding of the reasons for making the practical and ethical choices open to them. The first section below recaps some of the main shared principles of relating in each tradition. This is a preparatory step to discuss the role of person-centred therapists from a psychodynamic perspective, in an attempt to acknowledge the importance of the full range of feelings that arise for person-centred therapists. The aim is clarifying details of the core conditions and the use of therapist feeling to positive ends (Brazier, 1993, Tudor and Worrall, 1994).

The paper has three aims. The first is to compare and contrast the two approaches and note the main areas of difference and similarity with respect to practice. It is hoped to begin an informed debate of the importance of gaining a wide understanding of practice and theory. The second aim is to critique person-centred theory and practice, by way of this comparison and discussion, in order to develop and clarify it with respect to its key terms. The third aim is to note that both forms of therapy are psychodynamic in a broad sense: Both concern the changing dynamics of what comes to awareness, the changes in the processes of the mind and the dynamics of human relations. Only in the specialised sense does the word 'psychodynamic' refer to understanding conscious and unconscious phenomena, by recourse to evidence of unconscious processes.

This paper is written in response to debate on both sides of the Atlantic (Ellingham, 1995, Geller and Gould, 1996, Kahn, 1985, 1987, 1996, Wheeler and McLeod, 1995). Questions about the similarities and differences between person-centred and psychodynamic practice have been broached. The question of the psychodynamic equivalent of the transference and counter-transference relationship in person-centred therapy has arisen. It is impossible to cover all the areas entailed in this debate in meaningful detail. So, the subjects of congruence and negative therapist feeling, and the core conditions, have been chosen for detailed consideration. The following stages scrutinise the person-centred practice of prizing or unconditional positive regard (UPR) and the psychodynamic practice of attending to counter-transference (Boswell and Dodd, 1994). Other aspects of both forms of work are omitted.

In considering these points, it is argued below that both practices focus on theories of unconscious causation, defences and unconscious processes of empathic perception (Bornstein and Pittman, 1992, Gendlin, 1978, Rogers, 1959). McCleary and Lazarus originally wrote about empirical research into the subliminal recognition of words that was faster than the ability to speak. The results of experiments of momentary exposure were that: "the subject is … capable of responding in a discriminatory way … the level of perceptual activity indicated by this finding [should] be called *subception*", (1949, p 179). Villas-Boas Bowen describes such a process in therapy as concerning material that is radically different from the client's current self-concept that cannot be directly admitted to consciousness, similarly such material might be subceived (1986, p 299). Clearly, person-centred and psychodynamic practice acknowledge the presence of processes that bring to the conscious mind senses from an unknown source. Therefore, both approaches are psychodynamic in a broad sense. One neutral word to describe such senses is that they are 'pre-reflexive'. The feelings of self and other (empathy) are automatically created and are available to attention if a person wishes to reflect on them. However, defences may also alter or mask such feelings, changing their sense entirely.

Through the major channel of empathy and the 'dimly perceived' edge of awareness of oneself and one's reaction to clients (Rogers, 1961, p 33), both person-centred and psychodynamic therapists become aware of client defences, choices, habits and values. However, the major difference concerns how such awareness of self and other are used to make spoken interventions. This paper is written with the assumption that whether or not a theory of unconscious perception and communication is explicit or explained to clients, it is assumed that human beings have an implicit, preconscious knowledge about how to behave appropriately in different social situations (Bornstein and Pittman, 1992).

Person-centred and psychodynamic similarities

The starting place is to note the large areas of accord: The skills, values and qualities of relating in person-centred and psychodynamic practice share similarities: In both, the therapeutic actions and attitudes aim to facilitate insight and provide new experience. Re-evaluation and insight gained by clients exploring their issues and engaging with therapists may begin to change the old experiential gestalts of self-identity, the processes of consciousness and manner of relating to self and others (Laplanche and Pontalis, 1985, p 142, Rogers, 1951). Both styles demonstrate empathy by tuning-in to clients' overt and implied emotions, thoughts and motivations. It is interesting to compare the similarities and differences on empathy between Rogers and the psychodynamic writers (Beres and Arlow, 1974, Berger, 1987, Bowen, 1986, Glucksman, 1993, Kohut, 1982, Rogers, 1957, 1965, 1975, Rothenberg, 1987, Vanaerschot, 1990, 1993). Empathy enables clients to gain new learning and renegotiate the boundary between self and others, and move away from distress, towards more frequent, harmonious and tolerant relations with self and others. Potentially, both practices increase insight, ego-strength and help gain an inner locus of evaluation. These are forms of reality-tested experiential learning that may provide more accurate understanding of self and others, an on-going ability to cope with stress, and gain a greater range of action and feeling (Rogers, 1959, p 234). This attention to new learning in the field of insight and empathy, may help develop new forms of relating to self and other. The positive difference is that the new learnings are not mutually exclusive states, based on rigid and high ideals of self or superego, or dichotomies of love or hate, good or bad. Therefore, another way of studying the similarities is to regard both practices as therapeutic relationships made in the favour of clients.

But this is not all. There are other areas of overlap between person-centred and psychodynamic therapy. From the first session, setting boundaries occurs along with some form of assessment and setting aside preconceptions, as therapists from both schools strive to meet clients (Freud, 1913c, Rogers, 1942). From the first minute of contact, the therapeutic relationship is being initiated and both persons in it become aware of their own and the other's aims, values and lifestyle by mutual empathic attending. Both types of therapists may be warm and open, and to various degrees, natural and accepting. Person-centred and psychodynamic therapists are bidden to communicate a clear, respectful and valuing attitude towards clients (Rogers, 1961, p 34, p 194, Strupp and Binder, 1984). Both forms of practice share a commitment to creative silence and an ideal of attending and listening without impediment or bias (Rogers, 1961, p 34, Strupp and Binder, 1984). Both may use encouragers and attend to verbal and non-verbal communication, and pay attention to when verbal messages may not concur with meta-messages in feeling, voice tone or gesture. Both practices work by creating a therapeutic relationship, attending to clients' feelings and internal frames of reference. Both require the disclosure of some of the therapist's own reactions. Whether these are psychodynamic interpretations or reflections, both are based on "counter-transference" feelings. Both practices aim to set aside and work through non-therapeutic therapist feeling, through supervision and personal reflection.

However, if we compare those concepts and values that govern therapeutic decision-making, we see how the theory for practising connects with prior therapeutic experience. For instance, both might use an awareness of stages of the beginning, middle and end of therapeutic relationships (Jacobs, 1988, Rogers, 1942, pp. 30-45). Although both practices are embodiments of differing values and perspectives, they share working toward becoming reflective practitioners who are able to conceptualise and use their awareness of therapeutic process. Both work with awareness of endings and toward a final good ending by using an awareness of these points (Mearns and Thorne, 1988, Strupp and Binder, 1984). Also, an emphasis on saving the frame and maintaining therapeutic roles and boundaries occurs, allowing healthy rewards and frustrations for client and therapist alike. But, both methods differ in their ways of working with client material. Although both work with the therapeutic relationship, each practice maintains a different attention in responding to clients. The different attitudes, values and theoretical understanding create two, subtly different forms of practice. For instance, defences and transference are acknowledged to exist in both forms, but they are handled in different ways (Hoffman, 1983, Kahn, 1987, Rogers, 1986b, Zhurbin, 1991). It would be possible to go into more details about how the two forms are different at this stage in the exposition, but now the paper moves to focus on person-centred work. The aim in these sections is to appraise person-centred practice with an eye to adding greater theoretical and practical clarity. There are interesting overlaps between the two.

Moving into the details

For person-centred work, it is a requirement that the three core conditions are simultaneous (Rogers, 1975, p 9). At least, the core conditions describe an overall area of effective attitudes for a series of many behaviours. For the therapist, these attitudes comprise openness to self-experience; to the experience of the other; and a valuing of the other. Defences, repression and poor communications with clients prevent the core conditions from becoming established at a sufficient relational depth and quality of psychological contact (Mearns, 1997, personal communication). In 1985, Rogers and Sanford concluded that congruence is the most important fundamental condition (p 1378). At a level of honesty and openness to one's own reactions in the therapeutic situation, both models share a set of fundamental similarities concerning empathy and insight: Therapists should own their reactions and experience them, be it called congruence, genuineness, authenticity or honesty (Rogers, 1957, p 98) or the understanding of transference and counter-transference reactions (Laplanche and Pontalis, 1973, Strupp and Binder, 1984). Therefore, the following discussion and clarification starts with congruence in relation to other factors.

There is a fundamental tension between Rogers' emphasis that there should be egalitarian meetings with clients; whereas a strict psychodynamic approach is in favour of fixed roles and a 'specialisation of labour'. A major difference concerns psychodynamic interpretations that may appear as all-knowing and go beyond what is conscious to the client and be based on general theory rather than the specific experiences of a particular client. Also, psychodynamic interpretations may not make sense to clients (Thorne, 1996, p 135). Psychodynamic interpretation specifically concerns the naming of alleged unconscious reasons that cause current experience (Smith, 1987). Only in the general hermeneutic sense of "interpretation" does it mean making sense of things. Hermeneutics is making sense of situations. Whereas psychodynamic interpretation in the narrow sense is the most specific ingredient of psychodynamic therapy that tries to make positive changes for clients (Owen, 1992b). The topics of power, boundaries and psycho-dynamic interpretation are not new to person-centred debate but are rather its history that has been forgotten and not explored. These topics were covered by Rogers in 1942.

At that time, Rogers was clearly against the psychodynamic interpretation of transference and for the acceptance of underlying feeling instead (1942, p 38). He noted that spontaneous client insight into transference does occur (p 40). Inevitably, Rogers did make sense of the life-situation of clients, a hermeneutic interpretation of the client: For instance: "After two diagnostic contacts the situation was put to the mother as a difficulty in their relationships", (p 33). What this means is that a specific meaning was made of the presenting problem and this was discussed with the client. It is not clear whether the remark was phrased as a hypothesis about the cause of the client's distress and current behaviour. If it were, then it would be a psychodynamic interpretation (Smith, 1987).

But these remarks aside, there is a major problem because the person-centred therapist needs to be congruent and value the client. The problem concerns how it is possible for person-centred therapists to have negative "counter-transference" feelings about clients whilst prizing and empathising with them. The usual answer is that it is not a contradiction to empathise with a client and to value their humanity—and express ambivalence or disagreements. If the core conditions are in place, it is well within their scope to accept clients and disagree with the some of their opinions.

Problem 1: How are congruence, transference and counter-transference related in person-centred therapy?

There are a variety of perspectives on the nature of transference, counter-transference and how the two are linked. The specific perspective chosen here is a development of Freud (Hoffman, 1983, Sandler, 1976, Weisberg 1993). If we accept that transference is a major phenomenon in person-centred therapy, as well as in psychodynamic work, although it is not given the same conceptualisation or the same attention or emphasis, then what are the implications? This is the first question to be tackled.

The original Freudian view is that the unconscious is social and that each person is able to subceive empathically the unconscious of others: "everyone possesses in his own unconscious an instrument with which he can interpret the utterances of the unconscious of other people," (Freud, 1913i, p 320—more of this below). Thus, the transference of clients co-creates the counter-transference feelings and attitudes of therapists and there is a two-way inter-action between them. The specific choice of the definition of transference is that it is a complex form of inaccurate empathy and social behaviour, based on selective interpretation and attention:

> ... to certain facets of the therapist's behavior and personality; that he [the client] is compelled to choose one set of interpretations rather than others; that his emotional life and adaptation are unconsciously governed by and governing of the particular viewpoint he has adopted; and, perhaps most importantly, that he has behaved in such a way as to actually elicit overt and covert responses that are consistent with his view point and expectations. The transference represents a way of not only construing but also of constructing or shaping interpersonal relations in general and the relationship with the analyst [therapist] in particular ... [It includes a] sense of necessity that the patient [client] attaches to what he makes happen and to what he sees as happening between himself and the analyst [therapist].
> Hoffman, 1983, p 394.

The problem concerning how to understand transference and how to respond to it are based on the ability of the therapist to interpret appropriate emotion and behaviour. The crucial distinction in being able to employ the concept of transference at all concerns how to distinguish its occurrence in the first place. As one French analyst has pointed out, transference entails judging between what is appropriate to the current situation; as opposed to that which seems to be more relevant to a past one (Chertok, 1968, p 575). If it is not possible to make such a distinction, then transference as a phenomenon cannot be identified, and no action concerning it could be taken.

Both person-centred and psychodynamic approaches allow for therapists' negative reactions towards clients to be brought into awareness, to be accounted for and worked with, in a positive manner. On the one hand, the psychodynamic approach values creative silence and 'neutrality,' whilst allowing therapists to use negative feelings about clients to work out how the client may currently be evoking similar reactions in other people. The counter-transference to the transference is theoretically assumed to indicate long-lasting underlying attitudes towards other people, that lead clients to have the interpersonal difficulties that cause them distress. The purpose of neutrality is that it permits a full range of feelings about clients to arise, including negative feeling. On the other hand, if person-centred therapists are trying to prize clients, or are genuinely prizing them, might the prizing distort the full range of feeling that genuinely occurs? (Strupp, 1974, Quinn, 1993): A resulting ambivalence that person-centred therapists may have about clients is the balancing of a 'surface,' negative and ultimately, temporary dislike or negativity, with a stronger overall positivity about clients and human nature in general (Rogers, 1961, p 33). For person-centred therapists, there is the need to communicate unconditional positive regard (UPR), that might at times be in conflict with what therapists temporarily feel about clients. In other words, how do person-centred practitioners use congruence with a negative feeling about clients? I would like to leave this question hanging a while and move onto the next problem of theory and practice that requires clarification.

Problem 2: Is there a boundary to congruence?

At first glance, Rogers is apparently inconsistent in requiring congruence at all times. It would seem to be highly incongruent to try and blend *prizing* with *honesty about negative feeling*. It would contravene a general trend to be tactful with one's honesty. But such a strategy is not mentioned. There could be cases where to be utterly honest might be non-empathic and not providing UPR.

However, Mearns (1997, personal communication) states that the core conditions are fully cohesive, and at what he calls 'relational depth,' he claims no inconsistency can occur in the person-centred relationship. However, this claim is a recent occurrence and the first explicit statement of its kind in writing. What Mearns is stating is that at the relational depth of the mutual commitment, asserting oneself and expressing temporary disapproval or dislike of the others' actions are valid expressions of congruence and fully in-line with empathy and UPR. Mearns does not see any contradictions or the possibility of the non-simultaneity of the core conditions. Similarly, in Rogers' writings on congruence, it appears that honesty is always the best policy. Rogers and Mearns say nothing of how to work with a tactful or helpful honesty. There may be cases when to be tactlessly and destructively honest with clients would not be therapeutically helpful. In those situations, when the destructive reactions that clients can inculcate in therapists were congruently expressed, they would repeat the negative cycle of the maladaptive transference relating (Sandler, 1976, Weisberg, 1993). Such a repetition of hurting the client would mean that the therapist has come out of a therapeutic role and has missed the opportunity to empathise and explore the client's negativity and so make a positive difference.

Several authors have questioned the person-centred approach in its attempt to be congruent (Dolliver, 1995a, 1995b, Kirschenbaum, 1991, Masson, 1988, Mearns, 1997, pp. 144-5). In Rogers' 1957 meeting with Martin Buber (Buber and Rogers, 1960), and in Jeffrey Masson's critical remarks about person-centred practice in his tirade *Against Therapy* (1988), we read that not only is there an inevitable inequality between therapist and client, but also that either therapists are their congruent selves or they are not: If one *tries* to be oneself or uses taught skills to attempt this, it implies that one did not genuinely feel it. This raises several questions: (1) Can taught skills become so practised that they are a congruent part of oneself? (2) To what degree can a person be, or not be, his or her self? (3) How can someone deceive themselves and not realise it? And (4), if a client does not like a person-centred therapist—is it the real person of the therapist that is disliked or just the role and the skills used? Finally, at least one other problem arises: The person-centred approach implies, but does not directly state, that there is a difference between congruence in sessions—and ordinary life in the world. Congruence only pertains to sessions where the honesty of clients is met with the honesty of person-centred therapists (Mearns, 1997, personal communication).

However, there might be other cases where relational depth is insufficiently achieved with awkward, obtuse and antisocial clients, who are hostile and manifest 'negative transference,' the situation may be somewhat different. Furthermore, those clients who are aggressive and invasive may require therapists to set boundaries with them for personal safety and to enable the minimum requirements for the core conditions to take place. There is a dilemma: should therapists be immediately congruent with their feelings of hurt and anger? Or should they not express this at first, and encourage clients to explore their experiences first. Or should therapists describe the effects of the clients' actions from another perspective, that takes both their stances into account and may reflect the dilemma as therapists see it ("meta-communication", Bateson, 1972, p 178). The latter action would open clients to awareness of the feelings of hurt or anger of therapists in a way that meta-comments on the situation, calls for reflection on it, and aims towards understanding and solutions to conflict.

Therefore, I agree with Mearns' claim. There could be situations when firm statements about the therapeutic conditions should be told to clients and asking them to behave in sessions in a manner that is in-line with a minimum of desirable appropriate behaviour in sessions, as in life with others. (But these are not pathological conditions of worth). Such boundary-setting was clearly spelled out by Rogers (1942) but seems to have been overlooked in the intervening years. Allow a recap of Rogers' early position on boundaries to make the situation clear.

In 1942 Rogers referred to boundaries by the term "limits" and discussed this useful part of practice in a separate section of his first book (pp. 95-108). Not only did he feel that psychological instability and severe psychopathology were contra-indications (p 75), but he also reported that therapists fail when clients who were "never suitable" were worked with, when they should not have been (p 234). In an exceedingly contemporary attitude, Rogers mentioned that it is therapists' responsibility to be the keepers of therapeutic boundaries. Firstly, therapists should make the overall ground rules clear at the outset, which prevents disruption later on, to pre-empt disagreement. The boundaries that practitioners should be most concerned with are: (1) The responsibility of therapists in providing help to clients. (2) Setting the limit of the time spent together. (3) Therapists should set limits on the permissable aggressive action of child clients engaged in play therapy. (4) Rogers discussed the value of such limits to both clients and therapists.

So there does not seem to be a boundary to congruence in person-centred therapy during time with clients. But perhaps not all the details of the relations between congruence, transference and counter-transference have yet been brought out.

Problem 3: Is there conflict between UPR and counter-transference?

After the previous sections, it is now possible to return to comparing and contrasting psychodynamic and person-centred work. We can see now that there are tensions in person-centred approach between maintaining a balance between a professional role, working to a code of ethics and being congruent. There are further tensions between using techniques and being congruent and spontaneous, where the latter can never be a technique. What is fundamental for psychodynamic work is the assumption that a lack of self-awareness about the cycles of destructive relating can be corrected through clients' new insights and self-exploration gained by interpretation. What is fundamental for person-centred work is the assumption that to be heard, valued and accepted, begins positive change.

A difference may be noted in that person-centred therapy explicitly emphasizes the giving of esteem to clients as being curative (Rogers, 1975). Whereas the psychodynamic approach maintains an allegedly neutral professional role and is not overly concerned with a warm involvement but not opposed to such (Strupp and Binder, 1984). Psychodynamic therapy uses a free-floating association, with the ideal of getting to know clients as they understand themselves, through the use of silence and neutrality (Dorpat, 1977). But something similar occurs when person-centred therapists attend to clients at a feelings level and do not ask questions that might intrude into their experience (Thorne, 1996, p 133). Generally, both forms of therapy do not want to be directive or use or methods of steering clients towards where therapists want to go.

The person-centred approach insists on minimising the power differential, being non-authoritarian and highlighting how the congruence and the person of the therapist are introjected by clients. The idea is to work together in the direction of clients' greater congruence, self-expression and individuality. This drive towards individuality means reconsidering the introjections of family and society, and potentially re-evaluating the values and senses of self-esteem. The purpose is to help clients move further towards their own carefully considered sense of who they are. It has to be noted that the apparently overly-individualistic emphasis of Rogers has been criticised by contemporary person-centred writers (Holdstock, 1993). The point is that others and culture, *per se*, are not necessarily detrimental to the tendency for growth and development. What are pathological are unconsidered conditions of worth in producing inaccurate self-esteem and the internalisation of social conditions that cause self to turn against itself, in self-harming ways. The positive alternative is to turn towards others in increased empathy and become more tolerant of self and others. The direction towards a cure in contemporary person-centred theory is less based on a discourse of the self-contained Self and more concerned with helping clients gain considered choices about the person they wish to be with respect to others.

Problem 4: How are pre-reflexive psychodynamic processes understood?

The closing theme is how we empathise others. The psychodynamic literature has many accounts of this central psychological process and its relation to theories of defence against anxiety and unpleasant feeling. The person-centred tradition is more concerned with developing therapists who can empathise with clients, rather than developing an intellectually differentiated account of the possible psychodynamic processes that may be occurring. Here empathic feelings towards others are linked to the concept of pre-reflexiveness, in that some thoughts and feelings are or could become conscious, whilst other experiences are not immediately conscious. Coleman (1988) has suggested that an awareness of aspects of communication that are outside of consciousness could be added to person-centred practice and theory. But this is nothing new. In discussing his most intuitive moments, Rogers described them as:

> ... I am perhaps in a slightly altered state of consciousness, ind-
> welling in the client's world, completely in tune with that world.
> My nonconscious intellect takes over. I [nonconsciously] know
> much more than my conscious mind is aware of. I do not form
> my responses consciously, they simply arise in me, from my non-
> conscious sensing of the world of the other.
> Rogers, 1986a, p 206.

Let us compare this description above by Rogers, to that of Freud who wrote "everyone possesses in his own unconscious an instrument with which he can interpret the utterances of the unconscious of other people", (1913i, p 320). The quotation above could be considered as a turn to Freud rather than the beginning of a fourth condition (Rogers, 1986a, p 198), or a spiritual turn in person-cen-tred work, as has been claimed by other writers (p 199). I conclude that uncon-scious or pre-reflexive processes are present in person-centred therapy but their nature is not a subject for analysis.

Therefore, putting the pieces together, the generally psychodynamic aspects of person-centred practice are based on nonconscious, pre-reflexive empathic com-munication and the provision of psychological responsiveness towards clients. There is the connection to the relevance of empathy in general. It is interesting to note that we never have first-hand, direct experience of the thoughts and feelings of other people. We only have that experience of ourselves. Consequently, empa-thy occurs between selves. It is a form of insight into self that refers, accurately or inaccurately, to others. In psychodynamic terminology, empathy is projection. It is a sense generated from within oneself that is given to the other person. In a dif-ferent terminology, empathy is always capable of being present to our awareness. In its base form, it is pre-reflexive, an involuntary response to others that can be made more conscious and the subject of prolonged consideration (Owen, 1998). Rather than creating an understanding of an involved therapist and a projecting client, a more accurate picture of the situation may be to picture it as two people trying to tune-in to each other.

The consequence for person-centred therapy is that if the openness to clients' experience is used with an accepting neutrality, then it could enable clients to own sessions, present themselves in their own manner and set their own agenda. Rather than an enforced and strained positivity towards clients, a variable psycho-logical contact could be necessary. This would mean that person-centred thera-pists could note their own negative and positive reactions to clients that might form material for awareness-increasing reflections for the client. This involves the use of immediate or *post facto* insight and empathy, and the full range of counter-transference feelings in a helpful and respectful manner. It decreases the tendency to prize clients by feeling that one has to have positive feelings about them at all times.

Taking a critical position to person-centred work does not mean destroying it, but making a balance between genuine warmth and an accepting neutrality, by gauging an emotional distance that does not lead therapists to confluence with clients, so losing themselves in manipulations through being pulled out of the therapeutic role, which would do neither person any good (Mearns, 1992). Perhaps person-centred therapists need to find a balance between the core conditions and something like *neutrality*, as in the early days of 1942. Such an approach could appreciate how free association, free-floating attention and creative silence also operate in person-centred work and are implied in its guidelines for relating. The person-centred style of therapy could become more precise about certain areas of its theory and practice and so add greater flexibility, co-operation and explanation to practice, thereby providing clarity about the details and choices that awareness can occur in it.

In summary of this section, there are important similarities in these two forms of broadly psychodynamic therapy. Both agree that not the entire mind is conscious at any one time and that awareness can occur that is not always conscious. Both agree that relationships and events can be mis-interpreted (inaccurate empathy) by clients and therapists. Both practices have a reliance on empathy. Where they differ is how therapists react to vicarious feelings that are based on the imagined or remembered emotional understanding of themselves or another: This is a pre-reflexive connection between human beings that is called insight and empathy.

In closing

This paper ends by making two claims: Firstly, that therapy inevitably exaggerates and encourages some psychological processes and inhibits others. Depending on what effects specific therapists wish to create in their sessions, there may be possibilities to further develop the person-centred approach by an extended comparison with the psychodynamic perspective. An emphasizing of the systemic aspects of relating and social learning theory may also provide benefits: "individuals are culturally conditioned, rewarded, reinforced, for behaviours that are in fact perversions of the natural directions of the unitary actualizing tendency", (Rogers, 1977, p 247, Bott, 1990, 1992, 1994). Consequently, there is also a focus on communication and attitudes towards the systemic, mutual construction of patterns of transference and counter-transference, empathy and insight. Another major area for comparison is that each practice has its theory of child development and the attainment, perpetuation and cure of psychological problems. Secondly, I claim that a more cohesive, richer and detailed picture of person-centred work is produced when these thoughts are added to considerations of the process of any situation, and particularly making sense of self and others.

Both psychodynamic therapy and person-centred therapy agree that the release of trapped, hidden or forgotten, unchanging 'negative' emotions, enable self-esteem to be increased and the unconscious or organismic valuing process, to be contacted again. Perhaps Rogers is correct to assume that openness to self and other can be a starting point for acceptance and understanding. It is probable that person-centred and psychodynamic purists would find it untenable to think that any one style of working could be mixed with a single pure approach.

In conclusion, accurate empathy is a gift that may be entirely absent for some, damaged but capable of improvement in others and variable in its accuracy for all. Consequently, we can only properly validate empathy with those who we empathise. It is sobering to search for training manuals or research on the evidence into the key experiences of unconscious processes, insight and empathy. The fine details of the descriptions of these crucial experiences are often missing from the majority of the literature, as are detailed discussions of how to work with commonly recurring situations associated with these key terms. This state of affairs is even more striking in comparison to the law and jurisprudence. Overall, therapy has no equivalent of case law or a single philosophy of practice, but rather contains a fragmented series of case histories, theoretical and research perspectives. Therapists progress insightfully and empathically, according to the guidelines of ethics, research and theory, mixed with the experiences of supervision, personal therapy and work experience.

13

On existential psychotherapy: A hermeneutic and meta-representational perspective

Given that Heidegger criticised Sartre, and anyone who would begin philosophy with consciousness rather than thinking being, and that Heidegger disliked existentialism for its humanism, it could be possible to mis-understand the role of hermeneutics and intersubjectivity in the approaches to therapy that are existential. This paper answers these topics via the question "what is existential therapy?" Some of the many possible answers are considered en route to the favoured answer concerning hermeneutics, intentionality and intersubjectivity. Therapy cannot remove the past nor can it sometimes alter the current problem. What is offered minimally is an opportunity to change perspective and that invokes hermeneutics. With reference to other stances, these are also understood as hermeneutic and justificatory. One aim of the paper is to move towards practice and prepare for an appraisal and development of existential therapy. But before any retrieve, there is a need to come to terms with the history of the variegated set of positions called existential therapy. It is not possible to make an exhaustive analysis of all the writers who have been named "existential" nor discuss practice in detail. This paper appraises Sartre and Merleau-Ponty who are nominated as the most central proponents of existentialism because they base their stances on the original work of Husserl and Heidegger (amongst others). Reasons are provided to justify this selection. Another aim is contextualising the broad church of contemporary existential therapy. What follows is not an in-depth appraisal but a sketch of some of the most salient points. The term "meta-representation" is introduced in relation to the concept of intentionality and links are made to developmental psychology. Below, a number of questions are posed and not all of them are fully answered. The paper argues for a rejection of non-self-reflexive, non-hermeneutic and non-intentional stances. Not only are human beings and relationships intentional and intersubjective, but also meaning requires a specific stance in order to judge the accuracy of alternative theoretical accounts.

In order to refine practice and theory, what is required is a clearer understanding of the hermeneutic position of oneself with respect to the manifold of hermeneutic positions that exist in everyday life, as well as the tangle of 400 theories and practices (Karasu, 1986) that comprise the ensemble known as counselling, psychology and the psychotherapies. In order for each practitioner to know how to proceed with a client, it is argued that one should be able to account for how one interprets psychological situations between clients and ourselves, in relation to specific and general situations. It is argued that a minimally adequate account of the therapy situation is one that accounts for the different perspectives of client, therapist and other parties: this involves psychological meaningfulness. What stance or stances can be occupied to provide a proper perspective on the human condition that can account for these different perspectives? Or better, what conditions structure psychological meaningfulness and are capable of making it adequately understood? Not only is it necessary to understand how everyday psychological life makes sense, through its conditions of possibility, but it is necessary to understand how any therapy can be judged: For it is necessary to judge between different hermeneutic perspectives, hypotheses of cause and effect and ultimate justifications and preferences.

Existential therapy comprises a number of philosophical reflections on lived experience. The question "what is existential therapy" can become "whose work is included in existential therapy?" Is it just Heidegger's critique of Freud? Or is existential therapy a talking therapy that excludes the possibility of using specific interventions? The first answer offered to the question of the scope of existential therapy is that there are many writers within the area who do not define their practice with respect to Heidegger and Freud. It is true that Heidegger's critique of Freud has been very influential. But psychoanalysis is not the only form of therapy. And there is a great disparity between Heidegger and Freud on intentionality and consciousness. It could be argued that Heidegger's claim to have improved on Husserl (a preference for the being of Da-sein and the relation to being or other Da-sein) is not a help to the work of therapists who are caught up in the mass of questions concerning the presence of the past and helping clients become more comfortable with themselves and the nature of human existence. Nor does Heidegger's critique of Freud reflect the whole breadth of the field of existential therapy that is also sceptical and a critical space (eg Szasz, Laing). Nor does the Heidegger-Freud nexus say enough about the important role of hermeneutics.

A second look at the question "what is existential therapy?" could be to scrutinise its parts by asking "what is existential-phenomenological philosophy?" Or, even more generally by asking about its closest relative "what is Kantian philosophy and what does it do?" Answers to these questions then run into considerations of the extent of the research required to create a sufficient answer. "What is existential therapy" can become "which writers need to be understood in order to define the whole of existential phenomenology?" Or "which writers can be genuinely classed as existential even if they are not existential phenomenological?" As regards philosophy generally, the point of the application of philosophy to therapy means valuing philosophical stances as more pertinent to it than non-philosophical ones. To refine the question further would mean offering an answer to the question "who needs to be considered?" Indeed, would the work be done when the whole of what therapy does is understood? So let us consider the relationship between Heidegger and Sartre as a way of understanding a central facet of what it means to be existential.

The difference between Heidegger and existentialism

Heidegger criticised Sartre for his humanism and never classed himself as an existentialist. In 1945 Sartre gave a lecture that was published three years later in English as *Existentialism and Humanism*. In it Sartre made his stance on Husserl and Heidegger clear and claimed that his work was in accord with *Being and Time*. "Heidegger as well as the French existentialists and myself ... have in common is simply the fact that they believe that *existence* comes before *essence*—or, if you will, that we must begin from the subjective", (1948, p 26). Heidegger's reply is the *Letter on Humanism* where he wanted to take *Being and Time* back from the French reading of it.

> Sartre's key proposition about the priority of *existentia* over *essentia* does, however, justify using the name "existentialism" as an appropriate title for a philosophy of this sort. But the basic tenet of "existentialism" has nothing at all in common with the statement from *Being and Time*—apart from the fact that in *Being and Time* no statement about the relation of *essentia* and *existentia* can yet be expressed, since there it is still a question of preparing something precursory.
> Heidegger, 1993, p 232.

Caputo explains this difference as being due to Heidegger's development in thinking since 1927 (Caputo, 1999, pp. 229-231). The other phrases used to make this difference clear are that an "ontic" psychological, or anthropological, reading has been made of philosophy. For *essentia* to come before *existentia* means that possibility comes before actuality. What Heidegger concluded in 1947 was that thinking Being is "neither theoretical nor practical" nor a "conjunction" of them (1993, p 263) and that thinking is a return to a source, no longer in the style of previous philosophy, but more original than that (p 265). It is clear that *Being and Time* is not a book on psychology and should not be read as such.

The difference between Heidegger and French existentialism is as follows. Heidegger was strongly against the *intuitus*, which he thought was superficial. "The idea of the intuitus has guided all interpretation of knowledge ever since the beginnings of Greek ontology up to today, whether that intuition is actually attainable or not", (1996, §69b, p 328). "Phenomenology of Da-sein is *hermeneutics* in the original signification of that word, which designates the work of interpretation ... hermeneutics ... receives a specific third and, philosophically understood, *primary* meaning of an analysis of the existentiality of existence" of Da-sein as the conditions for the possibility of a phenomenological ontology and historical comparisons of the understanding of Being (§7c, p 33). But the penultimate footnote to the text of *Being and Time* reads: "Thus not existential philosophy" with respect to his evaluation of his own approach as a "hermeneutic of Da-sein" or "analytic of *existence*", (§ 83, p 397). So there is a good deal of difference between Heidegger and French existentialism (Sartre, Merleau-Ponty, Marcel and others).

Heidegger in *History of the Concept of Time* (original lectures given in 1924) argued that Husserl's treatment of consciousness and intentionality was insufficient and that considering being-in-the-world was the answer[1]. But there is a counter-argument because Heidegger never got to grips with a host of topics to his own satisfaction and rejected formal and logical methods of answering the question of Being, as section 83 of *Being and Time* shows. The closing pages of *Being and Time* show its author pouring doubt on the worth of his approach. But in what way did Heidegger make intentionality more understandable by considering Being? On the contrary, Heidegger did not further the understanding of intentionality by the five reductions[2] in *Being and Time*. Did the promise of *History of the Concept of Time,* repeated in *Being and Time,* ever come to fruition? An attempt to better understand intentionality did not occur. Furthermore, there is a question as to the usefulness of a discourse about Being and placing intentionality and contextuality in Da-sein's Being, because a discourse concerning mental processes is part of everyday understanding and speech and can be easily understood by clients.

In answer to these points, a first part-answer is supplied concerning what French existentialism believed: The work of Maurice Merleau-Ponty and Jean-Paul Sartre are selected as key writers who are definitive of existential phenomenology: This is because they focus on the work of Husserl and Heidegger in the main, and provide a reaction to the natural attitude specifically, in the assertion that human being is intentional being. Ricoeur also commented on existential phenomenology and his definition stipulated three core topics of the body (1967b, pp. 208-9), freedom (pp. 210-211) and the other (p 211), with the latter two themes broadly in agreement with Sartre.

Being and Nothingness is a crossover between Husserl and Heidegger (amongst others). Section two of the introduction states "Husserl has shown that an eidetic reduction is always possible … For Heidegger … it can always pass beyond the phenomenon toward its being", (1958, p xxiv). Sartre is in agreement with Heidegger when he asks for "the exact relation which unites the phenomenon of being to the being of the phenomenon" to be understood (p xxv). Some of the other relevant themes are as follows. Some passages in *Being and Nothingness* mirror Freud's attention to explaining symptoms and dreams by the force of wishes. Sartre made a parallel between Freud's interpretation of the unconscious amongst the conscious, and urged an existential psychoanalysis of the symbolic relation between the individual style of a conscious life—and the fundamental total structure that it indicates: as a developmental inquiry (p 569). Existential psychoanalysis focuses on the interpretative ability to understand the human condition that is prior to all understanding—and is tied to intersubjectivity. Sartre defined existential psychoanalysis as rediscovering, in each instance, the totality of each person. New positions on one's own past can be attained through the analysis of ongoing choices that are both free and determining of consciousness (p 573). Sartre also wrote of psychoanalysis that "its method is better than its principles", (Ibid). But whereas psychoanalytic interpretation should help clients understand themselves; existential analysis leaves that possibility to clients (p 574). The work of Sartre on intentionality (1970) and temporality (1960) is heavily influenced by Husserl.

The important 1945 commentary by Merleau-Ponty mentioning Sartre's *Being and Nothingness* is clear: Human being should not be considered only as the result of external forces that "shape him from the outside and make him one thing among many", (1964a, p 71). The existential view is one that "consists of recognizing an a-cosmic freedom … as he [human being] is spirit and represents to himself the very causes which supposedly act upon him", (p 72). A certain tension exists. On the one hand, "man," human being, "is part of the world; on the other, he is the constituting consciousness of the world", (Ibid). Equivalently, for Merleau-Ponty, the object is in a "*relationship of being*" to the subject (Ibid). But this focus does not to dismiss the rich number of other themes, nor the central attention to meaning and interpretation of what appears to consciousness. In these respects, Merleau-Ponty commented that "relativism … is an anthropological fact," (1964b, p 108) by which he meant that whilst one deals with human specifics then relativism ensues, because to stand outside of history is to claim an absolute perspective and that is unacceptable (p 109). *Phenomenology of Perception* has a thread running through it of the treatment of meaning: Because some meanings are ambiguous or manifold, and these occupy the region of meaning, altogether *meaning is an indeterminate region*[3] (1962, pp. 6, 24, 54, 169). The relation to intersubjectivity is that bodily perspective is involved: "my body appears to me as an attitude directed towards a certain existing or possible task", (p 100). Other people are an "inexhaustible ground", (p 361). Husserl, Sartre and Merleau-Ponty agreed that the body expresses consciousness.

The point is that existentialism, according to Sartre and Merleau-Ponty, deals with meaningful concrete instances in a way that sends knowledge and theory back to lived experience thus overcoming *dead reference*, the practical and conceptual clichés that inhabit manners of thinking, speaking and relating.

Hermeneutics as prior to cause and effect

This section considers some aspects of meaning and intersubjective understanding before providing some answers in the following two sections.

The view of existential therapy in this paper is that it is primarily hermeneutic phenomenological philosophy in application to the practice, research and supervision of therapy. All therapies are equal when understood as being hermeneutic, in inevitably occupying a stance towards psychological and intersubjective life. Possibly there are as many styles of practice as there are therapists and it would be pointless to try and create uniformity amongst a school of therapists as long as some minimum standards of deportment were attained. But it is noted that where existential therapy differs from other approaches is that it is mindful of the difference between conditions for understanding—and theories of cause and effect ("formulation" as it is sometimes called). This difference does not always appear in non-existential approaches, that focus on confused ideas about cause and effect. However, before considering the question concerning cause and effect that is preferred in this essay, two points are selected as being important.

(a) Existential therapy is primarily phenomenological philosophy applied to therapy, psychology and the human sciences in the manner of sceptical criticism—especially of the natural scientific, quantitative stances. This is not to say that qualitative psychological research can pass without critical comment.

(b) There is the historical importance of Kant's a priori style of argument as a backdrop within this approach to the philosophy of therapy[4] (Gardner, 1999). The style and content of work by Edelson, Popper, Grünbaum and Erwin does not help establish rules for distinguishing an accurate of understanding from its lack. Merleau-Ponty and Sartre occupy a place of opposition to Kant, yet the influence of Kant's demand to focus on the possible and thinkable, prior to the empirical and actual, is clear. The main thrust of philosophy after Kant is to work out how concepts are effective or not, and to understand how humans understand, from the safety of the philosophers' armchair. Philosophy is not the ultimate test of ideas about psychosocial reality. That is the job of empirical research. So in the philosophy of therapy, logical coherence becomes a discussion of emotional and relational coherence and the consequences of the practice of ideas.

A pertinent philosophical question is "how would we know whether a therapeutic concept worked or not?" The answer provided is that a concept would have to be related to the aims and nature of therapy and details would have to be specified. The question of how we would know whether a therapy concept worked or failed can also be asked in the context of how any understanding is shared. A pertinent question is then "how would we know whether therapy understood its clients or not?" (A question asked from the comfort of the armchair of thought, rather than in the heat of the moment, when therapists and clients can be confused and caught up in something they do not fully understand, emotionally nor rationally). The answer this paper provides is to claim that the key point is to have a theory of how the perspectives of clients and therapists correlate, in the same relationship and conversation, according to the same topic they discuss. Without such a theory, then the centrality of dialogue and the face-to-face encounter will be mis-represented. Such a perspective would be related to clients in a way that can create an adequate understanding of meaning. In order to appraise if existential therapy, or indeed any kind of transcendental philosophical approach to therapy, is sufficient or not, it would have to consider the conditions of possibility of therapy concepts as they lie between therapists and clients. This is with respect to understanding other persons, and so making tangible the nature of the influence of the past, the nature of emotional contact between the parties involved, and the way in which the relationship is understood that is neither wholly the clients' nor the therapists'. The topics under consideration usually focus on the generalised sense of other persons that clients have, "transference," an affective state or manner of mis-empathising, mis-relating and mis-interpreting, that can be interpreted from the presence of clients.

In the above, the role of hermeneutics appears: There is a whole; however difficult it is to state what is included in it. Therapists mark out a part of the whole as important, in order to identify something as crucial in terms of commenting on the problem as clients see it (as indeed, clients mark out a part of the whole as problematic). For this paper, hermeneutics and intentionality go hand in hand. There is a hermeneutic manifold of perspectives that can be taken towards any psychological event. Another way of stating this is to say that there are intersubjective conscious senses of any cultural object: what this means is that there are many publicly-accessible conscious understandings of any experience. Yet another way of stating the same is to write that meaning exists within the possibility of understanding not only one's own but also others' understandings of the same object. These statements are in-line with intentionality in that there is a shared pool of the lifeworld, of cultural life, that shows how two or more persons share the same perspective as one another[5].

To take points (a) and (b) above, about the influence of Kant in existential phenomenology a little further, the area of agreement for Husserl and Heidegger is the relation between concepts and everyday experience. For Husserl after 1931, description is referred to as a "new naïveté, that of simple descriptive act analysis", (Cairns, 1976, p 27), which implies an unclear hermeneutic position. For Heidegger, philosophy returns to the everyday as "the *point of departure* for the ontological problematic", (1996, §83, p 397). Heidegger's hermeneutic position is in-part a novel version of Dilthey and within the German tradition of hermeneutics.

But let us not lose sight of helping clients. In answer to the question, "what should therapy concepts do to aid practice?" One response is that they should enable therapists to meet clients and understand them. If concepts made a relational, affective or other distance, whereby clients could not get help, or therapists came to mis-understand, then a helpful encounter may not be achieved. (There might even be a purposeful role of intellectualising therapeutic work in order to keep the feelings of clients from 'contaminating therapists,' but that possibility must be dealt with elsewhere). In order to make this section more explicit, something needs to be said of the type of activities that occur in any therapy. Minimally but not exclusively, the following mutual tasks are meant:

• Understanding the problems of clients in new contexts, where what seems non-sensical or unrelated to them, is made clear by the affective and relational perspective of therapy: its psychological-hermeneutic stance. At heart, therapy is making sense of past occurrences, fearful anticipations, and problematic sensitivities in the present (etcetera).

• Making links between events, thoughts and feelings in a way that has not occurred for clients, but is apparent from the perspective of therapists. Interpreting in the psychodynamic sense occurs and is part of everyday cause and effect interpretation. Such thinking is suggesting possible 'causes' concerning influential or motivating factors for feeling and action. "It would seem not unreasonable—not qualitatively different from the ways in which we come to conclusions in ordinary living—for the therapist to point out to her patient the verbal and non-verbal behaviour that leads her to think" that such and such is the case (Lomas, 1987, p 33).

• Helping clients not miss their own strengths and reducing hurtful self-criticism. Helping clients to undo reifications of their self-image and their generalised senses of other people. Perhaps, through appreciating their own strengths rather than fixating on themselves as weak, under attack, unlovable, bad or useless.

• Entering into non-dogmatic dialogue and analysing emotional and relational situations with clients, including the immediate therapeutic one, with a view to enabling them to make better decisions and promote their quality of life.

Given that existential therapy is both hermeneutic and intentional, what do these terms mean?

If the differences between the therapies are differences of hermeneutic stance, then they employ some means of interpreting the intentionality of clients and self. But the importance of hermeneutics has generally been over-looked. One way of stating hermeneutics as a core concern is to understand it as the means of contextualising psychological problems and their treatment. For instance, one interpretation might be that problems are only a reaction to current stimuli because of pairing between stimulus and response. A second interpretation is that they are due to the accrual of the influence of the past, where past attachment difficulties, trauma and defensive choices and positions, have created specific lines of development. A third interpretation might be that psychological problems are due to the accrued effects of stress on the brain and the physiology of an individual. A fourth interpretation might account for physical predisposition that, through a first occurrence, is maintained by a variety of communications, implied requests and functions. These explanations begin with interpreting concepts out of everyday and therapeutic experience—and there is the relation between the part and the whole: But how do concepts refer to psychological experience as a whole?

Practice follows theory, in that the understanding of the problem orients therapists and clients in some way. The first question that follows is "how does psychological life make sense to anybody?" Because a hermeneutic stance is prior to ideas of cause and effect, the two should not be confused and hypothesising about cause and effect needs to be investigated. One piece of received wisdom is that if it is possible to know how a problem started, it will show how it originally solved or avoided a problematic consequence. A second piece of received wisdom is that if it is possible to know how a problem is maintained, it will show how to curtail the problem. But is it at all possible to judge developmental lines in a person's lifespan? Or to judge between resultant states as opposed to traits of the ego or personality? What are the most fundamental points that need to be taken into account when creating psychological understanding?

The opening pages of *Being and Nothingness* provide an answer that is fundamentally hermeneutic. Sartre wrote of the inter-relation between consciousness, the body and the cultural object that "abstraction is made when something not capable of existing in isolation is thought of as in an isolated state. The concrete by contrast is a totality which can exist by itself alone", (1958, p 3, a reading of Husserl, 1982, §15). What Sartre posited is the following: Psychological qualities, relations, affect, intentions are abstractions and do not exist apart from the bodies of self, others and community. Such qualities and relationships are interpretations and abstract nouns that indicate the inter-relationship between living persons. Consciousness is interpreted as intentional in meeting others in the lifeworld of everyday culture and society. Emotion, relating, thinking and complex co-occurrences concern different types of mental processes. None of them are "concrete" in the phenomenological sense. For existential phenomenology, the manifold of meanings of cultural objects, as cognised beings, is interpreted as the result of mental processes. If these cognitive-affective processes are not accounted for, this makes human being insufficiently understood. The point is that phenomenology is a self-reflexive stance and that wholism is required to understand intentionality and the implication of intentionality between people.

Accordingly, intentionality is a fundamental understanding and concepts about it are required to point to its nature and importance. Due to Brentano's influence on Freud and Husserl, there is the commonality that they use versions of the concept of intentionality. This is because Brentano lectured to both whilst they were students at the University of Vienna. Intentionality is held to be a good interpretative form because it includes multiple types of intentional relation to an object. The reason for this is that one has first-hand experience of one's own consciousness and it is acceptable to assume that other persons are conscious too. Without intentionality, object-senses are considered but there is no account of how people can have several senses of, and types of intentional relation to, the same referent. Thus, existentialism is opposed to forms of interpretation that deny the existence or usefulness of intentionality in explaining the sharable psychological life. Freud and Husserl shared intentionality as a base concept. So does the population at large who understand it in a less precise way. It is easy to discuss with clients how persons distract themselves, how a topic appears in their thoughts, or show how a person is frightened that something will happen, how a person is fixated on the past. Such communication concerns intentionality and not Being alone. Freud, Husserl and the everyday employ interpretation in the general sense. When we are with others, we infer that their speech, behaviour and emotions are in some way 'caused' by their consciousness: Such interpretation indicates the being of consciousness. One's own consciousness never fully appears to self. The consciousness of others never appears apart from its mediated occurrence in the living bodies of others. Consciousness and its intentionality concern the numbers of ways human beings can plan, remember, wish, play, love and hate … It is argued that this 'meta-representational' picture of the intentionality of consciousness has advantages over other types of theorising because it distinguishes between the manifold senses and their referent. (More will be made of this distinction below where meta-representation is more fully explained). Therefore, existential therapy is a legacy of taking consciousness seriously and being able to create a theoretical discourse about how people are aware of meaning and relate to the same meaningful objects in different ways[6].

But the therapies that follow the natural attitude confuse cause and effect with meaningfulness. It is in the existential and hermeneutic traditions that hermeneutics is given priority over cause and effect. Natural ideas of cause construe an effect as it being impossible for a specific human condition to be otherwise than it is, because of its specific cause. The existential view of 'cause' is the assertion that meaning is not at all caused in the way that matter is caused to change. When meanings change they are influenced between people. They are encouraged or chosen. They are associations and remembrances. There is the influence of the past and other sorts.

An allied question with respect to meaning can now be stated. 'What is the scope of therapy?' The answer given here is according to the actuality that there are intentional 'causes' and 'effects'. The psychological form of 'cause' is not the type of cause that operates within natural being, that an outcome cannot be otherwise. Rather in psychological 'cause' there is an influence or motivation between experiences and among people. Three kinds of cause can be identified after Kern (1986). His distinctions are necessary to take account of the complex inter-relation of these causes in specific instances:

1. Socially mediated motivations from contact with others, may become engrained, habituated and be understood by self, as parts of self that cannot change. They include the on-going presence of the social past. Socially mediated motivations are those of folk psychology, the ordinary understanding of emotional and relational life, understood in the context of the conditions of possibility of history, society and culture.

2. Personal choice, free will and personal preference exist in connection with habituated constraint in the individual (cf Sartre). Personal choice can be understood in the context of the conditions of possibility of personal conscience, social context and the effects of psychological trauma on the individual.

3. Cause in the material sense is due to physical inheritance and predisposition. Material cause (or "heritability") in human beings is understood in the context of the conditions of possibility shown by psychobiology that indicate mental and physical freedom and constraint.

These three types of cause co-occur and it is difficult to identify the precise influence of each in any client or their problems and potential answers to them. Any actual psychological influence implies an ethical question as to the value and extent that change might bring.

There could be further debate into the nature of philosophy and therapy. For these are regions without any consensus concerning how to proceed. There are a large number of writers who have contributed to the field of existential therapy and it is true that many writers have not been mentioned with respect to those who followed on since Sartre first published *Being and Nothingness*. Something does need to be said of the relation between these writers in order to make clear the stance of existential therapy to itself[7].

Talking and action as parts of the whole of psychological meaningfulness

This section discusses the scope of what existential thought can consider concerning speech and action.

Like the non-existential stances (of schools or individuals), the existential writers are those who comment on parts of everyday living, the whole of the ordinary psychological life of any human being. In everyday life, talking and action are moments of a whole, as are the specific parts of the whole, such as thinking, feeling, relating, planning, remembering so on and so forth. Talking and action are moments of the whole in therapy also. Despite whether change does or does not take place, emotion is linked to thought and action. Bodily sensation is linked to imagination and memory to habit and relating ... The point is that writers comment on parts of the whole with respect to the talking and action therapies, as representative of the whole of therapy. Practically speaking, talking therapy (psychodynamic, person-centred, interpersonal therapy, etc) is a part of the whole that focuses on the therapeutic relationship and meaningfulness. It seems to me that talking therapy is easiest for the largest part of the population to enter. Whereas action therapies (those demanding that clients occupy a specific hermeneutic stance and carry out specific instructions and actions) are not as accessible in the way that talking is. The point I wish to make here is not to mistake the part for the whole. Talking and relating are parts of the whole, as is action. But because of the ease of talking and relating, with respect to taking action, it seems to me that talking and relating come before 'interventionism' (cognitive behavioural therapy or any specific request to ask clients to do something in order for them to help themselves). Therefore, any choice of how to provide therapy needs to appraise non-specific talking and relating—as one approach to meaning—or to consider that there might be a specific way of directly changing the meaning and experience of some situation through clients taking action. Because existential therapy is a philosophically informed set of approaches, perhaps it can find some answers to the further questions that arise.

In a different terminology, I am claiming that the distinction between being and doing is a false one. This is shown by there being no guarantee that an intervention (which might only be verbal) will have any specific consequence. An intervention in relating may or may not produce any change. Alternatively, it might produce a number of changes to parts of the whole. For instance, a verbal-cognitive intervention might promote change in re-evaluating self-worth, and promote changes in becoming more assertive and leaving behind past influence and so tend to make clients anticipate a brighter future and be able to empathise others more accurately—or it may not.

What is being argued for is a future task of accounting for the talking and action therapies (such as cognitive-behavioural therapy and other specifically interventionist approaches[8]). On the one hand, the talking therapies are flexible and enable clients to take part in something towards understanding and helping themselves. (Perhaps the skills required for talking and relating cannot be wholly taught. In my experience of teaching post-graduate students, perhaps some trainees cannot be taught how to understand themselves in relation to others because their personality is disposed in another way). On the other hand, the action therapies are more specifically focused on teachable skills and require a specific focus for clients to take part in them. It seems that something of this dichotomy is also present in the broad grouping called existential therapy. The point is that if talking is more fundamental than action, in that clients and therapists have to communicate in order to understand and negotiate help; then the action therapies go a stage further. They are encouraging a second, less fundamental stage of actions and analyses built on the necessity of there having been prior talking and relating. If this is agreed, then the less fundamental, interventionist approaches need an account of talking and relating that is sufficient to engage clients in their therapeutic processes.

What have been stated so far are some exploratory steps in a philosophical approach to working out how concepts and experiences fit together or not. This is not identical with experimental methods in psychology. The next section furthers an exploration of psychological reality that connects with hermeneutics, intentionality and intersubjectivity.

Meta-representation as a fundamental concept

So, taking a step closer to practice, there arises the centrality of hermeneutics within the context of philosophical reflection on there being multiple, intersubjectively accessible stances, can be applied to meeting with clients. For understanding hermeneutics, for instance, there is the work of Rickman (1997, 1998) who bases his approach on Dilthey. Going further towards understanding the specifics of intersubjectivity, there is the experimental work of Perner (1991) and colleagues who have investigated the phenomena of shared meaning and the developmental changes that occur in children as they come to understand others and, for instance, the specific case that others can have false beliefs and what this means. The advantage of an intentional or meta-representational understanding of consciousness and intersubjectivity is that there are marked differences between:

• Perception or primary representation in the five senses of what is current—and—presentiation, or secondary representation, that occurs in empathy, recollection, anticipation, depiction or imagination, for instance.

• Mis-representation of differences, accuracy and inaccuracy, true or false, occur with respect to what is held to be the case—as opposed to what self or others believe to be the case.

• Meta-representation is the "ability to represent the *representing relation* itself," to represent representations, and specifically, to represent how others are representing a cultural object (Pylyshyn, 1978, p 593). This was explicit in Husserl's theorising about intentionality: For instance, picturing presentiation involves understanding visual works of art occurs through a "difference between "picture" and "depictured"", (Husserl, 1982, §99, p 245): Meaning that in the case of visual art, the canvass is perceived; whereas the scene that the painting is about is presentiated, depicted in the canvass. To make such distinctions requires an understanding of intentionality. Perner and colleagues have shown that major changes take place in children's understanding of themselves and the social world around three to four years of age. This understanding is related to a move from understanding specific situations, to an entry into an empathic and intersubjective understanding of the world and meaning in it, as publicly accessible and reliant on the perspective taken towards them.

In the case of therapy, meta-representation means to represent that another person is representing their perspective on an object in some specific way. Husserl, Gurwitsch and Merleau-Ponty agreed that intentionality involves such a meta-representative perspective of empathising another, as having a specific profile of an object, through some intentional relationship to it, which is different to our profile on it. It is argued that this specific point is a minimally accurate understanding of humanity. Perner has established an experimental position with respect to the referents of different types of mental process and the cognition of reality. The work of Perner and colleagues is a genuine example of intentionality in developmental psychology. Perner concludes that "metarepresentation is in fact indispensable for modelling the information-gathering process and thereby understanding how it works and how one can improve it so that the model of reality reflects as accurately as possible", (1991, p 40). Meta-representation is:

"Explicit understanding ... that one and the same representation can have different interpretations," (p 102) or perspectives, and this is compatible with hermeneutics. The empirical finding is that three-year-old children generally "cannot answer explicit questions about why a person knows or doesn't know something", (p 151). Perner and colleagues show that the adult experimenters' requirement for a verbal response from a four year-old can inhibit their ability to communicate their understanding. When three year-olds are permitted to point, or can answer by merely looking in the right direction, or are permitted to respond with physical activity, they point at the right answer in meta-representational experiments when they are three. The main finding was that children greater than three years old were able to make "a distinction between representing a fact and making a judgment about a fact", (Clements and Perner, 1994, p 377).

Wimmer and Perner (1983, p 103) noted that five to six year-olds could tell the difference between a lie and a mistaken assumption 94 per cent of the time as opposed to 28 per cent of the time for four to five year-old children. Peskin (1992, p 84) concluded that the "success of the older children in concealing information indicated their new representational understanding that to influence another's behavior, one must influence that person's mental state". Botterill and Carruthers conclude, on behalf of Perner, that the "theory of mind development cannot be explained in terms of quasi-scientific theorising, because scientific theorising would be entirely impossible without mind-reading ability", (1999, p 94). Meta-representation is a development of Brentano's intentionality and a genuinely useful development of it in a way that surpasses Heidegger's to turn to philosophy and being, because it accounts for the inter-relation of the perspectives of self and other.

'Mind reading' in an approximate sense, or better, empathy in the existential sense, is empathising within the intersubjective world about common referents and different perspectives on them. It is a condition for rationality and experimentation. For instance, it has been shown empirically that children who have more siblings are likely to understand when others have false beliefs earlier than those who have fewer siblings. One interpretation of this finding is to conclude that empathic ability, that employs imaginative transposal into the place of other persons, is further developed through early socialisation (Perner, Ruffman and Leekam, 1994). The point for therapy is that traumatic memories and associations are 'causative' of the current state of clients in terms of how they relate with others and how they live their lives according to the cognitive and affective senses they empathise. In childhood, or for adults who suffer trauma at an earlier time, there have been harmful experiences and forms of communication that have produced insecure attachment styles. Verbal and physical violence, and neglect of the needs and rights of children, contribute to a tendency to be unable to re-attach securely to their carers, even in those cases where it is not the carers who have been the perpetrators of the abuse. Generally, previous violations have the continuing effect that the adult becomes unable to soothe themselves and connect with others (there are a number of permutations on this theme). This factor often leads the traumatised adult to therapy in the first place, as they are unable to help themselves. Their ego-constancy, senses of others and ability to attach are damaged. They appear as strongly influenced by the past and have inaccurate understandings of themselves, others and the world, in that they treat the current situation according to the old one and expect that the future will be as harsh as their childhood.

Close

What the paper has argued for is the view that existential therapy is a wide church and sceptical of psychology as science. It is a critical space and the application of hermeneutic-phenomenological philosophy to therapy. The task of therapy's self-understanding is to account for permissable theoretical contributions and state what types are insufficient, in which ways. How do the interpretative stances work or not? How might some be more adequate than others? Why might one prefer concept A to concept B? Such are the type of questions that are at the heart of this tradition of philosophical thinking.

In a nutshell, it would be possible to show there are problems with both Husserl's and Heidegger's approaches to phenomenology. Husserl sidestepped hermeneutics in order to ascertain the a priori conditions of possibility for consciousness to constitute meaning with other consciousness. In so doing, he claimed it is possible to be absolute with respect to intersubjectivity in the sense that he could account for the infinite manifold of perspectives on the same cultural object because of the fundamental work of empathy, a mental process that quasi-gives the perspectives of other persons 'when we understand what they feel and experience'. This is an absolute perspective because it relates the founding whole of intersubjectivity to specific perspectives of self and other on the same object, and so accounts for different perspectives on it *and* the simultaneously different appearances of it, for more than one person. Heidegger sidestepped consciousness and intentionality in order to ascertain the a priori conditions of the possibility for Da-sein to manifest the meaning of Being with other Da-sein in history. In so doing, he claimed it is possible to refine hermeneutically one's approach with respect to meaning, in the sense that he achieved an absolute perspective on the primacy of Being. His perspective related the transcendence of Da-sein's Being in its everyday world and historically accruing senses of the meaning of Being. Husserl, Heidegger and Merleau-Ponty agreed that a philosophically-informed psychology must attend to everyday conscious experience.

When viewing the therapies, there is no consensus and therapy does not have a coherent theoretical account of the manifold of ideas and practices that comprises it. How can we account for the lack of consensus? Maybe there is no formulaic correspondence between concepts and experience because there is the possibility of hermeneutic differences and influences of interpretation at every stage of reckoning. But because of the lack of consensus, even in the field of self-reflexive approaches like existential therapy, there is a need to justify one's interpretations and actions. The first stage in doing this is to account for oneself and the approaches of others in some ubiquitous way, in addition to the help provided through personal reflection and supervision.

In summing up, there is a long and fruitful history of competing readings of Husserl and Heidegger, some of which are more accurate than others. The paper has argued that a development of intentionality, a meta-representational theory of mind, is acceptable because it supports hermeneutic understanding and differing perspectives. If the task of therapy is in-part a pragmatic one, and if clients are able to use what it offers, then one aim is to help them flexibly in numerous ways. A further question is "what ways are suitable, in what conditions?" On the one hand, dogmatism serves to reify and universalise ideas way outside of their context of applicability: for dogma there is only one acceptable theoretical-hermeneutic stance. On the other hand, the ability to account for the perspectives of others is a major topic for therapy and ordinary life. It is argued that there should be no slavish adherence to theory. If existential therapy is to follow its ability to be a critical philosophical approach, in scrutinising its own and other approaches, then it will have to account for the divide between talking therapy and working with the therapeutic relationship; and the more interventionist styles of working. The refusal of consciousness and intentionality smacks of radical behaviourism that refused to account for consciousness because it lies outside of that which can be measured and modelled by natural science.

Notes

1. Heidegger did not treat intentionality as intentionality but obscured Husserl's comments in *Ideas I* on intentional implication and modification and turned away from the phenomena to Greek philosophy. Specifically, he turned away from the phenomena of the different types of givenness and abandoned a possible critique and development of the investigation of noesis-noema correlates. In Heidegger's writing, Husserl's phenomenology is defined without mentioning the major focus on the intentional analysis of noeses and what that means in terms of stating how mental processes work (for instance Husserl, 1982, §§99, 111). It is not clear whether this was a purposeful mis-representation of Husserl's case or not. However, Heidegger's critique of Husserl made Heidegger's phenomenology into an object-related study in the context of ancient Greek philosophy rather than the relation of the being of Da-sein to the being of what exists and how it exists for Da-sein.

2. The first and most explicit reduction is a philosophical and historical one, the same as defined by Husserl in 1913 (1982, §18, p 34, cf Heidegger, 1996, §6, p 22). Heidegger's comments on the stripping away of the usual meaning and assumptions that occur when tools go missing are a reduction through the interruption of everyday unthematized experience. This 'mistake reduction' (§16, pp. 68-69) is a reduction by the accidental disclosure of an assumption. Reduction also happens through the experience of *Angst* in which the assumptions of having a home in a safe and well-known world are temporarily eradicated (§40, pp. 174-8). Fourth, there is the reduction to temporality and what that reveals as the ultimate horizon or ground of the Being of Da-sein and for Da-sein's understanding of Being: "existential-temporal analysis of Da-sein requires in its turn a new retrieve in the context of a fundamental discussion of the concept of being", (§66, p 306 and §79, pp. 276-7). Fifth, through semantic 'archaeology' it is possible to reactivate or make a reprise (*Wiederholung*), a rediscovery of original meaning (Kocklemans, 1977). Heidegger wanted ontology to begin a de-constructive comparison, where contemporary ties of meanings are held in abeyance and checked with respect to the original meanings, practices and the worldviews of the ancients. It is not clear what makes ancient understanding better than contemporary understanding and why that the ancient is always preferable.

3. Merleau-Ponty, particularly in *Phenomenology of Perception*, often expressed Husserl's stance in a more accessible way than Husserl did. This is not to say that Merleau-Ponty agreed with everything that Husserl wrote.

4. Gardner's portrayal of *Critique of Pure Reason* states a focus on finding the limits of rational thought—as opposed to how thought can be over-ambitious. Page after page concerns a focus on the competence of what reason can comprehend in relation to conscious experience. Since Kant, philosophy has the job of deciding on the proper extent of thought before taking action.

5. This is in answer to Kant's request to explore the "*a priori* conditions of possible experience in general are at the same time conditions for the possibility of the objects of experience", (1993, p 128/A 110). This means that the conditions of experience dictate the nature of the objects of experience and lead to the connection with intentionality, intersubjectivity and hermeneutics in relation to the manifold of possible meanings of one object, process or event.

6. The treatment of consciousness by natural psychological science falls roughly into two camps. Either consciousness is no special challenge to its methods and stance, and its difficulties fall within its dominion. Or consciousness is not an object capable of scientific scrutiny and it falls outside of its limits. Both of these positions are current in psychology and cognitive science and have also existed in therapy. Cognitive behaviour therapy does not clearly distinguish between the differing types of intentionality nor does it account for the intentional pairings of sense. For instance, the basic manoeuvre in behaviour therapy is to reduce avoidance and increase exposure to a feared object. What this often entails is breaking the composite meaning of a bodily reaction (eg panic) that is in a paired association with anticipatory meaning (say fear of dying). What behaviour therapy does is to help clients be able to experience a panic episode without the conditioned meaning. This reduces the occurrence and alters the meaning of panic. Furthermore, reframing is a hermeneutic procedure and stoicism is involved in asking people to overcome their fear of fear that has become habituated and generalised. Still the work of Fonagy (2003), Wells (1997) and Tarrier, Wells and Haddock (1998) warrant study.

7. There are five 'axes' that can be related to the centrality of Husserl and Heidegger. The first axis is to understand the relation of Husserl to his phenomenological philosophy peers of Scheler, the early Heidegger and Merleau-Ponty. This axis comprises the core phenomenological writers and this group would also include Sartre but to a lesser extent. Overall, Sartre had a broader focus and belongs continental philosophy. A second axis would compare Freud to the phenomenological influence on therapy of the sort initiated either by Boss, Ricoeur (1970, 1978) or Atwood and Stolorow. And there is the matter of how to read

Freud (Lohser and Newton, 1996). Lacan could be placed in this grouping because he was influenced by Merleau-Ponty on the importance of language but he did not follow phenomenology despite having been influenced by Heidegger (Roudinesco, 1990, p 299). A third axis moves from Husserl's influence to how it has been taken up by American phenomenological psychology, that is argued to be a rush headlong into non-a-priori experimentalism entirely against the instructions of the phenomenological philosophers who require self-reflexivity and analysis of justifications. A fourth axis lies in the direction towards hermeneutics. This path takes into account the specific contributions of Dilthey, Mannheim, Parsons, Ricoeur, Derrida and Gadamer, for instance. It is important, as it is a commonality within existentialism. There is a fifth axis toward the work of Levinas and ethics. There could be a more philosophical approach that would follow the trends from the Ancients, through Descartes to Kant and appraise Hegel, Nietzsche, Kierkegaarde, Sartre, Foucault and others.

8. Wilson (1996) is a representative of a movement towards the use of empirically-validated manualised treatments. What this means is that therapy should be practised in a universalised manner for all who have a specific disorder. For him, there is no need to attend to the unique details of someone's life because such material is incapable of validation in tests with inter-rater reliability. The upshot is that therapy should be practised according to manuals that dictate the results of treatments that have been experimentally proven to work.

PART III

The question of
psychology for
psychotherapy: Pure and
applied

This final part of the work explores various aspects of contemporary psychotherapy research by in empirical psychology and its consequences from the perspective of pure psychology.

Critical remarks

From the point of view of the natural sciences of physics, chemistry and biology, the claim that there is a viable empirical psychological science of complex meaningful events is nonsense. The problem is that in experiments, animate persons and meanings could never be suitably controlled and one input variable altered to show how an outcome varies. Large-scale studies can never produce findings that average out uncontrolled variables in a reliable manner either. So the natural psychological science approach includes the effects of uncontrolled variables and introduces context-specific results in quantitative research. Hence, empirical findings concern situations that can never have all the variables controlled and the cross-section of the population included in double-blind trials are never adequately representative of the population at large.

Furthermore, the phenomena 'measured' are time- and context-dependent meanings and wholistically connected to many influences. Within this whole there are no completely independent areas such as affect, relationships, behaviour, conceptual theory or ordinary thought. These are all aspects of a greater whole of meaning comprised of wholes of lesser sorts. Accordingly, because of the wholism of the nature of self and others in a meaningful world, there arises the need to understand how the pieces of a person's life fit together in general, for the specific case of helping an individual. The whole is mapped by a number of disciplines such as developmental psychopathology, social psychology, cultural anthropology, psychiatric anthropology and other disciplines that recognise the role of the social in creating and maintaining meaning. Altogether, natural psychological science looks through the telescope of understanding from the wrong end. It looks through the front lens of the telescope and only sees the pieces that comprise a whole. Then it puzzles over how the pieces could possibly create a greater whole. What phenomenology sees, when it looks through the telescope from the eyepiece, is primarily a whole of understanding. Only with care can the pieces be identified and inter-related according to a prolonged qualitative study of their inter-relationships. The differences between the qualitative experiences—and the way that quantitative psychology makes sense of them—can be summarised as follows.

In sum, natural scientific psychology concerns a realist approach to what is measurable, before considering how meaning works and what anything means. It assumes that nature is the primary substance that is causative. In some cases the view of meaning is that, if it is relevant at all, it is an epiphenomenal smoke-screen that cannot be given priority. What is preferred is hypothesis-testing, concerning small parts of the natural whole. Its stance is material reductivism that focuses on inanimate being. If it attends to consciousness at all, it reifies it and assumes the nature of cause and effect, in advance, as due to material cause only.

Apart from questions about the suitability of falsificationism and aspects of quantitative methodology, there are further problems in making participants able to respond in a standardised way. For instance, the use of questionnaires is suspect because participants would need training in order to know how to answer the questions. If the ways of answering are not standardised, then questions are not answered in a similar way. The reason is that participants will allocate all types of answers that are inaccurate. Hence, self-rating cannot form the base of a science and subjecting such data to statistics proves nothing.

What is not being suggested is the abandonment of empiricism but its reformation. What is being claimed is that only specific portions of natural psychological science are valid and warrant the use of statistics. Where there is something constant that can be measured, the claim of being scientific is justified. For instance, research into the influence of genetic factors of heritability and psychophysics both qualify for the title of psychology as science. But no amount of data will ever mean that statistics is suitable in understanding the basics of therapy and studying human development. From the phenomenological perspective, natural psychological science cannot answer every question practitioners need to know in order to practice. By itself, natural psychological science cannot help therapists be more effective. The basis of genuine understanding cannot be furthered by measurement and statistics alone. No matter what statistics tells us about what happens on average, it cannot specify what is happening in a specific case.

In overview, natural scientific psychology is the *problem of the naturalistic attitude* that is an excessive focus on material being. The problem of the naturalistic attitude is believing that empirical psychology is a sufficient procedure to provide all forms of understanding including ideal knowledge, like mathematics, logic and guiding ideas. The naturalistic attitude has also been called Scientism, physical reductivism, materialism, material reductionism and psychologism. Edmund Husserl countered psychologism in the *Logical Investigations,* first published in 1900 (Husserl, 1970a) by pointing out that there are both real and ideal types of knowledge. Phenomenology began in order to not rush hastily into empirical relativism as the sole answer to all questions. Some matters cannot be answered by this mode if inquiry.

What this third and final part does is place together a number of papers that consider core factors in the nature of a psychology that are pertinent to therapy practice. The clinical reality is that there are unique presentations and complex inter-actions between multiple disorders. There is a complex inter-action between the personal style of the ego, its social context and the developments between the person and the consequences of their problems, that cross-fertilise themselves across the lifespan. If research deals with specific single occurrences of one disorder at a time, then there is no empirical base on how to work with complex problems because the amount and degree of complexity defeat the ability of the empirical model. Hence, there is the need for proper assessment and the judicious use of theory and clinical judgement.

The naturalistic attitude is also problematic because therapists have no means of diagnosing or providing material changes in the brain, for instance. Therapy has no means of providing physical remedies to psychological matters. Even if natural causes genuinely do predominate in any specific case, that does not guarantee helping the practitioners of the psychological therapies. Practice concerns how to create actual outcomes with real people given their limitations, plus those of therapists and the situation as a whole. Practice primarily involves social skills and making things happen in any given situation. Practice is not based on a logical or technical know-how.

Pure psychology as indicating answers

Pure psychology makes theory about the conditions of possibility for the psychological meanings of generalised people in the real world. It is an idealising process that is built on private and public meaning and takes contexts of time, place and person into account. Pure psychology grounds and fundamentalises, in terms of justifying ideas and its own perspective before creating empirical procedures. It specifies how types of intentionalities create meanings that are conscious or preconscious. It starts with qualitative experiences and meaning. It moves from what appears, through what is possible, to what must be in terms of the intentionalities. Husserl argued by attending to parts and wholes of meaning of verbal and non-verbal kinds. He wanted consciousness to be explained through argument and discussion prior to action.

The most basic key of understanding is that intentionality has a temporal orientation, and through this understanding it becomes possible to grasp, for instance, how clients anticipate horrors that they have not yet actually experienced. When the temporal focus that goes with intentionality is understood, it becomes possible to understand how past occurrences are still influential. Both anxieties and defences are temporal in their orientation. Sometimes worry is focused on the anticipatory loss of a loved one. The worrier is focused on what will happen in the worst possible case. For instance, worry contributes to a large number of other problems such as health anxiety, eating disorders, anxiety and depression, attachment problems, bipolar mood disorder and obsessive compulsive disorder. If it was not possible to grasp the nature of psychological reality, as revealed by understanding the role of time, intentionality, place and person, then the orientation of clients to what they believe exists cannot be grasped. What this means is that it is necessary to interpret intentionality and hold intentionalities as 'causal' in the psychological sense: as motivating influences on meaning. It was Husserl who was first to point out that there are inter-relations between the parts of the whole of time and that such a whole is ever-present in the present (the "original temporal field") as the connections between past, present and future. The present is comprised of what is just about-to-be plus what has just been (1991, §3, p 11, §31, p 70, both from 1905, §12, p 33 (1908), §25, p 56 (1907-9), Appendix VI, p 117 (unknown date of writing)). Alternatively, to not understand that reality appears for consciousness in time is remaining unable to make distinctions between senses and the object to which they refer. There are many *truthful* senses of the same object. It is frequently the nature of the psychological problem that *one sense of an object is mistaken for an unchanging and unchangeable whole*—when it is not. Therapy theory must not succumb to the same mistake.

In conclusion, a great deal of what is currently claimed by empirical psychology has unclear legitimacy and cannot be used as the only proper justification for the practice of clinical reasoning and psychosocial skills. The use of open questions and a basic knowledge of classical conditioning, negative reinforcement and attachment theory are sufficient to guide individual formulation. Such questions are: "What happens when you ___?" "When does that start?" "What happened before that?" "What happened after that?" These and similar questions are sufficient to grasp the sequence and co-occurrence of the intentionalities that 'cause' the outcomes of obsessive compulsive disorder and low mood, for instance. The general form of the answers found is that the detail of the relation of intentionality to an object produces lived senses of it, of different sorts. As negative emotion and mood are the usual outcomes that people complain about, it can be seen that the ways in which these are created are that people remember, imagine or anticipate. They see to feel, hear to feel, and avoid doing something to prevent such feelings. These seem to be the basic processes that promote the maintenance of psychological disorders.

The papers of this final part include the following: *On the Status of Psychological Knowledge* sets the scene by commenting on the difference between qualitative and quantitative approaches in empirical psychology. *The Future of Psychotherapy in the UK: Discussing Clinical Governance* warns of the expediency of dealing with economic pressures on public therapy services by assessing the assumptions that drive evidence-based practice. *On "The Private Life of the Psychotherapist" and the Psychology of Caring* is a book review of an excellent overview of research papers that looked behind the scenes of what it means to practice. *Attachment and Intersubjectivity* applies phenomenological ideas to show how they make links between the empirical body of knowledge into intimate relationships (in the family and between adults) that is attachment research. It makes sense of relationship dynamics for practice. *Reference, Temporality and the Defences* re-thinks the defences as meaningful in relation to the orientation in time. The point of the exercise is the observation that many defences have a temporal function in that they take from the past, in order to prevent further mishap in the present and future. *Towards an Intentional Analysis of Consciousness?* applies the idea of intentionality to the experience of distress as a way to thinking through the larger themes contained within human psychological problems as a whole. Finally, *The Empirical Evidence Base as the Re-Appearance of the Problem of Psychologism* shows the problem of psychologism that phenomenology was originally created to avoid, in the contemporary therapy research.

14

On the status of psychological knowledge

This paper assesses the status of psychological knowledge within an area that seems to be diverging rather than converging. So it may be better to write about psychologies rather than psychology, as the field is fragmented and shares no universally agreed methods. A discussion of the specific differences between the quantitative and qualitative facets of psychology is made: In this analysis there appears to be no overall procedure for resolving the confusion, as each approach is antagonistic to the other. Given that part of the role of psychological knowledge within society is about the explanation of human nature, below are comments on the philosophical problems of psychology that lead to the current state of these competing justifications and claims.

The paper is written from the perspective of Husserlian phenomenology, a philosophy of consciousness and science. Its founder was Edmund Husserl (1859-1939) and his work answered questions about how cognition creates meaning, the world and the views of others (Husserl, 1973a, 1981a, Bernet, Kern and Marbach, 1993). The paper makes a brief definition of this approach and demonstrates how this perspective assesses the current state of play in the many facets of the creation, maintenance, development and destruction of psychological knowledge. For instance, a search of PsycLIT will show no comprehensive theory of empathy, discussions of how to interpret self or others, or methods of how to ground psychological knowledge. Thus the core activity of psychology carries on without a theory of empathy and insight, concerning how we know others in the overall context of the world.

The starting point acknowledges that cognition and perception meet the outside world, and notes that what appears in consciousness are appearances of the outside world (Husserl, 1973a). Consciousness cannot be solipsistic or we would never be connected to anyone or anything—and nothing could be co-ordinated, shared or disputed (Bernet, Kern and Marbach, 1993, p 54). There are three major questions for the establishment of psychological knowledge. How do we know with certainty that our empathy, a vicarious experience, truly reaches others in an accurate manner? Secondly, what conditions need to be in place to enable an accurate empathy to occur? Thirdly, what is the ability to judge this accuracy and hence to know the difference between accurate and less accurate knowledge of self and others?

According to Husserl, psychology has had a false start by not having a philosophical grounding. A base is required for psychology to be sufficiently grounded and cohesive in both its qualitative and quantitative aspects. For all forms of knowing others, there is the central problem of being able to make dependable yet empathic judgements about them (Stein, 1989). This problem exists at various levels, in different areas of the profession and its applications.

The phenomenological method in the years of 1907 to 1911 can be defined as consisting of three steps from *The Idea of Phenomenology* onwards (Husserl, 1973a). There is an attempt at setting aside all current assumptions and reconsidering a chosen subject or the process of a psychological act. Psychological knowledge is treated as a neutral phenomenon for study. All claims and assumptions are rejected for an attempt to understand reduced phenomena that are sensually present in relation to how other forms of meaning are implied. According to Husserl, this bases philosophy in a way that is indubitable about the conditions for knowledge, understanding and experience. When we observe or imagine the connection between intentionality and its object, in many different views, or many types of the same object, we can recognise how the correlation between act and object of this sort belongs to a certain class.

The data that remains, after attempting to reject prior understanding, is carefully considered for the possible conditions that enable it to be the way that it is. It is regarded in the light of possible inter-relations between its key characteristics that appear as constants. The process is an ideal generalising one where its answers are not in a current experience but across temporal duration of what meanings are present and those that are implied.

A final stage occurs in the publication, discussion and possible agreement of the details that have been found. What the process of reflection shows is that objects only make sense in the context of the outer world. Therefore, psychological knowledge like any other subject is viewed in a series of contexts, such as its function in society, its values, ethics and attitudes towards people and underlying assumptions. The contexts which are considered below are (1) objectivity and relativity, (2) circulation and interpretation, (3) the qualitative-quantitative debate, and (4) seeing psychological knowledge in the marketplace and the social functions to which it is put in the many areas in which it is applied.

Ideal objectivity and relativity

One of Husserl's points is that objectivity and the truth requirements for the sciences have not yet been properly considered. This is due to the movement of psychology away from philosophy, in order for it to sit with natural science and its approach to inanimate matter, physiology and biology. For him, an ideal was mathematics with its sets of axioms and universals that are the same for all places, times and persons.

The problem of the lack of understanding of ideal objectivity arises in trying to claim psychological knowledge. The problem concerns how subjective and relative personal truths can become objective, dependable, agreeable truths that can be reproduced on a regular basis as part of a human science. Husserl used the term "grounding" to mean the way in which any knowledge can be true for all persons and for all time, in the way that mathematics can be true (1981a, p 186). But there is a major difference between psychology and the ideals of mathematics: All those who know mathematics can agree that $1 + 1 = 2$. But these ideals only exists within mathematics, although maths are used within the sciences and the every day. Husserl's ideal objectivity is a requirement for Kantian transcendental argument. It is a requirement for something that is hard to deny, irrespective of time and context.

Husserl insisted in 1911 that the purpose of a science is to overcome relativism and establish agreed bases from which the community of workers called psychologists can progress (p 188). In 1911, Husserl argued that there is a circle between prior understanding and the knowledge created by the sciences (pp. 192-3). Philosophically ungrounded approaches produce assumptions that are projected in the habitual manners of natural quantitative science (p 178) and relativistic qualitative history (p 186). Husserl wished to steer between these and create a phenomenology that will ground both approaches and make them attend to the nature of their objects.

Husserl preferred idealism to relativism because he wished to overcome the immediate character of events that are seen according to the perspective of the viewer, particularly in accord with the culture and place in history of the viewer (Margolis, 1991, Harré and Krausz, 1996). Personal and relative truth for a person or people can become an ideal truth. But, knowledge also gets superseded and is only held until some better explanation arises. None of this serves to solve the fundamental philosophical and methodological problems of saving the profession from getting out of it's relativistic quagmire. If relativism cannot be overcome, all that exists are competing claims, none of which can be decided upon, because there is no overall accepted method for preferring a claim. Therefore, from the Husserlian point of view, no more time should be spent on ungrounded approaches to studying humanity: All interpretative procedures and methods of making psychological knowledge should be grounded.

Accordingly, there is also a tension between the personal-relativistic truth of one moment; compared to the possible existence of ideals that are true for all people and all times, as in mathematics. The ideals about human beings are their existential commonalities, such as all persons who are alive will die. All persons are embodied, live with others and understand meaning.

But the path ahead is split in two: If there are such things as ideals and reproducible methods that produce ideals for all people and all times, irrespective of context, then other approaches need to admit their use of ideals. Non-phenomenological methods and results have to be abandoned because by definition they are ungrounded. But, if there is no such thing as ideals and no standardised, reproducible methods, there can be no psychological science conceived along the lines of a natural science, a Hard science of psychology. For, if there is no ideal objectivity, there is no basis for justifying the beliefs and hence justifying the existence of the profession called psychology. In other words, if there is no means of distinguishing more certain knowledge, then all beliefs are equally supportable and all is uncertain.

Circulation and interpretation

This same approach can be used to describe the circulation and interpretation of what is accepted to be valid psychological knowledge in society. The sociology of knowledge is an approach that tries to evaluate and distinguish the overall character of a field of inquiry (Stark, 1958, Berger and Luckmann, 1966, Kuhn, 1970, Buss, 1979, Garcia, 1987). The sociology of knowledge, the history of ideas and social constructionism are practices that turn their attention to the ways in which ideas are used, initially justified and become further justifications to permit and dismiss specific social practices. In the remainder of the paper, the letter k is a shorthand notation for different types of psychological knowledge and truth claims that are in dispute.

The relationships between the places of k creation, its use and eventual obsolescence can be viewed as follows: Psychological k is invented, maintained and destroyed within academia and practice, and recorded by books and journals. Differing forms of k are taught at universities and k circulates along channels of communication and contact between universities and the places where it is used for assessing, discussing or changing others' behaviour. The circulation of k is like a game of Chinese whispers. A game where children sit in a circle and pass on a message by whispering it in another's ear. What happens is that the message soon becomes grossly distorted. Each time it circulates, it changes shape and gains new features, while others are taken away. If there is no method for the settlement of the debate between rival factions, then the conflict over the interpretative free play and the slippage in meaning about the definitions will continue to increase, until some change occurs within the overall system of relations. As Husserl pointed out in 1911, if k is without relation to Absolute Truth, it remains relativistic and ungrounded (1981a, p 172).

Example: A polarisation

After these prior clarifications, it is now possible to turn to the specific debate between qualitative and quantitative psychologies. Qualitative or quantitative research methods are two forms of legitimating k. The current state of psychology can be viewed as a polarisation between a qualitative, descriptive, meaning-oriented and philosophical aspect; and a quantitative, explanatory-causative, empirical-scientific aspect. Below, these opposing approaches are given the names qualitative and quantitative for ease of understanding. The quantitative approach works towards natural science, but this aim or ability is not accepted as possible or desirable by the qualitative approach.

Quantitative psychologists believe that they can never get into the minds of the other, to feel what others feel and see the world precisely as they see it. Such an aim is not their prime directive, for this psychology construes problems on the model of natural science and statistics. Hard science can, in some cases, accurately predict how inanimate things will behave in the future, as long as the overall system is not too complicated for it to model. Hard science psychology feels it can predict how human beings will behave in some circumstances. On the other hand, qualitative psychology aims to find the explicit or implicit meanings and understanding of others and may include a phase of consulting with those who have taken part in the research, to check that their meanings have been registered intact. Qualitative psychology does not aim at finding probability, but at finding the key experiences of its participants.

The dimensions over which qualitative and quantitative approaches struggle are claims about the depth of qualitative work versus the probability of quantitative; or the hermeneutic nature of the qualitative approach versus the straight-forward measurement of what can be rated by quantitative workers. The approaches differ according to claims and counter-claims of the varying amounts of subjectivity or probability, two items that are taken to be mutually exclusive. Other debates focus around rival claims to be reliable and portray human nature in general and concerning specific people. Both claim that the other degenerates into mere subjective opinion. The quantitative workers regard the qualitative approach as being unable to give any regular measure. However, both sets of workers use hermeneutically-based systems that construe the task, each in its own manner before it is even begun. Their debate does not address the source of these disagreements nor enable a way out of the conflict. Therefore, the relationship between the two methods needs further clarification.

Quantitative work keeps meaning only until numerical data replaces the original qualities. It rates people "objectively" without emotion and makes a factual interpretation. Then there is no longer meaning in its original sense, but its second interpretation and translation into numbers. A third process of interpretation occurs when the numerical calculations are finished. Qualitative psychology, on the other hand, is wholly interpretive and may consist of checking the interpretations that are made. So, qualitative methods ground the process of quantitative rating before numerical analysis. Qualitative methods come before quantitative methods because the fundamental starting point is the meeting of one set of people with those of another set who are to be understood. Therefore, if qualitative work is not grounded in ideal truth, and quantitative is based on qualitative, then both forms of knowledge are ungrounded. If qualitative psychology is a priori to quantitative, then the qualitative needs to be grounded first, before quantitative can begin.

Market forces

A final context for understanding psychological knowledge is that of the market place for jobs, products and services. Here, psychological k also operates inside relationships that are sold. People want to be successful in their dealings with others and they may feel they need to some k to help them in this. Employing this notation allows the consideration of the ways in which k is a product to be sold and exchanged. Psychological k circulates between those who want it and are willing to pay for it; and those who think they have it to sell. For instance, the psychological k that is sold to industry is used in the areas of job selection, management and problem-solving. There are psychological k makers, wholesalers, traders and consumers. For a new type of k to be successful in the marketplace means making a product that is convenient, easy and reliable as an interpretative system that works on social problems and provides explanation and rationale in legitimating certain forms of action.

Psychological k is also used to assess people, situations, verbal and written information and provides procedures for interpreting and acting differently in the world. What the buyers of these services are not aware of is the lack of grounding for these claims, as others dispute each perspective within the overall field. The effect of this plurality of perspective is that the k produced is relativistic, relative to the observers making the claims and their own theoretical stance. Each parochial area has to refuse to acknowledge the viewpoint of its rivals and the limitations of its own perspective. If they did believe that their own view was insufficient and incapable of possessing reliable error- and bias-free k, then each group would have to disband and take up a new viewpoint.

It might be the case that the rival factions within psychology try to destroy the legitimacy and justifications of their competitors. If this were so it would also happen in relation to the exchange of k for money, or in competition for access to the flows of money, as money is another symbol that is passed on in exchange. Therefore, to discredit the knowledge of others is to question the financial value of their knowledge in the marketplace.

Concluding remarks

In returning to the beginning again, this paper claims that psychology has no single well-defined theory concerning the source of its own knowledge claims that considers how the empathic acts of the psychologist meet the people on whom its attention focuses. Psychology needs to be grounded to help knowledge creators understand empathy and its relation to self-knowledge. Psychology can only get a true start if it sets itself problems that can be solved. The problems that it currently faces concern the issues of the reliability and trustworthiness of its knowledge, for any truth claims that psychology produces should be an accurate reflection of the views of others. The upshot of these points for psychology is to emphasise that the profession deals in relative personal, perspectival and relativistic truths and is not a hard science that is based on agreed methods, that accumulates a body of procedures and can count its successes, like chemistry or computing.

The yearning for justification within the sciences is such that it produces illusions of knowledge, because the alternative of relativism is nihilism and chaos. The choice of a qualitative or quantitative approach is also linked to the question about what makes a psychologist a member of their profession. The overall aim is to make an enterprise that justifies itself and delivers reliable knowledge that reflects the complexity of contradictory human qualities and changeable aspects, as well as the more fixed and unchanging aspects of human nature. Psychologists need to earn a living, but if they have no reliable knowledge to trade, they cannot fulfil this last requirement without dispute. This situation shows psychological approaches as erecting some defensive fabrication against meeting criticism and looking at their own grounding principles. Psychologists could investigate their own interpretative practices of creating and destroying meaning in their work. Meanwhile, the lay public and psychological knowledge users remain unaware of the lack of consensus.

15

The future of psychotherapy in the UK: Discussing clinical governance

The National Health Service Executive has set clinical governance as the future of psychotherapy in the National Health Service (NHS). This paper draws together some of the themes and aims of current discussions concerning clinical governance and other related issues inside the NHS. The movement towards evidence-based practice and the centrality of evidence-based theorising and management, "clinical governance," seems to be central to further developments throughout the NHS. The aim is to provide a brief outline of the aims of clinical governance and discuss how it may be accomplished within primary and secondary care. A critique of the standard paradigm of quantitative research is provided by two leading quantitative researchers who have called into question the applicability of the drug metaphor and the drug trial model for testing efficacy and finding of the psychoactive ingredients of therapy.

Since the publication of the paper *NHS Psychotherapy Services in England* by the NHS Executive in 1996, there has been a slow and sure movement towards its recommendations and implications (Parry and Richardson, 1996). A bevy of interlacing and overlapping terms have been developed in order to urge an overall movement towards evidence-based practice and theory. The guiding idea is that research should act as an overall monitor of the practice of individuals and departments. Research should inform both the knowledge-base that underpins practice and direct it towards safety and effectiveness. Funding and training should be made available in-line with a consensus about what has been proven to be effective and ethical practice. Such attention should aim at serving the greatest good of the actual needs of the local population of each Trust.

These aims are considered as laudable by the author and are not challenged in this paper. The paper recaps the work done so far and eventually presents various problems with the quantitative research model that is often assumed to be equitable. First of all, what is required is a recap of the position statement put forward by Parry and Richardson on behalf of the NHS Executive. But before that a terminological note needs to be made. There is a conceptual overlap between evidence-based practice and the term "clinical governance". Clinical governance is a more embracing term entailing clinical audit, risk management, quality development, the management of complaints, staff training and development and the analysis of trouble-cases (Owen, 1996). Clinical governance means overall clinical management with an eye to the development of good practice. The term "clinical governance" is the most all-embracing, as it includes the concept of "clinical reasoning," the justification and decision-making for interventions made by therapists. However, evidence-based practice, as a part of clinical governance, is the new watchword for all interventions within the NHS.

Parry and Richardson collated the discussions of approximately 60 interested organisations. The report states that within therapy there is a need to identify and prevent "inappropriate interventions and ineffective organisation and delivery of services which are wasteful of resources", (1996, p 5). Evidence-based practice means finding forms of practice that are justified by qualitative and quantitative research. It includes links to safe and ethical practice, the use of assessment and adequate supervision. Parry and Richardson state that those therapies that are shown to be ineffective "should not be persisted with", (p 7). This is something of an ultimatum. There are three overall aims of the NHS Executive that are being put forward. Firstly, empirical evidence is being requested in order to identify and justify the difference between helpful and unhelpful forms of practice and the overall organisation of NHS services (p 9). Those forms of practice and services that are ahead of the field in empirical research, into the compatibility of specific treatments for specific disorders, have a head start in this respect. Secondly, empirically-proven effectiveness and the safety of practice are not the only factors to be taken into consideration. Cost-effectiveness is also important. Consequently, it is also the case that treatment and services that cannot justify themselves in comparison to medication, or in comparison to combinations of medication and in-patient, or outpatient treatment, may need to be abandoned (pp. 54-55). Clinical governance requires the management of practice to assess the suitability of treatments by the dimension of cost. Thirdly, it is required that research should monitor the effectiveness of practice in gaining long-term symptom relief. Such results aim to be fedback into theory, training and the management and delivery of services to inform funding (p 56). This drive to accountability and quality assurance is progressing in all areas of health care.

However, it seems that particular difficulties arise in the consideration of therapy services because they are more fragmented than other forms of health care.

Overall, the Parry and Richardson report acknowledges that there is an insufficient basis on which to make the desired changes (p 10). The report declares that the underlying principles of the therapies remain unknown (p 16). On the one hand, there is a sufficient amount of reliable research in specific areas of therapy provision, but on the other hand ...

> ... psychotherapies have been more studied than many other health interventions ... Despite this, there is no doubt that basic and applied research in psychotherapy has had insufficient impact on the organisation and delivery of psychotherapy services. Which forms of therapy are provided and the ways patients are allocated to treatments at present owe very little to research evidence on effectiveness and far more to the personal allegiances of psychological therapists to different schools of therapy.
> p 41.

The attention to empirical justification is not evenly distributed throughout therapy provision (p 42). Indeed, most practices are not justified by research and these unjustified types seem in particular danger until they are deemed justified. "Much of the current diversity in practice is unjustified, and reflects badly on the ability of the field to reach consensus about the appropriate treatment approaches to patients with different mental health problems", (p 43). Furthermore, it is acknowledged that there is neither consensus concerning a shared evidence base nor any theoretical uniformity across the field (p 47). It is a concomitant that there is not a sufficient evidence base for enacting good practice. Thus, the general aims of the NHS Executive in therapy as a whole are currently incapable of being accomplished.

The above points are the main findings of the report and constitute a basis from which to organise therapy services according to the psychological needs of each region. The next two sections spell out what these guidelines could mean for future practice in the NHS. The first section provides more details of the scope of clinical governance and clinical reasoning. The second section spells out the entailments of clinical governance and clinical reasoning in the creation of local and national standards for practice.

The way forward

Lets take some points of reference from the guidelines that have been established for the NHS. Four general pointers arise from the Parry and Richardson report. (1) There should be a focus on client need in the local population. Funding and services should be primarily directed towards helping those persons with severe and enduring mental health problems. (2) The needs of the local population should be ascertained by market research and outreach. (3) Services should work toward meeting "marginal unmet need," that is, that which would provide the greatest benefit for the largest section of the population, if the actual needs of the population were capable of being met. (4) All services should employ on-going clinical audit and quality assurance to make sure that they are delivering the required services.

The term "clinical governance" is rising as the overall term for the control and management of health interventions by evidence-based research. The general aims of clinical governance are initially to develop a cohesive approach for staff from different yet allied professions, to enable them to work together towards clearly stated aims. Clinical governance is management by objectives. The force is for the establishment of consensus, particularly a shared body of research and ethical knowledge. What such a body of knowledge can entail is learning from local and national mishaps, difficulties and inquiries. The body of research knowledge should be based on qualitative and quantitative forms of analysis. Out of this ground there arises three main aims.

At the level of organisation and management structure, there should be an overall meeting of the community's psychological needs. This should entail guidelines for the management and promotion of therapy, ethics and health and safety issues. Secondly, at the level of clinical practice, and particularly within therapy, there is a need to appreciate a wide mix of skills and ensure a sufficient and cohesive number of staff for client needs in the local population. Evidence-based practice is the aim and this should have on-going research to evaluate its overall delivery and appraise the skills of staff. Thirdly, there is an aim to nurture effective staff through an investment in continuing professional development and by ensuring adequate supervision and training.

The way in which clinical governance will actually operate will differ according to the nature of the social context of primary and secondary care. Secondary care is perhaps the simpler situation where there may already be clearly accountable lines of management and responsibility. Generally, working life will be easier if there are clear management structures and clearly defined roles and processes for effective management and the distribution of responsibilities. The situation may be somewhat more complex in primary care because of the further complexities of self-employed, part-time staff and multiple professions working alongside each other. The situation is made more complex by the buying-in of external services that are not part of the NHS. Structures of accountability and systems for the management of complaints and other matters need to be in-place, according to the peculiarities of local demand.

In both primary and secondary care, the general aims for clinical governance are to establish agreed methods for practice, to help staff be fit for its practice and to create safe and helpful organisational practices. Such clinical governance systems need to be developed across each Trust and meet with primary care services. There should be specific roles and persons who are wholly responsible for the initiation and development of clinical governance in each Trust. The bottom line is that in a legal sense, when push comes to shove, there need be clearly identified persons who have the power to instruct and dismiss.

The next related topic to clinical governance is the concept of clinical reasoning. Again, in-line with evidence-based practice and its justification by empirical research, the argument is to create requirements for making sound decisions during practice and supervision. The aim is to create an adequate knowledge and research base that is sufficient to underpin good practice. At a meta-level, there should be effective use of such knowledge by individuals. The skills of good practice should be integrated into the person of the therapist. Also at the meta-level of the scrutiny of practice, there is a need for self-monitoring and formal evaluation of a service and its participation in clinical governance by each Trust.

The aims of clinical reasoning can be summarised as follows. With respect to therapy, the idea is to turn the basis of insight, empathy and a sixth sense for what might be happening between self and other, into more clearly defined rationales for intervening. Generally, it is hoped to be able to achieve an increased understanding of problems through more accurate decision-making. The expected greater accuracy of attention to the psychological state of clients will reduce individual bias and error on the part of therapists and sustain better communication with clients. In terms of practice, what is being urged is an ensured high level of skills, plus accurate insight and empathy as a basis for the use of skills. It is entailed that a more adequate knowledge of psychopathology and assessment will inform practice.

At this point, before moving onto a consideration of where the drive to clinical governance is taking therapy, there arises an aside to the many problems that could be encountered in attempts to enact the guidelines above. Because the

Parry and Richardson report refers to the therapies as unjustified and lacking a common research base, this means that unjustified, even "speculative" theories of the many therapy schools are being given credence and projected onto clients. The intellectual understanding that therapists are gaining from their empathic being-with clients is a subjective reality that has been intellectually hi-jacked by misnomer and lack of sound reasoning, according to Parry and Richardson. Another way of stating this same point is to express it in terms of hermeneutics. The history, signs and symptoms of distress that are being interpreted by therapists, in the hermeneutic sense of interpretation, are being overlaid with unjustified theoretical prejudices, personal values and individual preferences. In short, the Parry and Richardson report is a strong critique of the epistemology of theory and practice.

Local and national standards

However, back to the aims of clinical governance and what this actually means for the practice of therapy, locally and nationally. The future projects that are being urged on the whole of health care point in the direction of gaining consensus. The ultimate aims are the establishment of local and national standards for minimum good practice. These standards require the identification, justification and communication of good practice, for the individual and for services as a whole. The first task is the creation of research to initiate evidence-based practice and identify generic skills. Entailed within this enterprise is the working out of what constitutes a sufficient knowledge-base for the creation of a standardised set of tools for clinical governance. This might include computerised audit, statistics and data recording systems as in the CORE system devised by Psychological Therapies Research Centre, at the University of Leeds (CORE System Group, 1998). The standards would be guidelines for the minimum good practice of ethics, supervision, continuing professional development, quality assurance and the justification of practice by evidence-based research. This work requires much co-operation and future development. To describe its possible progress requires the frequent use of the words "should" and "might," because what I am describing currently does not exist and could only exist through consensus.

At a national level perhaps, there could be a set of general tasks and future projects concerning the creation of the appraisal of individuals and services. Links need to be made to create effective audit tools and allied data recording. Any standards for performance need to be attainable and individuals and services need to be given guidance on how to attain them. Such a framework for monitoring the delivery of standardised good practice could be linked with career and professional development in order to structure a progression between junior and senior levels of attainment. Generally, a major focus will be on identifying and justifying the difference between sufficient and insufficient knowledge and skills. Overall, there should be clearly identified ways of achieving the above. It is not enough to demand the change of well-established practices, even though they may be haphazard in the eyes of an outsider. Psychotherapy is a young profession. Rather than a pejorative attention to force change, there could be a facilitation of change in the direction of a genuine attention to client needs.

The ways in which these future projects could be carried out are by "away days," workshops and the use of external consultants, facilitators and trainers. At a local level, the way forward is to motivate grassroots practitioners into collating, analysing and presenting information in order to devise the desired standards at the local level. The specific tasks require working toward identifying the core skills for general practice and for the specialities of severe and enduring mental health, personality disorder, eating disorder, severe neuroses, phobias, anxiety and depression, so on and so forth. There is much scope for a consultative process here, nationally and locally, and for the involvement of universities and professional organisations. Rather than laying down the law from outside, it is better for each service to own the process of its development and take the opportunity to innovate and improve on past performance. There could be an on-going series of iterations between the agreement of standards, their assessment and further refinement, and then the publication of revised standards and revised systems for their monitoring. In an on-going process of refinement, it would be possible to meet national standards and the demands of the local situation.

Problems with quantitative research

But what Parry and Richardson do not address are the drawbacks and politics entailed in the provision of therapy. The political issues involve respecting the wishes of clients who want talking cures rather than drugs. This in itself is a large issue that is not going to be discussed, but rather mentioned in passing and let drop. However, what is addressed in more detail are the problems associated with quantitative research. The writers cited are well-respected mainstream psychologists who have many decades of experience between them. Parry and Richardson recommend the use of randomised control trials. But Stiles and Shapiro (1989) refer to this paradigm as the pharmacotherapy model or the "drug metaphor". The problem with quantitative research is that as a strategy it is too narrow and tends to destroy the meanings and experiences of clients. If psychological research has the general aim of capturing understanding about that which is most relevant to the research question, then according to Stiles and Shapiro, the quantitative model is severely flawed because, in philosophical terms, it entails unsuitable ontological consequences. Let us be precise about the nine ontological assumptions of the drug metaphor as identified by Stiles and Shapiro.

1. Outcome is assumed to be distinct from process and the relation between the two is assumed to include a direct and identifiable cause-effect relation. The ontological assumption entailed in this move is that there is a cause-effect distinction, such that outcome is a function of process. In other words, all consequences and changes that arise for clients are a result only of the therapeutic process, the input (p 526). The authors question the correct identification of cause-effect linkages. Secondly, they call into question the simplistic understanding that psychological health is an easily measurable outcome.

2. This same model assumes that psychotherapeutic "dosage" is the same and repeatable for different practitioners of the same type of work. It is assumed that the interventions and processes claimed by practitioners automatically refer to pure doses of the active ingredients that create measurable psychological change. In double blind drug trials, 100 mg of drug X is often similar in Mexico as it is in France. In therapy trials, it is assumed that claimed therapeutic process variables allegedly refer to pure doses of psychoactive ingredients. The authors point out that this assumption is unfounded. One hour with therapist A, practising therapy of brand X, is not the same as one hour with therapist B, practising the same brand. Apart from the powerful effects of placebo being ignored, the authors claim that this assumption is "absurd". Might it not be the case that the psychotherapeutic "dosage" is impure, a mixture of processes?

3. It is assumed that raters can distinguish inactive processes and they can accurately measure causative ingredients of therapy. Again, Stiles and Shapiro do not agree. Even in studies where manuals have been used to train therapists in order to make them work in a standard manner, there are still differences in interpretation of the manuals. The authors remark that therapy trials do not rule out placebo effects.

4. It is generally believed that therapists have psychoactive behaviours and attitudes—this contradicts the equivalence hypothesis as defined by Stiles, Shapiro and Elliott (1986) and supported by others. The "equivalence hypothesis" or "equivalence paradox" found that despite the many therapies having entirely different ideologies, attitudes, skills and techniques—generally the results for clients

were approximately similar. The meaning of this result might be that therapy is a form of faith healing, a placebo reaction.

5. When it comes to the interpretation of statistical results there is an assumption of linear interpolations between process and outcome (dose and response). On the other hand suggest Stiles and Shapiro, might it not be the case that there are optimum levels of receiving therapy interventions? The authors note that this is also the case with drugs that may have adverse side-effects as well as desired effects.

6. There is an assumption of the acceptability of the dominant psychological scientific trial and the use of statistics. Stiles (et al, 1995) note the model goes unchallenged, despite it being the case that drug trials only consider one variable: the drug and its absence. This is not so in therapy (Stiles and Shapiro, 1989, p 532).

7. In statistics, what does a positive correlation actually mean? If a therapy brand works, then each of its practitioners will be able to show that their process-inputs correlate positively with outcome. But a positive correlation does not necessarily imply cause-effect relations. Changes may be attributable to unidentified causative factors that are not being measured.

8. What does a null or insignificant correlation mean? In drug trials there is the way in which the dose gets absorbed and metabolised by the body due to the individual characteristics of the patients. In therapy, it is not clear what specifically helps clients to improve. Is it really the case that therapists alone cause changes to happen? It may be the case that different clients react differently to the same interventions.

9. The final assumption identified by Stiles and Shapiro concerns the way in which clients control their amount of self-disclosure and involvement. The authors suggest that clients monitor and judge what it is safe for therapists to work on. Rather than therapeutic input lying under the control of therapists, it is also the case that clients and their abilities play a part in regulating therapy and are active ingredients.

In the appraisal of research yet more general questions arise such as:

a) Precisely what level of training do practitioners have?

b) How have participants been included and excluded and do they have the same level of initial distress?

c) How were the raters trained indeed was there a training for the raters?

d) How are the interventions, concepts and processes defined? Are these the same?

e) What are the details of the experimental design? Might different designs help one therapy look more effective and others ineffective, because they are based on different client outcomes?

f) Does the research state a hypothesis for the purposes of its falsification or is it omitted?

g) Do the final conclusions drawn from the research tally with the methods and data that are shown?

But the final conclusion of Stiles and Shapiro is that traditional therapy research based on an unquestioned acceptance of the drug metaphor is an unsuitable source of evidence for changing practice and theory. Despite this challenge to the drug model for quantitative research, still the use of the model continues unabated. The drug model that has been unquestioningly accepted by therapy research has been criticised by calling attention to nine specific ontological assumptions that it contains. If this case of ontological critique is upheld, then evidence-based practice and the grand projects of clinical governance and clinical reasoning need to be put under wraps until the evidence for evidence can be agreed.

16

On "The Private Life of the Psychotherapist" *and the psychology of caring*

This paper is an extended book review of *The Private Life of the Psychotherapist* by James Guy. His book discusses the joys, stresses and realities of being a therapist. Below is an overview of joining, remaining in, and retiring from the profession. The next sections deal with the relation between the core skills of therapy and the psychological consequences that they are likely to produce.

Often members of the general public have a strong reaction to finding out that someone is a mental health professional. The range of reactions can include horror, fear, fascination, anxious jokes, the fear of being analysed, and occasionally, profound respect. Other reactions include dismay or disbelief that an anxious and awkward individual is attracted to a profession whose members, it is felt, should be self-assured perfect citizens, totally exempt from any imperfection.

Five hundred years before Patrick Casement and Robert Langs, the medieval doctor Paracelsus commented that physicians should throw away their books and learn from patients (cf Casement, 1985, 1991, Langs, 1988). It is interesting to ask what mental health professionals have actually learned from their contact with clients, their training, supervision, life and personal therapy.

The Private Life of the Psychotherapist is one of a small number of books that stands head and shoulders above the general run of therapy literature, and ahead of the section concerned with becoming a therapist (Balsam and Balsam, 1974, Goldberg, 1986, Kottler, 1986). Guy's book describes how work experience impacts on home life. Guy (1987, p 185) believes that the personal is equivalent to the professional, since much personal satisfaction and personal value and identity is found by mental health workers. The work is particularly demanding, right across the spectrum of professional groups that provide it. The demands of work and home can be in conflict. Below a few thoughts on the psychology of the car-

249

ing are offered. Full billing must be given to James Guy for compiling the papers and presenting them with consummate ease. The same ground is re-worked below with a view to identifying the processes at play and learning from them.

The starting point is to take the current impossibility of being able to distinguish between the causes of human behaviour. Whether mental illness and destructive "acting out" is caused mainly by DNA, mainly by social effects or a mixture of the two, people's behaviour can be classified according to their personality, their regular way of thinking, their relating and perceiving the world. Psychiatry gives us categories of personality types and may describe certain forms of abnormal behaviour. When candidates enter training, an overlay of new modes of relating, interpreting and responding to life are taught. Therapy ideologies have direct consequences as they can form the basis of ways of life.

Joining the profession

Guy comments that some applicants to the profession may be attracted to the work but unsuited to it by the presence or absence of various qualities. He considers the possibilities of both being interested and suited for the profession. He finds that the problem in training institutes is to extract those who are interested in therapy, but not emotionally and intellectually suited to it. Merklin and Little (1967) comment on the effects of training on psychiatrists who found they experienced moderate to severe anxiety and depression, short lived neurosis and psychosomatic disturbances.

The choice of theoretical orientation has been studied by Steiner (1978), who found that the most important factor mentioned was the influence of their own therapist. The second most influential factor was the course and the reading list of the institute. The third most influential factor was the orientation of superiors and colleagues. Finally, the next most influential was the orientation of the supervisor. The process of supervision is also discussed (Hutt, Scott and King, 1983).

The dynamics of the families of origin of therapists have been studied by Guy (1987, p 18) who concludes by saying that many enter the profession because of a need for intimacy due to a sense of isolation that was existent during their childhood, and that many therapists come from families marginalised by their socioeconomic status or religion, which heightens their initial sense of separation from mainstream society. The relationship between therapists and their mothers is said to be a key factor. It has been shown that therapists are used to playing a therapeutic role in their family, long before they entered training. They are characterised as satisfying their mothers' emotional needs, rather than their own, and so have early experiences of being self-denying.

The motivating forces on therapists are listed by Guy who classifies some positive ones as curiosity and inquisitiveness, a liking for listening to others, being capable of self-denial, empathic and understanding, insightful and tolerant of ambiguity, and being comfortable with power. He reckons some negative motivating forces are emotional distress, vicarious coping through clients, loneliness and isolation, desire for power, recognition and prestige, the need to love and a form of rebellion.

Reactions to work stress

Negative coping mechanisms for work stress include social withdrawal, depression, denial, drug and alcohol usage, displacement behaviour, obsessionality, and may be associated with a lack of initiative in seeking help. Of course, if therapists have a tendency to alcohol abuse or drug addiction, then the quality of therapy may be adversely effected (Thoreson et al, 1983).

The effects of practising on therapists are commented on under the classifications of the good and the bad. When people are faced with stress they react in ways that are common knowledge to psychologists. The discussion is further split into the headings of positive and negative coping mechanisms.

As a professional group, therapists have been noted to be loners. The friendships of therapists have been studied by Cogan (1977) who found that of those who had been practising more than ten years, they reported few friendships, when previously they had reported much enjoyment and satisfaction from many more. Friendships during the time of training were noted as being deep, intense and open. The respondents stated that they felt it was because of their work experience, that they had been enabled to participate more fully in friendship.

Also, Barron makes the statement that the doctrines of therapists are parochial and congruent, perhaps even indistinguishable, from the personality of the worker in question (Barron, 1978). "Psychological mindedness" is the term that Farber uses to talk about the ability of therapists to engage strangers in discussions about human motivation and the breaking of taboos (Farber, 1985a). Psychological mindedness is the demonstration of such reflections on the meaning and motive of one's own and others' acts. Farber believes psychological mindedness is the result of the inter-action of genetic endowment and environmental influences.

One reaction to believing one's interventions are useless, or losing confidence in oneself, is a destructive impact on clients. When distress is visible to clients, they may even end up giving care to therapists (Chiles, 1974). Laliotis and Grayson (1985) note that the rate of mental illness and chemical dependence amongst therapist ranges from five to 15 per cent. Other surveys have noted that up to 69 per cent of professionals know of mental illness amongst colleagues that was judged as impairment at work. Another study showed four per cent of respondents admitting to having mental illness in the preceding three years. Lack of therapeutic confidence is concomitant with feeling not being able to be as effective as one would like. Past mistakes and ineffective interventions can appear like ludicrous errors perpetrated on clients. The truth is that therapists did the best they could at the time but past mistakes cannot be rectified or forgotten.

The stress of providing therapy can include many escapes to negative coping mechanisms (Deutsch, 1984, Farber, 1983a, 1983b). The work has its own unique stressors. Clients can touch an aspect of oneself that is painful to acknowledge. At an intensely charged moment, the therapist can be confronted with his or her own strong emotional reaction to the subject being discussed. The intensity of therapy can also produce anxiety as we hear stories that are shocking and disturbing.

Therapist impairment can take the forms of past traumas, associations and therapy-associated trauma. Impairment can be due to many factors. Boxley, Drew and Rangel (1986) estimate that the rate of impairment may lie between 4 and 21 per cent of trainee clinical psychologists. The quality of relations between trainees and trainers is the most important aspect that determines trainee satisfaction and helps to promote the perception of professional confidence in the young therapist (Bradley and Olson, 1980). Deutsch (1985) surveyed 264 therapists and found that 82 per cent had relationship difficulties, 57 per cent were depressed, 11 per cent were involved in substance abuse, and 2 per cent had made suicide attempts. Kutz (1986) defines impairment by making a comparison to a time when professional functioning had been higher.

Norcross and Prochaska (1986a) found that nearly 80 per cent of women therapists had had at least one episode of high distress during the previous three years. Nearly 28 per cent were due to relationship problems, 16 per cent to work, 13 per cent family death, 10 per cent family illness, eight per cent birth of children, personal illness five per cent and "other" scored 10 per cent. The same researchers compared the rates at which women therapists entered personal therapy, to the rate at which women who had the same episodes of distress. Norcross and Prochaska (1986b) found that only 28 per cent of the therapists elected to have therapy, whereas 43 per cent of the lay population did.

Therapists can only give so much for so long, before requiring rest and replenishment. Positive coping reactions include an increased interest in activities outside of work. This may include seeking out the company of new friends who have no connection to the mental health or caring professions. Making a sharp alterna-tive to sedentary hours in intense conversation with challenging and distressed clients; spontaneous activities, sport and hobbies may provide regeneration. Bel-lack (1981) suggests that hours of continued inactivity can make a tendency to weight gain, high blood pressure, coronaries and back pain. In a similar prag-matic vein, Leighton and Roye (1984) suggest that therapists take part in a pro-gramme of exercise and good nutrition.

Freudenberger's term "burnout" is used to describe the most serious levels of depletion, helplessness, guilt and anxiety that can occur for practitioners (Farber, 1983c, Farber and Heifetz, 1982, Freudenberger, 1974). The therapists suffering burnout make themselves apparent by becoming increasingly intolerant, rigid, inflexible and closed to new experiences. It may follow that the ability to tolerate ambiguity will decrease. The person becomes more detached, bored, defensive, cynical, pessimistic, suspicious, de-personalised, or perhaps omnipotent and criti-cal (Watkins, 1983). When the level of stress exceeds the point of being an active stimulus, therapists can have their personal life and therapeutic ability impaired.

If therapists cannot contain feelings of anger and resentment about their choice of career, and the atmosphere they work in, this will also contribute to depletion. Specific focuses of displeasure may be the low pay for working in a psychology department, or the financial insecurity of private practice. Therapists may also feel lack of reward. If a private practice is not providing sufficient income, there may be the anguish at a perceived lack of recognition from referral sources. Therapists have to care and listen when clients can turn to no one else. An over-indulgence in the criticism of clients and their choices can be an indica-tor of burnout, as cynical attitudes are a way of therapists keeping themselves safe by being bored, hating and dismissing pain and need.

The main occupational problem that therapists report is isolation due to the intimate and behind closed doors nature of the work (Bermack, 1977). When this occurs it is felt as though one is 'alone' with clients all day. Another hazard is the effect of spending working time being introspective and silent, so that clients can also look at their own lives and reactions. Therapists model how clients will react in the session. Subtle clues can be picked up as to the expected behaviour that is appropriate for each therapist. The occupational hazards of therapy can result in therapists diversifying into other areas to take themselves out of the front line of providing care (Freudenberger and Robbins, 1979). Marmor (1953) points out that the poorly defined, complicated and ephemeral aspects of the job create random stresses that must be dealt with.

Positive aspects

Firstly, the positive benefit that practice provides according to Guy's round up of research is that job satisfaction can exist in a work environment that is deeply stressful and poorly paid, and, in institutional settings, possibly under-funded, undervalued and understaffed. There is literature on the positive effects that therapeutic work can provide its practitioners (Burton, 1975, Eisenhart and Ruff, 1983, Farber, 1985b, Farber and Heifetz, 1981, Ott, 1986). Holt (1959) stresses that during training, in addition to positive personality changes, trainees report leaving their institute with a strong and resilient commitment to their chosen vocation.

Good therapy is concomitant with a state of positive functioning and harmony between self and other that is learned from practice (Brenner, 1982). Dent (1978) comments that those who are good therapists are also likely to be interested in artistic and expressionistic activities, and disregard mechanistic and scientific ones.

Positive coping reactions can include the monitoring of self, colleagues and clients. A form of peer or co-evaluation of therapeutic performance could be one way of establishing a healthy balance. But these must not turnout to be destructive. Their remit should be towards the making of a consensus about individuals' subjective abilities. This in effect becomes a licensing by one's colleagues. It is carried out by mutual involvement rather than by coercion.

A round up of positive dimensions include independence to practice as one chooses, with the possibility of making a good income if the referral sources are generous, variety is ensured and needs for intellectual and emotional satisfaction will be met. Effects of personal enrichment and fulfilment can occur along with emotional change similar to those of paying for personal therapy oneself. Cray and Cray (1977) note that having children can serve to keep one's feet on the ground. These positive effects include the co-creation of, and participation with, clients and others, with a greater sense of ability, involvement and purpose in life.

Negative aspects

The down side of therapeutic work, being there for others, is a high degree of stress with the high possibility of burnout, something which is part of working in a job with a high degree of interpersonal contact. Such professions can include walks of life as the police force, nursing, teaching, sales and management (Maslach, 1982). The emotional effects of providing therapy can include anxiety (Schlicht, 1968) and a sudden moodiness and depression (Rippere and Williams,

1985). Displacement activities may be entered into where stressed therapists redirect their energies into some new pastime, love affair or other interest.

Emotional and intellectual tiredness and the need to sit still for 50 minutes at a time, takes its toll of the vitality of workers. Lost vitality must be replaced, and may be done by giving sufficient attention to friends and family, and making friendships with well-adjusted people who have nothing to do with caring or mental health work and may even have a healthily sceptical attitude towards it. There is a positive anchoring effect gained from engaging in small-talk about ordinary things, after hours of being with provocative and demanding clients.

The most serious form of desperation and self-loathing is suicide. Ables (1974) and Ballenger (1978) both reported that clients whose therapists had committed suicide were angry at having been abandoned, were more depressed and may have an increased tendency to suicidal ideation. Plus abandoned clients may suffer guilt at the thought that they may have played some part in the death and fear their own ability to cope with life. The rate of suicide amongst the mental health professions is noted as being the same or greater than that of the general population.

Incompetence and how to prevent and deal with it are discussed. One study by Clairborn (1982) found that there was no correlation between licensure and the rate of incompetence. If licensing is brought in, it does not reduce the amount of complaints made about practitioners. In America, few states believed that professional misconduct was grounds for state action, and fewer than half the state legislatures questioned, believed that professional negligence was grounds for investigation or punishment. One way of controlling incompetent and impaired practice is to license practitioners and revoke it if necessary. In proceedings of complaint by the public about therapists, there must be the right of clients to complain and be heard, and the right of therapists to make a proper defence. Maybe this activity is best left to the courts to decide.

Therapy has different stresses according to the social contexts in which it is situated, the ways in which entry to practice is controlled, and the ways in which the flows of money circulate. The fundamental attribution error is noted as the mistake of jumping to the conclusion that the motives for aberrant behaviour are entirely due to individual temperament and inherent character. When the fundamental attribution error occurs, it describes the tendency to attribute actions wholly to the individual in focus, without taking into consideration of the human context (Ross, 1977). This point will become more apparent below.

On leaving the profession

It was a conscious decision to enter the profession, and subsequent decisions are made to stay in it throughout the length of a career, as there will be times when therapists wish they had made a different career choice. There are several ways in which therapists retire, change career, reduce their number of therapy hours, or temporarily take-leave from practising because of a personal crisis. Discouragingly, Chessick (1978) found that despair and discouragement increase as therapists stay in practice.

There are other possibilities for people to leave the profession. For instance, someone may infringe the rules of professional conduct and be disbarred or cut off from referral networks, thus effectively stopping an incompetent therapist from practising. Sometimes stress can get so high, and for one reason or another, practitioners may decide to temporarily seek help and not let down clients, by temporarily withdrawing from practice until they have attended to their own needs.

There are many instances that impinge on the steady presence and professional availability of practitioners. These cases can include such instances as pregnancy and childbirth (Baum and Herring, 1975, Cole, 1980, Fine, 1980), change of job or moving premises, divorce, death or illness, bereavement and bankruptcy. In the event of personal illness, Abend (1982) recommends that therapists disclose the details during therapy. Sometimes impairment of the ability and quality of therapy may be only short-term, and the therapist will be able to engage clients again, after making an appropriate intervention. Possibilities for help can include self-monitoring, knowing when to admit the need for help of a specialist group (or creating a peer group) or seeking personal therapy.

If self-help programmes were available for wounded healers they would offer a form of caring that would be suitable for this high-stress profession. McCarley (1975) believes that therapists have unique insight into their own profession and are the best ones to help colleagues who are impaired. A "macho" element can exist and needs to be overcome. It implies that therapists who cannot take the pressure should not be doing the job. If therapists battle against the stigma of having their own mental health problems, it would be a less shameful event to take time off work and recover.

Retirement and changes of career into management, supervision, teaching, research or training are also issues that inevitably need to be addressed during a career. Retirement may come about when poor hearing, lack of visual acuity, slowness, or low energy levels at certain times of the day hinder therapists. Criticisms of elderly colleagues include their lack of knowledge about the current liter-ature and trends within the profession, and having the values of a prior generation. When a colleague dies after an illness, the associated transitions must be handled with care so that adequate time can be given for both therapists and clients to make an adequate goodbye (Cohen, 1983). Sudden death may require colleagues to step in and assist in the aftermath of bereavement.

Bad therapy

There are several ways in which therapy can be destructive for both parties. The most frequent victims of therapeutic work are clients who come with high hopes. The researcher and psychoanalytic therapist Robert Langs has done much to highlight the shortcomings and atrocities committed in the good name of therapy (Langs, 1985). Farber describes bad therapy, induced by stress or impairment, to be due to a tardiness in being able to recognise the possibilities and consequences of one's actions, with new and unknown clients, who could in fact behave in unpredictable ways (Farber, 1983d).

The effects of entering sexual relationships with clients before, during or after seeing them have recently been brought into the open, and there is some litera-ture available on it. It is also viewed as a form of incompetence. Under the head-ing of "bad therapy" come the abusers who persistently use seduction as a weapon of dominance and the fulfilment of their own needs (Holroyd and Brodsky, 1980).

One study noted the effect of taking advantage of clients and entering into destructive dual-role relationships with them (Zelen, 1985). Generally, dual-role relationships are regarded as unhealthy. This means that if a person acting as a therapist also sees the client outside the work setting, as a new friend, or an acquaintance of the family, then both parties may suffer from knowledge about the therapist's true or alleged actions and the exposure of the client's personal secrets.

One estimate of the number of clients in private therapy who have personality disorders lies between 30 and 40 per cent. This estimation in Guy's book inti-mates that therapists come from a similar or the same personality pool as some clients. When stress gets very high, therapists may share the same difficulties as the people they are trying to help. If this is so, it means that it is only the overlay of training and the use of positive coping skills make any difference. The situa-tion is one of therapists working within the confines of the professional role and clients electing to enter into this contact.

Possibly there is a link between immature personalities and the personality disorders. Perhaps the distinguishing mark is that those with the most severe personality disorders are totally un-amenable to change and therapy is not indicated for them. Less severe personality disorders may change over a period of years, but only through long-term therapy with a skilled individual. The lesser personality disorders and immature personalities should receive benefit from therapy and be able to use it as a chance to make the necessary adjustments for fitting in with the rest of the world. This is, of course, part of the argument for mandatory personal therapy for trainees. It becomes mandatory because it gives a chance for those who are stuck in their development to be facilitated by their chosen brand, or another form of therapy.

Core skills

Reading in-between the lines of Guy's work, one wonders if there is such a thing as a core set of skills that the disparate profession of therapists possess, in order that they may carry out their work effectively. It is implied that there is a need to offer creative silence, open ended questions and self-denial to make the space in which clients can be as much of themselves as possible.

There is also implied a responsibility to make a relationship with clients. Furthermore, it seems that what therapists provide is a relationship, or indeed, the possibility of having a relationship, which may or may not be taken up by clients, according to their prejudices, abilities and personal development. Therapists work in the atmosphere they co-create with their clientele. When therapeutic behaviour is carried over, outside of the therapy sessions, into all areas of life, that will be inappropriate.

If all aspects of thinking, feeling, doing and relating to others are linked, it follows that the core skills of offering space and accepting clients is one of having a chameleon-like flexibility yet a solidity that enables them to know they are cared for. Trusting clients know they meet someone who can cope with stress and who is trustworthy and dependable.

As a rule of thumb there are four grades of therapeutic change. Occasionally, a breakthrough is achieved that comes suddenly and is accompanied by aspects of positive psychological change. Sometimes success is achieved at a slower rate, and may be accompanied with discomfort. Thirdly, if the client is unwilling or unable to change, or his or her relationship ties are too strong, so no change occurs. Fourthly, at other times, extra hurts may be received by the therapy regardless of whether the therapist intended to hurt or not. The consequences of these processes are another emotional burden to be dealt with.

Therapists need to demonstrate constantly that they are listening and caring persons who are truly present. Another pre-requisite for practice is the need to keep on caring and control one's own emotions and impulses. If clients insult therapists they do not insult them back. When clients fail in their attempts after a spell of progress, therapists do not tell them that they were not yet ready. When clients cry we do not reinforce their despair by telling them that things can only get better, now that they have reached rock bottom. This is being "liberal" in the work with people in anguish and confusion. The occupational hazards of providing therapy arise from the need to be liberal in making the therapeutic relationship, and not respond to invitations to denigrate an attacking client. Because of this, therapists should curb their more usual reactions to provocation or reinforcing someone's negative behaviour. Part of this attitude involves making an alliance with clients in the direction of their own positive mental health.

The psychology of caring

The psychology of caring is an overview of the processes taking place. It could be called a meta-psychology, taken in the sense of being *about* the psychology of providing psychological help. Marston (1984) found that the desire for intense and intimate relationships was the over-riding motivating factor in becoming a therapist. Scott and Hawk (1986) are two authors who conclude that healers should start their professional life by healing themselves. Work experience can be the teacher. Gitelson (1952) has noted that at certain times the taboo on self-disclosure may be lifted to good effect. Guy and Liaboe (1986) have explored the effects of the "one-way intimacy" that occurs in the skewed relation of therapy, where therapists hear about clients but they hear nothing about the intimate life of therapists.

Members of the caring and health professions, and particularly therapy, need to practice self-denial in their work and during their training. Self-denial in different forms is required so that therapists care for clients, and put some of their own requirements aside. The degree to which caring moves between self and other can vary so much that some professionals entirely sacrifice their evenings, weekends, holidays and their energy in the pathological pursuit of clients, totally against the interests of their friends, family and their own need to re-energise themselves and keep a healthy perspective.

Others may exploit clients for their own concerns for money, through a need to be needed and recognised, for sex or nefarious emotional needs. In distinction, the non-caring professions revolve around the abilities to make a profit and have the work force efficiently carry out company policy. The psychology of altruism is part of that of caring. A leading question is to wonder why altruistic persons should take a job in caring for strangers, when the rest of the "non-caring" world goes about its business.

The guiding myth for the profession centres on the illusion of having a relationship that is permanent, stable and perfect. But, it is part of the nature of therapy to be a temporary relationship. Therapists get used to the steady procession of enquiries that end in no appointment, those who make first appointments but never appear and those who come once but never again. The number of meetings and departures in professional life take their toll on the security of the therapist. Guy comments that there is nothing so poignant than the sight of a therapist waiting for a late client to attend. From the previous papers mentioned in this review, therapists join the profession because they enjoy and crave intimacy but they must remain professionally distant, whilst still being warm, genuine and empathic.

In contrast to the myth of therapy mentioned above, there is its counterpart when clients find that their once great hopes and dreams for a cure have been let down and that the therapist, rather than being a wonderful calm and caring presence, turns out to be anxious and idiosyncratic and does not have an instant cure for their life of malaise. Idealisation and loss are a major part of the reality of being a therapist (Burton, 1970). Some clients have unrealistic expectations. How these hopes and disappointments are treated becomes a pivotal point of the therapy. Because, if disappointments are relieved, they could make a momentum for positive change. If hopes are discouraged, then they may have a depressing, frustrating or disillusioning effect.

An aspect of therapy is providing appropriate care and making an accurate appreciation of clients. But who can be said to have the clearest view of what is happening? If all ideologies and methods have a perspective, then they each emphasise some aspects and ignore others.

Wounded healers use their insight into themselves in order to help those who are troubled. They are wounded and may have transcended their earlier pain and inability. They have looked into their own motivations and gained insight that can be used to guess how others are similarly unable to change. The life of a therapist is however, aided to go into a positive direction. Because, it means submitting to a life of constant becoming. When clients are facilitated in their journey, therapists gain rewards of an increased tolerance for difference and acceptance.

Good enough therapy

Guy mentions Carl Jung as one writer who pointed out three relevant aspects of clinical practice, from which the profession must learn. Firstly, Jung believed that therapists must be able to face up to their own problems and contain themselves from acting out and hurting clients. Secondly, Jung mentioned an "unconscious infection" that therapists pick up from their contact with clients. This latter effect is also described under the heading of counter-transference reactions. Some sound advice is as follows:

> Avoid therapists who fail to show common courtesy in human interactions, who are overly zealous, who make extravagant claims, and who in general lack human qualities of warmth, concern, respect, understanding, and kindness. Beware of pompousness, hostility, harshness, lack of seriousness, seductiveness, inappropriate familiarity, and 'phoniness' of all kinds. Above all, make sure the therapist impresses you as a decent human being whom you can trust.
> Strupp, Hadley and Gomes-Schwartz, 1977, p 137.

From the quotation and the discussions above, it seems that although therapists are similar to clients, they must not let their wounds handicap the therapeutic relation. Guy refers to the third Jungian term "shadow" to describe what he feels is the direction of the cure. Jung's "shadow" means the thing that a person has no wish to be. It is the opposite of what we consciously want to be: we want to hide the shadow, but we do not know precisely what it is. But, it must not be pushed away. Usually, effort is made to avoid the shadow. But if only it can be valued and learned from. If this can be done, professionals could regain their sense of balance and become anchored in the everyday world. We need to acknowledge the effects of the shadow that we bring to our work, and the collective shadow that consists in impaired colleagues who are permitted to carry on, despite disability. The shadow of therapy for Guy concerns the ability of the profession to deal with the negative consequences of the psychology of caring.

However, good enough therapists are neither self-indulgent nor self-obsessed. They realise that other people may not be as psychologically-minded as they. Good enough therapists accept and trust ordinary people with their foibles. They know that therapists are not the sole heirs to the knowledge of humanity. They can turn off the ability to be with profundity and can talk about inconsequentialities also. They can set boundaries but are not dogmatic or authoritarian. They make good parents, are not patronising and may not necessarily have children or be married. They are self-denying during work but not outside of it. They can help friends and not "therap" them. Their families get their proper share of attention. Good enough therapists are self-confident but not grandiose or omnipotent. They can live with uncertainty and ambiguity.

Conclusion

Bugental makes an apposite comment that Guy quotes: "there can be little doubt that the prime variable affecting psychotherapy (outside the patient, himself, of course) is the psychotherapist.... the personality, sensitivity, and skills of the therapist are of crucial importance", (1964, p 272). Bugental re-emphasises the personal nature of the work. Therapists each have the right to express themselves. Yet this expression must not interfere in the development of clients. As part of the scope is to understand others, therapists should start by understanding themselves. Also, if Guy is correct in his statement about the shadow of therapy, then more work needs to be done on delineating the processes of healing and hurting, as they take place within the profession. The truism that it is impossible to do good therapy without a stable and happy home life is born out. Also, this discussion lends new meaning to the saying "you don't have to be mad to work here, but it helps". Fortunately and unfortunately, therapists are mortals with feet of clay like everybody else.

Theory comes from experience but is not the whole truth. It can be learned from, absorbed and used as a vocabulary for describing the experience of providing care. Therapists are not the only experts on human behaviour. If all therapy theories and their practitioners disappeared from the world overnight, life would carry on. Therapy ideologies sit uneasily with the other explanations of the human sciences. The difference between the two is that therapy has a job to do, whereas human science has the luxury of making abstractions.

17

Attachment and intersubjectivity

To say one's practice is influenced by attachment research is a respectable claim. Yet the understanding of attachment is often muddied by natural psychological science's focus on material being. Thus, conscious psychological senses and processes are discussed in terms of causative neurological development. Gaining an accurate understanding of attachment has an important role in addressing complex psychological phenomena, particularly when there is no consensus on how to proceed. How are attachment and intersubjectivity accurately identifiable? *Intersubjectivity* is capable of explaining *attachment* yet both terms need better definition and inter-relation. This paper does not solve the problem of how to understand attachment and intersubjectivity. Rather, it attempts to demonstrate a series of problems in understanding attachment, everyday life and therapy as intersubjective. Scepticism is held concerning interpreting unconscious objects without relation to conscious ones. Consciousness is not an epiphenomenon. It is what needs explaining.

Introduction

There have been attempts by Husserl (Allen, 1976), Merleau-Ponty (1964c), Bowlby (1980), Hesse and Main (1999) and Stern (1985) to capture the inter-responsive nature of the meaningful world of children. The paper argues for an attendance to the phenomena of attachment and intersubjectivity, in order to distinguish each. It argues that the position of Stein (et al, 2002) is capable of supporting speculative theorising that can generate further findings. What is of concern is understanding how therapeutic practice, research and theory relate to the conscious experiences of one individual. For instance, the stance called behaviourism refused any but the most simple of mental processes. But it is untrue to say that it refused to interpret observable events without acknowledging consciousness altogether. It did focus on the association between a cultural object and emotion (often anxiety, fear or frustration). Behaviourism believes that negative reinforcement provides temporary relief from conditioned emotions so any avoidance or temporary relief maintains the emotion. What is of concern is interpreting mental processes between two or more persons that are specifically about significant attachments rather than non-attachment forms of relationship. If basic distinctions cannot be made, and a form of theorising arises that does not relate to conscious phenomena, then the study of attachment and its use in therapy will be hampered. An argument is put forward that concludes with the assertion that attachment only relates to specific intimate relationships but these are not authoritatively defined.

This paper raises a number of questions about the use of attachment and intersubjectivity as ideas capable of justifying therapy. One question that is raised but not answered is "what does attachment explain in adult relationships?" Any idea about relating should be capable of directing therapists in the heat of the moment. A further question concerns whether attachment, as it is currently understood, is capable of identifying specific causes and effects. Such thinking is close to understanding the defences as they appear in relationships. Attachment exists in relation to the fear of abandonment and how adults 'protect themselves' from others. The repeated frustrations of children who need to be attached, and the insecure forms of attachment that can occur, accumulate for individuals and co-exist with more secure forms of relating. Crittenden, for instance, has concluded (1) that avoidant infants are unable to interpret or use emotional communication. (2) That ambivalent infants have not socially learned to regulate their carers. And (3), that disorganised infants are unable to anticipate the responses that their carers make and remain angry and anxious (cited in McCluskey, 2005, p 67). If theory cannot suggest guidelines, then choosing action will remain unclear.

Attachment theory shows empirically that there are specific sorts of relationship processes that occur between a child and its carers—before, during and after a temporary separation (Ainsworth and Wittig, 1969). Attachment refers to formative intersubjective habits and 'positions' that can influence the adult in creating a tendency for being confident, gregarious and able to enjoy harmonious relations with others—or in conflict, retreat and dissatisfaction. Attachment can refer to the effects of disruption in adulthood (Brisch, 1999, Heard and Lake, 1986, 1997). Attachment as a whole includes its disappointment (in anticipatory fear, avoidance, betrayal and ambivalence). The influence across time is such that some form of presence of the past can be discerned, but always as empathies of the first-hand experience of others. It is not controversial to believe that the past influences the present. It is difficult to pinpoint the nature of the influence though.

This paper is a reflection on the relation between attachment, theoretical stance and methodologically-derived outcome. If anything, it asks more questions than it solves. If it were the case that a theoretical stance was inappropriate for the phenomena, then the guiding ideas produced would increase the occurrence of mistaken actions. Because there is a lack of overall consensus within the field of attachment research and its theorising, as there is within all psychology, there is a need for some shared terms of reference and practice. "Internal working model," "schema" and other such terms show what sort of theoretical stance has developed towards the observable situation of child and carer inter-actions. The aim is to present theoretical work in progress and promote collegiate debate about how to investigate the key phenomena.

Attachment is intersubjective. But intersubjectivity includes meaning, understanding communication and relating. But what is attachment? How is it possible to fend off unsuitable characterisations of attachment? (There are further questions concerning the extent and inter-relation between observable phenomena that cannot be answered here). The first section problematises attachment through raising some unanswered questions. Second, there is a speculation concerning the possible correlations between attachment and its defences or 'management' in dismissing or being preoccupied (following Stein et al, 2002). The third section concerns how to interpret the intentionalities inherent in attachment. Finally, a conclusion is provided.

Unanswered questions

Intersubjectivity is a contemporary watchword for the inter-relation of changes in psychological meaningfulness and responsiveness in psychoanalysis (Renik, 2004), therapy generally (Diamond and Marrone, 2003) and infant research in child development (Stern, 1985). Most accounts deal with it in terms of the development of neurological changes in the child's brain rather than the specifics of how it is possible to understand psychological meaningfulness and responsiveness, within the overall context of the ability to inter-act with respect to the point of view of others. Intersubjectivity is literally what lies between subjectivities, egos or personalities. It is often taken to mean the immediate inter-responsive nature of human communion. Whether the contact is between infants and carers or two or more adults. However, it is insufficient to define attachment by stating it is intersubjective without defining what both are, and how each may be distinguished and interpreted. When "intersubjectivity" is adopted as a watchword, a complex number of assumptions and necessities are invoked. What follows is a selection of comments on intersubjectivity. Next some comments are made that define attachment.

• Intersubjectivity is the basic form of inter-connection between people within specific social contexts and relationships (Owen, 2000b, 2003). Although Husserl's account of intersubjectivity was an argument about the conditions for the public meaningfulness and being in a shared world of meaning, his ideas on inter-relation are capable of accounting for non-verbal affective communication also.

• Intersubjectivity includes reciprocal and non-reciprocal aspects of inter-relating. Some aspects of roles may be complementary and not have exclusive tasks or duties. Whilst others might be complementary because tasks are reserved for one person in a pair or group and not available to others. For instance, in care-seeking for infants, it is only the adults who are carers. But in adult, intimate relationships and some occupational relationships, the caring could be more mutual.

• Intersubjectivity concerns the performance of specific roles in home or occupational life. Sometimes such roles are specialised, mutually exclusive or predetermined by values and the cultural traditions of social convention. Some persons may be permitted or excluded from occupying roles by specific reasons of cultural markers such as profession, social class or race. Some rules may determine aspects of home or occupational life. There may be boundaries to the entering or leaving of social groups of various sorts.

• Intersubjectivity is about the effects of social rules, about constraint or social freedom, according to specific customs and practices of various cultures.

Attachment has been defined in a number of ways. The central research question of attachment research is understanding how fear of abandonment and its avoidance, feature in the four forms[1] of attachment. The four forms are:

(1) secure attachment and its form of coping with separation (Ainsworth et al, 1978, Bowlby, 1988, Main, 1985, Sroufe, 1983).

(2) preoccupied attachment anxiety and its type of defence (Ainsworth et al, 1978).

(3), dismissing attachment and its type of defence (Ibid, Bowlby, 1977a, 1977b, 1980, Main, 1985).

(4), fearful attachment as exhibited in anxiety and avoidance (Bartholomew, 1990, 1997).

It was the conclusion of Bowlby that neither nature nor nurture was predominant in attachment. They always co-occur and cannot be observed singly (Bowlby, 1958, p 358). He believed that sense-material from different perceptual fields becomes the sense of the other at about five to six months (p 361).

In understanding attachment phenomena as the end-products of intentional processes, it becomes necessary to overcome the non-intersubjective entailments of attachment theory. This is because therapy practice should not be based on 'naturalised' attachment research and methods of research that do not fit the conscious experiences of attachment or intersubjectivity or wish to avoid psychological meaningfulness altogether. Attachment is noting discrete, repetitious types of relationship between people in family, loving and sexual relationships, in work and friendship. Attachment is about potentially observable inter-relations where specific persons can be identified as having problematic or secure anticipations, abilities to engage or attempt to avoid engagement by actions or influences.

Bowlby stated that attachment is not immature physiological dependence (p 371, 1988, p 12). His position can be read as making a distinction between emotional felt-senses and intellectual thought about a referent. Intentionality of a composite sort is what creates the attachment bond, either securely or defensively. Attachment has been noted as a person-specific type of relating (Allen et al, 2001, p 437). This suggests that attachment is not constant or ubiquitous but discretely different according to a specific understanding of a specific other person. Simpson and Rholes (1998, pp. 4-9) note that secure parents often have secure children. Whereas dismissing parents may have anxious-avoidant children. And preoccupied parents have anxious-ambivalent children. They also note that secure adults are able to self-regulate and discuss their emotions more than insecure ones. Such ability shows that persons who can often create secure processes around them, first know and then trust what they feel. Generally, emotion and emotional expression are a call on care-givers to respond. This means that people understand emotion as the felt-sense of a *fundamental form of relation of self to other*, a most basic form of co-empathy and intersubjectivity. A special case is where the other is turned to self, as it occurs in two-person relationships and as it momentarily occurs in any larger group.

Hesse and Main (1999, p 500) have provided details of specific examples of inter-actions between children and carers. They conclude that secure adults are co-operative and have infants that are secure. Secure infants might be distressed on separation but they become secure once the adult returns. Dismissing adults are overly self-reliant or controlling of others, dismissive of their own thoughts, feelings and past relationships, and have infants who are likely not to show distress on separation, and ignore or avoid their parents on return. Nor do the infants of dismissing adults show anger at having been separated. Preoccupied parents have a preoccupation with their past relationships that might include a mood of anger, passivity or fearfulness. They are believed to have infants who are wary before separation and cannot settle on reunion. Thus, the preoccupation is passed on.

Brennan, Clark and Shaver (1998, p 69) conclude that attachment as conceived by Ainsworth (et al 1978) was correct in a two-dimensional view of the combinations of secure coping; preoccupied anxiety and approach; fearful anxiety and avoidance; and avoidance with no anxiety. Marris has called attachment "not, essentially, a relationship the child has learned to be predictably nurturing, but an innate pattern of bonding which ... very quickly becomes identified with the unique figures who thereafter become intensely important ... The way the attachment develops into a relationship will be learned, but not the attachment itself", (1996, p 54). This view would seem to be supportive of a two-step process between nature and nurture, but states nothing about the mediating, affective and cognitive processes by which care-giving persons and contexts arise.

Possibly, attachment is intimate bonding like love, its disappointments and frustrations in close personal relationships and not the general form of relating in society. Attachment is not just about the caring between infants and care-givers. The core focus for infants and adults is the developmental definition of empathy as emotional communication (Bowlby, 1958, pp. 369-370). What appears is that emotional attunement leads to lived senses where people know what they feel (validation) and can identify new occurrences due to knowing themselves well in relation to others. This type of accuracy is touched on by Rogers (1959) as an organismic valuing potential. Self-recognition and the ability to empathise are found to go hand in hand by Bischof-Köhler (1988, cited in Perner, 1991, p 132). Accurate self and other understanding are the fundament of good social learning, emotional intelligence and psychological mindedness. Emotional mis-attunement leads to alexithymia where infants are unable to know or trust what they feel and that may be connected to defences that modify, distract or obliterate unbearable feelings of loss, shame at having needs and other situations. In adults, higher intellectual beliefs about what and how things exist, are linguistically-expressed, and can drive emotions and actions. But still it may be possible to contact the base lived experience of intersubjective relationships as emotion[2]. When the care-seeking needs of infants are met, security of attachment is achieved. When the needs remain unmet, an insecure form of attachment appears.

Insecure attachment as defence shows varying abilities to make connection with, or remain distant from, others who could be closer and more constant in their quality of response. It is claimed that to develop Bowlby's initial aims requires working out cause and effect, due to differing forms of intentionality, the mental processes that can be interpreted as constituting attaching, insecurity and absence of attachment.

There are research questions concerning the understanding of movements between *one place* and *another* among the various types of attachment relationship.

1. Concerning the genesis of psychopathology as insecurity of attachment, how is insecurity first achieved? And later maintained?

2. Concerning the genesis of a cure through therapy (from insecurity to security) how is security first achieved and thereafter maintained?

3. What are the psychological conditions that need to be in place to enable movements of sorts 1 and 2?

4. How do relationships with specific others compare to a person's general overall, 'default,' attachment style? Do people occupy a region of several styles? Do they do this through conscious preference or unconscious habit? How is it the case that individuals have access to more than one attachment style? Are some forms of attachment mutually exclusive? How do secure and insecure processes co-exist?

5. How do attachment styles change across the lifespan? What are the actual relations between infant, child, adolescent and adult forms of attachment? Are the infant and adult types largely the same? Or do they differ in complexity and organisation?

6. How do early and adult attachment styles co-exist such that, at moments of stress, the later adult style is abandoned in favour of a much earlier one?

7. Attachment in non-nuclear families is much more diffuse as grandparents, aunts, uncles and others provide caring for much longer periods of time than in Western parenting (Marris, 1996, pp. 62-3). There is an anthropological dimension to attachment research, of understanding it as a panhuman phenomenon rather than confusing it with its culturally-bound instances.

Where behavioural, intrapsychic and other natural scientific formulations fall down is that they are incapable of relating self to the other, intersubjectively[3]. Their form of thinking is a 'one person psychology' that cannot properly represent the nature of human relationship except to state that there is conditioning and its negative reinforcement over time. Attachment as part of a phenomenological theory of mind has an advantage in that it identifies meaningful types of relationship and posits how their intentionalities are different (Perner, 1991). Thinking about intersubjectivity is a problem of accounting for a complex and infinitely variegated number of phenomena. To do so requires some explicit type of reasoning about inter-responsiveness, verbally and non-verbally. These questions are left hanging in favour of investigating a theoretical research question concerning how expressive human bodies indicate that attachment and intersubjective communication are present.

The next section ascertains how attachment styles comprise a whole, following the work of Stein (et al, 2002). A two-person relationship can be interpreted as two, inter-related halves of what is observable. The back and forth sequences of inter-action between the two parties is an abstraction from the whole. Furthermore, it is possible to work out how selves come to treat themselves, because of the cumulative effect of previous inter-actions[4]. The over-arching theoretical research question is precisely how do researchers make sense of what is observed?

A speculation after Stein

The original purpose of Stein and her team was to map "the relationship between underlying constructs of attachment insecurity and strategy for coping … confusion remains about what the questionnaires actually measure", (et al, 2002, pp. 77-78). Stein and colleagues investigated the inter-relation between avoidance and anxiety. The plot on page 84 of that paper can be read as suggesting there are two major dimensions that map attachment. Accordingly, a two-dimensional space maps an infinite set of possibilities by positing attachment, and its absence, as a fundamental cause in relating. The team's effort was to "expand thinking about attachment along multiple dimensions instead of the usual two," of anxiety and avoidance, it was "not our intention to create a new typology". The plot of their findings "is a heuristic description of the underlying dimension of security," (Stein, personal communication, 2004).

Stein and colleagues explore similar topics to Brennan (et al, 1998) who focused on Ainsworth's view of attachment according to the self-rating of the avoidance of attachment and separation anxiety (et al, 1978). Brennan and colleagues found that there might be two types of preoccupied attachment, a high-anxiety low-avoidance sort and a medium anxiety sort (p 59). Brennan and colleagues replicated Ainsworth's original two-dimensional analysis of attachment. In short, secure children are gregarious and cope well with separation and reunite easily with their responsive parents. Preoccupied children are anxious and ambivalent. Disorganised children are anxious, resistant to care and avoidant. Whilst dismissing children are avoidant and do not connect with carers. Allen (et al, 2001) compared two measures of attachment with one population. They noted that one adult can have relationships with others that are discretely different in attachment style (p 437). This would seem to be confirmation of Ainsworth's "phase four" of multiple attachments that can be attained after nine months of age (1970). Phase four concerns the formation of a reciprocal relationship, where the infant infers motives concerning the primary caregiver's actions. The intentional explanation of this is that the empathic object of the carer is the infant self who is simultaneously empathising the carer.

Stein's research suggests a potential hypothesis about cause and effect in that it suggests some evidence that dismissing and preoccupied attachment are "strategies" that try to deal with being attached. The two dimensions are coherent in representing the whole of co-empathic representations. Stein's paper can be understood as claiming that secure attaching is an independent variable; and that its absence occurs in fearfulness. It also suggests a dependent variable of the manner or strategy of attachment. There is the possibility of investigating associated hypotheses, when there is clarity about the basic assumption that is being explored. The combinations of attachment and its lack, and preoccupied or dismissive "strategy," provide a conceptual structure for testing hypotheses and interpreting what appears as attachment relationships. There is the hope of gaining a consensus within research and theorising. Results can be understood as reciprocal or "circular" forms of cause and effect that operate within intersubjectivity.

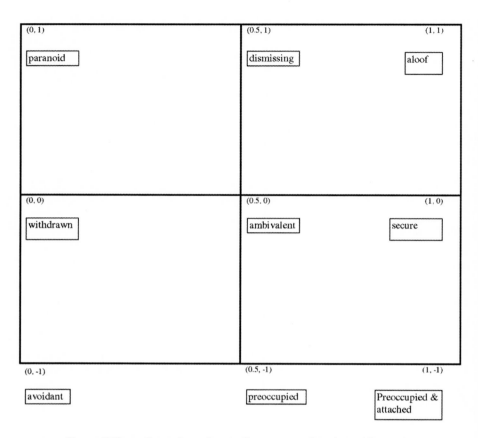

Figure 5-The y dimension refers to the manner of coping with attachment from dismissing (top) to preoccupied (bottom). It is possible to
posit attachment as an input variable that constitutes a specific outcome
that can be ascertained empirically. The horizontal x co-ordinate is the
independent variable of the amount of attachment from 0, avoidant, to
+1, attached. The vertical y co-ordinate is the dependent variable of the
strategy of dealing with the amount of attachment from + 1, dismissing,
to -1, preoccupied.

Although the original plot made by Stein (et al, 2002, p 84) was a two-dimensional square where secure attachment was placed on the left hand side, along the
length of a whole range of y values (see Figure 5 for a re-presentation of this). The
re-writing of it in Figure 5 inverts this arrangement to place security on the right
hand side, in-line with the standard manner of showing (x, y) co-ordinates.
Instead of allocating the score of -1 to secure, and +1 to insecure along the x-axis.

Figure 5 allocates zero to non-attachment and +1 to secure attachment. The y dimension is maintained as it was in Stein's original paper but inverted. The y dimension now refers to +1 for dismissing or dominance, and -1 for preoccupied (sensitive, unregulated, submissive) attachment. Both may be considered as strategies for dealing with the degree of attachment, a quantified amount of attachment on the x co-ordinate, the independent variable or input. The y dimension is compressed to maintain the square shape. To repeat, the x dimension is from avoidant, non-attachment to securely attaching, left to right. What Figure 5 shows is a set of possible positions that comprise the whole of attachment actualities. The point is trying to imagine what the combinations of Stein's work means prior to their further empirical investigation.

Rather than there just being a focus on the relation of the fear of abandonment and its avoidance, there are several allied research questions concerning how emotions and repeating problems become part of a developmentally increasing problem in relating with others. In being able to get around the social world without doing harm of various kinds to others and oneself, there is the question of how to interpret feelings. Regardless of the developmental phases of each of the participants and their physical ages, what the points in the two-dimensional space mean are as follows. The following remarks are tentative, hence the question marks in brackets. Moving from the bottom left corner to the bottom right corner:

(0, -1) Avoids and does not attach. (Is this despair? Being beyond protest?).

(0.5, -1) Preoccupied with separation, abandonment, rejection or receiving disapproval. Some attachment and some social anxiety. Maintains relationships.

(1, -1) Preoccupied but can attach securely. Has strong social skills but is focused on others in the past thus providing a sense of loss that may influence present relationships.

Moving from middle left to mid right:

(0, 0) Withdrawn and does not attach. Ambivalence not achieved.

(0.5, 0) Ambivalent with some avoidance and desire to be attached that can be successfully maintained or broken off if necessary.

(1, 0) Securely attaching without unnecessary anxiety: gregarious, resilient, resourceful, co-operative, friendly and relaxed in company. Secure persons have good self-esteem and the ability to understand themselves and others accurately. They have no unnecessary fear, hatred or need to control. Neither are they preoccupied with the past nor unduly fearful of the future. Securely attaching people are understood as a model of good psychological health.

Moving from top left to top right:

(0, 1) Paranoid protest and anxiety, but overall not attaching due to anticipated, interpreted or actually experienced hostility from others. Anticipates attacks and may interpret and empathise that attacks have taken place when there have been none.

(0.5, 1) Dismisses and controls others with some avoidance and attachment.

(1, 1) Aloof, dominant and dismisses but may require being in control in order to attach. This position may also include being intimidating or powerful.

With the testing of the predictions above, it is hoped to become more precise about how the overall combinations and fundamental parameters vary. One way of understanding attachment is to seek out its basic forms and work out how not only cause and effect, but also psychological meaningfulness operate. Attachment relationships are co-empathic and intersubjective but not all relationships concern attachment.

'Grid reference'	Self	Intersubjectivity	Sense of other & possible responses
(0, -1) Avoidant, schizoid	Withdrawn, no distress	Not achieved	Avoided. Other withdraws or feels ignored.
(0.5, -1) Preoccupied with separation, anger or loss	Fearful of rejection, sulking or loss	Preoccupied angry, or fearful	Empathised to be unavailable. Other feels attacked and could respond in a variety of ways.
(1, -1) Preoccupied distracted	Distracted, reparative to others	Preoccupied, not wholly involved	Can connect.
(0, 0) Withdrawn	Avoids care giving	Not attaching	Others are good but avoided.
(0.5, 0) Ambivalent, fearful & approaching	Socially anxious, fears rejection	Some attaching	Ambivalent: Feared, avoided & wanted. Other may feel anxious also.
(1, 0) Secure	Ego constant, self-regulated, self-worth achieved, accurate understanding, gregarious, good social skills	Secure, open	Non-threatening senses of others and accurate anticipations of the actions of others. Except when there is actual threat. Satisfying relationship established.
(0, 1) Paranoid	Paranoid, dysregulated responses to 'attacks'	Wary, attacking	Feared, attacked, rejected or out of reach. Other feels attacked and could respond in a variety of ways.
(0.5, 1) Controlling, dismissing	Self-reliant, controlling	Not reciprocal	Dismissed, conditions of worth applied. Other feels controlled, attacked, manipulated, ignored.
(1, 1) Aloof dominant, dismissing	Controlling	Not mutual	Controlled or fighting control or ignored.
Disorganised	Pan-anxiety, dysregulated	A tendency towards not attaching, co-occurring with other types	A tendency to be influenced by the prior attachments. Other feels confused, attacked, anxious.
Meta-representational context	Reflection on total of self experience and comparison to others	Total of co-empathic manners of being-with	Total of felt senses of empathised others

Table 1 - A sketch of some factors concerning an intersubjective theory of attachment. The aim is to specify which intentionalities predominate in any specific form. The remarks above are tentative ones.

Table 1 is a sketch of some factors towards the theorising and empirical investigation of attachment as attachment, rather than construing it around material and neurological factors. What needs to happen is some further thinking through of the relations between consciousness and the material aspect of human being. Further factors co-occurring with the basic terms above can be found after further conceptual discussion and experimentation. Only empirical research can show what the contingent connections are between associated factors such as anxiety, defensive type and the role of meaning in guiding sought-for outcomes.

The speculation derived from the work of Stein and colleagues is that further research is required on how secure attachment is different to the insecure forms. Secure attachment is different in that some mental processes occur that enable self-soothing, self-cohesion and a confident openness to others. It means that 'uninterpreted emotions' are capable of being found that are potentially accurate lived senses of what is happening between self and other, in the past, present or future. Attachment security implies coherency and trusting the senses of general and specific others. If a secure person is fearful of another, it is more likely due to their being at actual risk rather than the inaccurate empathising of risk where there is none. The problem of understanding attachment is how to interpret the results of various experiments and phenomena that are taken as meaningful. Avoidance, anxiety and security are not clearly apparent in relation to the mental processes that are occurring. Particularly, it is unclear how the same infant or adult employs different types of attachment style. In security, the emotions are trustworthy, co-operative, affiliative and pro-social. The senses of the other are accurate with respect to the long-term knowledge of a person. The other's sense of oneself occurs in a relationship where distress is attenuated and accurate psychological understandings have accrued. Thus, accurate apperception occurs and the self understands itself.

When it comes to understanding attachment between infants and adults, there are further unanswered questions. First, intersubjectivity indicates the inter-responsiveness between two or more people but needs to go further in specifying those inter-actions.

Second, each empathic experience of another person is an instance, a single perspective on the referent of being together that comprises a whole of such senses. Understanding others attends to the part and the whole. There are theoretical parameters concerning the conditions of empathy and intersubjectivity. There is an appreciation of the actual whole—call it intersubjectivity as a conscious phenomenon.

Third, if self-regulation is understood as a feedback system, then such an interpretation should be based on the perceptual and empathic observation of how children and adults behave. Such matters require clarity about the theoretical stance adopted. What will compound faulty conclusions are theoretical assumptions that direct empirical attention towards biological and neurological phases of development because of the belief that defences are biologically-based, rather than attending to anxiety as a meaningful learned threat, due to the past actuality or anticipated occurrences in a relationship. There is a temporal aspect to attachment because the past influences how the present and future are empathised.

Interpreting mental processes

One question is how to interpret mental processes within what appears. A further problematic appears concerning the complex set of inter-actions between various sorts of intentionality—namely separation anxiety, defence, approach in order to satisfy needs; and avoidance of anticipated abandonment or actual rejection (see below). Both Freud (1926d) and behaviourism have provided answers. These are now compared with respect to finding a more intersubjective way of looking at this situation. Natural scientific psychology is unqualified to make comments on meaningfulness[5]. The diagram could be criticised for conflating behaviourism and psychoanalysis (Figure 6). But surprisingly the two stances are remarkably similar.

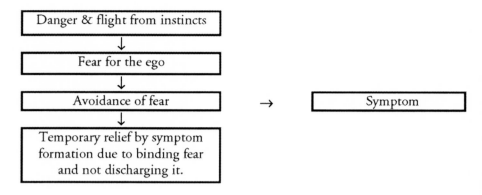

Freud's (1926d) formulation of the causes of symptoms and the relation to childhood relationships.

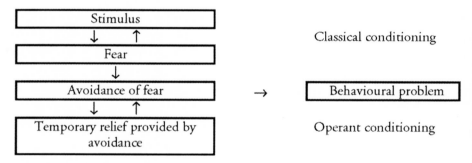

A behavioural formulation applicable to many forms of conditioned problem. The on-set of the problem is due to classical conditioning (top half). The maintenance of the problem is through negative reinforcement, in the bottom half.

> Figure 6-Comparison of the psychoanalytic and behavioural formulations of anxiety and defence as similar alternatives for interpreting attachment. The problem is how to take observable inter-actions and infer that specific composite forms of intentionality are occurring between care-seeking and care-giving.

On close inspection of what is asserted by Freud (1926d, pp. 144-5) and behaviourism with its empirical support (Walker, 1984, 1987), there seems to be much in common. Figure 6 expresses these two different views of cause and effect, in the production of psychological problems. It might be the case that attachment could be interpreted in a similar way. One question often touched on in passing, is based on Freud's view that defences 'wipe out' or reduce fear about instinctual impulses through distraction from, or alteration of, conscious meaning caused by libidinal impulses. For Freud, anxiety is a signal in order to avoid danger. It has a function of negative reinforcement when the ego avoids the danger, thereby rewarding itself with less discomfort (1926d, p 138, p 156).

There are other views of this situation though. One such view would be to believe that fear might be maintained because it is negatively reinforced, as Skinner suggested was the case in operant conditioning (Figure 6). Pavlov and Skinner offered a minimal understanding of the basic processes of learning. Classical conditioning and operant conditioning (negative reinforcement), are empirically validated (Walker, 1984, 1987). Please allow a brief explanation of these views.

In classical conditioning, a stimulus is connected with a response. The way it is portrayed, in the top half of figure 6, is that a cause is established originally, in the perceptual presence of the stimulus, that becomes paired when the subject becomes hypersensitive to it and selectively attends to it with anxious anticipation. In the particular case of the strange situation, anxieties of specific sorts could be conditioned through the repeated absences of carers. A repeated type of intersubjective event, on re-establishing contact, could be sufficient to maintain insecure attachment. Negative reinforcement can also occur when children act on the motivating force of the anxiety produced. Specifically, in the bottom half of figure 6, it is believed that the accrual of anxiety is sufficient to motivate a behaviour that provides temporary relief from anxiety. The overall behavioural outcome, because of the child's attachment need, is the adoption of some characteristic behaviour as a result of the repeated reward of having done something to reduce anxiety and gain temporary relief. Such is the stance of behaviourism and it is useful as a minimal positing of some (not all) of the mental processes at stake in child and adult attachment.

Discussion

Whatever the differences and similarities between attachment and intersubjectivity, there is a need to make clear how specific phenomena are being interpreted. For instance, is it the case that the interpretation of attachment that currently occurs is a misguided technical and evolutionary psychological reading of love between parents and children? Attachment as a phenomenon is not co-extensive with all relationships in society because some relationships are not psychologically important. The term "ego" has been used to denote intersubjective style, which is one possibility. Whereas others prefer to interpret beliefs about others as causative. Whilst the psychodynamic tradition prefers metaphors of the projection of unconscious senses into real others to create their conscious senses (which are not recognised as having arisen in self).

When it comes to practice and the everyday life for that matter, there are some major differences in how to understand what we feel. Emotion is fundamental lived experience of self-other inter-relation. But there are other possibilities of how emotions arise. Some emotions could be improper representations of the relationship in that they are either conditioned or otherwise inaccurate with respect to the whole of the relationship. This is an abstract comment that needs illustration. An inaccurate sense of a relationship is one where fear might be present yet there is 'nothing' in it that warrants the fear. The point is that conscious emotions occur in the living body, in its current context of relating, and may also be influenced by a past relation or be influenced by the object of current feeling or discussion. Emotions are a form of intentionality, a basic form of understanding, a code of communication and expression. Emotions may also be learned.

Another form of emotion is when linguistically-directed beliefs, internalised speech, discussion or theory create emotion. The basic claim here is that verbal thought can create emotion (and once it is felt, it could be evidence for further thoughts about those feelings). Language could construct feelings helpfully where earned secure thinking could provide a framework for overcoming emotions that, if they were acted on, would be damaging to the person's well-being overall. There could be unhelpful versions of causative internalised speech in social phobia where people tell themselves what will happen, and side with the feeling that they produced, and so avoid the feared situation, never entering it and not having a fuller experience of what it is like. What transpires is a fixed attitude, idea or relationship between self and the other, as the object of attention. This is an impoverished representation of what the relationship is and can be.

In practice, attachments are felt-senses. The conscious communications that occur are fundamentally about non-verbal affect and how it is communicated through perception and empathy of what is perceived in social learning. There is an implication of intentionality between people. In the case where self and other are turned towards each other, there is a simultaneous co-empathising. The referent is the shared relationship and reality testing occurs across time, so that in the special case of secure attachment, there is the outcome of gaining accurate representations of what self and others are capable of feeling and doing. Attachment processes are face-to-face. The outcome is that some feelings are veridical and worthy of being trusted, whilst others may not be at all accurate. Or, in some worst-case scenarios, what it is felt may be entirely irrelevant to what is happening. This is not a re-invention of transference and counter-transference but an entirely different explanation of the conscious inter-action between people. A meta-representational approach is one that spots the differences between secure openness and its ease of communication and specifies the role of fear and inhibition. It shows that insufficient emotional experiences can become more capable of being felt and expressed in a more relaxed manner. There may be different sources of different forms of emotion. One consequence is that it is possible to judge when emotion is mis-interpreted but that requires knowing in a reliable fashion what situations emotions are about. Only careful and prolonged consideration through discussion and keeping the evidence open before drawing a conclusion can help spot reliable differences.

Intentionality	'Grid reference'	Attachment process
Avoidance, no care-seeking made & no care-giving accepted.	(0, -1)	Not achieved. Care-giving avoided.
Anxious ambivalence & preoccupation.	(0.5, -1)	Preoccupied, some dysregulation, semi-gregarious, anxious, clingy or angry.
Preoccupied, depressed & attached. Care-seeking deficient.	(1, -1)	Preoccupied, depressed & neurotic attachment.
Paranoid hostile care-seeking. Needs remain unmet.	(0, 1)	Paranoid pre-emptive attacks on mis-empathised carer so care-giving possibly defeated.
Controlling, angry dominance.	(0.5, 1)	Dismissing, controlling.
Aloof, dominant & attached.	(1, 1)	Aloof, dismissing.
Care-seeking inactive. Care-giving not received.	(0,0)	Not achieved.
Ambivalence of anxiety, retreat & approach.	(0.5, 0)	Attachment positively & negatively valued.
Secure regulation, mutual satisfaction & supportive context for exploration, care-giving accepted.	(1, 0)	Secure, open, rewards itself, care-seeking accepted and satisfied.
Failure of coherence between emotion and understanding—or coherence not yet attained. Pan-anxiety, not capable of attaching	An insecure tendency, co-occurring with others forms.	Disorganised & ineffective care-seeking tangles, rejects or defeats care-givers.

Table 2-A second attempt at thinking through the relations between care-seeking and care-giving. Some notes on possible connections between the forms of intentionality and the sense of the referent of the shared relationship.

Conclusion

Through the identification of attachment phenomena, it may be possible to assess how a talking therapy will be suitable and provide treatment (of talking and relating) according to some ideas of how attaching has become damaged and how it can be restored. The problem is how the promise of attachment can be delivered for the practice of therapy. Secure forms of attachment are more mutual than the insecure sorts. Insecure attachment types are also attempts to understand the common relationship between infants and carers. Secure attachment is when good social learning occurs with self-regulation. Conditioned meanings and emotions may exist in some situations. But not all meanings are conditioned. Social learning influences how people interpret various situations. But how to treat meaning and emotions in attachment remains an open question.

One point is noting that empirical findings do not give birth to themselves. Rather, empirical research employs non-empirical, hermeneutic and theoretical reasoning and assumptions. It employs such assumptions to design the research method and interpret its results[6]. Stein's work is seen as pivotal because of the way it investigated the relationship between attaching and its lack, and the manoeuvres for dealing with the degree and quality of attachment created.

What is being asserted is that it might be possible to distinguish how the "pieces of attachment" fit together in a coherent way. A view of attachment as intersubjectivity is entailed in distinguishing the various forms of mental process, as they present different senses of the same referent. This view makes clear the problems of natural empirical research, because interpretation of what appears is currently outside of its scope. However, a self-reflexive understanding of the position taken could show what parts of theory are more or less accurate with respect to the phenomena. The point is that therapists provide psychological influence and work within that medium. They do not provide psychosurgery or drugs to alter neurological functioning. A focus on the material substrate of psychological meaningfulness is not a focus on psychological meaningfulness or its 'causes' in intentionality. It is unclear what readers are meant to do with findings about neurological development.

This paper assumes that a specific sense of one referent, the accumulated impact from one or more carers or significant adult others, can be distinguished with respect to the whole set of senses concerning them. Theory and experimental methods need to bear that in mind or they risk misconstruing the topic under consideration. Attachment requires thinking about co-empathic intentionality and the manners of representing the first-hand experiences of others. Something that can never become first-hand for self.

Possibly attachment research does assume an inaccurate picture of attachment before beginning its work. What is understood is always a phenomenon from some perspective, rather than some non-interpreted reality-in-itself. It is further assumed that it is necessary to make distinct the inter-relation between any particular attachment phenomenon; the theory and meta-theoretical understanding supplied (in such a way as to help theory correct itself with respect to the phenomenon); and to make sure that appropriate empirical methods can be devised. But this leads on to show what it means to understand attachment as intersubjectivity: as intellectual analysis that relates to what is observed or experienced (Owen, 2003).

The central focus for this paper has been a theoretical research question. It is a pressing concern to create a consensually agreed means of recognising how two human expressive bodies, in non-verbal affective inter-relation and speech, can be understood as indicating that attachment phenomena of discrete sorts are occurring. The paper has noted how phenomena exist relative to the theoretical stance taken. The theoretical problem is how to occupy a position that has benefits in that it reveals the core phenomena of attachment. The role of empirical research is to test such understanding, in a wide sense of the word "test" not necessarily including testing predictions by using statistics. The role of theory is to organise the data in a meaningful way. The lived experience of being attached and intersubjective should not be confused with neurological development and the psycho-physics of what may co-occur in meaningful relationships. If empirical psychology is not just methodology, devoid of the influence of assumptions, theory and interpretative stance—then the burden is on empirical psychology to show how it makes sense of what appears. Some people have read attachment as part of evolutionary psychology or as showing the development of the brains of children rather than what it originally meant: that child and carer were attached to each other.

Intersubjectivity is not co-extensive with attachment. It is likely that attachment phenomena may only happen in psychologically important relationships where intimacy is either achieved or its previous betrayal haunts the present and the future. These may concern the 'five drives' of care-seeking, care-giving, defence, sexuality and interest sharing (Heard and Lake, 1986). Attachment is a distinguishable part of intersubjectivity in society. Attachment is not a form of relating that concerns social traditions, duties or roles towards specific others. Although cross-culturally, there are different child-rearing practices that mould it. Any ultimate conclusions are referred to further empirical research. When attachment is understood as part of the whole set of actualities that are intersubjective, it challenges researchers, theorists and practitioners of therapy, to grasp its core qualities. One way of defining attachment is as co-empathic intersubjectivity that happens between child and carer. Attachment can be understood adequately within its whole set of manners of inter-relating. Assumptions play a role in interpreting mental processes and this topic is opened up for discussion without it being possible to make any concluding remarks.

Notes

1. Across the spectrum of attachment research, it is unclear how many basic forms of attachment exist. Hardy (et al, 2004) believe there are only three major types. Attachment is arguably a natural scientific way of understanding love and its disappointments. Love, when understood intersubjectively, is about how two or more people become positively and negatively involved with each other.

2. Thanks to Yvonne Agazarian of the Systems Centered Therapy Institute, Philadelphia, for showing me the force of a psychological reduction in attending to emotions as important sources of information. It is all too easy to think about these topics and not feel them.

3. Other ways of interpreting the nature of self is to see it as intrinsic with others in relation to shared public or cultural objects (Owen, 2000b). What this means for attachment is that self and other are turned toward each other, so that the mutual cultural object is their relationship. The infant emotes and expresses itself in relation to its needs. The carer empathises the child's needs and satisfies them to some degree or not. It is argued that research requires clear statements concerning its own theoretical commitments, for it to devise suitable experiments that explicate the phenomena.

4. Basically, the ego is the object of oneself for oneself, oneself for others and it is empathised by others. Tyson (1996, p 172) has theorised that there is a progression towards types of egoic constancy in child development. Namely, there are three types of egoic constancy in (1) self-esteem, (2) an overall apperceptive coherence of self-recognition and identity, and (3), in learning to act towards itself in a specific manner.

5. Aitken and Trevarthen, for instance, hold the belief that development is "guided by regulatory mechanisms in the brain that formulate a behavior field for the individual acting practically in relation to the objective world, and socially related fields of subjective expression for a self and one or more others", (1997, p 672). Whilst this may be generally true, it says nothing about specific psychological intersubjective processes that have conscious senses. This is the sort of problem that intersubjectivity as a watchword should overcome by being able to have a language for discussing the relation to conscious senses. Aitken and Trevarthen (p 669) also note that "joint awareness" and "joint referencing" exist as part of affective non-verbal communication. Joint awareness and joint referencing occur in the type of conceptual intentionality inherent in speech and language as well as

non-verbal communication and emotion. Aitken and Trevarthen urge the creation of theory that does adequately address "both cognitive (individualist) and intersubjective (communitarian) aspects in the formulation of an adequate theory of the emergence of human mental functions", (p 655). Specific phenomena need to be recognised within observable inter-actions and mental processes must be interpreted to explain them.

6. Attachment needs to be properly contextualised. Fonagy points out that there is a question about how to represent relationships (1999a, p 457, 1999b). Blatt, Auerbach and Levy seem to be at least some way to stating how the conscious objects of consciousness, self and other, are central to psychological development (1997, pp. 355-6). They relate secure attachment to a positive sense of others and a positive sense of self. When this happens it can be seen as a response within the greater whole of child development, cultural acquisition and participation in an intersubjective life of responding to the responses of others.

18

Reference, temporality and the defences

This paper aims to apply an awareness of temporality and reference for understanding the defences. The processes called defences are a pre-emptive wiping away of anxiety or an attempt at combating unpleasant emotions or thoughts. The aim of the paper is to apply temporal understanding to reveal underlying attitudes within the defences as a beginning to understanding temporality within the full range of experience. Reference and temporality are linked to the covering over and revealing of experience. It is not possible to tell the whole story of associated themes, so some aspects have been omitted through the necessity of limited space.

Introduction

This paper does not fully define the Husserlian or Heideggerian approaches to temporal experience for that would take many thousands of words. But it is possible to gain an overview of the major findings by considering the work of those who have studied Husserl's research papers (Kern, 1993b) and have gained an understanding of the original work of Husserl. For Husserl and Heidegger, temporality and reference, meaning and signification, are core themes (Thurnher, 1995). If it is agreed that an original phenomenological approach to understanding humanity is suitable, it follows that references and temporality are central issues. The consequence for the human sciences and therapy is that references and meanings are understood as temporally changing phenomena. From such a position it would follows that psychological change, can also be understood within the context of temporality and the reference of intentionality.

A series of introductory comments must come first. One topic to be set in place is the belief of one leading contemporary phenomenologist that the descriptions given by Freud and Lacan are valid and in-line with those of Husserl. To support this, it is necessary to explain the connection between the ego and the acts of higher volition and involuntary aspects of consciousness and the passive syntheses. When phenomenology is applied to therapy, it means that after an agreed grounding of the central concepts with others, it would be possible to make more detailed comments on defence and other experiences by following the path laid down by other writers, for instance Jaspers in 1913 (Jaspers, 1963). The purpose of such a future project is not to pathologise, but understand personal and fundamental attitudes towards living and being with others.

Let us consider a practical example before going any further. It is often the case that our knowledge of another person changes, as does our knowledge of ourselves. Instead of employing modes of understanding that would reify our experience of another or self, it would be more accurate, and probably more complex, to adopt an initial framework for understanding that was able to account for temporal change[1]. Husserl was the first person to attempt such a perspective, and how he could be judged as being successful in this or not does not matter, for it is the overall sense of his perspective that is important.

The standpoint and method of seeing employed

Temporality is of the utmost importance. Husserl and Heidegger classed it as the most constitutive framework for consciousness and the intersubjective constitution of meaning[2]. Consequently, Husserl's *On the Phenomenology of Inner Time Consciousness*, referred to below as the "*Time* book" for short (1991), is both a test case for phenomenology to see if Husserl actually did what he wrote about (1973a) and for phenomenologists who wish to have an introduction to the actual practice of the transcendental reduction and seeing the evidence of universal essences of temporality[3]: The point of this exercise for contemporary therapists is that Husserl argued that empirical research should be based on a sound understanding of temporal experience. He hoped that concepts and methods would take into account the overall homogenous, co-ordinated relation between recollection and retention of the past (an automatic or involuntary form of memory, following Locke, 1961, p 117), perception of the present, imagining and the anticipation of the future.

But the main standpoint for this paper is a general position on temporality, half-way between Husserl and Heidegger, because Heidegger adopted a modified version of Husserl's theory of temporality within Division Two of *Being and Time*. Consequently, it is possible to set aside the many introductory comments of Division One and attend more fully to the reintroduction of them within the second Division. The "existentials" are all related to *sich-zeitigen*, self-temporalizing temporality within the second Division[4]. This is a belief in the self-generation of Da-sein as it flows through time whilst being in the world.

The key items to aid understanding are those comments that mention time as the horizon for the interpretation of the manifold modes of being. What this means is that there are many ways in which the meaning of being appears within the being of Da-sein. But the most important thing is to understand that Da-sein's temporality is the sufficient basis for the many possibilities and actual combinations of human being to occur for specific persons. Another way of stating this conclusion, at the level of everyday psychological life, is to write that knowledge of ourselves, of each other and things appear within a world-horizon. The meanings of the beings that can be interpreted are a result of our specific attitudes of temporal approach that occur at a fundamental being-level, that constitute the world-horizon, and from that, conscious psychological awareness and ordinary experience occurs. If this is correct then the first, the most constitutive, "temporal attitudes" of manners of relatedness to the world-horizon are most important.

The method of seeing involved is to follow Husserl's method as laid out in the *Time* book (§9, texts 51, 52, 54) and to use self-analysis and free association to allow the themes and gestalt-objects to appear. The largely qualitative research method I have used to analyse one of my own defences is provided below. This is also called the apperception[5] of one's own absolute constituting "flow" that appears through one's own past history (Descartes, 1986, Leibniz, 1973). The process of Husserlian seeing is similar to a form of self-analysis that has been added to imaginative variation of what appears, to find the invariant aspects of it.

It would be wrong to dismiss the unconscious as not being represented within Husserl. The implication of the self-constitution of conscious experience by the passive, non-egoic "flow" of absolute consciousness is that we do not consciously do anything to make ourselves exist as conscious beings. The most appropriate term for such a process of consciousness is to call it a synthesis. What this means is that consciousness as a whole is comprised of egoic, active striving plus the higher intentionality of thought, speech and rationality. But temporality and the constitutions of the matter of the five senses are achieved passively by syntheses, without the action of the ego. When consciousness is turned towards the blue of the sky, for instance, it passively receives the sensual blue that is presented to visual sensation. However, Husserl maintained that the blue is constituted by consciousness. Importantly, other aspects of consciousness are, to a degree, passive as well, such as our involuntary empathic connections to others and the involuntary syntheses of defence and the creation of emotions such as anxiety[6]. Also, in-line with sketching the Husserlian picture of consciousness, it is important to note the work of a current writer who supports the Freudian-Lacanian hypothesis concerning defences. This also needs to be explained before going any further.

Recently there have been comments by Rudolf Bernet that have clearly supported the Freudian-Lacanian picture of defences and repression as a key part of consciousness (Bernet, 1996). Bernet, a Director of the *Husserl Archives* in Leuven and a practising psychoanalyst, endorses the Freudian-Lacanian view of defences. This position may be described as follows: For Freud and Lacan, there are two major spheres within consciousness as a whole. The intellectual sphere of conceptual intentionality is characterised by the term secondary process that is a fairly fixed type of reference of the associations between thought, speech and emotion, a semi-permanent cathexis (charging) of emotion to linguistic meaning, in-line with the definitions of culture. On the other hand, there is a primary process sphere that is characterised by a free-flowing connection between thought and emotion, whereby a more simple, analogous and symbolic type of "thought" occurs, of the type associated with dreaming, daydreams and free association. Bernet also points out an agreement between Freud and Husserl: the object is an experiential one that is expressed in both their writings as *Vorstellung*, representation (translated most often by Strachey as "idea").

For Freud, the intentional object is originally a combination of thought and emotion. Trauma of a general kind causes the degradation of a specific object, such that thought and emotion become disconnected. When this occurs, the remaining emotion becomes transformed into a different type, which may include unpleasant anxiety. The remaining split-off representations are forced into the primary process domain and become cathected with primary process, free-flowing "unconscious" psychological energy. The split-off, deformed and repressed representations then appear in attempts to gain readmission to consciousness, where they recur in attempts to express themselves via further connections with other, whole intentional objects. When the deformed representations eventually do recombine with an intentional object and become expressed sufficiently-well through speech and secondary process thought, the deformed representations lose their ability to disrupt the secondary process level of the ego. When such an eventual recombination with the sphere of consciousness awareness occurs, insight and symptom-relief may also occur for the individual. The account of this can be found in Freud in *A Note on the Unconscious in Psychoanalysis, Instincts and Their Vicissitudes, Repression, The Unconscious,* and the *Splitting of the Ego in the Process of Defence* (Freud, 1984). What the remainder of this paper does is explore two things: reference and temporality.

Some introductory comments should be made on the nature of references. Husserl regarded references as intentionalities that enable meaning in the world with others. So consciousness is both immanent, or inward; and transcendent, outward looking, insomuch that it can represent the outside world and other people within itself. Husserl believed that empathy and intersubjectivity were at base temporally co-ordinated, so that the acts of creating the sense of another within oneself were achieved within the totality of past, retained intersubjective experience. As a further aspect of sharing a world with others, empathy then forms the basis for the higher intentionality of shared objects in the world. The term for fitting together these acts and syntheses is "implication". This makes phenomenology a learning theory but of an entirely different sort to the type of natural science learning theory carried out by Bandura (1986). Husserl's learning theory is best portrayed within *Cartesian Meditations* with reference to anticipation (1977b, §52, p 114).

What this means is that at some point in childhood we learn how to share the set of cultural meanings from social experience within the family and within early socialisation. On top of such a base, meanings and references become layered. Whenever we meet a person or a thing we "appresent" (add what is not present) of the past retained meanings to the current perceptual-sensations, when we recognize the current perceptual object to be the same or similar to ones we already know, we carry within ourselves, within our preconscious retentional memories, prior experience. Thus what occurs within memory is that our perceptual connections with the world and others are made meaningful now, within the stream of concrete lived experience, by consciousness passively assembling and selecting the meanings already held which are quasi-present. Such processes occur in insight and defensively fail to occur within the non-recognition or mis-recognition of defensive attitudes that prevent previously united representation and emotion from recombining.

The temporality of one type of defence

It would be possible to make detailed comparison of Husserl's original method, standpoint and results of his researches on temporality and compare them to similar work by Jaspers, Heidegger, Sartre, Merleau-Ponty, Derrida and others[7]. But this would take the paper into a detailed analysis. On the other hand, it is not possible to simply ignore the previous comments by phenomenological writers, so the work of Jaspers has been chosen for a brief mention of someone who tried to explore the subjective experiences of temporality as a ground for understanding a wider field of experience. Jasper's (1963) subjective descriptions parallel

Husserl's project. Unlike Husserl's transcendental attitude explorations of temporal experience, Jaspers focused on some of the psychopathological phenomena of changed awareness (pp. 60-78), alterations in the senses of time and space (pp. 79-87), changes in the senses of lived bodiliness (pp. 88-92), alterations in perception (pp. 93-107), emotion (pp. 108-115), fluctuations in motivation (pp. 117-119), different awarenesses of self (pp. 121-128), self-reflection (pp. 131-133) and attention (pp. 138-143). Such a laying out of the ground can be turned to good effect by using temporality to compare and contrast the fluctuations noticeable in the defences, as part of human personality and within the area called psychopathology. However, what is missing from the perspective of Bernet above are the details of the temporal changes that are entailed in the changes of the senses of self that occur in the enactment of a defence. The comments in this section of the paper are derived from a direct seeing of my own experiences and a study of the experiences of others.

Firstly, at time one, there is the usual sense of ego ("ego_1" for short) which is an owned egoic sense of unity. Around the sense of self there is the everyday connection with others and the usual fluctuations in the sense of self, brought about through ordinary living. There might also be parts of self that are disowned and projected onto others and not admitted to consciousness. But these are not initially problematic. In this first position, the ego is mostly intellectual and volitional; but there are also unconscious intellectual, associational and emotional processes that are emerging above the threshold of consciousness, which find expression in the conscious part of the mind in desires and wishes for behaviours that are not part of ego_1. With an increase in the admittance of the desires and wishes to consciousness, ego_1 changes its boundary to own or include the eruption of defensiveness, so the sense ego_1 is no longer maintained.

Secondly, a change in the psychodynamics of the individual has occurred such that there is a transition period, time two. During this time there is a loss of ego_1, but the establishment of a widened sense of self, whereby the old inhibitions have decreased and the defences of ego_1 have fallen, so that a sense of inner conflict and anxiety arises. In this state of tension, there may be the consideration of actions or behaviours that lie outside of the usual repertoire of ego_1. During a first phase of the second time period, there is an increase in drive conflict and anxiety, with concordant changes in the behaviours associated with a new sense of self, ego_2. This change means that a previously ego-dystonic part of self has been brought inside the old ego boundary and is now owned.

However, there is a second phase to time two, when the new behaviour that has been contemplated is selected and enacted. This often leads to a decrease in anxiety, that reduces temporarily the sense of inner conflict that had arisen. Overall, in the second phase of time two, anxiety decreases. A discharge of cathexis is achieved, that was associated with the previous state of unpleasure, to use Freudian language. Generally, this phase is associated with reduced tension and anxiety, which in some way serves a function of expressing previously preconscious aspects of ego_1 that are seeking expression and admission within consciousness and by the ego. If they cannot do so by speech, thought and discussion with others, it seems they do so via symptoms, anxiety, habituated behaviours and other aspects that are not under control of the conscious ego_1, the "I can" of the first sense of the ego.

However, there is a third sense of the ego that emerges during a third stretch of time. This ego_3 is similar to ego_1 but different because in time three, ego_3 may feel guilty over its own actions as carried out by the temporary sense of ego_2. Potentially, ego_3 may feel that it needs to make atonement for the actions and behaviours associated with the second phase of time two above. Ego_3 has achieved satisfaction of its drives and expressed material that was outside of the ego-boundary of ego_1. But sometimes there may be confusion about what has been lost or gained. Overall, the unpleasure of anxiety at time one, which peaked during the first phase of time two, has now been dissipated. But ego_3 may have become guilty because of its actions in time two. The sense that consciousness gives to itself as ego_3 is that it has to take further actions in order to regain an adequate sense of self-worth, in order to make reparations for its relaxation and pleasure gained during the second phase of time two. These reparations may involve further actions with others and the establishment of an ego_3-boundary, once more, with the actions of ego_2 outside of ego_3, similarly as they were for ego_1. As time passes by and the needs of the aspects of consciousness associated with ego_1 accumulate again, and if no other way of expressing or changing them is brought into play by ego_1, then the cycle may continue unabated.

Therefore, psychological change can occur spontaneously or through egoic action or understanding. When this happens the meaning and the motivations of the primary process sphere are in some way changed so that the need to repeat is lessened. What this leads to is understanding the place of hiding and revealing meaning in the three stages above and in other occurrences of defences.

In the analysis above, we can see the following theme appears with respect to the revealing and covering over of references and meanings. On the one hand, some defences serve a purpose of hiding what would be disturbing within ourselves from ourselves. Indeed, such reconnections may not begin to reappear for years. This is an example of temporally-rooted defences trying to prevent references to retained experience occurring, in such a way to reduce further anxiety and unpleasant emotion within current consciousness. Defences have several forms, but the characteristic that they have in common is that they attempt to prevent harm whether in the face of actual threat or merely anticipated threat due to past learning. On the other hand, references can be restored or revived to lost retained material, and this might be either painful or a joyful experience. In either case, the achievement of a moment of insight may or may not lead to symptom reduction or behavioural change, but may lead to an enhancing of the sense of self.

Directions for future research

Another avenue for exploration is that problems arise when many feelings, thoughts and behaviours get repeated and the same meanings arise—yet the new moment is always upon us. The psychological baggage of the past gets carried forwards into the new moment. Some of the baggage is helpful but the rest might be jettisoned without loss. If only it could. The new moment is always new. The future, to agree with Heidegger, is what we have left: The inexorable movement towards a fate that is both personal and shared. A major question to be investigated concerns how new, helpful learning occurs—alongside the change in the retained objects. One way of looking at psychological change, apart from viewing it as the reuniting of representations and emotion (following Freud, Lacan and Bernet) is to study how inappropriate meanings within consciousness get left behind and how more helpful meanings[8] and associated behaviours get up-dated and taken forward, to feature in the repertoire of behaviours and meanings that are useable within the new moment. In doing this, it is necessary to study the changing relation between past, self- and other-destructive behaviours and meanings, and to see how persons move towards a better future. There are further consequences of the phenomenological understandings[9].

However, the point of therapy in the style of a talking cure is that thoughts and emotions are allowed to surface and potentially recombine, and that therapists act to facilitate a certain sort of relationship and state of mind in clients, whereby such material can surface, be described again and again if necessary, until such re-combinations occur spontaneously, or are aided to occur with the help of careful interventions. It will take further research and discussion to develop a clear understanding of temporality for use in practice, supervision, empirical research, personality and psychopathology, human development and the human sciences in general. The understanding of temporality within meaning-creation and repression in self-experience, is a starting point.

Notes

1. This is nothing new for such attempts have been tried several times before. Within psychoanalysis Theodore Reik noted that the sense of the ego varies between actual experiences or imagined fears of "ego-horror" as well as the "ego ideal", (Reik, 1948, p 174). These are two extremes of psychological potential and actuality. Also, in connection with this variability, the importance of empathy for Husserl should not be under-estimated either. Husserl believed that we never have direct access to another's consciousness. But for him, we do have experiences of the other within ourselves as constitutions that we ourselves first produced with respect to our adult carers when we were infants. This first experience then becomes the basis for more differentiated experience that we gain as adults. For Husserl, it is always the case that we create the empathic senses of others and appresent (add them) to other persons.

2. Temporality is the most fundamental Being-structure of Da-sein. But Heidegger presented an incoherent picture of temporality in *Being and Time* (1996). It is incoherent because at several points he referred to the equi-primordiality of the three ecstases or raptures that are three types of "intentionality" towards the future, present or past. At other points, he clearly stated the primacy of the authentic future, of living towards a finite human existence with others. Therefore, it is unclear which takes preference. If it is the future, he should have stated it plainly and refrained from comments on equi-primordiality.

3. The labyrinthine collection of lectures, appendices and supplementary sketches published as volume 10 of *Husserliana Gesammelte Werke*, most of which are translated as *On the Phenomenology of the Consciousness of Internal Time* (Husserl, 1991), is a starting place for a deep understanding of the method and maturation of phenomenology. Major explanatory works that have been of use in understanding Husserl's mature theory of time include Bernet (1994b), Marbach (1993), Cairns (1976), Brough (1977, 1989, 1991) and Seebohm (1992). Bernet, Kern and Marbach (1993) and Kern (1993b) have been of particular use in delineating the overall dimensions of the time phenomena that Husserl considered in the context of his overall stance (1981a).

4. The theme of the self-temporalization of temporality in Heidegger's *Being and Time* is similar to what Husserl called the "flow" of absolute consciousness in his papers on temporality up to 1917. Therefore, when seen neutrally, in the transcendental attitude of not attending to the sense of usual reality and trying to set

aside previous assumptions, it can be stated that time constituting consciousness self-reflexively constitutes appearances of flowing consciousness itself. Or to state this in simpler language: as each moment comes and goes, consciousness makes appearances, and, more often than not, makes them meaningful. It does this automatically without the activities of the ego. But the constituting consciousness also flows along. Therefore, it constitutes itself.

5. Descartes' six meditations (1986) are a guiding image for Husserl's reductions and close to the reductions given by Heidegger in *Being and Time*. Also, to understand Husserl's claim to have direct insight into the structure of consciousness, it is important to note what apperception is: "Thus it is well to distinguish between *perception*, which is the inner state of the monad representing external things, and *apperception*, which is *consciousness*, or the reflective knowledge of this inner state, and which is not given to all souls, nor at all times to the same soul", (Leibniz, 1973, p 197). Such a theme also appeared in Descartes' "mental scrutiny" of himself and is similar to the revelations of Da-sein in the forced reduction by *Angst* (Heidegger, 1996, §40).

6. This is a relevant aside, but one that cannot be explored within the confines of this paper. For instance, the ego is basically associated with conscious volition, "the I can" as Husserl called it. But there are several other aspects to it. The ego is active and passive, conscious and concerns out of awareness, and reflexive and pre-reflexive aspects. The ego has parts that are constitutions of thought, belief and the carriers of meaning, including the value of self-worth. It has out of awareness intellectual capabilities because it is capable of solving complex problems whilst the conscious mind is asleep, or solving a problem whilst not giving it conscious attention: Such is problem-solving and creativity.

7. Jaspers was perhaps first to write on the subjective experiences of temporality in psychopathology but not from a Husserlian perspective. Jaspers achieved these comments through an empathic understanding of those in his care as a psychiatrist. Comments before the publication of *Husserliana X* were made Husserl's 1928 publication (Husserl, 1991, "Part A"). Heidegger also commented incoherently on Husserl's theory of temporality in *Being and Time* and made other comments across the years 1924 to 1934 which did not fit together either. (*The Concept of Time, History of the Concept of Time, Metaphysical Foundations of Logic*, Heidegger, 1984, 1985, 1992). Sartre also commented on Husserl's theory of temporality but in a confused manner (*The Transcendence of the Ego*, 1960, pp. 32-36). Merleau-Ponty wrote on Husserl's ideas of temporality via the 1928 pub-

lication, and Fink's *Sixth Cartesian Meditation*, enabled Merleau-Ponty to prepare the *Phenomenology of Perception*. In 1946, Roman Ingarden published part one of his work on *The Controversy Over the Existence of the World*, parts of which were translated as *Time and Modes of Being*, (1964). Alfred Schutz (1967) also drew on temporality when he was discussing the most fundamental aspects of empathy and intersubjectivity. (*The Phenomenology of the Social World*, Chapter 2: *The Constitution of Meaningful Lived Experience in the Constitutor's Own Stream of Consciousness*). Jacques Derrida has also written on Husserl's theory of temporality, finding it replete with the metaphysics of presence, when this reading runs entirely against Husserl's text that clearly shows the inter-relationship of past, present and future.

8. Objects are experiential meanings that are complexes of meaning, behaviour, relating to others, thought, feeling and such. They are similar to the use of part-objects in psychoanalysis, but different insomuch that they carry none of the associations of reification, parts of a person, or the psychoanalytic theory of child development. There are still further connections between Husserl's theory of the senses of self and others, that could be gained from a more thorough discussion of meaning-objects within the flow of temporal consciousness, as opposed to the senses of parts of others, or the senses of others, within the preconscious.

9. When persons say that "they haven't got the time" it means they never allocated the time to make something a priority. They never gave it sufficient attention to recollect it from their past, to make it present in their life or to plan towards it. What arises are the allied themes of desiring, wishing, valuing, choosing, wanting. In other words, there is a tension between egoic will versus out of awareness, perhaps habituated forms of wanting and desiring.

19

Towards an intentional analysis of consciousness?

Apart from the meaning and relationship-oriented types of problems that are brought to therapists, there is the way psychological distress is presented in psychopathology. This paper sets aside the problems of lifespan development, close and family relationships, health, finances and work, in order to focus on the nature of consciousness as revealed by an intentional analysis of 12 of the disorders within the American Psychiatric Association's *Diagnostic and Statistical Manual of Mental Disorders, Fourth Edition, "DSM IV"* and Glen Gabbard's *Psychodynamic Psychiatry in Clinical Practice.* This paper agrees that therapy should justify itself according to the phenomena of distress, interpreted in some way, and so gain an adequate understanding of its aims and objects. The approach is to analyse *DSM IV* in order to provide some guiding thoughts concerning repeating patterns within the whole. The hope is that therapists will turn accurately to the distress that they seek to alleviate. It is useful to theorise about motivations and the relation between self and other, as portrayed in these leading works. Although psychological classifications are written to serve a number of purposes, they also indicate the forms of intentionality that occur. The themes found are co-occurring and complex. The reader is encouraged to think with the author in trying to note the processes of psychological suffering.

This paper attends to the innate characteristics of human suffering to understand the foreground and the background, the whole and its elements. It begins an intentional analysis for preparatory theoretical research. The theoretical stance is briefly defined and then applied. The forms of suffering considered defy strict categorisation and show the co-occurrence of several basic elements. Some clarity is required concerning how the analysis is made. Of course, not everything can be noted and worthwhile discussions about nature and nurture, the use of terms such as "disorder," "personality," "object constancy," "security of attachment" and "ego," within a perspective of contextuality, are simply omitted for the sake of simplicity (Marbach, 2000, Kern and Marbach, 2001). The paper does not concern itself with the dangers of categorisation, labelling, the deconstruction of psychopathology[1] or the difficulties and misuse of diagnosis (Roy et al, 1997).

Getting started

The first problem is wondering where to start. Psychodynamics has come to be associated with a moribund tradition that sees its theory more than the client. The phenomenological approach is the contrary of such an outcome: openness to the phenomena informs the specific nature of theory, research justifications and practice. Indeed, phenomenology holds that theory, research and practice are closer than other traditions recognise. The phenomenological tradition holds that consciousness is intentionally related to objects, senses and meanings. There are many types of cognitive and affective processes that create these senses. One object may have many processes concurrent in producing a specific sense. The medical and scientist-practitioner models do not fully account for meaning and clients' perspectives. A lack of a focus on meaning is a shortcoming to be rectified. The following points are believed to be important in understanding psychological problems because they indicate human nature and how therapy can help:

• Ethical discussion is not a starting point because it is deemed too non-specific a perspective. The point of the paper is to focus on human nature as a source for considering relationship-dynamics and cognitive-affective dynamics in therapy.

• Attending to the needs of clients and their world means attending to their individual needs, understood against the backdrop of human nature generally. What is normative for Husserl was idealising theory. His stance against logical psychologism was a focus on epistemology that finds ideal universals, "a priori essences," of the conditions for the possibility of some phenomenon and its creation by consciousness with other consciousness (Bernet, Kern and Marbach, 1993, pp. 28-30).

• Fundamentally, it is claimed that the understanding of how to inter-act with clients should be of the same type as understanding clients generally. Even simple concepts such as defence and anxiety are difficult to pinpoint. The point of the exercise is clarifying concepts to make sure they fit their experiences. This is a difficult task given the nature of the region they comprise.

• It is deemed important to attend to the pertinent phenomena of suffering and recovery rather than focusing on irrelevant or inaccurate theoretical interpretations. Intentionality is useful because it includes types of intentional relation to an object. Without intentionality, there are objects but no account of how consciousness has several types of relation to them.

• Pure psychology includes consideration of the contextual factor of motivations between persons. Thus, there arises the importance of understanding psychodynamics within a social context where there are two opposing forces: There is the tendency of the distressed individual to become habituated and have similar generalised beliefs, attachments and behaviours that are fairly constant irrespective of context—versus the tendency for contextual differences and the ability to attend to novel experience. These two factors might be acting in opposition to each other.

To a degree, there are the semi-constant aspects of the life-context of clients, that through years of fixity produce an anticipation of specific generalised object-senses and over-usage of specific cognitive-affective processes. To a degree, there are the differences between the current psychodynamics of the client, at home and in specific social contexts, and what occurs with the therapist. The therapist is generally more constant and secure, through having reflected on their own lives and having made alterations accordingly through their personal therapy, their chance for recovery.

The phenomenological approach stated below makes the assumption that what arises in adulthood is due to the inter-action between stressors in the social environment and an accumulation of vulnerabilities in the individual. At this time in the history of psychology and therapy, it is not possible to make definitive comments about the aetiology of psychological distress or to know without doubt how therapy works. A guiding idea is to proceed with caution and not jump to any conclusions about material causes or the specific workings of intersubjective motivations. Currently, it is impossible to state whether a specific person or a specific disorder is caused by any single factor. It is most wise to support stress-vulnerability models that account for both possibilities in inter-action with each other (Plomin et al, 2000).

One way of orienting the work of therapy is to focus on the experiences of clients. In order to help them, it would be useful to have an accurate set of concepts that relate to their experiences. If therapists were to have inaccurate understanding, such concepts would take attention away from the concerns of clients. Accordingly, this paper tries to think about the conditions for having concepts that are accurate in attending to human nature. Further work is required for thinking about the various conditions for conceptualising. For instance, what needs to be known, with what degree of certainty, in order to know how to carry out this type of conceptualising? This paper claims that a first attention should go to the experiences referred to by *DSM IV* in order to maintain a therapeutic attention on the consciousness of the other. A judicious selection of personality types is considered as a means of sketching the whole. This paper seeks to extend the work of Jaspers (1963, 1968), Binswanger (1963) and Minkowsky (1970) that has attempted to understand 'psychopathology' through phenomenology.

The manner of thinking involved is informed by Husserl's *Third Logical Investigation* (1970a, §§7, 14, 17, 21). There is interplay between understanding the part and understanding the whole. Specific turns to understand the part occur within the accumulating understanding of the whole. Specifically, the empirical instance of understanding a client is adequately interpreted within the whole of the personal experience of meeting others. The feelings and experiences in this nexus are understood as meanings. They can be interpreted differently according to backgrounds. An intentional analysis explicates the processes, understood as ideals, that create the everyday senses that people have of self and other. The great task of theory is to reflect on both happiness and unhappiness. If there is only a focus on unhappiness, then there is no connection to the direction in which therapy wishes to go. The experiences of happiness and unhappiness, health and distress, make sense in the much wider contexts of culture and society (Pilgrim and Rogers, 1999).

But there always is the presence of some type of interpretation onto the phenomena under discussion. This is the case in the recording of the mere phenomena of psychopathology, as elsewhere in the field of psychology, therapy and the human sciences[2]. Following these thoughts a little further means understanding the interplay between the time-dependent phenomenon of the change-ability, constancy and recognition of the same in human experiencing. The paper needs to make its position on psychological health clear. Here, the assumption of psychological health is that object constancy and security of attachment are taken as accurate descriptive languages. A brief characterisation of happiness is called for at this point. The experience of happiness seems to include senses of capability, control, expansiveness and spontaneity. The sense of happiness is often called "confidence" or being "together". The sense of the object constant ego is resilient to stress and not usually threatened by contact with others and the world. It is without generalised and pervasive self-doubt or a sense of attack. It is easy to describe happiness in terms of the lack of the bad, but such a terminology would say nothing about a sense of sufficiency that can be characterised as 'object constancy' and 'secure attachment' (Marris, 1996). Although generally there is a lack of understanding of the fine variations that comprise everyday happiness of the end-states that therapy would like to bring about. Conversely, unhappiness is adequately characterised by object inconstancy and insecurity of attachment. Unhappiness is a myriad of states, some of which are described by specific understandings of how consciousness has worked in a faulty manner, more of this below. It is important to consider the whole and find out if this region of evidence, reveals its own nature rather than importing any external means of construing it. But the terms "ego" and "self" are used interchangeably and refer to the everyday usage of them by the public in speech and action[3]. The term "apperception" is used as a technical term for the perception of the sense of self or ego. The overviews in tables 3 and 4 are provided in an attempt to understand the whole set of phenomena.

	Temporal fluctuations	Givenness of self	Givenness of other
Schizophrenia	Variable	Weak, chaotic, fantasising	Disorganised, chaotic other
Paranoid personality disorder	Constant	Persecuted, projects anxiety	Persecuted by other, hostile
Bipolar	Bistable	Ambivalent, chaotic, partitioned	Limited & changeable with respect to other
Borderline personality disorder	Bistable	Weak, chaotic, anxious, histrionic	Volatile other
PTSD	Single occurrence	Hypervigilant, masochistic	Limited relation to other, anxious
Major depressive disorder	Bistable	Masochistic, fixed, negative	Good, capable other
Dissociative identity disorder	Multistable	Defensive, changeable, partitioned	Discretely changing relation to other
Simple phobia	Constant	Irrationally fearful, masochistic	Limited relation to other, anxious
Generalised anxiety disorder	Constant	Weak, masochistic, hypervigilant	Other may be 'persecutory'
Obsessive compulsive personality disorder	Constant	Masochistic, punitive, unrealistic	Other must obey self, projective, hostile
Antisocial personality disorder	Constant	Ruthless, insightless, violent, narcissistic	Attacks and hates other
Obsessive comp disorder	Constant	Masochistic, punitive, rigid	Unable to comply, anxious

Table 3-Focussing on the whole set of object-senses, the givenness of self and other in *DSM IV* with respect to temporal fluctuations. The column 'temporal fluctuations' tries to describe the variations that take place between opposing positions within the person. The number of changing forces at play varies according to how the phenomena are observed. Husserl believed that phenomenology elucidated or inferred the invariant nature of intentional processes. These are a priori or universal essences for him.

The evidence to be considered

The psychoses are a set of experiences that appear in a variety of forms and may only occur once in a lifetime, or in other cases, may appear for long periods of time and contribute to a low quality of life. The following commentary is a sketch of the intentional worlds of each problem selected. The commentary briefly touches on each of several different types of problem that have been selected to show the wide range of psychological problems that need to be accounted for by explanations of intentionality and intersubjectivity. What is presented is a whistle stop tour in order to make comparisons and spot commonalities.

Schizophrenia is claimed to be the archetypal psychosis. Its main features are hallucinations and delusions although several other definitive aspects can be present such as disorganised speech, disorganised behaviour or catatonia, and flattening of affect, loss of speech or lack of motivation. Hallucinations are imaginings that are sufficiently vivid that they could be believed to be perceptions. Although in less vivid cases, the hallucinations have a flimsy quality or are clearly superimposed over perceptions of the current context. Delusions are beliefs that are maintained without evidence or despite evidence to the contrary. (This is not referring to tacit beliefs or other received understanding). Overall, there are constitutions of hallucinatory and non-hallucinatory object-senses, for there are periods where no hallucinations occur. But when hallucinating, there is a disruption of consciousness and a chaotic type of object inconstancy[4]. Constituted meanings and experiences occur that do not reflect consensus in the perceptual field, or the cultural and societal world of other persons. When hallucinating, the productions of consciousness are focused on the personal themes of the individual. In a way, hallucination can be likened to a form of dreaming or the imagination run riot. The experience of schizophrenia may serve a defensive function in that it provides a retreat from the stresses of the social world. A great deal could be written about schizophrenia. For the purposes of this exercise some aspects are considered central and attention is omitted from others. Accordingly, the intentional experience of schizophrenia is portrayed in brief in tables 3 and 4.

Paranoid personality disorder is exemplary of paranoia. Lesser types of paranoid experience also occur. These can be called "quasi-paranoid". In paranoia, the sense of the other is inaccurate in a regular way. There are different degrees and types of paranoid empathic interpretation though. The difference between the full-blown experience that is called paranoid personality disorder; as opposed to the lesser types is the strength of the fearfulness of being judged negatively, and apperceiving oneself negatively.

Paranoid personality disorder mis-attributes the source of its anxiety. Paranoia refuses to be open to current contextual influences and can be antisocial[5]. Paranoia looks for disapproval and rejection from others and can interpret a neutral or irrelevant event as one that is proof of the bad intentions of others towards self. The constitutions in paranoid ideation concern the theme that others are empathised as attacking self. Clearly, interpretation and evocation are at work. The paranoid self generally empathises attack when there is none apparent to other persons. The general tendency of the cognitions and affects produce a 'projective,' persecutory anxiety and the mistaken attempt to defend self against 'attack'. Other persons are empathised as having the sense that they are attacking self, when in fact they are not. The general quality of the psychological energy at play is empathising others as sadistic in relation to self. There is no actual attack from others, at least at first. However, paranoid persons maintain an on-going sense of imagined attack, that after expression and repetition, brings about an actual lack of trust from others. Those around the paranoiac may feel that they are being unnecessarily attacked and accused of being attacking and antagonistic. So eventually, others may counter-attack the paranoid self, so fulfilling the paranoid empathy and anticipation.

Ego inconstancy is an identifiable experience that can be defined as chronic ego-object inconstancy. Such an inability to maintain a secure sense of self was referred to by Laing as "ontological insecurity". He defined its ontological security as the person who can "encounter all the hazards of life, social, ethical, spiritual, biological, from a centrally firm sense of his own and other people's reality and identity. It is often difficult ... to transpose himself into the world of an individual whose experiences may be utterly lacking in any questionable self-validating certainties", (1959, p 40). The following selections of problematic experiences show variations around this theme. The nature of the fluctuations vary, yet some of the processes may be the same. In order to discern the characteristics of ego inconstancy, the cases of bipolar disorder, borderline personality disorder, post-traumatic stress disorder major depressive disorder, and dissociative identity disorder are analysed.

Bipolar II disorder can include psychotic experiences and is characterisable as a gross lack of self-regulation. Generally, it is a movement between the alternations: depressed and elated. Or there may be a third, coping in a steady state between the two extremes. There is little or no personal control over the fluctuations. The general sense of the manner of production is that of alterations between the three steady states and the maintenance of an inability to form a more cohesive sense of self. There is a lack of defensive strategies to cope with anxiety. Persons with bipolar disorder are either caught up with anxiety or oppressed by it in depression. Mania, cyclothymia and bipolar disorder share the qualities of elation, dissociation and ambiguity that involve a distancing from other experiences. There is a major loss of self-regulation in them. Bipolar disorder or mania may occur after a period of prior depression (Gabbard, 2000, p 216) and so bipolar II disorder, as representative of ego inconstancy, seems to indicate some type of dissociation between sub-egos.

Borderline personality disorder is characteristic of gross ego inconstancy but is a rough grouping of four personality variants (Grinker, Werble and Drye, 1968, p 90). The span of this diagnosis includes four separate groupings[6] that share the following intentional characters: regular instability since adolescence, pervasive anger and self-harm, emotional dys-regulation of mood in relation to little provocation (object inconstancy), impulsiveness and risk-taking, chaotic relationships including idealisation and denigration and attempts to prevent, or fear of, abandonment. Plus inconsistent self-identity including a pervasive sense of emptiness. In the original research there were approximately four separate groupings. (1) A group that were depressed, blandly passive and fairly adapted. They were vague, unemotional, socially withdrawn, avoidant or very selective in relating with others. (2) A group who had an inconstant ego and suffered loss of identity and were in and out of attachment relationships and did not attach. They became angry on getting close and were depressed when they retreated. (3) A group who were unable to gain a sense of self and experienced vacillations that appeared as low self-esteem and neurotic depression. (4) A group with the failure of ego constancy who become temporarily psychotic and paranoid in a way that is indifferent to context. It understands self and other as highly inconstant and shows an excessive variability that is incoherent. They were clingy, impulsive, angry and antisocial. Borderline personality disorder indicates an inability to identify the constant aspects of self and other, although there are constancies apparent to others. The general act of understanding is such that large fluctuations of meaning occur, that cannot and are not held together. They cannot produce a more cohesive sense of self and other. The general quality of the psychological energy demonstrates an irregularity and incoherence across time. Thus, the types of constitution, of self and other, suggest great difficulty in achieving an overall sense of cohesion with variation. The type of attachment is clingy, disorganised and chaotic.

Post-traumatic stress disorder (PTSD) can be understood as a mood disorder that includes inconstancy of the ego (Gabbard, 2000, p 252). It is similar to anxiety and depression and may be quasi-paranoid, like social phobia and agoraphobia. PTSD features the repetition of trauma and its consequences. A previous trauma is maintained and re-lived, through the on-going effect of involuntary memory. The traumatic repetitions occur over a much longer period than is usually the case for mere shock. Possibly, the self is protecting itself through the maintenance of a state of hyper-vigilance in the on-going repetition of trauma and associated experiences. The strength of PTSD is linked to the subjective importance of the shock of the trauma.

Major depressive disorder occurs when the ego apperceives itself as incomplete and shows a failure to empathise a sense of contact and warmth in the company of others. It may be the case that there are distinctly different types of major depression. The definitive phenomena are a gross sense of loss, guilt that masochistically persecutes self and the inability to re-establish loving relations with others. The depressed self apperceives itself as lacking the necessary strengths and abilities to cope with the stresses and strains of ordinary living. It interprets itself as being unable to cope and gives itself a negative, masochistic valence. As such, major depressive disorder is the 'opposite' of narcissism: low self-esteem. When depressed, the manner of object constitution is regular and consistent. Dissociation operates where turning against the self occurs. The self apperceives itself as bad and one part tortures another through cognitive acts of obsessing over real and imagined shortcomings, while excluding evidence to the contrary. There is a general constitution of masochism that is perpetuated through blocking out evidence to the contrary. The maintenance of a depressive focus thereby brings true the depressive prophecy that self is inadequate. There is a strong and consistent negativity about the self's abilities, worth and past, plus an anticipatory hopelessness concerning the future.

Dissociative identity disorder has a variable relation to others, which makes it archetypal of the processes of defence through its constant ego structure (p 276). The telling point of dissociative identity disorder is that it shows that consciousness can produce semi-autonomous 'sub-egos' that have different access to state-dependent memory, learning and behaviour. The cognitive-affective processes in the constitution of self and other, for each dissociated sub-ego, show that the ego constitutions are both separate and connected: The overall system of sub-egos thereby manages anxiety, avoids intrapsychic conflict and reduces awareness of potentially painful material. Behaviour towards others is variable, indicating the constitution of multiple, senses of others in "splitting". One way of regarding this defensive manoeuvre is to see it as the successful creation of the breaking of references to, and awareness of, painful material. This may have had an originally defensive purpose and may have become habituated since childhood trauma. It may be the case that the reason for choosing one specific type of distress might have arisen as a method of preventing prior hurts that were even more painful than the current level of distress. Dissociative identity disorder is the production of an inconstant self and a specific way of splitting the ego that is shared by other types of distress. There are parallel sets of relationships with people that remain un-integrated. The sub-egos may function in the roles of victim, abuser, rescuer and uninvolved spectator (p 284).

Anxiety may be focused on some non-specific random event or it may be a highly specific fear. Either way, anxiety is an experience of preparatory arousal that sometimes may be excessive in that it prevents action and experiences, rather than being discharged in useful actions. Anxiety may also prevent a wider range of experiences and actions in that people may respond with avoidance of feared situations. Two cases are considered, one specific and the other general.

In simple or specific phobia, consciousness constitutes high levels of anxiety in the absence of actual threat. The manner of constitution is experiencing specific phobic objects as terrifying and apperceiving self as terrified in relation to them. The general quality of phobic anxiety is the constant constitution of the feared object, event or person. In other situations, the phobic affective intentionality varies giving rise to ambivalent attitudes towards the same object of attention.

In generalised anxiety disorder, the worried manner of fearfulness is different and free-floating. The constitution is a general attack on self whereby energy is turned against self in a disruptive and masochistic manner (p 258). A general sense of fear permeates life events, alongside the occurrence of multiple, specific anxieties. There is a disruption of an inconstant self by self. Others, things and events are the means of the expression of a deeper sense of vulnerability and inadequacy. Generalised anxiety disorder may involve a quasi-paranoia about family and self, plus the presence of distracting worries that may turn attention away from the possibility of even more disturbing topics becoming conscious.

The final theme considered is the occurrence of an excessively constant ego structure. The opposite tendency to ego-inconstancy perhaps, is an excessive constancy of the ego in the production of a relatively impervious and unrelated ego that can be present alongside a faulty connection to others and the social world. Three forms are chosen for the analysis of how they display their rigidity with respect to context and adaptive forces.

Obsessive-compulsive personality disorder shows egoic rigidity in respect of the relations towards other persons and with respect to obsessive-compulsive disorder[7]. The personal ideals worked towards are, at times, incapable of being achieved. The general quality of constitution shows self-denial, masochism and the narrowing of self in order to achieve self-worth. There is internal conflict between compulsive ritualised thoughts and actions that alleviate anxiety, in conflict with obsessive thoughts.

Antisocial personality disorder occurs when others are empathised as being capable of manipulation and control. The antisocial ego may empathise others as deserving an impulsive attack when they do not meet the needs of this potentially violent self. Others are the focus for the interpretation that they have affronted the antisocial self. The antisocial ego is close to narcissism[8], paranoia, dishonesty and evil. There is a maximally hostile relation towards others for the purpose of self-aggrandisement. Others' actions are slights on self and sufficient to justify attack and retaliation. Antisocial consciousness empathises a sense of threat and unfairness directed toward self and responds with hate, anger, violence, jealousy and envy. As such, it is interpretative in a manner that may evoke a hostile counter-response. Others are not valued and are empathised in a way that includes lacks of conscience, control and the readiness to blame others; through to narcissism with antisocial behaviour (pp. 499-501). Antisocial personality disorder is not merely an unjustified anger, antisocial behaviour or criminality. Research indicates that therapy is not indicated and that the ability to be a good actor and successful manipulator is such that this sort of person can run rings around a large section of the general population including experienced clinicians.

Obsessive-compulsive disorder features conflict between two, dissociated sub-egos. The obsessions are experienced as irresistible and excessive thoughts, impulses or imaginings. They are felt to be untypical of self yet are apperceived as egoic and reduce anxiety; whereas the obsessions are experienced as ego-syntonic yet invasive expressions of specific anxieties. Compulsions are behaviours like counting or checking that are excessive or too strong to resist, so they have to be repeated many times over because previous repetitions have not provided an effective defence against anxiety. Obsessive-compulsive disorder is fearful like the phobias, but a different quality of fear is present. The self is lived and understood in a rigid manner: it must be able to achieve its fixed ideals in order to attain self-worth. However, these ideals are unrelated to the requirements of general living or work. For instance, showering for six hours a day in order to attain the feeling of personal hygiene shows that the general quality of the psychological energy at work is toward the production of a self-punitive, conflicted and split self. The conflicted parts of self do not resolve their conflict but maintain it. As such, they can be described as being disconnected and similar to the case of dissociative identity disorder, in this respect.

The remarks in this section are presented in tables 3 and 4 in order to compare the parts that sketch some of the whole. This comparison is a good point at which to move further towards seeing the types of mental process that seem to be occurring.

	Degree & type of ego inconstancy	Manner to self	Degree and type of object constancy of the other	Manner and attachment to the other
Schizophrenia	High, hallucinatory	Chaotic, lost	Chaotic	Chaotic
Paranoid p d	Projective	Projective, defensive	Projective	Hostile
Bipolar	Ambivalent, split	Ambivalent	Dissociative, changeable	Variable
Borderline p d	High	Turning against self and other	Irregular	Chaotic
PTSD	Inaccurate	Maintenance of vigilance	Good	Saving, demanding
Major depressive disorder	Inaccurate	Masochistic, turning against self	Good	Loss of contact
Dissociative identity disorder	Dissociated	Dissociation, co-ordination	Dissociative changes	Attacks can be dealt with
Simple phobia	Inaccurate, projective	Fearful	Good	Saving, demanding
Generalised anxiety disorder	Inaccurate	Restricted	Disrupts self	Saving, feared
Obsessive compulsive p d	Inaccurate	Rigid, restricted	Needs to accommodate self	Demanding, rigid
Antisocial p d	Inaccurate	Uninhibited	Hostile, controlling	Hateful, demanding
Obsessive comp disorder	Split	Rigid, restricted	Needs to accommodate self	Unchanging

Table 4-The major dimensions of the whole in *DSM IV* interpreted to provide a comparison of the types of intentionality.

Discussion

The amount of detail in the ways of living is complex and begs an analysis. But at this point, I hesitate before going further into a detailed analysis, and in preference, make some points for readers who may like to think about how the material above can be used in therapy. The evidence base for a phenomenological therapy concerns the experiences of providing and receiving therapy, and providing and receiving supervision. It would take further work to immerse oneself in these experiences and reflect on the commonalities, the pushes and pulls of being client, therapist and supervisor. But making an attempt at a Husserlian analysis requires further comparison. The tables 3 and 4 are hesitantly constructed as a rough means of suggesting some of the main object-senses in common. The tables should not be taken as final reductions of the complexity of the whole, but merely as aids towards useful thinking about the nature of, and relations between, the major concepts that refer to these intentional experiences. But even at this point, there have been condensations of client material, gross generalisations and a specific interpretation of the clinical material. So a dilemma ensues with this form of analysis, as it would with any other. What I am hesitating about is the link between the forms of knowing the evidence and how that rests with the ethical domain. The approach in these pages explicitly prefers the epistemological to the ethical. This is not to say that ethics is rejected.

On the one hand, there is the need to attempt what Husserl asked. To compare the manners of givenness of, say, the empathic sense of others and to work out how the empathic synthesis that created them. (A specific notation for phenomenological description has been laid down by Marbach (1993) that will be commented on shortly). But, on the other hand, to compare these descriptions of the object of empathy requires comparisons of specific aspects. To aid this, it becomes easier to think about the details through further condensation of their full senses. Such thinking can further serve to reduce the accuracy of description of each part, yet is required in order to gain some sense of the whole. The whole is comprised of parts. Yet the detail of the parts exceeds the ability to write precisely about general themes of the whole. The whole includes laying out ideas about suffering and psychological well-being.

Again, the account needs to relate distress to happiness, as a successful outcome for therapy. What becomes apparent is that concepts that refer to the nature of distress and health need to be adequately accurate in their reference to a huge range of the experiences of clients.

Table 3 focuses on common elements of the senses expressed in *DSM IV*. When the columns, givenness of self and givenness of other, are compared it is possible to note interesting similarities, progressions and differences. Table 3 shows how different senses of self and other are constituted in regular ways. None of which include the possibility that the self is worthwhile and mature and the sense that the other is benign, potentially helpful and co-operative.

Table 4 is one attempt to focus on a selection of major themes that occur for the common elements of the manner of treating self and other—and the type of object constancy of self and other. Once more, interesting similarities, progressions and differences are noticed in these generalised statements. Table 4 shows further details that are all relevant to the same processes of affect, value and sense that together, indicate the panoply of senses that can arise for human beings.

The often cyclic nature of the on-set and the remission of distress, plus the steady tendency for inertia to increase over the lifespan, are two facets that may prompt some future research into the progression between childhood, adolescent and adult developments and how these may relate to the experiences of distress and health in later life. However, the aim of the presentation is a general one. A full analysis is not provided. A brief attention is given to two major points that could be further revealed through a much longer analysis. The reader is encouraged to reflect on tables 3 and 4. If it is the case that specific cognitive and affective processes are occurring, their commonalities might be inferred from comparing the senses that occur within the columns.

The nature of intentional analysis and towards making a conclusion

Intentionality is a key concept because it treats meaning-objects as achievements of consciousness. This means it attends to the way specific meanings are constituted and alter, according to the perspective taken. The aim is to make a picture of the workings of consciousness, by attending to the experiences of clients, and not by importing unsuitable material from outside the region of the phenomenon. To make the presentation clear, the paper summarises an argument that is in-line with Husserl's phenomenology and various types of thinking in therapy.

The standpoint of the theoretician is to think about consciousness. The findings of such thinking are concepts that relate to the whole, natural attitude everyday understanding of psychological experience, as people generally experience themselves and others (Husserl, 1977a, §45). Specifically, in the context of theory, the aim is to think about the whole set of object senses, self and other, to find some clinically useful concepts that relate to the phenomena experienced by clients. The purpose of a concept is to mark out what is potentially experienceable or inferable by others. Concepts are significant because they are the technical terms of the work that set the tone for the allegedly sufficient interpretation of material of a specific sort. Action follows these concepts. So for 'pure' or theoretical therapy, some debate is required to agree any results that could be used to provide help. The overall aim of Husserl is to 'see ideas,' a priori essences. Despite the difficulties in this, it is possible to understand essences as that which marks the difference between the professional understandings of therapy; as opposed to the everyday or folk understanding of the public. If no such demarcation can be made—then therapy is conceptually no different to the everyday. It then becomes unclear if the profession has an advantage over the layperson in understanding distress.

Husserl's intentional analysis compares the way that objects appear[9] in conscious awareness and indicates the processes of consciousness that made them (Husserl, 1982, §§130-2, §§150-151, Marbach, 1992; Bernet, Kern and Marbach, 1993, p 124, Ströker, 1993, p 109). The different types of objects, of the generalised self and the generalised other, are *Leitfaden*, "guiding clues" to understand the egoic acts and involuntary syntheses that made them. Thus, Husserl's method is parallel to psychoanalytic and cognitive forms of the inference and derivation of the acts and syntheses of consciousness. The use of the term "object" by no means implies that persons, or our consciousness of them, are reified. The important item to note is that it is easy to focus on the object side, the 'end products' of consciousness and omit Husserl's intention to deduce the ways in which the processes of consciousness created them. The derivation of the processes of consciousness may be useful for providing psychological help. The method of analysis reflects on the senses, of generalised self and others, and considers these as motivations for action in intersubjective occurrences and social situations. And with the consideration of the details, there come immense difficulties: It is as though something just intelligible is always out of sight. There are three hints of an answer.

Firstly, the disciplines of psychology, psychoanalysis and phenomenology are in agreement that the term "object" refers to meanings. The object is a regular self-same, a recognisable identifiable meaning of any sort. Objects may be deformed or can be experienced as ambivalent in a way that their two meanings cannot be brought together into a cohesive, meaningful whole. Alternatively, the fragmentary parts or profiles of 'the same object' might be so diverse that only with difficulty might meaningful experiences of 'the same object' be recognised as such. The easiest way to think about the variability of the whole series of profiles of an object is to think in visual terms. There is a level of generality being used here where the highly general term "object" of attention can be used to refer to a sense of a person, or the overall sense of a person or people in general. 'Object' best fits with people, in its application in therapy and psychology, but it need not be limited to people alone. Some senses that the term "object" can express are:

• There is a constant, regular, cohesive object. The senses of empathising others or apperceiving oneself might be rigid and restricted: they do not include other aspects that might have appeared.

• There is an irregular, poorly bounded object-sense. In the case of knowing oneself, and one's reactions to others, there is included a degree of inaccuracy and alexithymia. The sense of self or others might be inconstant in other specific ways.

• Ambivalence: There are two views of the same object but each is understood separately and not brought together to be understood as one object.

• There are at least two objects that seem to be similar but are understood as two or more different objects. There might be constant multiple senses of other persons or of oneself[10].

Secondly, the evolution of therapy thinking about the structure of consciousness, the ego and defence began with Freud who was the first to commence a discussion of the relation between anxiety and defence. He concluded that elements of one person's consciousness are in conflict with each other. He liked to think in a manner that assumes that there are pairs of opposing forces in play. But a look at tables 3 and 4 shows that what does appear through comparison and reflection on the disorders is that anxiety has a generally *defensive* function. Anxiety may be for the purpose of preparing consciousness to be able to meet anticipated threat and demand and so keep the individual safe. Accordingly, the previous understanding that anxiety and defence are opposed is wrong.

Thirdly, Marbach points out that the aim of intentional analysis is to understand the constant aspects of the processes of consciousness. Marbach suggests that perception is the "mental activity of perceiving … any individual, spatio-temporally located object (thing, event, etc.)", (1993, p 181), whereas recollection is quite different. It is a presentation of an object that is not currently present. Recollection is what has been perceptual or intellectual. Anticipation is similarly like the imagination of what will be perceptual, and the imagination of what could be perceptual, at some time. Marbach concludes that recollection is:

"I represent x with belief by means of representing a perceiving of x believed to have actually occurred in the past", (p 81).

Therefore, the distinction between recollection and perception is an explanatory manoeuvre to define empathic presentation and move to an evaluative level: Given that the empathic process creates the quasi-presence or mediated presence of the other's consciousness. This is because Husserl believed that we never have a first-hand experience of other consciousness, as those others experience it. The impressions that we do have of others must be created by ourselves. Thus, empathy may be defined as: (1) I, a separate person, (2) whilst perceiving the other's physical body, (3), have perceptual awareness of it in my current perceptual horizon, whilst grounded in my own living body (*Leib*), and consciousness. My consciousness (4) automatically re-constitutes the sense of the never-fulfilled empathy of my first-ever sense of another human being within myself when I perceive another human body. Thus, myself constitutes the empathic sense I have of the other for the other. (5) The sense of the other is an addition that occurs through a series of well-habituated appresentations and anticipations, of lower and higher order types. This is because of the intersubjective nature of consciousness, in producing cohesive cultural worlds, is based on the repetition of previous learning. (7) Thus my ordinary natural attitude experience, that the other is somewhat like me, alive and in a meaningful world with me, is constituted. Therefore, (8) with belief, my consciousness and my sense of unity are appresented to others. Consciousness automatically appresents these senses. We each have an automatic recognition that we are both human beings, because we both have human bodies so we find ourselves in the believed, natural attitude world.

If Husserl's stance is useful, this ideal understanding will apply to 'psychopathology' and will be true there as well as for any other case. If there are problems with intentional analysis, then pure psychology may need to be reconfigured in some way. This process would require a comparison of the statement above to consider how the most basic sense of the constitution of the other could shed some light on the generalised senses of other people, as indicated by the senses of the other as shown in the 'disorders' of distress. Such a move might open up thinking in psychology and therapy.

A full intentional analysis of distress shows that the types of outcome about cognitive-affective processes are:

• Imagination is a quasi-perceptual presence without belief in the existence of the object.

• Hallucination is also a quasi-perceptual presence that may occur with the modality of belief in the existence of the hallucinated object or not.

• Delusion is a belief that is held without evidence that is observable by others or despite evidence to the contrary.

• Affect and defence concern how an object comes into and out of awareness. The object of anxiety and distress is at times present, and at other times not so present or absent to consciousness. The processes involved may be both egoic and voluntary, and non-egoic and involuntary, occurring without conscious commission or control.

Imagination and hallucination are both forms of presentation. Delusion is expressed in the linguistic higher intentionality of thought and speech that meet the object for the deluded thinker but not for other persons. Affect and defences are affective processes that show the imposition of presentation on perception. This latter case needs further thought.

The point is to discern the nature of the egoic actions and the non-egoic processes. This makes Husserl's approach parallel to psychodynamic and cognitive practices. Freud, for instance, theorised that emotions could become repressed and still remain influential or motivational, covered over and yet potentially available to reflection on them and a potentially greater experiencing of them. It would be possible to go much further towards the details of what is available to inference in tables 3 and 4. But suffice to say, thinking through these details in sufficient detail is time consuming. Alternatively to Freud, it may be possible to conclude that meaning can come in and out of consciousness and take up different appearances according to the perspective taken.

The remainder of the paper changes focus to the consideration of the intersubjective and ethical concerns and then considers the topic of hermeneutic factors generally. These matters are in connection with considering how any learning from experience can occur, what errors limit accuracy and how intentional analysis can be carried out in specific therapeutic relationships.

Intersubjective and ethical considerations

It is important to comment on the use of the stance that is being set forward. A number of issues are important in addition to working out how consciousness functions. The knowledge gained, if any, could be used against clients or be put to work in unforeseen ways. The aim is to use this knowledge only for therapeutic purposes. Therefore, some view of the therapeutic ends need to be made. Below are some points concerning further topics that shape the way therapy is delivered. These points are not thought through thoroughly but are sketched in a hasty manner.

Perhaps most importantly are the links between intersubjectivity and ethics. Therapeutic work sits in the surrounding context of everyday experience. What intersubjectivity implies is that there is mutuality in meaning and that people are entitled to have their feelings and experiences taken as real. None of the comments above are for the purpose of invalidating the experiences of clients. But all the same, intersubjectivity also includes the possibility that the mutuality of meaning is not always reciprocal. One person may accept the meanings of the other. The point concerning the variability in perspective with respect to what appears is that people are not solely rational, neither should they be scorned because they are not rational. The rejection of client-difference and giving it a taboo meaning is not part of the therapeutic enterprise. Self and others both contain the novel and the different, as well as the identity of the selfsame and the constant. A good deal of Husserl's original writings is able to provide examples of how to treat the unique singular and the theorised whole or universal.

There are also the problems of material cause and intersubjective motivation. Ordinary people may have their own ideas of what has caused them to be as they are. To a degree, motivational factors and material cause comes from both the individual and the communal, working together in a nexus of motivation and causation. The external public world is inside and acting within the private space of the individual. 'Either/or' thinking about the public and the private is a misunderstanding of this nexus.

Possibly, the ethics of therapy begins with tolerance and compassion towards the other. One aim is to help clients help themselves. Facilitation, the fostering of independence and informed consent have their place. It might be a conscious intention that there is no place for alienating the client through verbal and non-verbal communication that gives them ammunition to stay away from receiving help. But communication overall can be ambiguous. The legal situation is unclear (Kennedy and Jones, 1995). If there is a legal duty of care towards clients this means perhaps, before ethics, there are a set of legal parameters that require therapists not to influence their clients unduly. And particularly in the case of negligence, there is the need to avoid creating foreseeable damage to them. Given the general acceptance that some clients can be self-harming, in a wide sense of this term, a keen absorption in the range of clues that show clients who are about to drop out of therapy, without their needs being met, is one case where feedback could be asked for about how well the sessions are meeting their needs.

One good part of becoming a therapist is that there should be less stigma about psychological distress. "Recovery" is well-known for therapists, as they are persons who have had their training therapy and so have had the chance to experience first-hand how the concepts of their theoretical stance are meaningful. The obverse also applies. If training has not been able to demonstrate what its concepts refer to, then its terms, values and ideals, have no experiential referent. Another facet is the possibility of there being future legal necessities to obtain consensus about how to avoid foreseeable harm and the types of harm that could be avoided for clients. Therefore, the mission is to produce a clinical reasoning that is over and above the immediate and intuitive response. Not that there is anything wrong with intuitive pre-reflective experience. But rather the aim is to justify our actions to others and ourselves.

Different types of interpretation

There are a number of points concerning how to interpret the experiences above. The hermeneutic factors can be grouped as follows.

For phenomenology, the natural scientific means of finding answers does not apply. But there is no ultimate control over how the experiences above can be interpreted. Each way of interpreting them ends up with an ethical consequence. The way of psychiatry and the scientist-practitioner stance in clinical psychology often has legal overtones. *DSM IV* sits in the psychological complex and the role of psychiatrists in taking away the liberty of clients 'for their own good'. The categories in *DSM IV* read like checklists but at times of stress, people may experience the phenomena of these categories and that might earn a person a diagnosis of mental illness. Also, there is no meaning-oriented account for the multiple co-occurrences of the experiences of suffering. Overall, therapy is destined to empower clients and it is valuable to include clients in ways that provide them with real choices.

Perhaps, the direction is towards placing clients in the right part of the services on offer for them. Historically, phenomenology has been in favour of a first-hand understanding of the experiences that the mental health services seek to alleviate. For instance, the requirement is to understand *DSM IV* from the inside and so empathise clients accurately. There is a great deal of difference between stigmatising the individual, and the possibilities of social exclusion and other unacceptable tendencies that have plagued the legal use of *DSM IV*.

Experiencing and understanding all forms of suffering first-hand is an impossibility. We cannot have first-hand experiences of all the types of suffering listed in *DSM IV*. Yet the phenomenological aim remains as stretching out to the other and the social world, whilst not losing track of the individual nor our own experiences. There may be regulative ideas about the types, limits and possibilities of intersubjective relationships with others that can be seen within the evidence. If social learning is occurring, then the ways of thinking and feeling about self and others are the outcomes of life-long learning across many social situations. Such experiences may become habituated for the individual, yet show the presence and inter-action with others.

DSM IV is a cultural-historical product, as are all forms of psychological understanding. Originally, Jaspers made a number of innovative contributions to the study of psychopathology (1963, 1968). Since then, there have been a number of critical perspectives on it. These seem to warn against a simplistic understanding and wish to take the understanding of distress out of the hands of the legal system and mandatory psychiatric treatment (Grob, 1991, Gaines, 1992, Parker et al, 1995, Mishara, 1994). Other works deal with the meaningful end-product of mysterious processes (Neimeyer and Raskin, 2000). But there are many questions raised in this area concerning the inter-action between the biological, psychological and the social that need a careful consideration (Rutter, 1987). It is not acceptable to regard these elements of the social whole, solely in the terms of the individual, to be understood outside of powerfully motivating, ubiquitous social practices (Rose, 1989, 1998). The history of psychiatric and psychoanalytic hegemony in the USA shows the rise to power of the concepts and practices of psychiatry in relation to the profession's treatment of the public who '*need*' such services. Many of the concepts noted above have a social history in that they occur within or enable certain medico-legal practices to exist. Although a Foucaultian critical perspective is relevant, it is not the focus of this paper.

However, a more equitable approach to the phenomena of distress and health requires making clear its own interpretative conditions. For instance, there is the case of different forms of interpretation that could be made of the *DSM IV* selection. Even, if we accept the Husserlian style of thinking, it is not the only form of construing mental life. What I am alluding to are the assumptions that have to be made to justify Husserlian reasoning as a line of thought. What makes it possible are a set of assumptions that include there being a connection between the end-product and the processes that made it. I can give two examples of the influence of different initial understandings.

For instance, one form of therapy thinking is material reductivist. It uses falsificationist empiricism to be certain about what it has empirically disproved. It assumes specific cause-effect links between an identifiable causative factor that can be controlled and excluded from one set of persons, but can be created in measurable units within another set. Material reductivism is closely linked to rationality and realism. They assume that consciousness and meanings for consciousness are measurable and statistically determinate. It is assumed that the use of statistics will show what is occurring, allegedly, because it 'accurately represents' the causative factors. The problem is that the concepts taken to the object under research, and the relationships to them, might have been decided in advance of the work to be done. This is a problem of construing the parameters and the nature of the work in advance of a long-term encounter with the object.

Another form of therapy thinking is one that urges that concepts should become more appropriate to the phenomena. Phenomenology believes that parts and wholes of different and similar sorts can be determined from out of the meaningful data itself. The latter focus is on what meaningfully appears within regions of the human world and specific lives within it. Theorising, action and ethics could attend to such referent experiences. Phenomenology asserts that the concepts can only be gained after a prolonged attempt at meeting and understanding the object. Any forthcoming concepts can only be asserted after understanding the object, from a variety of perspectives, and working out its inherent parameters, dimensions and context. Such an approach aims to set aside pre-conceptions in favour of the qualitative and experiential discovery of the qualities of the object in relation to other objects and in relation to other sets of persons.

If there is one reason to be sceptical about therapy concepts or practice, then it is because of a lack of consensus of its most basic terms. Many concepts that structure and guide the meetings with clients are unclear. If a conceptual focus is not valued therapy will continue to be inaccurate: To the extent that its concepts are haphazard, so are its ability to help and be able to describe what it is doing. Helping would then be a matter of chance rather than skilled accomplishment.

Concluding comments

The paper has begun a Husserlian intentional analytic approach to psychological well-being and distress. There are many interesting options that could be selected. It would be interesting to find the links between Husserl, Heidegger and Boss, who each felt he revealed human nature. But rather than go further along the track of looking for common assumptions in the history of thinking 'psychopathology' or disclosing the history of how therapists have acted with respect to how a psychological problem has been construed, there is now a close to the paper. Readers are purposefully left to contemplate what clinically useful thoughts arise from thinking about happiness and unhappiness, as revealed through *DSM IV* or other means.

The above is a sketch prior to contemplating interventions and how to commence, continue and deepen the therapeutic relationship. What the above attempts is a theoretical map that describes the whole country of psychological experience, in order to meet with clients in a more accurate manner. In comparison to reactive attachment disorder in childhood, it may be the case that the fundamental process of the constitution of a constant self and other, and a secure relationship between them, are like *tasks of mature development.* In order to attain benign, accurate and sufficient constitutions, it may be necessary to overcome the difficulties that arise with specific inconstant senses and insecure attachment. Accordingly, the difficulties encountered in empathising other persons can be expressed in a different way according to how many, and which, types of fundamental cognitive-affective processes are encountered by clients. Such estimation is adequately understood in the context of a theorisation of the whole of suffering and health.

Husserlian phenomenology is broadly 'cognitive,' 'psychodynamic,' 'intersubjective' and 'experiential' in the sense of attending to intentionality, or more accurately, intersubjective intentionality. The broad sense of 'cognition' refers to the emotional, linguistic, affective and motivational characteristics, understood as the products of consciousness. Accordingly, four points arise that guide the analysis.

a) Theory is an understanding about objectively identifiable phenomena. They appear not just for one person. Something that is objective in this sense is public.

b) The concomitant is that if a theory is not about an identifiable phenomenon, it will not be possible to provide psychological help in an accurate fashion.

c) A theory that is sufficiently accurate about a phenomenon can be easily demonstrated to colleagues, clients, supervisors and trainees.

d) Not only might phenomena-accurate theory promote the effectiveness of therapy, it might be clearly related to the relationship dynamics and experiences of providing and receiving psychological help.

The above is the promise of intentional analysis in its role for pure therapy not applied. When this approach stays within an understanding of the full set of suffering, it becomes possible to focus more clearly on the concerns of clients. So, such an approach may help engage clients in therapy. It follows that specific clients are inadequately known unless they are interpreted against the background of an understanding of health and distress. Only when this is achieved is there an indication of what the specific phenomena of psychopathology and well-being are for a client. If the therapy profession cannot agree its basic terms, then it is a matter of debate as to how the therapy process works.

Phenomenology is in an attempt to be accurate with respect to the phenomena that are observable by oneself and others. It goes towards the idealised things themselves and tries to see ideas. Such an attention to the phenomena could help therapists move forward with clients through changing psychodynamic habits and intersubjective dynamics. But doubts arise. Clarity of aim is apparent but the difficulty and amount of detailed thinking and reasoning required is daunting. Marbach has laid out guidelines for the attainment of intentional analysis. There are difficulties in taking his lead and applying it more fully to therapy. Future work might be able to identify fluctuations and variations that occur, in the senses of others and self, as they changed and are experienced within sessions.

Notes

1. It is difficult to deconstruct a topic when there is no consensus across the profession in the first place (cf Parker et al, 1995). Most deconstruction turns out to be old-fashioned scepticism. Previous estimates of the accuracy of diagnostic categories during the 1960s were as low as 50 per cent (Holmes, 1997, p 56). As far as the topic of the use of *DSM IV*, this deserves further detailed consideration.

2. For instance, there are different understandings of narcissism according to Kohut (1971) and Kernberg (1970). Kohut maintains that all distress, including depression, is a result of becoming an insecure object as a child, and hence this occurs for the adult. Depression may arise when others no longer affirm the insecure ego, then fragmentation and despair may follow. The phenomenon of depression is different according to Freud (1917e/1963, 1923b/1961), Klein (1940/1975), Bibring (1953), Jacobson (1971) and Arieti (1977). Workers in the cognitive and behavioural therapy understand the phenomenon of depression differently. The case of the different rendings of the same phenomenon shows how each theorist takes their own view of the same thing.

3. The constitution of the sense of oneself, what we discuss when we say "I ..." is an interpretation of the psychological domain. This is the main purpose of pure therapy and Husserl provided an example of what it is intended to achieve: "phenomenological pure psychology is absolutely necessary as the foundation for the building up of an "exact" empirical psychology ... The fundamental meaning of "exactness" ... lies in its being founded on an apriori form-system ... psychology ... can only draw its "rigor" ("exactness") from the rationality of that which is in accordance with its essence. The uncovering of the a priori set of types without which "I," "we," "consciousness," "the objectivity of consciousness," and therewith psychic being as such, would be inconceivable", (Husserl, 1997c, §5, pp. 165-6). What this means is that the task of theorising is to enable accurate empirical practice that will understand and connect with clients experiences, as they understand themselves in their home contexts. For Husserl, psychological theory is a promised land of making accurate understanding of others and the psychological world. Yet the whole to be considered is vast.

4. A number of the forms of distress share common elements. The aim is to compare the qualitative types and not venture into making quantitative estimates of the strengths of these elements. For instance, schizophrenia is similar to borderline personality disorder insomuch that both are highly object-inconstant and

entail problems of attachment and inconstancy of affect. It would not be acceptable to estimate the quantity of different phenomena but rather to delineate if a specific phenomenon was there or not.

5. Empirically, paranoia co-occurs in half the cases of panic disorder (Gabbard, 2000, p 386). Gabbard has found that the psychodynamics at play include the creation of ambivalent sub-egos. A demanding, narcissistic, driven, paranoid 'top dog' tries to hide the fearful, timid, inaccurately empathic 'bottom dog'. The top dog may become antisocial, verbally and physically. The causation of paranoia may be a prior attack. Thus paranoia may be linked to post traumatic stress disorder (PTSD). In PTSD there once was an attack but the paranoid person may have become stuck in a state of anticipatory fearfulness.

6. Borderline personality disorder is an empirical mish-mash first established in 1968 (Grinker, Werble and Drye, 1968). Four sub-types were put together to create one diagnostic category. There was no commentary in connection with post-traumatic stress disorder or multiple reactions to stress in childhood. The aetiology was noted as multifactorial (p 141). In more recent years it might be the case that self-harm is more prevalent than it was 40 years ago and in itself is not a key indicator of borderline personality disorder.

7. The constitutions of obsessive-compulsive personality disorder and obsessive-compulsive disorder share the characteristics of unrealistically high standards that are generally not open to reflection and change. They show imperviousness to new experiences and are productions of an on-going rigidity. Gabbard believes that three sets of cognitions and cognitive processes occur, whereby three or more aspects of self are in conflict. It may be the case that there are conflicts between a public facade; a private face and hidden controlling, sadistic and excessively punitive moral standards (Gabbard, 2000, pp. 552-3). He believes that relations with others may vary between obsequious masochism to controlling sadism. Without external help, these conflicts remain and may become more engrained.

8. Narcissistic personality disorder shows a degree of egoic fixity and a requirement for others to appreciate self. The narcissistic self, and its relation to others, can be seen as excessive attempts to be loved, admired and respected. Others are empathised, exhorted and encouraged to admire self and so achieve the loved self-ideal. The quality of narcissistic psychological energy requires overcoming failures at attempts to gain the desired response. But rather than giving up when the desired response is not forthcoming, attempts to gain admiration continue. The

case of narcissism is central for Kernberg and Kohut, but in this analysis it is seen as a lesser case of what happens in antisocial personality disorder.

9. The senses, *self* and *other*, are objects in the same sense as they are for psycho-analysis and psychology: an object of attention of one of the many types of aware-ness (Freud, 1905d, pp. 135-6). Psychodynamic writers have trod a similar path. Federn is one person who has contributed and emphasized the part played by cathexis, the emotional investment placed in objects of various sorts (1977). "Psy-chodynamics" was used by Weiss to describe the Freudian study of want and desire and their links to satisfaction, frustration, repression and mental forces 'within' the individual: "Every human being is aware of inner driving forces whenever wishes, feelings or emotions impel him to act; frequently, also, he is aware of opposing forces which restrain him from acting ... Psychodynamics is the science which describes and explains the manifestations and the consequences of the interaction of mental forces within the human being", (Weiss, 1950, p 1).

10. This type of thinking is wholly concordant with Husserl who allowed for the ambiguous figure-ground experience: "The thing "suggests itself" as possibly a man. Then a contrary seeming possible occurs: it could be a tree which, in the darkness of the forest, looks like a man who is moving. Now, however, the "weight" of the one "possibility" becomes considerably greater", (1982, §103, p 250). Husserl also wrote several times concerning the "exploding noema" where a previously clear sense might suddenly break apart when a new relevant element is recognised with respect to the previous whole. In the case of ambiguity and lack of clarity of sense: "the whole perception, so to speak, *explodes* and splits up into *"conflicting physical thing-apprehensions"* ... on the one hand, a continuation of experience is possible ... always in the manner of a *thoroughgoing harmonious ful-filling with a steadily increasing rational power*. On the other hand, it must make clear the contrary possibilities, the *cases of fusion or polythetical syntheses of discor-dancy*, the *"determination otherwise""*, (§138, p 332). What the above refers to is the consideration of the unstable gestalt of meaning that could be Edgar Rubin's vase, as it could an ambiguous understanding of a person or social situation. Some interpretative processes are at play and show their outcome in the bi-stable ambivalent experience.

20

The empirical evidence base as the re-appearance of the problem of psychologism

This paper comments on the problem of psychologism as it exists in the empirical outcome evidence base that is dominated by findings for cognitive behavioural therapy. The paper thinks through some aspects of the overall process with reference to the psychological meanings at stake. In brief, the findings seem to show that only cognitive behavioural therapy is effective. In exploring the reasons for this finding, four sections are provided. First, the general nature of the empirical model is laid out. Second, three guideline papers from the Department of Health and National Institute for Clinical Excellence (NICE) are discussed. Third, various criteria for understanding the empirical model are mentioned. And fourth, a general discussion ensues.

Phenomenology was created to solve the problem of psychologism. The problem of psychologism is putting the cart before the horse. Specifically, the cart of empirical research cannot pull itself along without guiding aims and theoretical ideals. Psychologism is the problem of making no distinction between a priori understanding of consciousness in a general sense—and the psychological actuality of the manifold of specific instances of being conscious. In the *Logical Investigations*, psychologism is a "mix up" of "the realm of psychological laws of thought with those of pure logic", (Husserl, 1970a, Prolegomena, §40, p 161). It is a failure to judge between theory and practice in a specific way. Phenomenology should not "ignore the fundamental essential, never-to-be-bridged gulf between ideal and real laws, between normative and causal regulation, between logical and real necessity, between logical and real grounds", (§22, p 104). The original point of phenomenology was to create theory. Of course theory and practice are interrelated. It is necessary to know how they fit together.

In more recent years a number of non-phenomenological psychologists have made the same or similar criticisms but without mentioning the specific term "psychologism". For instance, several have gone on record in stating that statistics cannot justify theory (Cohen, 1994, Gigerenzer et al, 1989, Glymour, 1980, Loftus, 1991, 1996, Lykken, 1991, Meehl, 1978, 1990, Morrison and Henkel, 1970). Others have stated that number-crunching is not primarily relevant (Cohen, 1990). And that statistics in itself has no meaning (Maltz, 1994).

Phenomenology is an answer by creating an a priori philosophical preparation for empirical methods that will relate consciousness, through its intentional forms, to conscious senses and referents. Specifically, applied phenomenological psychology is the relationship of justified concepts that will provide accurate action by relating pure a priori possibilities and necessities to the infinite manifold of conscious phenomena, lived experiences (Husserl, 1980, §8, p 42). Hence the focus on the imagination of possibilities and conditions of possibility in the case of therapy, concerns identifying the most pertinent factors that will create psychosocial skills for practice. Once these distinctions are in place it becomes possible to unpack the problem of the excessive hastiness of the natural psychological scientific approach and how it mis-represents the process and outcome of therapy. There could be theory for practice about psychosocial skills and aims. There could be research into the effectiveness of therapists. But what is in doubt is the current model of natural psychological science to deliver what is useful for practice or effectiveness.

The problem of practice from the perspective of empiricism

A number of documents have been published by national organisations on both sides of the Atlantic that refer to a burgeoning evidence base for therapy outcome research. What is at stake is a set of justifications for practice. Within the UK, the organisations that have been at the forefront of this type of innovation have been the Department of Health and NICE (NICE, 2004a, 2004b, 2005). Both have taken to their heart the idea that the practice should exist according to the *impartial results* of empirical research. The research process would seem to be even handed: Any therapy could be practised as long as it has been proven to be effective. The best means of showing such effectiveness is the double blind randomised control trial. A Department of Health guideline classifies five types of empirical justification, where type I is the best and most reliable form of evidence.

> **Type I evidence**—at least one good systematic review, including at least one randomised controlled trial
> **II**—at least one good randomised controlled trial
> **III**—at least one well designed intervention study without randomization
> **IV**—at least one well designed observational study
> **V**—expert opinion, including the opinion of service users and carers.
> Department of Health, 1999a, p 6.

In the listing above, philosophy and personal experience have no part. The empirical research model can be boiled down to three major parts.

1. A philosophical position comes first: Psychological theory of the type called natural psychological science is the means of interpreting the psychosocial. It is a focus on the inanimate in a way that distorts the biopsychosocial whole, in particular, conscious sense and meaning.

2. Empirical data is found through experimentation and interpretation according to (1).

3. The psychosocial aims of practice are found from (1) and (2).

For phenomenology, it is the case that justified concepts concern finding a priori in reflection on a posteriori findings (Husserl, 1980, §9, p 48). What this means is finding a priori pure ideas of theory about generality that are held to be true—that are about actual situations and specific people. For Husserl, the practice of any empirical psychology requires interpretation of a priori conditions of possibility that pertain to the infinite number of actual instances (Marbach, 2005). For quantitative natural psychological science, its function is to provide information that influences what clients and referrers ask for and what can be funded within the National Health Service (NHS) itself. The same preferences influence decisions about who will be employed and what is practised. As for private practice and the practice of voluntary organisations, then they too might be influenced by the same documents and findings from the evidence base. Particularly when clients have accessed such recommendations through the Internet and from other key influences.

Let us consider the following five databases and what they contain. Generally, outcome research considers quantitative evidence that shows what is curative for clients with a single psychological problem. Currently, it answers one major research question. "Research question 1: How should therapists practice with specific single disorders?" The brief overview below is proposed as a self-reflexive step in finding out how far outcome research has got in answering research question 1. The answer to this is provided by five nationally approved or otherwise renowned evidence-bases. These are from the American Psychiatric Association (Gabbard, 1995), Roth and Fonagy (1996), Nathan and Gorman (1998), the Clinical Psychology Division of the American Psychological Association (Chambless et al, 1998) and the Department of Health (2001b). The evidence base converges when more than one recommendation concludes that the same type of therapy, for a single disorder, is effective. Of the 186 papers cited by the five evidence bases, 164 (88.2 per cent) are cognitive, behavioural or cognitive-behavioural, eight (4.3 per cent) are psychodynamic and six (3.2 per cent) recommend interpersonal therapy. The remaining eight papers suggest relaxation skills, social skills, brief therapy and educational approaches as having been shown effective with specific disorders.

The most obvious conclusion is that cognitive behavioural therapy (CBT) is the most effective *so far*. But this is because it is the most researched type of practice. One reading of the evidence base is that it could produce crowing about the effectiveness of CBT. But the *excellent* result in fact says nothing of the effectiveness of other types of therapy because they have not been researched. If it is believed that CBT is supremely effective, then it might follow that other types of practice are outmoded and should be abandoned because they are ineffective and obsolete. Therefore at first glance, the empirical evidence base would seem to show one thing: that CBT is the only form of helpful practice.

The next section makes specific comments on three of the UK Department of Health guidelines from the perspective of assessing their quality for practice.

Comments on specific papers

Three quick reference guidelines have been produced by the Department of Health that sum up each of the much longer overviews provided by National Institute for Clinical Excellence. The comments of this section are academic comment in relation to the evidence base, as noted above, and with respect to my practice since 1987 and is accordingly limited. One response to the empirical research is to say "hands off my practice". But this is an immediate dismissal of the authority that is being called upon. Let us look at some of the documentation itself that is being foisted on NHS employees.

The guidelines for anxiety cover panic disorder and generalised anxiety disorder (worry). It is noted that the management of panic disorder can be achieved in primary care. What this means is that panic disorder, of less than one or two years duration, or the irregular occurrence of panic episodes, are what could be treated successfully in six sessions (Department of Health, 2004a, pp. 6-7). It seems to me that seven to 14 hours of CBT for a successful outcome with panic disorder would only possible in cases of medium severity with no other complicating factors. If there is agoraphobia, depression and low self-esteem or panic in connection with health anxiety, or if panic is part of the after-effects of rape or sexual abuse, then I do not believe that it could be treated in only 14 hours. Some people might well be helped in less than seven hours of CBT for panic disorder alone. But that would probably say more about clients' insight and characteristics than the therapy provided.

Generalised anxiety disorder (GAD) is a technical way of referring to what common sense calls worry. It is linguistically- or anticipation-driven anxiety that can be about any object. Worry may have a number of different forms or emphases. In my experience, I have found that GAD is often not recognised by general practitioners and even consultant psychiatrists. For treatment to be possible in a short amount of time, then success would only be for the most intelligent, self-caring and insightful clients (pp. 8-9). The recommendation for 16 to 20 hours of CBT is acceptable if it were ever to be present as a single disorder. However, GAD often appears as part of a much more complex history and overall interaction between attachment style, anxiety, depression, low self-esteem and other factors. Such factors increase the time needed for a successful outcome.

The Department of Health has produced a quick-reference guideline for the treatment of depression (2004b). Where problems arise with this document is that depression is treated as a unitary item, a continuum from mild to severe, with no sub-types or co-morbidity. Nothing is said of how depression inter-acts with other factors, particularly when there is a long-standing inability to look after self. No comment is made about depression as an outcome that inter-acts with other psychological disorders. Page six discusses assessment but says nothing of how to estimate complexity and how depression can be inter-acting with what appears as 'personality'. The guideline makes no note that a person who has had depression for decades will have its consequences in their lifestyle that affect their functioning and family system. Eating disorders and other major psychological problems co-exist with depression, yet no comment is made about how they co-exist. Depression can be part of a chronic inability to reflect on self and understand self as having needs that are capable of being satisfied. Whether this is causative of depression, or an outcome of it, is an interesting question. Although mild depression is discussed, no examples of it are defined (p 7). I would think that role change; medium complex grief and loss would qualify as forms of mild depression. But more complex and long-standing losses co-occurring with sub-stance abuse, would not be mild depression. Psychotic depression would necessi-tate psychiatric assessment and treatment or specialist cognitive therapy.

CBT for depression is the most frequently mentioned treatment (p 11). The only talking therapy mentioned is interpersonal therapy. This is true as a research finding but says nothing of the applicability of talking for understanding complex situations. Severe depression is also mentioned but not defined. The problem here is that CBT and the talking therapies require clients to begin to look after themselves, think about themselves, speak about their feelings, and be able to reflect and act, without home visits. There is no mention of the factors that should be noted at assessment for the psychological treatment of depression. Page 12 refers to crisis resolution teams that will be provided by the National Health Service for the most severe types of depression and suicidal intent. Again, CBT is the treatment of choice. However, depressed clients need to be able to use what is being offered them. There is no point offering something that cannot meet their needs and abilities.

The final Department of Health document that I would like to comment on is the one for post-traumatic stress disorder (PTSD) (Department of Health, 2005). Page six states some examples of PTSD, but the full list of its possible causes and the main part of the phenomenon itself, are missing with respect the *DSM IV* definition, which to my mind is much more accurate (American Psychiatric Asso-ciation, 1994, p 427). Namely, sudden death of a loved one is omitted. And para-noia, social anxiety and social phobia can co-occur with PTSD in the case of attack. Another cause of PTSD is rape but that is omitted and no notes are pro-vided on how to help survivors. On page 12, the recommendation is for early intervention for PTSD within one month of the trauma itself, but this is a con-tradiction in terms since PTSD does not officially start until after one month of trauma symptoms. For some people, trauma symptoms may subside without treatment. For others, if PTSD remains untreated it can lead to psychosis, major depression and debility, substance mis-use, agoraphobia and major negative con-sequences can ensue.

I am also particularly concerned by the lack of commentary on PTSD in childhood in the event of sexual abuse and the physical attack of children. This is because it may take their development into a completely different direction. This concerns me because if justifiable anger is an unrecognised effect, then children are mistakenly empathised as being bad, rather than them having some understandable reaction of anger and quarrelsomeness. The historical failure of various professionals to identify and supply treatment in this case seems to me to be excusable through lack of knowledge in previous decades. However, I do not see it as an excusable omission from national guidelines today.

Spotting the assumptions

By what criteria have the evidence bases so far been interpreted? The method, the quality of the statistics and the methodology used in each one of the 186 papers would have to be scrutinised in minute detail in order to ascertain the degree of quality of the science involved. One thing that is obscured is that the three guidelines and the 186 papers show what is effective for single psychological disorders. However, what is not noted is that single disorders are a rarity. The most frequent clinical situation of severity and complexity are not addressed by current empirical therapy research. Therefore, the research noted above does not help practice and does not show what is effective when there are two or more disorders concurrent. Nor do they advise how to help when there are 10 concurrent disorders that have been current for 30 years or more.

Practice requires a firm understanding of psychopathology in a developmental view, in relation to understanding the process of recovery from complex psychological problems. In other words, the problem towards which empiricism hastily directs itself is primarily a problem of understanding psychological meanings and human development. Fundamentally, it concerns how to interpret psychological objects, contexts and processes. A hermeneutics that helps therapy know what it is doing in terms of conscious meanings, aims and avoidances is required. The worth of a hermeneutic phenomenological perspective is noting differences in intentional relations. It concerns understanding how to find a central focus for sessions that will produce results. When it comes to empirical research questions, the following points are relevant and need to be asked in addition to research question 1 noted above.

Research question 2. How should psychological services, and access to them, be structured? This question could be answered according to some estimate of the severity of disability, distress and co-morbidity of psychological disorders and the so-called personality disorders across the lifespan.

Research question 3. How can qualitative research into therapeutic processes and relapse prevention be given a remit with respect to quantitative outcome research?

Research question 4. How can identifiably different clients use which specific types of therapy? In addition, for what optimum length of time should an approach be used? The question concerns how to best place clients within the full range of services that are on offer: What is best for them?

Research question 5. How can process and outcome findings be used to inform therapy concerning how the troubled mind works and suggest how therapy helps with different forms of distress? I suggest that the inner track of how to practice any therapy is intentionality and hermeneutics—not pseudo-science and poor quality psychological science.

What are hidden in the empirical model are a number of problems with natural psychological science and the use of statistics. Although statistics may have its strong points and its uses, there are other areas it cannot cover. The point of phenomenology is that it is against psychologism but not against empiricism. Phenomenology is a philosophical approach to begin a more appropriate applied psychology that places conscious meanings and forms of intentionality in the centre of attention.

Problem 1: There is poor science at large amongst outcome research in therapy. Time and again, researchers break the basic rules of reasoning between hypothesis testing, the representative sample tested and in making inferences about the population at large (Cohen, Sargent and Sechrest, 1986, Morrow-Bradley and Elliott, 1986, Dar, Serlin and Omer, 1994).

One reading of the evidence base so far is to consider that uncontrolled variables are at play. Possibly, there is something amiss with the appliance of science in the creation of an evidence base for practice, funding, training and research: Because there is no guarantee that extraneous variables have been controlled to the same degree in each paper. There are concerns about non-standardised use of statistics and the inclusion and exclusion criteria for the participants and other matters. The scrutiny of these pertinent details is questioning the quality of the standards employed in the creation of research itself. To be precise about the claims given would take much more detailed comment than can be afforded in this introductory paper. Methodological evaluation could play a much greater role in research, and that requirement is raised by this brief analysis.

But just because a number of therapeutic approaches to a specific disorder may not have been researched, it does not mean that those approaches should be discontinued. Nor just because a single RCT study has occurred, does it mean that a specific form of therapy is a treatment of choice. Such a conclusion could only occur at the end of a standardised set of comparisons. Similarly, just because a specific brand name of therapy has been researched, it should not be concluded that it is the only suitable form of therapy for a specific disorder.

If meaning-oriented and qualitative-research methods for assessment and therapy process are not valued, and, if they are not well-organised, then they are not able to argue their case. Within the five evidence bases there is an absence of attention to therapeutic process, particularly with respect to the increase in complexity of co-morbidity and the increase in inertia to change across the lifespan. One solution is to pose answerable research questions and use methods that temper the findings of outcome research. A useable result is one that could be rigorous about therapeutic process and the assessment of client abilities. Three further problems are mentioned in passing.

Problem 2: There is a further distance between RCT outcome research and research into therapeutic process across the lifetime of clients with co-morbidity. Such questions can only be asked through a different type of question and answer. Accordingly, because RCT outcome findings are not focused on meaning and process, they cannot answer the more detailed questions that practitioners would like to know: those about assessment and client suitability for specific types of therapy.

Problem 3: There is no place for a self-reflexive understanding of how to interpret the results of outcome research currently. What perspective qualifies as an answer? It is the place of inference and methods of the interpretation of results to weigh up meanings and emphases.

Problem 4: There is no consensus on what constitutes the appraisal process of statistics and interpreting the findings of outcome research. There are no standard forms of analysing meta-analyses, providing systematic reviews and creating RCTs in the first place. This type of research needs to be standardised or there is no cohesive body of outcome findings.

In the view of this paper, it is the role of RCT research to make one type of contribution that needs to be aided by contributions from qualitative, psycho-pathological and service-provision perspectives. It is also necessary to consider how clients appear with novel patterns of need, ability and personal history. There are implied research questions posed in assessment and answered by refer-ral. What is required is the justification of assessment and the clinical reasoning that accompanies it.

Discussion

It might be possible to conclude that the Department of Health is mistaken about the effectiveness of CBT, that the Department of Health mis-represents the nature of psychopathology and the means of providing therapy of any sort. But many sorts of interpretations are possible in relation to the evidence base as it stands. For instance, one would be the view that the quality of the therapeutic relationship is not particularly relevant because it is interventions that count. But for a hermeneutic psychology, some decision has to be made about what counts and how to interpret. What interpretative factors need an account? The answer suggested is that working out how to practice is much more complex than finding out if a specific therapy is more or less effective with a single disorder. From the perspective of phenomenology, there is a confusion that can be identified as fol-lows.

An initial question is to ask "to what degree is it possible to do empirical research of any qualitative or quantitative sort?" To be accurate empirically is to know how meanings are understandable and classifiable prior to allocating num-bers to specific psychological events and processes of the same sort. This is the realm of a priori philosophy in the service of empirical research and practice. It puts the horse of thinking before the cart of action.

Philosophical psychology of the phenomenological sort focuses on conscious meanings in relation to intentionality and is hermeneutic. Its aim is to under-stand psychological meanings and it is self-reflexive in accounting for its own the-oretical position. It aims to help the needs of clients, through making sense of psychological situations generally.

The role of statistics and the natural psychological model is where logic is appropriate. It has been shown that questionnaires have a much higher degree of precision in being able to predict outcome whereas therapists routinely under-estimate their ability to help. This is the difference between theory for practice (the real psychological world as it is multiply interpreted)—and the actuality of practice.

Practice is about *making things happen with specific clients*. In some situations the means of making things happen is to make the relationship ripe for open discussion, where spontaneous changes in meaning can occur. At others times, therapists need to take a lead in helping clients to get to a better place in understanding or in action. Psychological problems are about complexity of inter-action between mood, 'personality' and various disorders that have an on/off nature that can re-occur for no apparent reason to clients or those who study psychopathology. Psychological disorders have an unusual temporal manner of being. The PTSD effect is an excellent example of what I mean. For children who have been physically or sexually attacked, or have experienced any form of trauma, its effects can last for decades. Even when treated by any form of therapy, the negative effects of abuse and maltreatment are still present to some degree. Even the best functioning adult survivors of abuse still have some after-effects. The temporal nature of the abuse began in childhood yet it stretches across time in a biopsychosocial way. There is a complex inter-action between the material part of the individual in relation to intentionality, the personal set of choices and the social context itself. In conclusion, the evidence base so far does not reflect the highly complex nature of unique individuals.

It might be possible to conclude prematurely, that as a consequence of the evidence base, that CBT is opposed to other forms of therapy. It is still interesting to think about what part of CBT practice and theory is causative of its success. It is a matter of interpretation to think about tendencies that appear between the lines of what has been shown effective. Perhaps, CBT contains within it principles that define good practice for other forms of individual therapy. For instance, encouraging clients to be self-caring, becoming informed about the principles of their therapy and being active outside of the session are general principles that might make other forms more effective (Bordin, 1979). Reviewing clients' perspectives at the end of each session, and asking them to recap the principles by which they understand cause and effect operating in their problems, might also help. Another possibility is that clients may need to test themselves and their beliefs in problematic situations by reducing defences and increasing exposure to 'unbearable' emotions and thoughts. If such interventions were accepted as core principles for any therapy, it would mean that all therapy might include some behavioural task-setting as part of the work.

More importantly, there is the problem of what to do with the emotions that are generated by practising. I would claim that it is impossible to talk about the family of origin with a person who has had a bad childhood and not feel strong emotion of some sort in relation to what they say and what it implies. For cognitive behavioural therapy, for instance, there is no place for what is called counter-transference. An inevitable part of doing any therapy is how to understand the emotions felt by therapists that are the inevitable side-effect of doing the work. First and foremost, the need is to understand those emotions, then know what to do with them. To be blunt, the emotional contagion of practice is part of a process of taking out the rubbish. Clients are burdened by their negative emotions and therapists get an emotional reaction in connection to theirs. A model that has no understanding of these emotions is incomplete and can only leave its practitioners confused. Without a proper means of understanding emotions, there will be no ability to process them and allow them to dissipate. Without an intersubjective theory, there is no means of dis-entangling the place of our own sensitivities, in relation to the resonance felt because of our own personal history in relation to those of clients: For example, if any two people who have had early trauma and were to discuss it, then both might feel shocked, sad and angry. When this is the case for therapist and client, the discussion of the client's early trauma can be effective for the client but may re-connect the therapist with their trauma, during or after the session. What I draw from this is that therapists are qualified to help clients to the level that they feel comfortable with the amount of distress that is generated as the inevitable occupational hazard of doing the work.

Conclusion

CBT itself should not be an object for anxiety. CBT does have its strong points. It is interesting to specify what these are and how they work in terms of the intentional and hermeneutic differences they create. The function and area of applicability of CBT is to overcome conditioned negative emotions and negative reinforcement. Conditioning exists and needs to be overcome. What would be better is a compromise position to bring CBT ideas and practice to what is currently called working with transference and counter-transference. There are unanswered questions as to which parts of any practice are effective and how to structure future empirical research. A therapy without a self-reflexive understanding of its necessities and limitations would mean that the model was insufficient. It would not be able to specify psychosocial aims for particular situations and that would lead its practitioners into disarray and not deliver changes in understanding and action for clients.

Theory for practice can follow a tradition that attends to meaning for self and other; rather than referring meaning and cause to inanimate being. The function of theory is to link between instances, provide direction for action and point to what is important. Theoretical statements serve the purpose of commenting on any specific instance within their region of applicability.

Rather than *impartial* research to find out if a brand name therapy is effective or not. It is better to think about what components of therapy hit their mark. The function of talk is to understand. But discussion itself needs to be understood. This is the matter for philosophical psychology and specifically a hermeneutic approach. There are many ways of interpreting psychological problems. Which is best and why? The guiding research question of Paul needs to be recast. Originally he stated it as: "*What* treatment, by *whom*, is most effective for *this* individual, with *that* specific problem, and under *which* set of life circumstances", (1967, p 111). It could become: "*What* principles of cause and effect, for *which unique inter-action of problems* are most effective for *this* individual's ability to participate in *what* type of therapy and in *which* set of life circumstances?" The inclusion of more practical concerns would further the theory and practice.

So far the evidence base does not include many forms of practice. The omissions are the talking, relationship and meaning-oriented types. For me, arguments between brands of therapy are mistaken because there cannot possibly be such sharp distinctions. But for the dominant model of research, *talking and relating are not yet proven effective or ineffective. If so perhaps they should be abandoned as obsolete and ineffective.*

References

Abend, S.M. (1982) Serious illness in the analyst: Countertransference considerations. *Journal of the American Psychoanalytic Association,* 30, 365-379.

Abercrombie, N., Hill, S., & Turner, B.S. (1988) *The Penguin dictionary of sociology (2nd ed)*. Harmondsworth: Penguin.

Ables, B.S. (1974) The loss of a therapist through suicide. *Journal of the American Academy of Child Psychiatry,* 13, 143-152.

Ainsworth, M.D.S. (1970) Object relations, dependency and attachment: A theoretical review of the infant-mother relationship. *Child Development,* 40, 969-1025.

Ainsworth, M.D.S., Blehar, M.C., Waters, E. & Wall, S. (1978) *Patterns of attachment: A psychological study of the strange situation.* Hillsdale: Lawrence Erlbaum.

Ainsworth, M.D.S. & Wittig, B.A. (1969) Attachment and the exploratory behavior of one-year olds in a strange situation. In B.M. Foss (Ed) *Determinants of infant behaviour, Vol. 4.* (pp. 113-136). London: Methuen.

Aitken, K.J. & Trevarthen, C. (1997) Self/other organization in human psychological development. *Development and Psychopathology,* 9, 653-677.

Akhtar, S. (1994) Object constancy and adult psychopathology. *International Journal of Psycho-Analysis,* 75, 441-455.

Allen, J. (1976) A Husserlian phenomenology of the child. *Journal of Phenomenological Psychology,* 6, 164-179.

Allen, J.G., Huntoon, J., Fultz, J., Stein, H., Fonagy, P. & Evans, R.B. (2001) A model for brief assessment of attachment and its application to women in inpatient treatment for trauma-related psychiatric disorders. *Journal of Personality Assessment,* 76, 421-447.

American Psychiatric Association (1994) *Diagnostic and statistical manual of mental disorders (4th ed)*. Washington: American Psychiatric Association.

Ardener, S. (1981) *Defining females: The nature of women in society*. New York: Wiley.

Arieti, S. (1977) Psychotherapy of severe depression. *American Journal of Psychiatry*, 134, 864-868.

Atwell, J.E. (1969) Husserl on signification and object. *American Philosophical Quarterly*, 6, 312-317.

Bakhurst, D. (1990) Social memory in Soviet thought. In D. Middleton & D. Edwards (Eds) *Collective remembering* (pp. 203-226). London: Sage Publications.

Ballenger, J.C. (1978) Patients' reaction to the suicide of their psychiatrist. *Journal of Nervous and Mental Disease*, 166, 859-867.

Balsam, A. & Balsam, R. (Eds) (1974) *Becoming a psychotherapist*. Chicago: University of Chicago Press.

Bandura, A. (1986) *Social foundations of thought and action: A social cognitive theory*. Englewood Cliffs: Prentice-Hall.

Baron, C. (1987) *Asylum to anarchy*. London: Free Association Books.

Barron, J. (1978) A prolegomenon to the personality of the psychotherapist: Choices and changes. *Psychotherapy: Theory, Research and Practice*, 15, 309-313.

Bartholomew, K. (1990) Avoidance of intimacy: An attachment perspective. *Journal of Social and Personal Relationships*, 7, 147-178.

_____ (1997) Adult attachment processes: Individual and couple perspectives. *British Journal of Medical Psychology*, 70, 249-263.

Bateson, G. (1972) *Steps to an ecology of mind*. New York: Balantine Books.

Baum, O.E. & Herring, C. (1975) The pregnant psychotherapist in training: Some preliminary findings and impressions. *American Journal of Psychiatry*, 132, 419-422.

Bellack, L. (1981) *Crises and special problems in psychoanalysis and psychotherapy.* New York: Brunner-Mazel.

Beres, D. & Arlow, J.A. (1974) Fantasy and identification in empathy. *Psychoanalytic Quarterly,* 43, 4-25.

Berger, D.M. (1987) *Clinical empathy.* New York: Jason Aronson.

Berger, P. & Luckmann, T. (1966) *The social construction of reality: A treatise in the sociology of knowledge.* Harmondsworth: Penguin.

Bermack, G.E. (1977) Do psychiatrists have special emotional problems? *American Journal of Psychoanalysis,* 37, 141-146.

Bernet, R. (1979) Perception as a teleological process of cognition. In A.-T. Tymieniecka (Ed) *The teleologies in Husserlian phenomenology.* (pp. 119-132). Dordrecht: Kluwer.

_____ (1994a) Phenomenological reduction and the double life of the subject. In T. Kisiel & J. van Buren (Eds) *Reading Heidegger from the start.* (pp. 245-267). Albany: SUNY.

_____ (1994b) An intentionality without subject or object? (Trans M. Newman). *Man and World,* 27, 231-255.

_____ (1996) The unconscious between representation and drive: Freud, Husserl, and Schopenhauer. In J.J. Drummond & J.G. Hart (Eds) *The Truthful and the good: Essays in honor of Robert Sokolowski.* (pp. 81-95). (Trans M. Brockman). Dordrecht: Kluwer Academic.

Bernet, R., Kern, I. & Marbach, E. (1993) *An introduction to Husserlian phenomenology.* Evanston: Northwestern University Press.

Bibring, E. (1953) The mechanism of depression. In P. Greenacre (Ed) *Affective disorders: Psychoanalytic contributions to their study.* (pp. 13-48). New York: International Universities Press.

Binswanger, L. (1963) Psychopathology. In *Selected papers of Ludwig Binswanger: Being in the world.* (pp. 102-119). New York: Condor.

Bischof-Köhler D. (1988) Uber den zusammenhang von empathie und der fahigkeit, sich in spiegel zu erkennen. *Schweizerische Zeitschift fur Psychologie*, 47, 147-159.

Blatt, S.J. (1995) Representational structures in psychopathology. In D. Cicchetti & S. Toth (Eds) *Rochester Symposium on Developmental Psychopathology, Vol. 6: Emotion, Cognition, and Representation.* (pp. 1-33). Rochester: University of Rochester Press.

Blatt, S.J., Auerbach, J.S. & Levy, K.N. (1997) Mental representations in personality development, psychopathology, and the therapeutic process. *Review of General Psychology*, 1, 351-374.

Blatt, S.J. & Blass, R.B. (1990) Attachment and separateness: A dialectical model of the products and processes of psychological development. *Psychoanalytic Study of the Child*, 45, 107-127.

_____ (1996) Relatedness and self definition: A dialectical model of personality development. In G.G. Noam & K.W. Fischer (Eds) *Development and vulnerabilities in close relationships.* (pp. 309-338). Hillsdale: Erlbaum.

Blatt, S.J. & Shichman, S. (1983) Two primary configurations of psychopathology. *Psychoanalysis and Contemporary Thought*, 6, 187-254.

Boer, T. De (1978) *The development of Husserl's thought.* (Trans T. Platinga). The Hague: Martinus Nijhoff.

Bohart, A., O'Hara, M. & Leitner, L. (1998) Empirically violated treatments: Disenfranchisement of humanistic and other psychotherapies. *Psychotherapy Research*, 8, 141-157.

Bond, T. (1993) *Standards and ethics for counselling in action.* London: Sage.

Bordin, E. (1979) The generalizability of the psychoanalytic concept of the working alliance. *Psychotherapy: Theory, Research and Practice*, 16, 252-260.

Bornstein, R.F. & Pittman, T.S. (1992) *Perception without awareness.* New York: Guilford Press.

Boswell, D.L. & Dodd, D.K. (1994) Balance theory: A social psychological explanation of the value of unconditional positive regard. *Journal of Psychology,* 128, 101-109.

Bott, D. (1990) Epistemology: The place of systems theory in an integrated model of counselling. *Counselling,* 1, 23-25.

_____ (1992) "Can I help you help me change?" Systemic intervention in an integrated model of counselling. *Counselling,* 3, 31-33.

_____ (1994) A family systems framework for interventions with individuals. *Counselling Psychology Quarterly,* 7, 105-115.

Botterill, G. & Carruthers, P. (1999) *The philosophy of psychology.* Cambridge: Cambridge University Press.

Bowen, M.V. (1986) On the nature of intuition. Unpublished conference paper, Intuition and the Person-Centred Approach.

Bowlby, J. (1958) The nature of the child's tie to his mother. *International Journal of Psycho-Analysis,* 39, 350-373.

_____ (1977a) The making and breaking of affectional bonds, I: Aetiology and psychopathology in the light of attachment theory. *British Journal of Psychiatry,* 130, 201-210.

_____ (1977b) The making and breaking of affectional bonds, II: Some principles of psychotherapy. *British Journal of Psychiatry,* 130, 421-431.

_____ (1980) *Attachment and loss, Vol. 3: Loss, sadness and depression.* New York: Basic Books.

_____ (1988) *A secure base.* New York: Basic Books.

Boxley, R., Drew, C.R. & Rangel, D.M. (1986) Clinical trainee impairment in APA approved internship programs. *Clinical Psychologist,* 39, 49-52.

Bradley, J.R. & Olson, J.K. (1980) Training factors influencing felt psychotherapeutic competence of psychology trainees. *Professional Psychology,* 11, 930-934.

Brazier, D. (Ed)(1993) *Beyond Carl Rogers.* London: Constable.

Breda, H.L., van (1977) A note on reduction and authenticity according to Husserl. In F.A. Elliston & P. McCormick (Eds) *Husserl: Expositions and appraisals.* (pp. 124-125). Notre Dame: University of Notre Dame Press.

Brennan, K.A., Clark, C.L., & Shaver, P.R. (1998) Self-report measurement of adult attachment: An integrative overview. In J.A. Simpson & W.S. Rholes (Eds) *Attachment theory and close relationships.* (pp. 46-75). New York: Guilford.

Brenner, D. (1982) *The effective psychotherapist: Conclusions from practice and research.* New York: Pergammon.

Brisch, K.H. (1999) *Treating attachment disorders: From theory to therapy.* New York: Guilford.

Brough, J.B. (1977) The emergence of an absolute consciousness in Husserl's early writings on time-consciousness. In F.A. Elliston & P. McCormick (Eds) *Husserl: Expositions and appraisals.* (pp. 83-100). Notre Dame: University of Notre Dame Press.

_____ (1989) Husserl's phenomenology of time-consciousness. In J.N. Mohanty & W.R. McKenna (Eds) *Husserl's phenomenology: A textbook.* (pp. 249-290). Washington: Center for Advanced Research in Phenomenology & University Press of America.

_____ (1991) Translator's introduction. In E. Husserl *On the phenomenology of the consciousness of internal time (1893-1917).* (pp. xi-lvii). Dordrecht: Kluwer Academic.

Buber, M. & Rogers, C.R. (1960) Dialogue between Martin Buber and Carl Rogers. *Psychologia,* 3, 208-221.

Bugental, J.F.T. (1964) The person who is the psychotherapist. *Journal of Consulting Psychology*, 28, 272-277.

Burton, A. (1970) The adoration of the patient and its disillusionment. *American Journal of Psychoanalysis*, 24, 494-498.

_____ (1975) Therapist satisfaction. *American Journal of Psychoanalysis*, 35, 115-122.

Burwick, D.M. (1999) *How to implement the CMM*. Fort Knox: Business Process Solutions Publications.

Buss, A.R. (1979) The emerging field of the sociology of psychological knowledge. In A.R. Buss (Ed) *Psychology in a social context*. (pp. 1-24). New York: Irvington.

Cairns, D. (Ed) (1976) *Conversations with Husserl and Fink*. The Hague: Nijhoff.

Caputo, J.D. (1999) Heidegger. In S. Critchley & W.R. Schroeder (Eds) *A companion to continental philosophy*. (pp. 223-233). Oxford: Blackwell.

Carr, D. (1973) The fifth meditation and Husserl's Cartesianism. *Philosophy and Phenomenological Research*, 34, 14-35.

Casement, P. (1985) *On learning from the patient*. London: Tavistock.

_____ (1991) *Further learning from the patient*. London: Tavistock.

Cassell, E.J. (1976) *The Healer's art: A new approach to the doctor-patient relationship*. Harmondsworth: Penguin Books.

Chambless, D.L., Baker, M.J., Baumcom, D.H., Beutler, L.E., Calhoun, K.S., Crits-Christoph, P., Daiuto, A., DeRubeis, R., Detweller, J., Haaga, D.A.F., Johnson, S.B., McCurry, S., Mueser, K.T., Pope, K.S., Sanderson, W.C., Shoham, V., Stickle, T., Williams, W.C. & Woody, S.R. (1998) Update on empirically validated therapies II. *The Clinical Psychologist*, 51, 3-16.

Chertok, L. (1968) The discovery of the transference. *International Journal of Psycho-Analysis*, 49, 560-576.

Chessick, R.D. (1978) The sad soul of the psychiatrist. *Bulletin of the Menninger Clinic*, 42, 1-9.

Chiles, J. A. (1974) Patient reactions to the suicide of a therapist. *American Journal of Psychiatry*, 130, 463-468.

Chodoff, P. & Lyons, H. (1955) Hysteria, the hysterical personality and hysterical conversion. *American Journal of Psychiatry*, 114, 734-740.

Clairborn, W.L. (1982) The problem of professional incompetence. *Professional Psychology*, 13, 153-158.

Clements, W. & Perner, J. (1994) Implicit understanding of belief. *Cognitive Development*, 9, 377-395.

Cogan, T. (1977) A study of friendship among psychotherapists. Doctoral Dissertation, Illinois Institute of Technology. *Dissertation Abstracts International*, 78, 859.

Cohen, J. (1983) Psychotherapists preparing for death: Denial and action. *American Journal of Psychotherapy*, 37, 222-226.

_____ (1990) Things I have learned so far. *American Psychologist*, 45, 1304-1312.

_____ (1994) The earth is round (p<0.5). *American Psychologist*, 49, 997-1003.

Cohen, L.H., Sargent, M.M. & Sechrest, L.B. (1986) Use of psychotherapy research by professional psychologists. *American Psychologist*, 41, 198-206.

Cohn, H.W. (1984) An existential approach to psychotherapy. *British Journal of Medical Psychology*, 57, 311-318.

_____ (1985) Existential aspects of group therapy. *Group Analysis*, 18, 217-220.

_____ (1990) *Matrix and intersubjectivity: Phenomenological aspects of group analysis*. London, Group Analytic Society. Unpublished in English.

Cole, D.S. (1980) Therapeutic issues arising from the pregnancy of the therapist. *Psychotherapy: Theory, Research, and Practice*, 17, 210-213.

Coleman, E.Z. (1988) Room to grow. *British Journal of Guidance and Counselling*, 16, 21-32.

CORE System Group (1998) *CORE system user manual*. Leeds: CORE System Group.

Corsini, R. (Ed) (1981) *Innovative psychotherapies*. New York: Wiley.

Cray, C. & Cray, M. (1977) Stresses and rewards within the psychiatrist's family. *The American Journal of Psychoanalysis*, 37, 337-341.

Cushman, P. (1995) *Constructing the self, constructing America: A cultural history of psychotherapy.* Reading: Addison-Wesley.

Dar, R. Serlin, R.C. & Omer, H. (1994) Misuse of statistical tests in three decades of psychotherapy research. *Journal of Consulting and Clinical Psychology*, 62, 75-82.

Dent, J.K. (1978) Exploring the psycho-social therapies through the personalities of effective therapists. Baltimore: U.S. Department of Health, Education, and Welfare, National Institute of Mental Health.

Department of Health (1995) *A first class service: Quality in the new NHS.* London: Department of Health.

_____ (1999a) *Clinical governance practice guidelines.* London: Department of Health.

_____ (1999b) *National service framework for mental health: Modern standards and service models.* London: Department of Health.

_____ (1999c) *Modernising mental health services: NHS Modernisation fund for mental health services and mental health grant 1999/2002.* London: Department of Health.

_____ (1999d) *Services for patients with depression.* London: Department of Health.

_____ (2001a) *12 Key points on consent: The law in England.* London: Department of Health.

_____ (2001b) *Treatment choice in the psychological therapies and counselling: Evidence based clinical practice guideline.* London: Department of Health.

_____ (2004a) *Anxiety: Management of anxiety (panic disorder, with or without agoraphobia, and generalised anxiety disorder) in adults in primary, secondary and community care.* London: Department of Health.

_____ (2004b) *Depression: Management of depression in primary and secondary care.* London: Department of Health.

_____ (2005) *Post-traumatic stress disorder (PTSD): The management of PTSD in adults and children in primary and secondary care.* London: Department of Health.

Descartes, R. (1641/1986) *Meditations on first philosophy.* (Trans J. Cottingham). Cambridge: Cambridge University Press.

Deurzen-Smith, E. van (1994) Questioning the power of psychotherapy: Is Jeffrey Masson on to something? *Journal of the Society for Existential Analysis*, 5, 36-44.

Deutsch, C.J. (1984) Self-reported sources of stress among psychotherapists. *Professional Psychology: Research and Practice*, 15, 833-845.

_____ (1985) A survey of therapists' personal problems and treatment. *Professional Psychology: Research and Practice*, 16, 305-315.

Diamond, N. & Marrone, M. (2003) *Attachment and intersubjectivity.* London: Whurr.

Dilthey, W. (H.P. Rickman Ed) (1976) *W. Dilthey: Selected writings.* Cambridge: Cambridge University Press.

Dolliver, R.H. (1995a) Carl Roger's personality theory and psychotherapy as a reflection of his life experience and personality. *Journal of Humanistic Psychology,* 35, 111-128.

_____ (1995b) Carl Roger's emphasis on his own direct experience. *Journal of Humanistic Psychology*, 35, 129-139.

Dorpat, T.L. (1977) On neutrality. *International Journal of Psychoanalytic Psychotherapy,* 6, 39-64.

Douglas, M. (1978) *Cultural bias.* London: The Royal Anthropological Institute.

Dow, J. (1986) Universal aspects of symbolic healing. *American Anthropologist*, 88, 56—69.

Drüe, H. (1963) *Edmund Husserls system der phänomologischen psychologie*. Berlin: De Gruyter.

Eisenberg, L. (1977) Disease and illness distinctions between professional and popular ideas of sickness. *Culture, Medicine and Psychiatry*, 1, 9-23.

_____ (1988) The social construction of mental illness. *Psychological Medicine*, 18, 1-9.

Eisenbruch, M. (1984a) Cross-cultural aspects of bereavement I: A conceptual framework for comparative analysis. *Culture, Medicine and Psychiatry*, 8, 283-309.

_____ (1984b) Cross-cultural aspects of bereavement II: Ethnic and cultural variations in the development of bereavement practices. *Culture, Medicine and Psychiatry*, 8, 315-347.

Eisenhart, M.A. & Ruff, T.C. (1983) The meaning of doing a good job: Findings from a study of rural and urban mental health centres in the south. *Journal of Community Psychology*, 11, 48-57.

Ellenberger, H.F. (1970) *The discovery of the unconscious*. New York: Basic Books.

Ellingham, I. (1995) Quest for a paradigm: Person-centred counselling/psychotherapy versus psychodynamic counselling and psychotherapy. *Counselling*, 6, 288-290.

Elliott, R. (1998) Editor's introduction: A guide to the empirically supported treatments controversy. *Psychotherapy Research*, 8, 115-125.

Evans, F. (1977) The placebo control of pain: A paradigm for investigating non-specific effects in psychotherapy. In J. Brady, J. Mendels, W. Reiger, & M. Orne (Eds) *Psychiatry: Areas of promise and advancement*. (pp. 215-228). New York: Spectrum.

Farber, B.A. (1983a) The effects of psychotherapeutic practice upon psychotherapists. *Psychotherapy: Theory, Research and Practice*, 20, 174-182.

_____ (1983b) Psychotherapists' perceptions of stressful patient behaviour. *Professional Psychology: Research and Practice*, 14, 697-705.

_____ (1983c) Introduction: A critical perspective on burnout. In B.A. Farber (Ed) *Stress and burnout in the human service professions.* (pp. 1-20). New York: Pergammon.

_____ (1983d) Dysfunctional aspects of the psychotherapeutic role. In B.A. Farber (Ed) *Stress and burnout in the human service professions.* (pp. 97-118). New York: Pergammon.

_____ (1985a) Clinical psychologists' perceptions of psychotherapeutic work. *Clinical Psychologist*, 38, 10-13.

_____ (1985b) The genesis, development, and implications of psycho-logical-mindedness in psychotherapists. *Psychotherapy*, 22, 170-177.

Farber, B.A., Brink, D.C. & Raskin, P.M. (1996) *The psychotherapy of Carl Rogers.* New York: Guilford Press.

Farber, B.A. & Heifetz, L.J. (1981) The satisfactions and stresses of psychothera-peutic work: A factor analytic study. *Professional Psychology*, 12, 621-630.

_____ (1982) The process and dimensions of burnout in psychotherapists. *Professional Psychology*, 13, 293-301.

Federn, P. (1938/1977) *Ego psychology and the psychoses.* (Trans E. Weiss). London: Maresfield Reprints.

Fine, H.J. (1980) Despair and depletion in the therapist. *Psychotherapy: Theory, Research and Practice*, 17, 392-395.

Fink, E. (1933/1970) The phenomenological philosophy of Edmund Husserl and contemporary criticism. In R.O. Elveton (Ed and Trans) *The phenomenology of Husserl: Selected critical readings.* (pp. 73-147). Chicago: Quadrangle Books.

_____ (1934/1972) What does the phenomenology of Edmund Husserl want to accomplish? (The phenomenological idea of laying-a-ground). *Research in Phenomenology*, 2, 5-27.

_____ (1939/1981) The problem of the phenomenology of Edmund Husserl. In W. McKenna, R.E.M. Harlan, L.E. Winters & J.N. Mohanty (Eds) *Apriori and world.* (pp. 21-55). The Hague: Nijhoff.

Fluckiger, F. & Sullivan, J. (1965) Husserl's conception of a pure psychology. *Journal of the History of the Behavioral Sciences*, 1, 135-148.

Fonagy, P. (1999a) Points of contact and divergence between psychoanalytic and attachment theories: Is psychoanalytic theory truly different. *Psychoanalytic Inquiry*, 19, 448-480.

_____ (1999b) Psychoanalytic theory from the viewpoint of attachment theory and research. In J. Cassidy & P.R. Shaver (Eds) *Handbook of attachment: Theory, research, and clinical applications*. (pp. 595-624). New York: Guilford.

_____ (2003) The development of psychopathology from infancy to adulthood: The mysterious unfolding of disturbance in time. *Infant Mental Health Journal*, 24, 212-239.

Foucault, M. (1987) *History of sexuality, Vol 2*. Harmondsworth: Penguin.

Foulkes, S.H. (1948) *Introduction to group-analytic therapy: Studies in the social integration of individuals and groups*. London: Heinemann.

Fraiberg, S. (1969) Object constancy and mental representation. *The Psychoanalytic Study of the Child*, 24, 9-47.

Frankl, V.E. (1964) *Man's search for meaning*. (Trans I. Lasch). London: Hodder and Stoughton.

_____ (1967) *Psychotherapy and existentialism*. New York: Pocket Books.

_____ (1973) *The doctor and the soul*. (Trans R. Winston & C. Winston). New York: Vintage.

Freud, S. (1905d/1953) Three essays on the theory of sexuality. In J. Strachey (Ed & Trans) *The standard edition of the complete psychological works of Sigmund Freud, Vol. 7*. (pp. 123-243). London: Hogarth Press.

_____ (1905e/1953) Fragment of an analysis of a case of hysteria. In J. Strachey (Ed & Trans) *The standard edition of the complete works of Sigmund Freud, Vol 7*. (pp. 1-122). London: Hogarth Press.

_____ (1913c/1958) On beginning the treatment. In J. Strachey (Ed & Trans) *The standard edition of the complete psychological works of Sigmund Freud, Vol 12*. (pp. 121-144). London: Hogarth.

_____ (1913i/1958) The disposition to obsessional neurosis. In J. Strachey (Ed & Trans) *The standard edition of the complete psychological works of Sigmund Freud, Vol 12*. (pp. 311-326). London: Hogarth.

_____ (1917e/1963) Mourning and melancholia. In J. Strachey (Ed & Trans) *The standard edition of the complete psychological works of Sigmund Freud, Vol 14*. (pp. 237-260). London: Hogarth.

_____ (1923b/1961) The ego and the id. In J. Strachey (Ed & Trans) *The standard edition of the complete psychological works of Sigmund Freud, Vol 19*. (pp. 3-69). London: Hogarth.

_____ (1926d/1959) Inhibitions, symptoms and anxiety. In J. Strachey (Ed & Trans) *The standard edition of the complete psychological works of Sigmund Freud, Vol 20*. (pp. 87-175). London: Hogarth.

_____ (1940a/1964) An outline of psycho-analysis. In J. Strachey (Ed & Trans) *The standard edition of the complete psychological works of Sigmund Freud, Vol 23*. (pp. 144-207). London: Hogarth.

_____ (1984) *On metapsychology*. (Trans J. Strachey). Harmondsworth: Pelican.

_____ (Masson, J.M. Ed) (1986) *Complete letters to Wilhelm Fliess, 1887-1904*. (Trans J.M. Masson). Cambridge: Harvard University Press.

Freudenberger, H.J. (1974) Staff burnout. *Journal of Social Issues*, 30, 159-165.

Freundenberger, H.J. & Robbins, A. (1979) The hazards of being a psychoanalyst. *Psychoanalytic Review*, 66, 275-295.

Gabbard, G.O. (Ed) (1995) *Treatments of psychiatric disorders, 2 Vols (2nd ed)*. Washington: American Psychiatric Press.

_____ (2000) *Psychodynamic psychiatry in clinical practice (3rd ed)*. Washington: American Psychiatric Press.

Gadamer, H.-G. (1976) *Philosophical hermeneutics.* (Trans D.E. Linge). Berkeley: University of California Press.

Gaines, A.D. (1992) From DSM-I to III-R; voices of self, mastery and the other: A cultural constructivist reading of U.S. psychiatric classification. *Social Science and Medicine,* 35, 3-24.

Garcia, R. (1987) Sociology of science and sociogenesis of knowledge. In B. Inhelder, D. de Caprona & A. Cornu-Wells (Eds) *Piaget today.* (pp. 125-140). Hove: Lawrence Erlbaum.

Gardner, S. (1999) *Kant and the* Critique of pure reason. London: Routledge.

Garner, D.M. & Garfinkel, P.E. (1980) Socio-cultural factors in the development of anorexia nervosa. *Psychological Medicine,* 10, 647-656.

Geller, J.D. & Gould, E. (1996) A contemporary psychoanalytic perspective: Rogers' brief psychotherapy with Mary Jane Tilden. In B.A. Farber, D.C. Brink, & P.M. Raskin (Eds) *The psychotherapy of Carl Rogers.* (pp. 211-238). New York: Guilford Press.

Gendlin, E.T. (1978) *Focusing.* New York: Everest House.

Gergen, K.J. (1985) The social constructionist movement in modern psychology. *American Psychologist,* 40, 266-275.

Gigerenzer, G., Swijtink, Z., Port, T., Daston, L., Beatty, J. & Kruger, L. (1989) *The empire of chance: How probability changed science and everyday life.* Cambridge: Cambridge University Press.

Gitelson, M. (1952) The emotional positions of the analyst in the psycho-analytic situation. *International Journal of Psycho-Analysis,* 33, 1-10.

Glucksman, M.L. (1993) Insight, empathy, and internalization: Elements of clinical change. *Journal of the American Academy of Psychoanalysis,* 21, 163-181.

Glymour, C. (1980) Hypothetico-deductivism is hopeless. *Philosophy of Science,* 47, 322-325.

Goldberg, C. (1986) *On being a psychotherapist: The journey of the healer.* New York: Gardner Press.

Goldfried, M.R. & Newman, C.F. (1992) A history of psychotherapy integration. In J.C. Norcross & M.R. Goldfried (Eds) *Handbook of psychotherapy integration.* (pp. 46-93). New York: Basic Books.

Gorovitz, S., Hintikka, M., Provenence, D. & Williams, R.G. (1963) *Philosophical analysis.* New York: Random House.

Grieder, A. (1988) What did Heidegger mean by 'essence'? *Journal of the British Society for Phenomenology,* 19, 64-89.

Grinker, R.R., Werble, B., Drye, R.C. (1968) *The borderline syndrome: A behavioral study of ego-functions.* New York: Basic Books.

Grob, G.N. (1991) Origins of *DSM-I*: A study in appearance and reality. *American Journal of Psychiatry,* 148, 421-431.

Gurwitsch, A. (1974) *Phenomenology and the theory of science.* Evanston: Northwestern University Press.

Guy, J.D. (1987) *The private life of the psychotherapist.* London: Wiley.

Guy, J.D. & Liaboe, G.P. (1986) The impact of conducting psychotherapy on the psychotherapists' interpersonal functioning. *Professional Psychology: Research and Practice,* 17, 111-114.

Haar, M. (1993) *Heidegger and the essence of man.* (Trans W. McNeill). New York: SUNY.

Hall, E. T. (1977) *Beyond culture.* New York: Anchor Books.

Hardy, G.E., Aldridge, J., Davidson, C., Rowe, C. & Reilly, S. (2004) Assessing and formulating attachment issues and styles in psychotherapy. *British Journal of Psychotherapy,* 20, 493-512.

Harré, R. (1984) Social elements as mind. *British Journal of Medical Psychology,* 57, 127–135.

_____ (Ed) (1988) *The social construction of emotions.* Oxford: Basil Blackwell.

Harré, R. & Krausz, M. (1996) *Varieties of relativism.* Oxford: Blackwell.

Heard, D.H. & Lake, B. (1986) The attachment dynamic in adult life. *British Journal of Psychiatry*, 149, 430-438.

———————————— (1997) *The challenge of attachment for care giving.* London: Routledge.

Heidegger, M. (1927/1962) *Being and time.* (Trans J. Macquarrie & E. Robinson). Oxford: Blackwell.

———————————— (1927/1982) *The basic problems of phenomenology.* (Trans A. Hofstadter). Bloomington: Indiana University Press.

———————————— (1984/1984) *The metaphysical foundations of logic.* (Trans M. Heim). Bloomington: Indiana University Press.

———————————— (1979/1985) *History of the concept of time.* (Trans T. Kisiel). Bloomington: Indiana University Press.

———————————— (1989/1992) *The concept of time.* (Trans W. McNeill). Oxford: Blackwell.

———————————— (1947/1993) Letter on humanism. In D.F. Krell (Ed) *Basic writings: From* Being and Time *(1927) to* The Task of Thinking *(1964).* (pp. 217-265). London: Routledge.

———————————— (1927/1996) *Being and time.* (Trans J. Stambaugh). New York: SUNY.

———————————— (1968/1997) "Phenomenology," the *Encyclopaedia Britannica* article, draft B ("attempt at a second draft"). In T. Sheehan & R.E. Palmer (Eds & Trans) *Psychological and transcendental phenomenology and the confrontation with Heidegger (1927-1931).* (pp. 107-116). Dordrecht: Kluwer.

———————————— (M. Boss Ed)(1987/2001) *Zollikon seminars: Protocols-conversations-letters.* (Trans F. Mayr & R. Askay). Evanston: Northwestern University Press.

Helman, C. (1985) Psyche, soma, and society: The social construction of psychesomatic disorders. *Culture, Medicine and Psychiatry*, 6, 347-361.

_____ (1987) Heart disease and the cultural construction of time: The type A behaviour pattern as a Western culture-bound syndrome. *Social Science and Medicine*, 25, 969-979.

_____ (1990) *Culture, health and illness (2nd ed)*. Oxford: Butterworth-Heinemann.

Herrmann, F.-W., von (1996) Way and method: Hermeneutic phenomenology in thinking the history of being. In C. Macann (Ed) *Critical Heidegger*. (pp. 171-190). London: Routledge.

Hesse, E. & Main, M. (1999) Second-generation effects of unresolved trauma in nonmaltreating parents: Dissociated, frightened, and threatening parental behavior. *Psychoanalytic Inquiry*, 19, 481-540.

Hoffman. I.Z. (1983) The patient as interpreter of the analyst's experience. *Contemporary Psychoanalysis*, 19, 389-422.

Holdstock, L. (1993) Can we afford not to revision the person-centred concept of self? In D. Brazier (Ed) *Beyond Carl Rogers*. (pp. 229-252). London: Constable.

Holland, D. & Skinner, D. (1987) Prestige and intimacy: The cultural models behind Americans' talk about gender types. In D. Holland & N. Quinn (Eds) *Cultural models in language and thought*. (pp. 78-111). Cambridge: Cambridge University Press.

Holmes, D.S. (1997) *Abnormal psychology (3rd ed)*. New York: Longman.

Holmes, R.H. (1975) Explication of Husserl's theory of noema. *Research in Phenomenology*, 5, 143-153.

Holroyd, J.C. & Brodsky, A.M. (1980) Does touching patients lead to sexual intercourse? *Professional Psychology*, 11, 807-811.

Holt, R.R. (1959) Personality growth in psychiatry residents. *AMA Archives of Neurology and Psychiatry*, 81, 203-215.

Hughes, C.C. & Simons, R.C. (Eds) (1985) *The culture-bound psychiatric syndromes: Folk illnesses of psychiatric and anthropological interest*. Dordrecht: Reidel.

Hunsdahl, J. (1967) Concerning *Einfühlung* (Empathy): A concept analysis of its original and early development. *Journal of the History of the Behavioral Sciences, 3,* 180-191.

Husserl, E. (1950) *Pariser vortrage und Cartesianische meditationem.* The Hague: Nijhoff.

_____ (1956) *Erste philosophie (1923/1924), erster teil: Kritische ideenge-schichte.* Den Haag: Martinus Nijhoff.

_____ (1929/1969) *Formal and transcendental logic.* (Trans D. Cairns). The Hague: Martinus Nijhoff.

_____ (1921/1970a) *Logical Investigations, 2 Vols.* (Trans J. N. Findlay). London: RKP.

_____ (1956/1970b) *The crisis of European sciences and transcendental phe-nomenology.* (Trans D. Carr). Evanston: Northwestern University Press.

_____ (1973/1973a) *The idea of phenomenology.* (Trans W.P. Alston & G. Nakhnikian). The Hague: Martinus Nijhoff.

_____ (1973b) *Zur phänomenologie der intersubjektivität, texte aus dem Nachlass, erster teil: 1905-1920.* Dordrecht: Kluwer.

_____ (1973c) *Zur phänomenologie der intersubjektivität, texte aus dem Nachlass, zweiter teil: 1921-1928.* Dordrecht: Kluwer.

_____ (1973d) *Zur Phänomenologie der Intersubjektivität, texte aus dem Nachlass, dritter teil: 1929-1935.* Dordrecht: Kluwer.

_____ (1913/1975) A draft of a "preface" to the Logical Investigations. In *Introduction to the Logical Investigations.* (Trans P.J. Bossert & C. H. Peters). (pp. 11-61). The Hague: Martinus Nijhoff.

_____ (1968/1977a) *Phenomenological psychology: Lectures, summer semester, 1925.* (Trans J. Scanlon). The Hague: Nijhoff.

_____ (1950/1977b) *Cartesian meditations: An introduction to phenomenol-ogy.* (Trans D. Cairns). The Hague: Nijhoff.

_____ (1952/1980) *Phenomenology and the foundations of the sciences: Third book ideas pertaining to a pure phenomenology and to a phenomenological philosophy.* (Trans T.E. Klein and W.E. Pohl). The Hague: Nijhoff.

_____ (1911/1981a) Philosophy as rigorous science. In P. McCormick & F.A. Elliston (Eds & Trans). *Husserl: Shorter works.* (pp. 166-197). Notre Dame: Notre Dame University Press.

_____ (1941/1981b) Phenomenology and anthropology. In P. McCormick & F.A. Elliston (Eds) *Husserl: Shorter works.* (pp. 315-323). Notre Dame: University of Notre Dame Press.

_____ (1913/1982) *Ideas pertaining to a pure phenomenology and to a phenomenological philosophy: First book.* (Trans F. Kersten). Dordrecht: Kluwer.

_____ (1952/1989) *Ideas pertaining to a pure phenomenology and to a phenomenological philosophy: Second book.* (Trans R. Rojcewicz & A. Schuwer). Dordrecht: Kluwer.

_____ (1966/1991) *On the phenomenology of the consciousness of internal time (1893-1917).* (Trans J. Brough). Dordrecht: Kluwer.

_____ (1973/1997a) *Thing and space: Lectures of 1907.* (Trans R. Rojcewicz). Dordrecht: Kluwer.

_____ (1968/1997b) "Phenomenology," The *Encyclopaedia Brittanica* article, Draft A. In T. Sheehan & R.E. Palmer (Eds and Trans) *Psychological and transcendental phenomenology and the confrontation with Heidegger (1927-1931).* (pp. 83-105). Dordrecht: Kluwer.

_____ (1968/1997c) "Phenomenology," *Encyclopaedia Brittanica* article, Draft D. In T. Sheehan & R.E. Palmer (Eds and Trans) *Psychological and transcendental phenomenology and the confrontation with Heidegger (1927-1931).* (pp. 159-179). Dordrecht: Kluwer.

_____ (1968/1997d) The Amsterdam lectures <on> phenomenological psychology. In T. Sheehan & R.E. Palmer (Eds and Trans) *Psychological and transcendental phenomenology and the confrontation with Heidegger (1927-1931).* (pp. 213-253). Dordrecht: Kluwer.

_____ (1941/1997e) Phenomenology and anthropology. In T. Sheehan & R.E. Palmer (Eds & Trans) *Psychological and transcendental phenomenology and the confrontation with Heidegger (1927-1931).* (pp. 485-500). Dordrecht: Kluwer Academic.

_____ (1973/1999) *The idea of phenomenology.* (Trans L. Hardy). The Hague: Nijhoff.

Hutt, C.H., Scott, J. & King, M. (1983) A phenomenological study of supervisees' positive and negative experiences in supervision. *Psychotherapy: Theory, Research, and Practice,* 20, 118-123.

Ingarden, R. (1964) *Time and modes of being.* (Trans H.R. Michejda). Springfield: C.C. Thomas.

Jacobs, M. (1988) *Psychodynamic counselling in action.* London: Sage.

Jacobson, E. (Ed) (1971) *Depression: Comparative studies of normal, neurotic, and psychotic conditions.* New York: International Universities Press.

Jaspers. K. (1963) *General psychopathology.* (Trans J. Hoenig & M.W. Hamilton). Manchester: Manchester University Press.

_____ (1968) The phenomenological approach in psychopathology. *British Journal of Psychiatry,* 114, 1313-1323.

Jennings, J. (1986) Husserl revisited: The forgotten distinction between psychology and phenomenology. *American Psychologist,* 41, 1231-1240.

Joint Home Office/Department of Health Working Group (1999) *Managing dangerous people with severe personality disorder: Proposals for policy development.* London: Department of Health.

Kahn, E. (1985) Heinz Kohut and Carl Rogers: A timely comparison. *American Psychologist,* 40, 893-904.

_____ (1987) On the therapeutic value of both the "real" and the "transference" relationship. *Person-Centred Review,* 2, 471-475.

_____ (1996) The intersubjective perspective and the client-centred approach: Are they one at their core? *Psychotherapy,* 33, 30-42.

Kant, I. (1993) *Critique of pure reason*. (Trans J.M.D. Meiklejohn & V. Politis). London: Dent.

Karasu, T.B. (1986) The specificity versus nonspecificity dilemma: Toward identifying therapeutic change agents. *American Journal of Psychiatry*, 143, 687-695.

Keesing, R. M. (1981) *Cultural anthropology: A contemporary perspective*. New York: Holt, Rinehart & Winston.

Kennedy, M. & Jones, E. (1995) Violence from patients in the community: Will UK courts impose a duty of care on mental health professionals? *Criminal Behaviour and Mental Health*, 3, 209-217.

Kern, I. (1977) The three ways to the transcendental phenomenological reduction in the philosophy of Edmund Husserl. In F.A. Elliston & P. McCormick (Eds) *Husserl: Expositions and appraisals*. (pp. 126-149). Notre Dame: Notre Dame University Press.

_____ (1986) Trinity: Theological reflections of a phenomenologist. In S.W. Laycock & J.G. Hart (Eds) *Essays in phenomenological theology*. (pp. 23-37). Albany: SUNY Press.

_____ (1993a) Our experience of the other. In R. Bernet, I. Kern & E. Marbach *An introduction to Husserlian phenomenology*. (pp. 154-165). Evanston: Northwestern University Press.

_____ (1993b) Time-consciousness. In R. Bernet, I. Kern, & E. Marbach *An introduction to Husserlian phenomenology*. (pp. 101-114). Evanston: Northwestern University Press.

Kern, I. & Marbach, E. (2001) Understanding the representational mind: A prerequisite for intersubjectivity proper. *Journal of Consciousness Studies*, 8, 69-82.

Kernberg, O.F. (1970) Factors in the psychoanalytic treatment of narcissistic personalities. *Journal of the American Psychoanalytic Association*, 18, 51-85.

_____ (1977) Boundaries and structure in love relations. *Journal of the American Psychoanalytic Association*, 25, 81-114.

Kiesler, D.J. (1966) Some myths of psychotherapy research and the search for a paradigm. *Psychological Bulletin*, 65, 110-136.

Kirschenbaum, H. (1991) Denigrating Carl Rogers: William Coulson's last crusade. *Journal of Counseling Development,* 69, 411-413.

Kisiel, T.J. (1993) *The genesis of Heidegger's Being and Time.* Berkeley: University of California Press.

Kitzinger, C. (1994) Rough treatment for therapists. *The Times Higher Educational Supplement,* 1105, 7 January, 15.

Klein, M. (1940/1975) Mourning and its relation to manic-depressive states. In *Love, guilt and reparation and other works, 1921-1945.* (pp. 344-369). New York: Free Press.

Kleinman, A. & Good, B. (1986) *Culture and depression: Studies in the anthropology and cross-cultural psychiatry of affect and disorder.* Berkeley: University of California Press.

Kocklemans, J.J. (1977) Destructive retrieve and hermeneutic phenomenology in 'Being and Time'. *Research in Phenomenology,* 7, 106-137.

Kohut, H. (A. Goldberg Ed)(1971) *How does analysis cure?* Chicago: University of Chicago Press.

_____ (1982) Introspection, empathy, and the semi-circle of mental health. *International Journal of Psycho-Analysis,* 63, 395-407.

Kottler, J.A. (1986) *On being a therapist.* San Francisco: Jossey Bass.

Kreitman, N. & Schreiber, M. (1979) Parasuicide in young Edinburgh women. *Psychological Medicine,* 9, 469-419.

Kuhn, T.S. (1970) *The structure of scientific revolutions (2nd ed).* Chicago: Chicago University Press.

Küng, G. (1975) The phenomenological reduction as "epoche" and as explication. *Monist,* 59, 63-80.

Kutz, S.L. (1986) Defining "impaired" psychologist. *American Psychologist,* 41, 220.

Laing, R.D. (1959) *The divided self: An existential study in sanity and madness.* London: Tavistock.

Laliotsis, D.A. & Grayson, J.H. (1985) Psychologist heal thyself. *American Psychologist,* 40, 84-96.

Langs, R. (1985) *Madness and cure.* Emerson: Newconcept.

_____ (1979) *The therapeutic environment.* New York: Jason Aronson.

_____ (1988) *A primer of psychotherapy.* New York: Gardner Press.

_____ (1989) *The technique of psychoanalytic therapy, Vol. 1.* New York: Jason Aronson.

Laplanche, J. & Pontalis, J.-B. (1985) *The language of psycho-analysis.* (Trans D. Nicholson-Smith). London: Hogarth Press.

Larabee, M.J. (1986) The noema in Husserl's phenomenology. *Husserl Studies,* 3, 209-230.

Lazarus, A.A. (1976) *Multimodal behavior therapy.* New York: Springer.

_____ (1986) Multimodal therapy. In J.C. Norcross (Ed.) *Handbook of eclectic psychotherapy.* (pp. 65-93). New York: Guilford Press.

Leach, E. (1982) *Social anthropology.* Glasgow: Fontana.

Leibniz, G.W. (1714/1973) Principles of nature and of grace, founded on reason. In G.H.R. Parkinson (Ed) *Leibniz: Philosophical writings.* (Trans M. Morris & G.H.R. Parkinson). (pp. 195-204). London: Dent.

Leighton, S.L. & Roye, A.K. (1984) Prevention and self-care for professional burnout. *Family and Community Health,* 12, 44-55.

Lex, B. (1974) Voodoo death: New thoughts for an old explanation. *American Anthropologist,* 76, 818-823.

Linehan, M.M. (1993) *Cognitive-behavioral treatment of borderline personality disorder.* New York: Guilford Press.

Lipps, T. (1893) *Grundzüge der logik.* Hamburg: Voss.

_____ (1903a) *Leitfaden der psychologie.* Leipzig: Engelmann.

_____ (1903b) *Ästhetik: Psychologie des schönen und der kunst, Vol 1.* Leipzig: Voss.

_____ (1907) *Das wissen von fremden ichen. Psychologische Untersuchungen,* 1, 694-722.

Littlewood, R. & Lipsedge, M. (1987) The butterfly and the serpent. *Culture, Medicine and Psychiatry,* 11, 289-235.

Locke, J. (1689/1961) *An essay concerning human understanding, Vol. 1.* London: Dent.

Loftus, G.R. (1991) On the tyranny of hypothesis testing in the social sciences. *Contemporary Psychology,* 36, 102-105.

_____ (1996) Psychology will be a much better science when we change the way we analyze data. *Current Directions in Psychological Science,* 5, 161-171.

Lohser, B. & Newton, P.M. (1996) *Unorthodox Freud: The view from the couch.* New York: Guilford.

Lomas, P. (1987) *The limits of interpretation: What's wrong with psychoanalysis?* Harmondsworth: Penguin.

Luborsky, L. (1994) Therapeutic alliances as predictors of psychotherapy outcomes: Factors explaining the predictive success. In A.O. Horvath & L.S. Greenberg (Eds) *The working alliance.* (pp. 38-50). New York: Wiley.

Luborsky, L., Singer, B. & Luborsky, L. (1975) Comparative studies of psychotherapies: Is it true that "everybody has won and all must have prizes"? *Archives of General Psychiatry,* 32, 995-1008.

Lutz, C. (1987) Goals, events, and understanding in Ifaluk emotion theory. In D. Holland & N. Quinn (Eds) *Cultural models in language and thought.* (pp. 290-312). Cambridge: Cambridge University Press.

Lykken, D.T. (1991) What's wrong with psychology anyway? In D. Cicchetti & W.M. Grove (Eds) *Thinking clearly about psychology, Vol. 1.* (pp. 3-39). Minneapolis: University of Minnesota.

Maddox, R.I. (1983) Hermeneutic circle—vicious or victorious. *Philosophy Today*, 27, 66-76.

Main, M. (1985) An adult attachment classification system: Its relation to infant-parent attachment. Biennial Meeting of the Society for Research in Child Development, Toronto, April.

Maltz, M.D. (1994) Deviating from the mean: The declining significance of significance. *Journal of Research in Crime and Delinquency*, 31, 434-436.

Marbach, E. (1992) What does noematic intentionality tell us about the ontological status of the noema? In J.J. Drummond & L. Embree (Eds) *The phenomenology of the noema*. (pp. 137-155). Dordrecht: Kluwer Academic.

_____ (1993) *Mental representation and consciousness: Towards a phenomenological theory of representation and reference*. Norwell. Kluwer Academic.

_____ (1999) Building materials for the explanatory bridge. *Journal of Consciousness Studies*, 6(2-3), 252-257.

_____ (2000) The place for an ego in current research. In D. Zahavi (Ed) *Exploring the self: Philosophical and psychopathological perspectives on self-experience*. (pp. 75-94). Amsterdam: John Benjamins.

_____ (2005) On bringing consciousness into the house of science—with the help of Husserlian phenomenology. *Angelaki: Journal of the Theoretical Humanities*, 10, 145-162.

Margolis, J. (1991) *The truth about relativism*. Oxford: Blackwell.

Marmor, J. (1953) The feeling of superiority: An occupational hazard in the practice of psychotherapy. *American Journal of Psychiatry*, 110, 370-376.

Marris, P. (1996) *The politics of uncertainty: Attachment in private and public life*. London: Routledge.

Mars, G. (1994) *Cheats at work: An anthropology of workplace crime*. London: Dartmouth.

Marston, A.R. (1984) What makes therapists run? A model for analysis of motivational styles. *Psychotherapy*, 21, 456-459.

Marx, K. (1972) The critique of political economy. In R.T. De George & F.M. De George (Eds & Trans) *The structuralists: From Marx to Levi-Strauss.* (pp. 2-6). New York: Anchor Books.

Maslach, C. (1982) *Burnout—The cost of caring.* New York: Prentice Hall.

Masson, J.M. (1984) *The assault on truth: Freud's suppression of the seduction theory.* Harmondsworth: Penguin.

—————————— (1988) *Against therapy.* London: Fontana/Collins.

—————————— (1993a) *My father's guru.* London: HarperCollins.

—————————— (1993b) Issues of power in the psychotherapeutic relationship. Sixth Conference of the Society for Existential Analysis, London November.

—————————— (1994) The question of power in psychotherapy. *Journal of the Society for Existential Analysis*, 5, 24-35.

McCarley, T. (1975) The psychotherapists' search for self-renewal. *American Journal of Psychiatry*, 132, 221-224.

McCleary, R.A. & Lazarus, R.S. (1949) Autonomic discrimination without awareness. *Journal of Personality*, 18, 171-179.

McCluskey, U. (2005) *To be met as a person: The dynamics of attachment in professional encounters.* London: Karnac.

McEvedy, C.P. & Beard, A.W. (1970) The Royal Free epidemic of 1955: A reconsideration. *British Medical Journal*, 3 January, pp. 7-11.

Mearns, D. (1992) On the dangers of under- and over-involvement. In W. Dryden (Ed) *Hard-earned lessons from counselling in action.* (pp. 77-79). London: Sage.

————————— (1994) *Developing person-centred counselling.* London: Sage.

————————— (1996) Working at relational depth with clients in person-centred therapy. *Counselling*, 7, 306-311.

————————— (1997) *Person-centred counsellor training.* London: Sage.

Mearns, D. & Thorne, B. (1988) *Person-centred counselling in action*. London: Sage.

Meehl, P.E. (1978) Theoretical risks and tabular asterisks: Sir Karl, Sir Ronald and the slow progress of soft psychology. *Journal of Consulting and Clinical Psychology*, 46, 1-42.

_____ (1990) Appraising and amending theories: The strategy of Lakatosian defense and two principles that warrant it. *Psychological Inquiry*, 1, 108-141.

Merklin, L. & Little, R.B. (1967) Beginning psychiatry training syndrome. *American Journal of Psychiatry*, 124, 193-197.

Merleau-Ponty, M. (1962) *Phenomenology of perception*. (Trans C. Smith). London: Routledge.

_____ (1963) The structure of behavior. (Trans A.L. Fisher) Pittsburgh: Duquesne University Press.

_____ (1964a) The battle over existentialism. In *Sense and non-sense*. (Trans H. Dreyfus). (pp. 71-82). Evanston: Northwestern University Press.

_____ (1964b) The philosopher and sociology. In *Signs*. (Trans R.C. McCleary). (pp. 98-113). Evanston: Northwestern University Press.

_____ (1964c) The child's relations with others. In J.M. Edie (Ed) *The primacy of perception: And other essays on phenomenological psychology, the philosophy of art, history and politics*. (W. Cobb Trans). (pp. 96-155). Evanston: Northwestern University Press.

Merry, T. (1990) Client-centred therapy: Some trends and some troubles. *Counselling*, 1, 17–18.

Millman, M. (1974) *Such a pretty face: Being fat in America*. New York: Norton.

Minkowsky, E. (1970) *Lived time*. (Trans N. Mekel). Evanston: Northwestern University Press.

Mishara, A.L. (1994) A phenomenological critique of commonsensical assumptions in *DSM III R*: The avoidance of the patient's subjectivity. In J.Z. Sadler,

O.P. Wiggins, M.A. Schwartz (Eds) *Philosophical perspectives on psychiatric diagnostic classification.* (pp. 129-147). Baltimore: John Hopkins.

Moerman, D.E. (1972) Anthropology of symbolic healing. *Current Anthropology*, 20, 59—80.

Moran, D. (2000) *Introduction to phenomenology.* London: Routledge.

Morrison, D.E. & Henkel, R.E. (Eds) (1970) *The significance test controversy.* Chicago: Aldine.

Morrow-Bradley, C. & Elliott, R. (1986) Utilization of psychotherapy research. *American Psychologist*, 41, 188-197.

Nathan, P.E. & Gorman, J.M. (1998) *A guide to treatments that work.* New York: Oxford University Press.

National Institute for Clinical Excellence (2004a) *Anxiety: Management of anxiety (panic disorder, with or without agoraphobia, and generalised anxiety disorder) in adults in primary, secondary and community care.* London: National Institute for Clinical Excellence.

_____ (2004b) *Depression: Management of depression in primary and secondary care.* London: National Institute for Clinical Excellence.

_____ (2005) *Post-traumatic stress disorder: The management of PTSD in adults and children in primary and secondary care.* London: National Institute for Clinical Excellence.

Neimeyer, R.A. & Raskin, J.D. (Eds) (2000) *Constructions of disorder: Meaning-making frameworks for psychotherapy.* Washington: American Psychological Association.

Nelson-Jones, R. (1982) The counsellor as decision-maker: Role, treatment and responding decisions. *British Journal of Guidance and Counselling*, 10, 113-124.

_____ (1985) Eclecticism, integration and comprehensiveness in counselling theory and practice. *British Journal of Guidance and Counselling*, 13, 129-138.

_____ (1988) Choice therapy. *Counselling Psychology Quarterly*, 1, 43-55.

Norcross, J.C. (Ed) (1986) *Handbook of eclectic psychotherapy*. New York: Brunner/Mazel.

Norcross, J.C. & Goldfried, M.R. (1992) *Handbook of psychotherapy integration*. New York: Basic Books.

Norcross, J.C. & Newman, C.F. (1992) Psychotherapy integration: Setting the context. In J.C. Norcross, & M.R. Goldfried *Handbook of psychotherapy integration*. (pp. 3-45). New York: Basic Books.

Norcross, J.C. & Prochaska, J.O. (1986a) Psychotherapist heal thyself—I. The psychological distress and self change of psychologists, counselors, and laypersons. *Psychotherapy*, 23, 102-114.

_____ (1986b) Psychotherapist heal thyself—II. The self-initiated and therapy-facilitated change of psychological distress. *Psychotherapy*, 23, 155-168.

Omer, H. & London, P. (1988) Metamorphosis in psychotherapy: End of the systems era. *Psychotherapy*, 25, 171-180.

Onians, R.B. (1951) *The origins of European thought about the body, mind, the soul, the world, time and fate*. Cambridge: Cambridge University Press.

Ott, D.B. (1986) Factors related to job satisfaction among psychotherapists. Unpublished doctoral research paper, Rosemead School of Psychology, La Mirada, CA.

Owen, I.R. (1989) The application of some ideas from anthropology to counseling, therapy and cross-cultural counseling. In E.L. Herr & Mc Fadden, J. (Eds) (1991) *Challenges of Cultural and Racial Diversity to Counseling*. (pp. 37-40). Alexandria, VA: American Association for Counseling Development.

_____ (1991) *Cultural theory, the politics of desire, and the social construction of psychotherapy*. London, Antioch University, unpublished Masters thesis.

_____ (1992a) Applying social constructionism to psychotherapy. *Counselling Psychology Quarterly*, 5, 385-402.

_____ (1992b) What you say is what you do. *Changes,* 10, 35-40.

_____ (1993) On "*The private life of the psychotherapist*" and the psychology of caring. *Counselling Psychology Quarterly,* 6, 251-264.

_____ (1994) Introducing an existential-phenomenological approach: Basic phenomenological theory and research—Part I. *Counselling Psychology Quarterly,* 7, 261-273.

_____ (1996) Are we before or after integration? Discussing guidelines for integrative practice via clinical audit. *Counselling Psychology Review,* 11, 12-18.

_____ (1997) On the status of psychological knowledge. *Changes,* 15, 100-106.

_____ (1998) Reference, temporality and the defences. *Journal of the Society for Existential Analysis,* 9, 84-97.

_____ (1999) The future of psychotherapy in the UK: Discussing clinical governance. *British Journal of Psychotherapy,* 16, 197-207.

_____ (2000a) Using the experience of gender to explain the difference between Husserlian and Heideggerian phenomenology. *Phenomenological Inquiry,* 23, 86-106.

_____ (2000b) Husserl's theory of meaning: Meaning arrives with the other. *Journal of the Society for Existential Analysis,* 11, 11-31.

_____ (2003) What the analysis of empathy in the Fifth Cartesian Meditation reveals for psychotherapy. Unpublished doctoral thesis. London: Regents College, School of Psychotherapy and Counselling.

_____ (2006) *Psychotherapy and phenomenology: On Freud, Husserl and Heidegger.* Lincoln: iUniverse.

Owen, I.R. & Morris, N. (1999) The Husserlian phenomenology of consciousness and cognitive science: We can see the path but nobody is on it. *Journal of Consciousness Studies,* 6 (2-3), 269-272.

Palmer-Barnes, F. (1998) *Complaints and grievances in psychotherapy: A handbook of ethical practice.* London: Routledge.

Parker, I., Georgaca, E., Harper, D., McLaughlin, T. & Smith, M. (1995) *Deconstructing psychopathology*. London: Sage.

Parloff, M.B., London, P. & Wolfe, B. (1986) Individual psychotherapy and behavior change. *Annual Review of Psychology*, 37, 371-349.

Parry, G. & Richardson, A. (1996) *NHS Psychotherapy services in England: Review of strategic policy*. London: Department of Health.

Paul, G.L. (1967) Strategy outcome research in psychotherapy. *Journal of Consulting Psychology*, 31, 109-119.

Perner, J. (1991) *Understanding the representational mind*. Massachusetts: MIT Press.

Perner, J., Ruffman, T. & Leekam, S. (1994) Theory of mind is contagious: You catch it from your sibs. *Child Development*, 65, 1228-1238.

Peskin, J. (1992) Ruse and representations: On children's ability to conceal information. *Developmental Psychology*, 28, 84-89.

Phillips, J. (1996) Key concepts: Hermeneutics. *Philosophy, Psychiatry, and Psychology*, 3, 61-69.

Pilgrim, D. & Rogers, A. (1999) *A sociology of mental health and illness (2nd ed)*. Buckingham: Open University Press.

Plomin, R., DeFries, J.C., McClearn, G.E. & Rutter, M. (1997) *Behavioral genetics (3rd ed)*. New York: Freeman.

Plomin, R., DeFries, J.C., McClearn, G.E. & McGuffin, P. (2000) *Behavioral genetics (4th ed)*. New York: Freeman.

Prince, R.H. (1976) Psychotherapy as the manipulation of endogenous healing mechanisms: A transcultural survey. *Transcultural Psychiatric Research Review*, 13, 115 -133.

_____ (1983) Is anorexia nervosa a culture-bound syndrome? *Transcultural Psychiatric Research Review*, 20, 299-300.

Prochaska, J.O. & Diclemente, C.C. (1992) The transtheoretical approach. In J.C. Norcross & M.R. Goldfried (Eds) *Handbook of psychotherapy integration.* (pp. 300-334). New York: Basic Books.

Pylyshyn, Z.W. (1978) When is attribution of beliefs justified? *Behavioral and Brain Sciences,* 1, 592-593.

Quinn, R.H. (1933) Confronting Carl Rogers: A developmental-interactional approach to person-centered therapy. *Journal of Humanistic Psychology,* 33, 6-23.

Rachman, S. (1981) The primacy of affect: Some theoretical implications. *Behaviour Research and Therapy,* 19, 279-290.

Reik, T. (1948) *Listening with the third ear: The inner experience of a psychoanalyst.* New York: Forrar & Strauss.

Renik, O. (2004) Intersubjectivity in psychoanalysis. *International Journal of Psychoanalysis,* 85, 1053-1056.

Rennie, D.L. (1998) *Person-centred counselling: An experiential approach.* London: Sage.

Rice, L.N. & Sapeira, E.P. (1984) Task analysis of the resolution of problematic reactions. In L.N. Rice & L.S. Greenberg (Eds) *Patterns of change.* (pp. 29-66). New York: Guilford Press.

Richards, G. (1996) *Putting psychology in its place: An introduction from a critical historical perspective.* London: Routledge.

Rickman, H.P. (1997) Dilthey's hermeneutics. *Journal of the Society for Existential Analysis,* 8, 46-55.

_____ (1998) Deconstruction: The unacceptable face of hermeneutics. *Journal of the British Society for Phenomenology,* 29, 299-313.

_____ (2004) *The riddle of the sphinx: Interpreting the human world.* Madison: Farleigh Dickinson University Press.

Ricoeur, P. (1967a) *Husserl: An analysis of his phenomenology.* Evanston: Northwestern University Press.

_____ (1967b) Existential phenomenology. In *Husserl: An analysis of his phenomenology*. (Trans E.G. Ballard & L.E. Embree). (pp. 202-212). Evanston: Northwestern University Press.

_____ (1970) *Freud and philosophy: An essay on interpretation*. (Trans D. Savage). New Haven: Yale.

_____ (1978) *The rule of metaphor: Multidisciplinary studies in the creation of meaning*. (Trans R. Czerny, K. McLaughlin & J. Costello). London: RKP.

Rippere, V. & Williams, R. (1985) *Wounded healers: Mental health workers' experiences of depression*. New York: Wiley.

Rittenbaugh, C. (1982) Obesity as a culture-bound syndrome. *Culture, Medicine and Psychiatry*, 6, 347-361.

Rogers, C.R. (1942) *Counseling and psychotherapy*. Boston: Houghton Mifflin.

_____ (1951) *Client-centred therapy*. Boston: Houghton.

_____ (1957) The necessary and sufficient conditions of therapeutic personality change. *Journal of Consulting Psychology*, 21, 95-103.

_____ (1959) A theory of therapy, personality, and interpersonal relationships, as developed in the client-centred framework. In S. Koch (Ed.) *Psychology: A study of a science, Vol. 3*. (pp. 184-256). New York: McGraw Hill.

_____ (1961) *On becoming a person*. Boston: Houghton.

_____ (1965) *Client-centred therapy: Its current practice, implications and theory*. London: Constable.

_____ (1975) Empathic: An unappreciated way of being. *The Counseling Psychologist*, 5, 2-10.

_____ (1977) *Carl Rogers on personal power*. London: Constable.

_____ (1986a) Client-centred therapy. In I.L. Kutash & A. Wolf (Eds.) *Psychotherapists' casebook: Theory and technique in the practice of modern therapies*. (pp. 197-208). San Francisco: Jossey Bass.

_____ (1986b) Reflection on feelings. *Person-Centred Review*, 1, 375-377.

_____ (H. Kirschenbaum & V.L. Henderson Eds)(1990) Do we need "a" reality? In *The Carl Rogers Reader*. (pp. 420-429). London: Constable.

Rogers, C.R. & Sanford, R.C. (1985) Client-centred psychotherapy. In H.J. Kaplan & I. Sadock (Eds) *Comprehensive textbook of psychiatry, Vol. 2*. (pp. 1374-1388). Baltimore: William & Wilkins.

Rose, N. (1989) *Governing the soul*. London: Routledge.

_____ (1998) *Inventing ourselves: Psychology, power and personhood*. Cambridge: CUP.

Ross, L.D. (1977) The intuitive psychologist and his shortcomings: Distortions in the attribution process. In L. Berkowitz (Ed) *Advances in experimental social psychology, Vol. 10*. (pp. 173-220). New York: Academic Press.

Roth, A. & Fonagy P. (1996) *What works for whom? A critical review of psychotherapy Research*. New York: Guilford Press.

Rothenberg, A. (1987) Empathy as a creative process. *International Review of Psycho-Analysis*, 14, 445-463.

Roudinesco, E. (1990) *Jacques Lacan & Co.: A history of psychoanalysis in France, 1925-1985*. (Trans J. Mehlman). London: Free Association Books.

Rowan, J. (1988) The psychology of furniture. *Counselling*, 64, 21-24.

Roy, M.-A., Lanctot, G., Merette, C., Cliche, D., Fournier, J.-P., Boutin, P., Rodrigue, C., Charron, L., Turgeon, M., Hamel, M., Montgrain, N., Nicole, L., Pires, A., Wallot, H., Ponton, A.-M., Garneau, Y., Dion, C., Lavallee, J.-C., Potvin, A., Szatmari, P., Maziade, M. (1997) Clinical and methodological factors related to reliability of the best-estimate diagnostic procedure. *American Journal of Psychiatry*, 154, 1726-1733.

Rutter, M. (1987) Temperament, personality and personality disorder. *British Journal of Psychiatry*, 150, 443-458.

Salmon, C.V. (1929) The starting-point of Husserl's philosophy. *Proceedings of the Aristotelian Society*, 30, 55-78.

Sandler, J. (1976) Countertransference and role-responsiveness. *International Review of Psycho-Analysis,* 3, 43-47.

Sartre, J.-P. (1948) *Existentialism and humanism.* (Trans P. Mairet). London: Methuen.

_____ (1958) *Being and nothingness: An essay on phenomenological ontology.* (Trans H.E. Barnes). London: Methuen.

_____ (1960) *The transcendence of the ego: An existentialist theory of consciousness.* (Trans F. Williams & R. Kirkpatrick). New York: Hill and Wang.

_____ (1970) Intentionality: A fundamental idea of Husserl's phenomenology. *Journal of the British Society for Phenomenology,* 1, 4-5.

Scanlon, J.D. (1972) The epoche and phenomenological anthropology. *Research in Phenomenology,* 2, 95-109.

Scheler, M. (1954) *The nature of sympathy.* (Trans P. Heath). London: RKP.

Schimek, J.G. (1987) Fact and fantasy in the seduction theory: A historical review. *Journal of the American Psychoanalytic Association,* 35, 937-965.

Schlicht, W.J. (1968) The anxieties of the psychotherapist. *Mental Hygiene,* 52, 439-444.

Schwartz, L. (1986) Anorexia nervosa as a culture-bound syndrome. *Social Science and Medicine,* 20, 725-730.

Schutz, A. (1967) *The phenomenology of the social world.* (Trans G. Walsh & F. Lehnert). Evanston: Northwestern University Press.

Scott, C.D. & Hawk, J. (1986) *Heal thyself: The health of health care professionals.* New York: Brunner/Mazel.

Seebohm, T. (1992) The preconscious, the unconscious, and the subconscious: A phenomenological explication. *Man and World,* 25, 505-520.

Semin, G.R. & Gergen, K.J. (Eds) (1990) *Everyday understanding: Social and scientific implications.* London: Sage.

Shapiro, A.K. (1971) Placebo effects in medicine, psychotherapy and psychoanalysis. In A. Bergin & S. Garfield (Eds) *Handbook of psychotherapy and behavior change: An empirical analysis.* (pp. 437-473). New York: Wiley.

Shaughnessy, P. (1995) Empathy and the working alliance: The mistranslation of Freud's *Einfühlung. Psychoanalytic Psychology,* 12, 221-231.

Simpson, J.A. & Rholes, W.S. (1998) Attachment in adulthood. In J.A. Simpson & W.S. Rholes (Eds) *Attachment theory and close relationships.* (pp. 3-21). New York: Guilford Press.

Smith, D.L. (1987) Formulating and evaluating hypotheses in psychoanalytic psychotherapy. *British Journal of Medical Psychology,* 60, 313-317.

Smith, Q. (1977) A phenomenological examination of Husserl's theory of hyletic data. *Philosophy Today,* 21, 356-367.

Sokolowski, R. (2000) *Introduction to phenomenology.* Cambridge: Cambridge University Press.

Solnit, A.J. (1982) Developmental perspectives on self and object constancy. *The Psychoanalytic Study of the Child,* 37, 201-218.

Solnit, A.J. & Neubauer, P.B. (1986) Object constancy and early triadic relationships. *Journal of the American Academy of Child Psychiatry,* 25, 23-29.

Spader, P.H. (1995) Phenomenology and the claiming of essential knowledge. *Husserl Studies,* 11, 169-199.

Sroufe, L.A. (1983) Infant-caregiver attachment and patterns of attachment in pre-school: The roots of maladaptive competence. In M. Perlmutter (Ed) *Minnesota symposium on child psychology, Vol. 16.* (pp. 41-83). Hillsdale: Lawrence Erlbaum.

Stark, W. (1958) *The sociology of knowledge: An essay in aid of deeper understanding of the history of ideas.* London: Routledge & Kegan Paul.

Stein, E. (1989) *On the problem of empathy.* (Trans W. Stein). Washington: ICS Publications.

_____ (1922) Beiträge zur Philosophischen Begründung der Psychologie und der Gesiteswissenschaften. *Jahrbuch für Philosophie und Phänomenologische Forschung*, 5, 1-283.

Stein, H., Koontz, A.D., Fonagy, P., Allen J.G., Fultz, J., Brethour, J.R., Allen, D. & Evans, R.B. (2002) Adult attachment: What are the underlying dimensions? *Psychology and Psychotherapy: Theory, Research and Practice*, 75, 77-91.

Steiner, G.L. (1978) A survey to identify factors in the therapists' selection of a therapeutic orientation. *Psychotherapy: Theory, Research and Practice*, 15, 371-374.

Stern, D.N. (1985) *The interpersonal world of the infant: A view from psychoanalysis and developmental psychology*. New York: Basic Books.

Stern, P. (1898) *Einfühlung und association in der neuren asthetik*. Hamburg: Voss.

Stiles, W.B. & Shapiro, D.A. (1989) Abuse of the drug metaphor in psychotherapy process-outcome research. *Clinical Psychology Review*, 9, 521-543.

Stiles, W.B., Shapiro, D.A. & Elliott, R. (1986) Are all psychotherapies equivalent? *American Psychologist*, 41, 165-180.

Stiles, W.B., Shapiro, D.A., Harper, H., & Morrison, L.A. (1995) Therapist contributions to psychotherapeutic assimilation: An alternative to the drug metaphor. *British Journal of Medical Psychology*, 68, 1-13.

Ströker, E. (L. Hardy Ed)(1987) *The Husserlian foundations of science*. Washington: Center for Advanced Study in Phenomenology and the University Press of America.

_____ (1993) *Husserl's transcendental phenomenology*. (Trans L. Hardy). Stanford: Stanford University Press.

Strupp H.H. (1974) Some observations on the fallacy of value-free psychotherapy. *Journal of Abnormal Psychology*, 83, 199-201.

Strupp, H.H. & Binder, J.L. (1984) *Psychotherapy in a new key*. New York: Basic Books.

Strupp, H.H., Hadley, S.W. & Gomes-Schwartz, B. (1977) *Psychotherapy for better or worse*. New York: Jason Aronson.

Swaan, A. de (1981) The politics of agoraphobia. *Theory and Society*, 10, 359-385.

Tarrier, N., Wells, A. & Haddock, G. (Eds) (1998) *Treating complex cases: The cognitive behaviour therapy approach*. Chichester: Wiley.

Thoreson, R.W., Nathan, P.E., Skorina, J.K., & Kilburg, R.R. (1983) The alcoholic psychologist: Issues, problems, and implications for the professional. *Professional Psychology: Research and Practice*, 14, 670-684.

Thorne, B. (1992) *Carl Rogers*. London: Sage.

_____ (1996) Person-centred therapy. In W. Dryden (Ed) *Handbook of individual therapy*. (pp. 121-146). London: Sage.

Thurnher, R. (1995) Heidegger's conception of phenomenology with reference to Husserl. Postgraduate seminar. London: City University.

Torrey, E.F. (1986) *Witch doctors and psychiatrists*. Northvale: Jason Aronson.

Trân D.T. (1986) *Phenomenology and dialectical materialism*. (Trans. D.J. Herman & D.V. Morano). Dordrecht: Kluwer.

Tudor, K. & Worrall, M. (1994) Congruence reconsidered. *British Journal of Guidance and Counselling*, 22, 197-206.

Tyson, P. (1996) Object relations, affect management, and psychic structure formation: The concept of object constancy. *Psychoanalytic Study of the Child*, 51, 172-189.

Vanaerschot, G. (1990) The process of empathy: holding and letting go. In G. Lieater, J. Rombauts & R. Van Balen (Eds)(1991) *Client-centered and experiential psychotherapy in the nineties*. (pp. 269-293). Leuven: University of Leuven Press.

_____ (1993) Empathy as releasing several micro-processes in the client. In D. Brazier (Ed) *Beyond Carl Rogers*. (pp. 47-71). London: Constable.

Villas-Boas Bowen, M.C. (1986) Personality differences and person-centred supervision. *Person Centered Review*, 1, 291-309.

Vygotsky, L. (1978) *Mind in society.* Cambridge: Harvard University Press.

Walker, S.F. (1984) *Learning theory and behaviour modification.* London: Methuen.

_____ (1987) *Animal learning theory: An introduction.* London: R & KP.

Watkins, C.E. (1983) Burnout in counseling practice: Some potential professional and personal hazards of becoming a counselor. *Personnel and Guidance Journal*, 61, 304-308.

Weisberg, I. (1993) Transference and countertransference vs. role evocation and response: a commentary on the writings of Frank P. Troise. *International Journal of Communicative Psychoanalysis and Psychotherapy*, 8, 65-66.

Weiss, E. (1950) *Principles of psychodynamics.* New York: Grune Stratton.

Wells, A. (1997) *Cognitive therapy of anxiety disorders.* Chichester: Wiley.

Wertsch, J.V. (1985) *Vygotsky and the social formation of mind.* Cambridge: Harvard University Press.

Westerman, M.A. (1993) A hermeneutic approach to integration: Psychotherapy within the circle of practical activity. In G. Stricker, G. & J.R. Gold (Eds) *Comprehensive handbook of psychotherapy integration.* (pp. 187-216). New York: Plenum Press.

Wheeler, S. & McLeod, J. (1995) Person-centred and psychodynamic counselling: A dialogue. *Counselling*, 6, 283-287.

Wilson, G.T. (1996) Manual-based treatment: The clinical application of research findings. *Behaviour Research and Therapy*, 34, 295-314.

Wimmer, H. & Perner, J. (1983) Beliefs about beliefs: Representation and constraining function of wrong beliefs in young children's understanding of deception. *Cognition*, 13, 103-128.

Woolfe, R. & Dryden, W. (1996) *Handbook of counselling psychology.* London: Sage.

Young, J.E. & Klosko, J. (1994) *Reinventing your life.* New York: Plume.

Zajonc, R. (1980) Feeling and thinking. *American Psychologist,* 35, 151-175.

Zelen, S.L. (1985) Sexualization of therapeutic relationships: The dual vulnerability of patient and therapist. *Psychotherapy,* 22, 178-185.

Zhurbin, V.I. (1991) The notion of psychological defense in Freud and Rogers. *Soviet Psychology,* 29, 58-72.

978-0-595-45573-7
0-595-45573-5

Printed in the United Kingdom
by Lightning Source UK Ltd.
121976UK00002B/103-135/A